MARBLES

"I have always admired Ellen Forney's humor and honesty, but *Marbles* is a major leap forward. It's a hilarious memoir about mental illness, yes, but it's also an incisive study of what it means to be human and how we ache to become better humans. Amazing stuff."

— e Indian

"Dense with intellectual and emotional power, Forney's book is a treasure—as a memoir, as an artwork, and as a beautifully conceived and executed commentary on both mental experience and the creative life. With wit, humor, a wicked sense of the absurd, and eloquent insight into the beauty that shines through the mercurial life of the mind, this graphic memoir explores its subject with a particular precision and power. Forney should be read."

—Marya Hornbacher, author of *Madness: A Bipolar Life*

"Ellen Forney's memoir of her bipolar diagnosis and long pharmacopic trek toward balance is painfully honest and joyously exuberant. Her drawings evoke the neuron-crackling high of mania and the schematic bleakness of depression with deft immediacy. Forney is at the height of her powers as she explores the tenuous line between mood disorders and creativity itself."

—Alison Bechdel, author of *Fun Home: A Family Tragicomic*

"Eisner-nominee Forney confesses her struggles with being diagnosed as bipolar in this witty and insightful memoir. Forney allows her art to chronicle her outer life while revealing her inner state of mind. . . . Readers struggling with their own mania or depression will find Forney good company, and others searching for insight into the minds of troubled artists will find Forney an engaging storyteller."

—*Publishers Weekly* (Starred Review)

"[A]s engaging and informative as it is inspirational. Not only does her conversational intimacy draw readers in but her drawings perfectly capture the exhilarating frenzy of mania and the dark void of depression. Forney's story should resonate with those grappling with similar issues, while her artistry should appeal to a wide readership."

—*Kirkus Reviews* (Starred Review)

"Until she was thirty, Forney took for granted her creative spark, her love of life, her obsessive exercise, her impulsive, polymorphous sexuality. They were just who she were. Then she was diagnosed with bipolar disorder, and suddenly she found herself having to figure out where her mental illness ended and she began and whether her art was separable from her madness." —*Time*

"Sprinkled with plenty of self-deprecating humor, Forney's story is relatable and entertaining, in spite of its heavy subject matter." —*Seattle*

"In *Marbles*, cartoonist Ellen Forney's life-altering journey through mental illness is graphically exposed in more ways than one. . . . Forney's quest to discover whether her mental illness is necessary to her art is a timeless, not to mention relevant, one." —*Bust Magazine*

"Forney, with a darkly funny honesty and powerful imagery, illustrates what it means to have a disease that affects only 1 or 2 percent of the adult population—but that most people are afraid to talk about. . . . Forney depicts depression elegantly." —*Curve*

"Ellen's work has always been hilarious and sharp, but *Marbles* has an emotional resonance that shows new depth as an artist and a writer. This is an extremely personal, brave, and rewarding book."
—Dan Savage, author of *It Gets Better* and *The Kid*

"Ellen Forney's *Marbles* provides an insightful, unapologetic view into a mind blessed and tormented by bipolar disorder. By tackling some of the most difficult questions about the disease, including its relation to creativity and the role of medication and therapy, Forney pulls her readers into uncomfortable terrain and miraculously gets them to enjoy every minute of it."
—Melody Moezzi, award-winning author and *bp Magazine* columnist

"Who knew that an adventure into one of the murkiest ideas of our time—bipolar disorder—would turn out to be an epic comic thriller in which all of creativity since the Renaissance hangs in the balance? *Marbles* is like one of those really early comics where Lex Luther threatens total destruction of the world while Superman sits in the Fortress of Solitude wondering, Which superpower will get us out of this jam? Only by Superman, I mean Ellen Forney, and by Lex Luther, I mean manic depression, and by superpower, I mean her Amazon Pencil of Armor-Piercing Wit."
—Jack Hitt, author of *Bunch of Amateurs: A Search for the American Character*

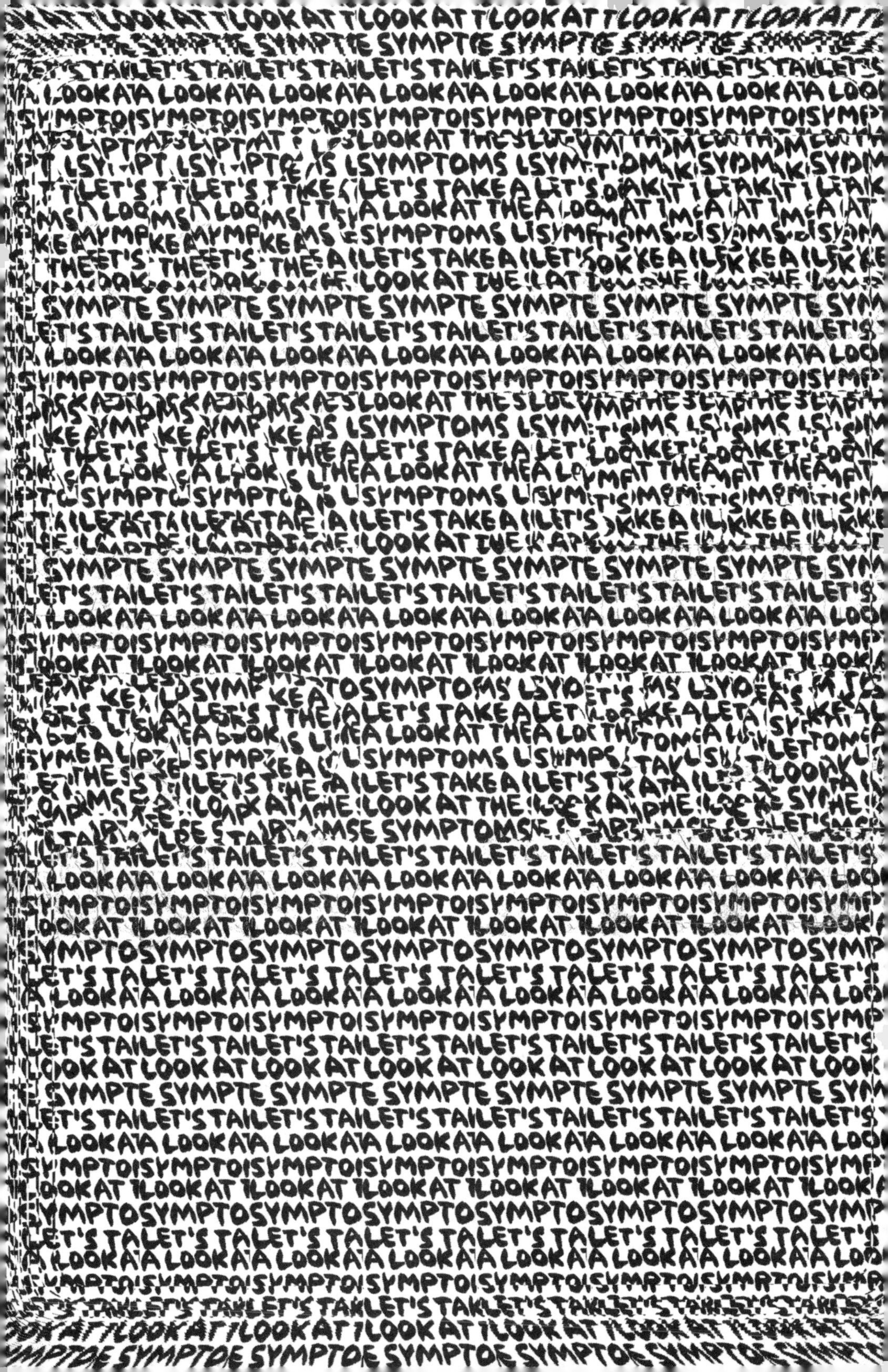
LET'S TAKE A LOOK AT THE SYMPTOMS

MARBLES

MANIA, DEPRESSION, MICHELANGELO, & ME
A GRAPHIC MEMOIR BY ellen forney

GOTHAM
BOOKS

GOTHAM BOOKS
Published by Penguin Group (USA) Inc.
375 Hudson Street, New York, New York 10014, U.S.A.
Penguin Group (Canada), 90 Eglinton Avenue East, Suite 700, Toronto, Ontario M4P 2Y3, Canada (a division of Pearson Penguin Canada Inc.); Penguin Books Ltd, 80 Strand, London WC2R 0RL, England; Penguin Ireland, 25 St Stephen's Green, Dublin 2, Ireland (a division of Penguin Books Ltd); Penguin Group (Australia), 250 Camberwell Road, Camberwell, Victoria 3124, Australia (a division of Pearson Australia Group Pty Ltd); Penguin Books India Pvt Ltd, 11 Community Centre, Panchsheel Park, New Delhi–110 017, India; Penguin Group (NZ), 67 Apollo Drive, Rosedale, Auckland 0632, New Zealand (a division of Pearson New Zealand Ltd); Penguin Books (South Africa) (Pty) Ltd, 24 Sturdee Avenue, Rosebank, Johannesburg 2196, South Africa

Penguin Books Ltd, Registered Offices: 80 Strand, London WC2R 0RL, England

Published by Gotham Books, a member of Penguin Group (USA) Inc.

First printing, November 2012
5 7 9 10 8 6

LIBRARY OF CONGRESS CATALOGING-IN-PUBLICATION DATA
has been applied for.

ISBN 978-1-592-40732-3

Printed in the United States of America

Some names and identifying characteristics have been changed to protect the privacy of the individuals involved.

While the author has made every effort to provide accurate telephone numbers, Internet addresses, and other contact information at the time of publication, neither the publisher nor the author assumes any responsibility for errors, or for changes that occur after publication. Further, the publisher does not have any control over and does not assume any responsibility for author or third-party websites or their content.

Penguin is committed to publishing works of quality and integrity.
In that spirit, we are proud to offer this book to our readers;
however, the story, the experiences, and the words
are the author's alone.

ALWAYS LEARNING   PEARSON

DEDICATED WITH
IMMENSE GRATITUDE
TO MY MOTHER
& TO MY PSYCHIATRIST

CHAPTER 1

EVERY TIME OWEN TRACED A NEW LINE WITH HIS NEEDLE,

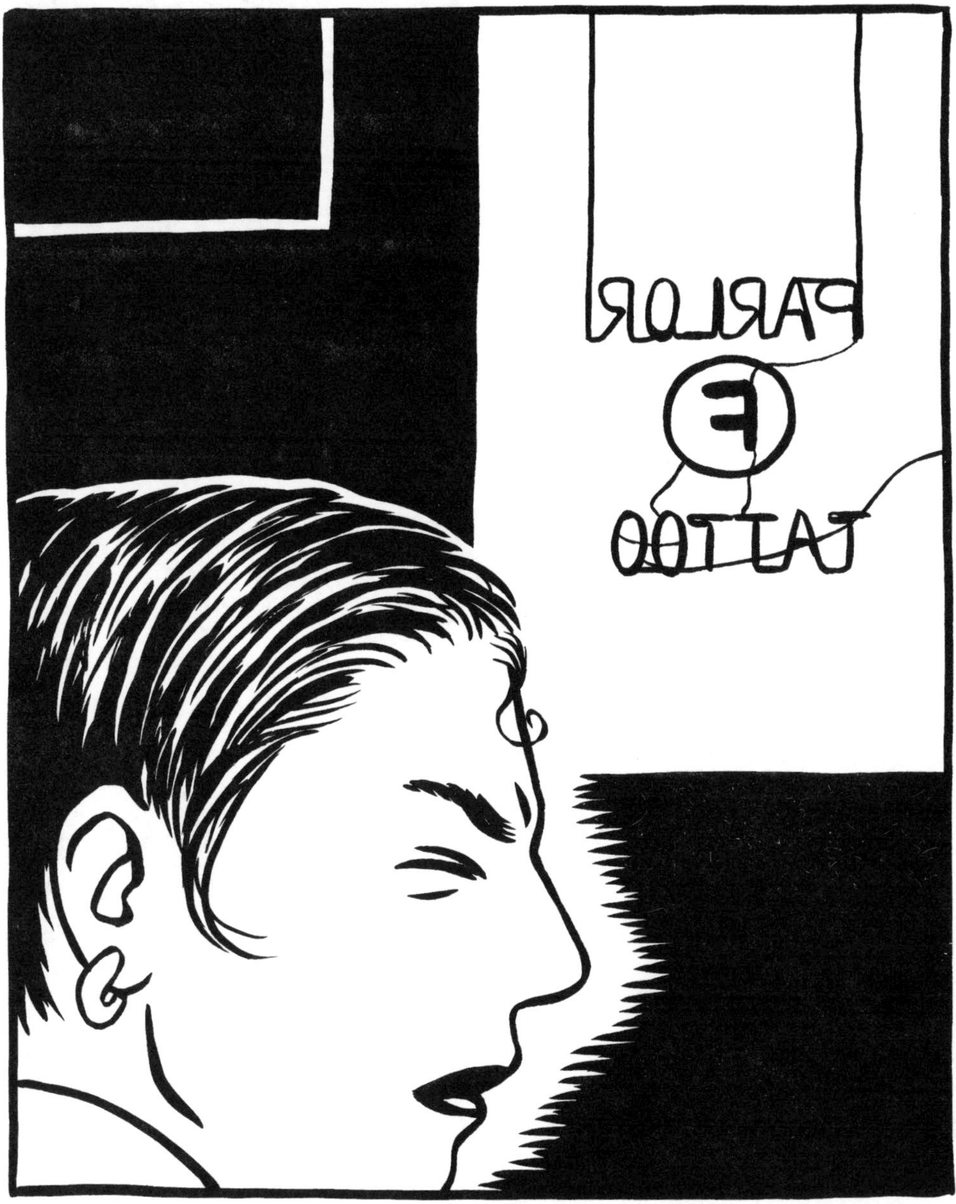
PARLOR
TATTOO

I COULD SEE THE SENSATION — A BRIGHT WHITE LIGHT, AN ELECTRICAL CHARGE, UP & TO THE RIGHT.

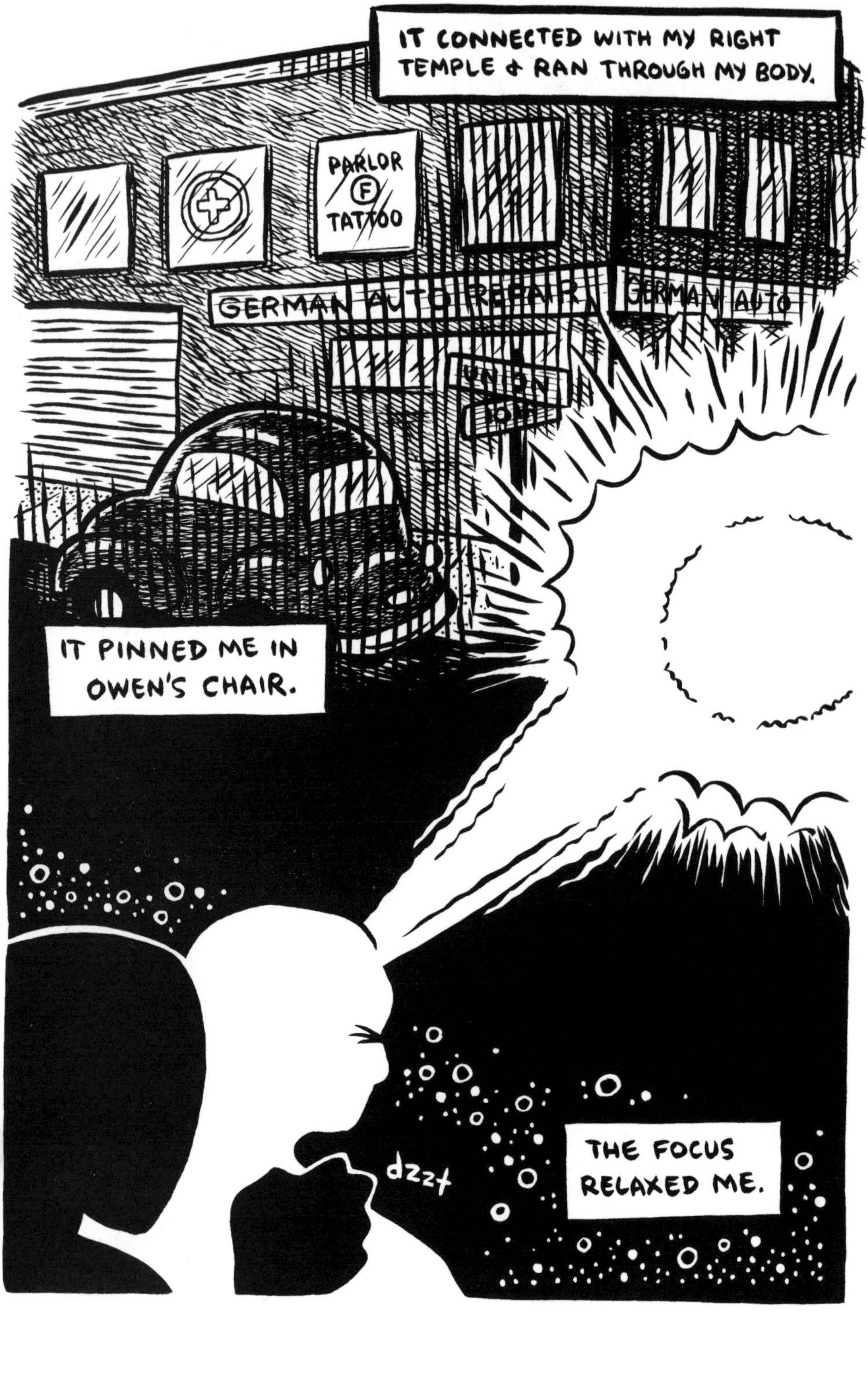
IT CONNECTED WITH MY RIGHT TEMPLE & RAN THROUGH MY BODY.
PARLOR
F
TATTOO
GERMAN AUTO REPAIR
GERMAN AUTO
IT PINNED ME IN OWEN'S CHAIR.
dzzt
THE FOCUS RELAXED ME.

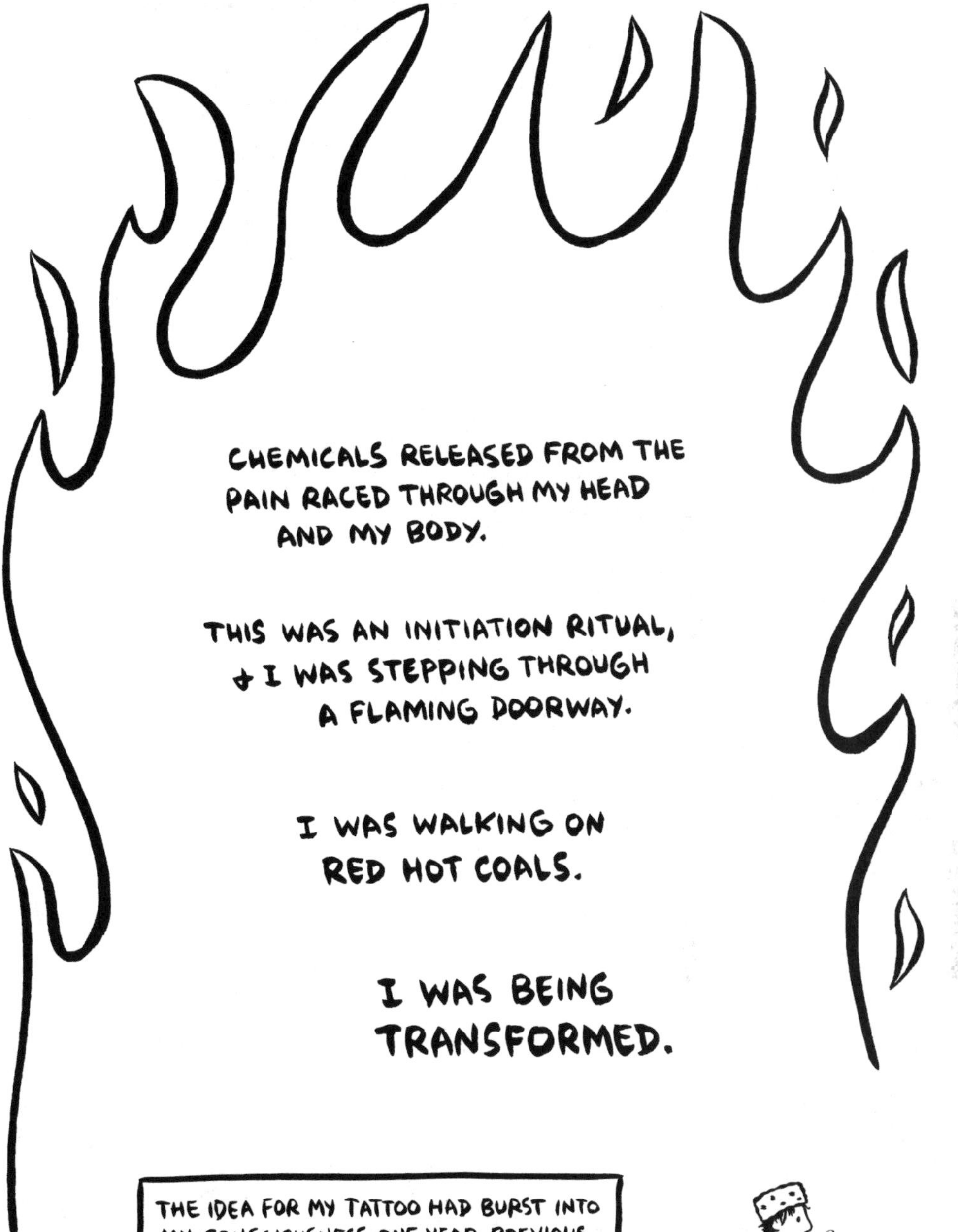
CHEMICALS RELEASED FROM THE PAIN RACED THROUGH MY HEAD AND MY BODY.
THIS WAS AN INITIATION RITUAL, & I WAS STEPPING THROUGH A FLAMING DOORWAY.
I WAS WALKING ON RED HOT COALS.
I WAS BEING TRANSFORMED.
THE IDEA FOR MY TATTOO HAD BURST INTO MY CONSCIOUSNESS ONE YEAR PREVIOUS, ON ONE OF MY LONG, BRISK WALKS.

I'D BEEN MUSING ABOUT THE WHAT AND WHERE FOR MY FIRST—AND, I RESOLVED, ONLY—TATTOO. I WANTED IT TO BE MEANINGFUL.
SUDDENLY, A NETWORK IN MY HEAD LIT UP!!
KRAK!!
gasp!
ping!
ping!
Where:
MY WHOLE BACK
dzzzt!
ping!
ping ping!
FULL-BACK TATTOOS LOOK BADASS
WITH ENERGY GOING UP
SITE-SPECIFIC FIT
POSITIVE, JOYFUL
HOW?
BURST PIPE?
FOUNTAIN?
TRANSFORMING MY LEAST FAVORITE BODY PART
SCARS FROM YEARS OF BAD SKIN

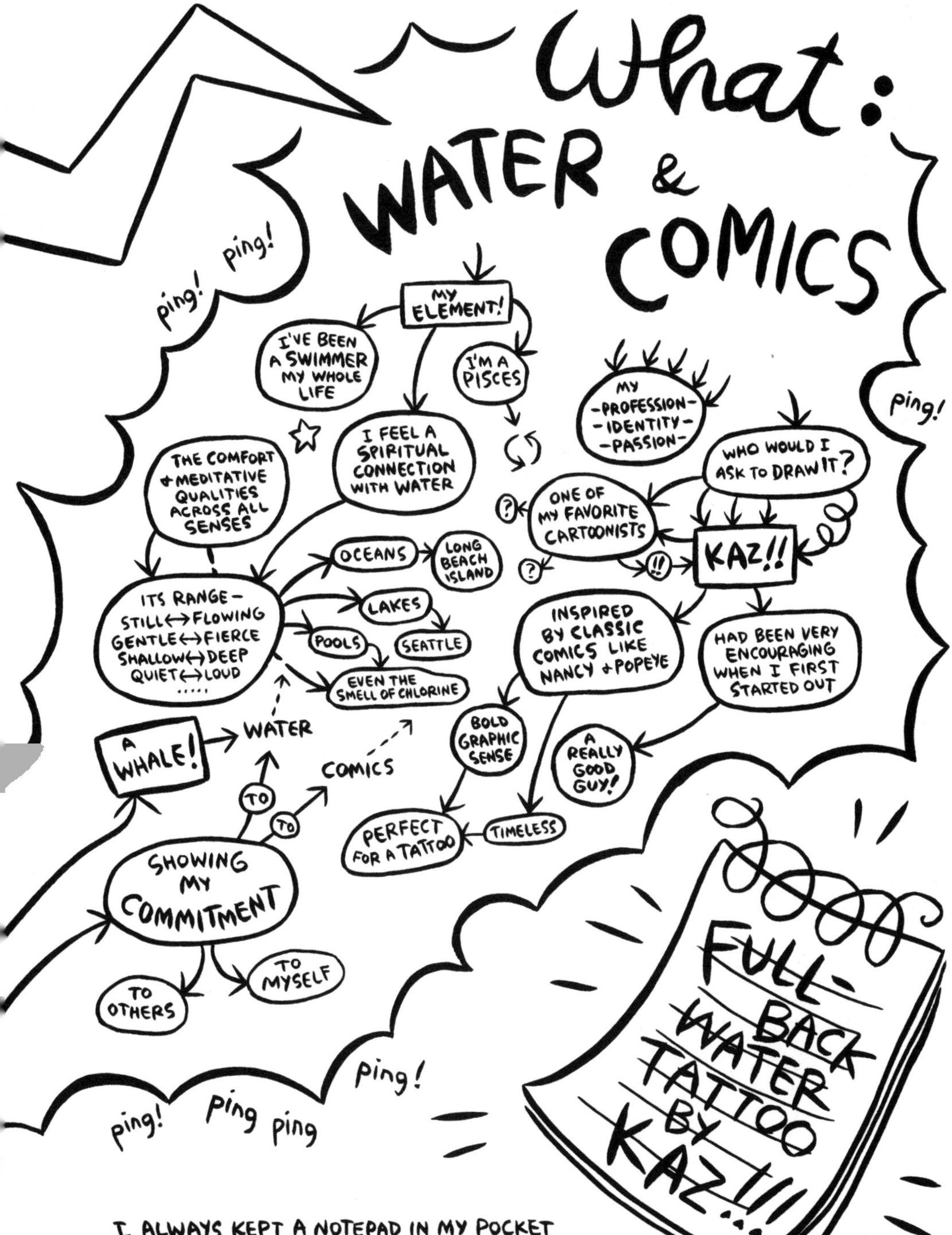
What:
WATER & COMICS
MY ELEMENT!
I'VE BEEN A SWIMMER MY WHOLE LIFE
I'M A PISCES
I FEEL A SPIRITUAL CONNECTION WITH WATER
THE COMFORT & MEDITATIVE QUALITIES ACROSS ALL SENSES
ITS RANGE— STILL↔FLOWING GENTLE↔FIERCE SHALLOW↔DEEP QUIET↔LOUD .....
OCEANS
LONG BEACH ISLAND
LAKES
SEATTLE
POOLS
EVEN THE SMELL OF CHLORINE
A WHALE!
WATER
COMICS
TO
TO
SHOWING MY COMMITMENT
TO OTHERS
TO MYSELF
MY -PROFESSION- -IDENTITY- -PASSION-
WHO WOULD I ASK TO DRAW IT?
ONE OF MY FAVORITE CARTOONISTS
KAZ!!
INSPIRED BY CLASSIC COMICS LIKE NANCY & POPEYE
HAD BEEN VERY ENCOURAGING WHEN I FIRST STARTED OUT
BOLD GRAPHIC SENSE
A REALLY GOOD GUY!
PERFECT FOR A TATTOO
TIMELESS
FULL BACK WATER TATTOO BY KAZ!!!
ping! ping! ping! ping! ping! ping ping

I ALWAYS KEPT A NOTEPAD IN MY POCKET BECAUSE I HAD IDEAS LIKE POPCORN, & I'D FORGET THEM IF I DIDN'T WRITE THEM DOWN.

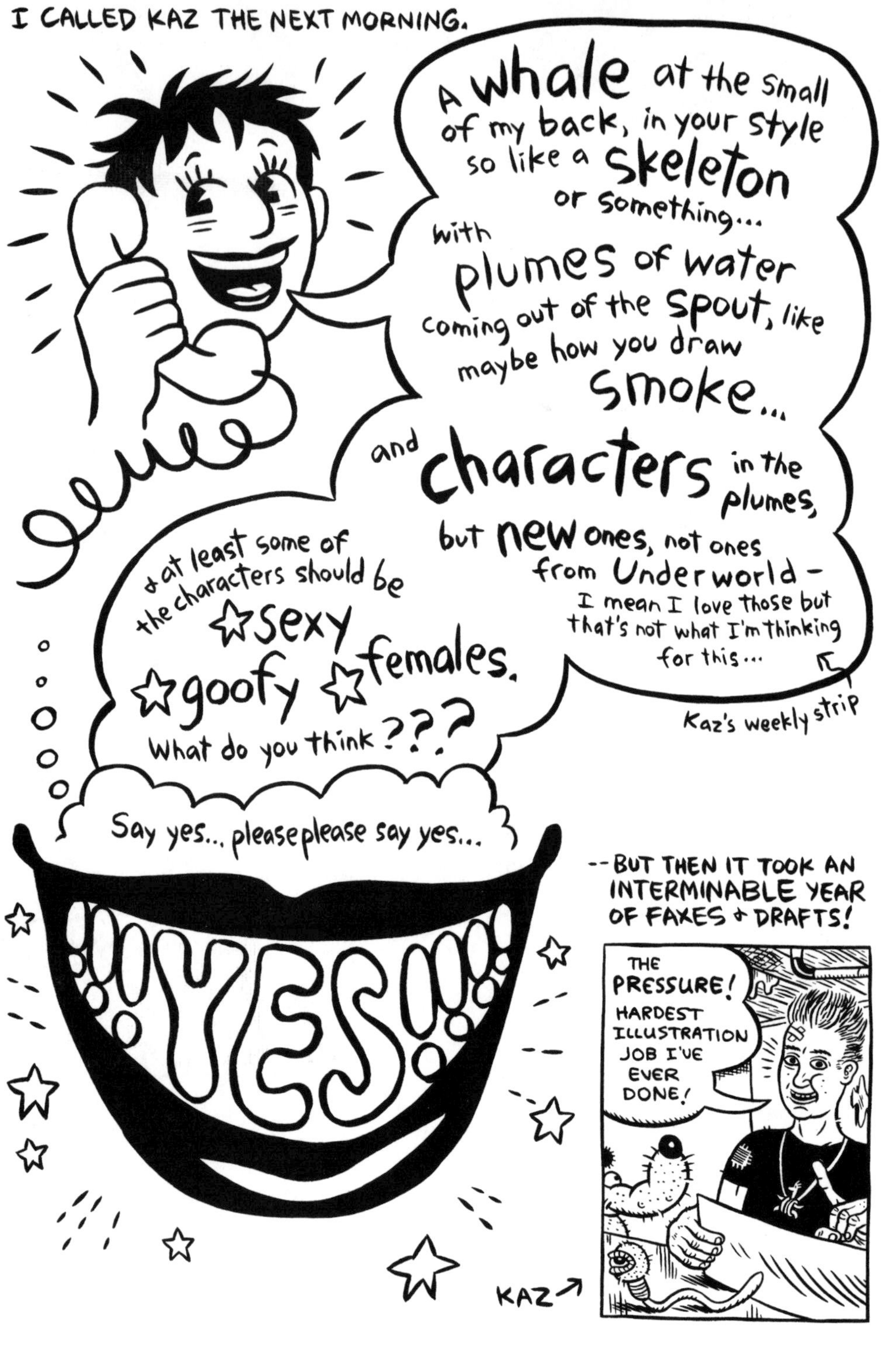
I CALLED KAZ THE NEXT MORNING.
A whale at the small of my back, in your style so like a skeleton or something... with plumes of water coming out of the spout, like maybe how you draw smoke... and characters in the plumes, but new ones, not ones from Underworld - I mean I love those but that's not what I'm thinking for this...
Kaz's weekly strip
& at least some of the characters should be sexy goofy females. What do you think???
Say yes... pleaseplease say yes...
YES!!!!!!
--BUT THEN IT TOOK AN INTERMINABLE YEAR OF FAXES & DRAFTS!
THE PRESSURE! HARDEST ILLUSTRATION JOB I'VE EVER DONE!
KAZ

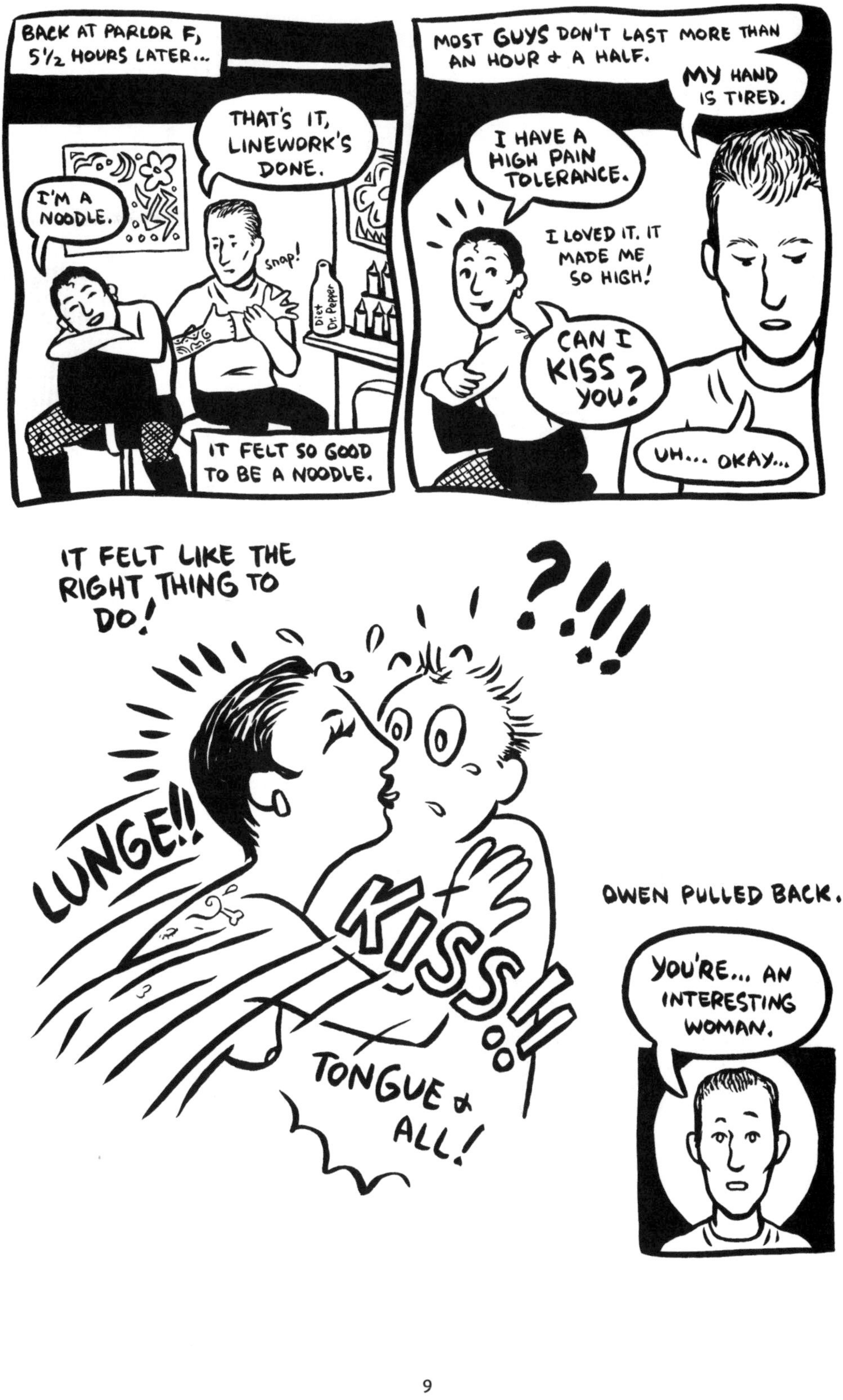
BACK AT PARLOR F, 5½ HOURS LATER...
THAT'S IT, LINEWORK'S DONE.
I'M A NOODLE.
snap!
Diet Dr. Pepper
IT FELT SO GOOD TO BE A NOODLE.
MOST GUYS DON'T LAST MORE THAN AN HOUR & A HALF.
MY HAND IS TIRED.
I HAVE A HIGH PAIN TOLERANCE.
I LOVED IT. IT MADE ME SO HIGH!
CAN I KISS YOU?
UH... OKAY...
IT FELT LIKE THE RIGHT THING TO DO!
?!!!
LUNGE!!
KISS!!
TONGUE & ALL!
OWEN PULLED BACK.
YOU'RE... AN INTERESTING WOMAN.

OWEN ASKED FOR A PHOTO BEFORE I LEFT.

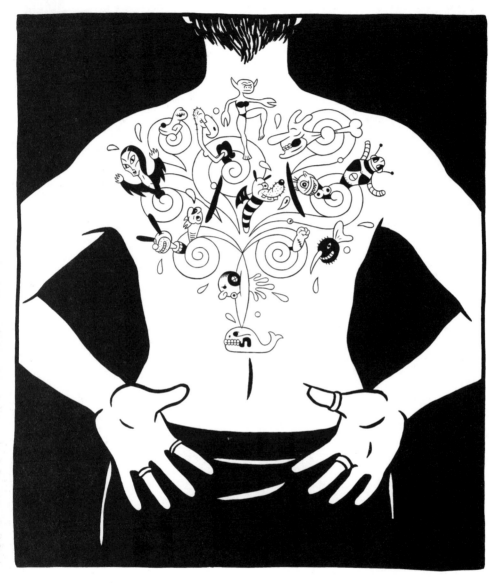

HE SAID HE LOVED THE WAY
TATTOOS LOOK WHEN THEY'RE
NEW, WHEN THE LINEWORK'S
ALL RAISED.

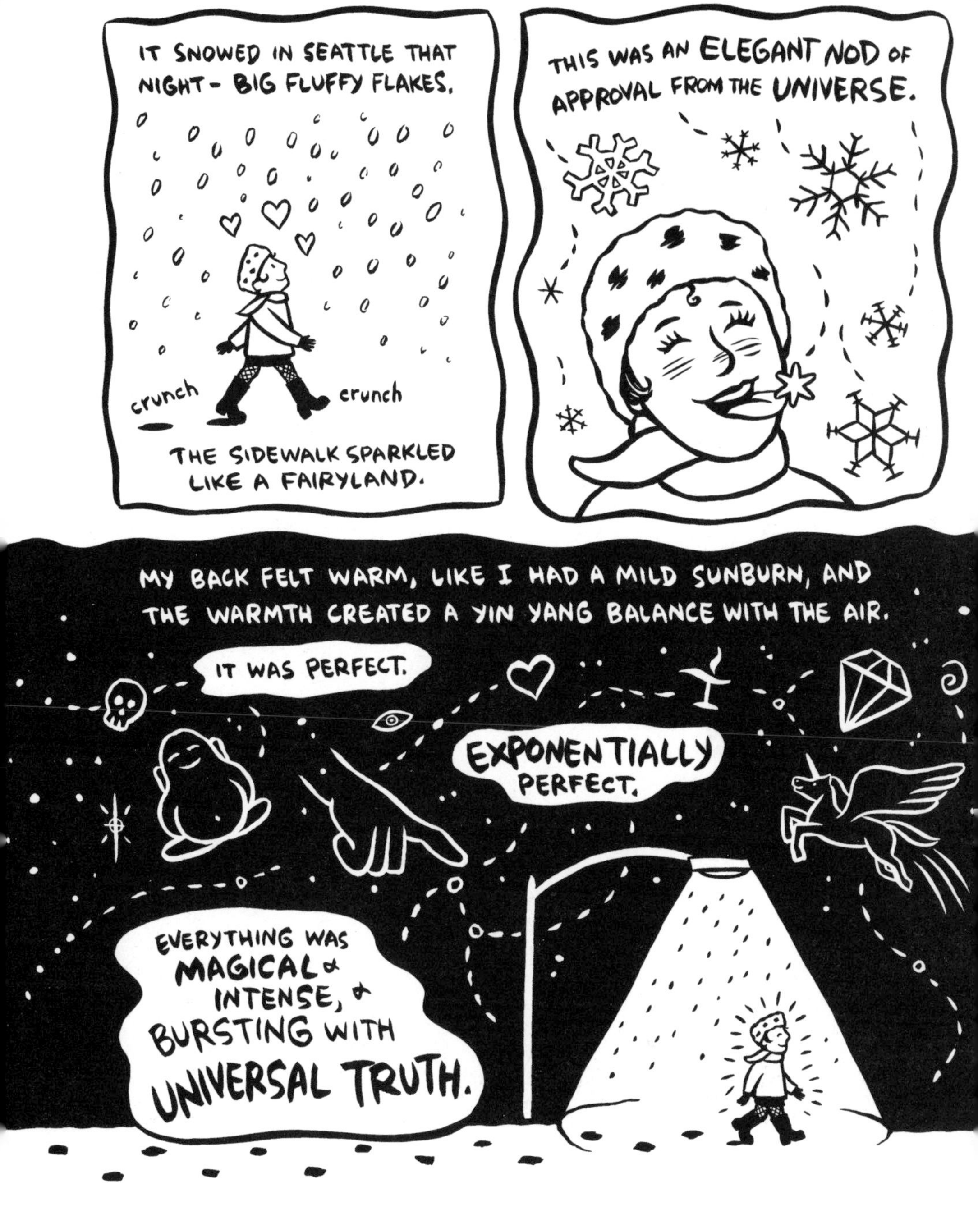
IT SNOWED IN SEATTLE THAT NIGHT - BIG FLUFFY FLAKES.
crunch
crunch
THE SIDEWALK SPARKLED LIKE A FAIRYLAND.
THIS WAS AN ELEGANT NOD OF APPROVAL FROM THE UNIVERSE.
MY BACK FELT WARM, LIKE I HAD A MILD SUNBURN, AND THE WARMTH CREATED A YIN YANG BALANCE WITH THE AIR.
IT WAS PERFECT.
EXPONENTIALLY PERFECT.
EVERYTHING WAS MAGICAL & INTENSE, & BURSTING WITH UNIVERSAL TRUTH.

CHAPTER 2

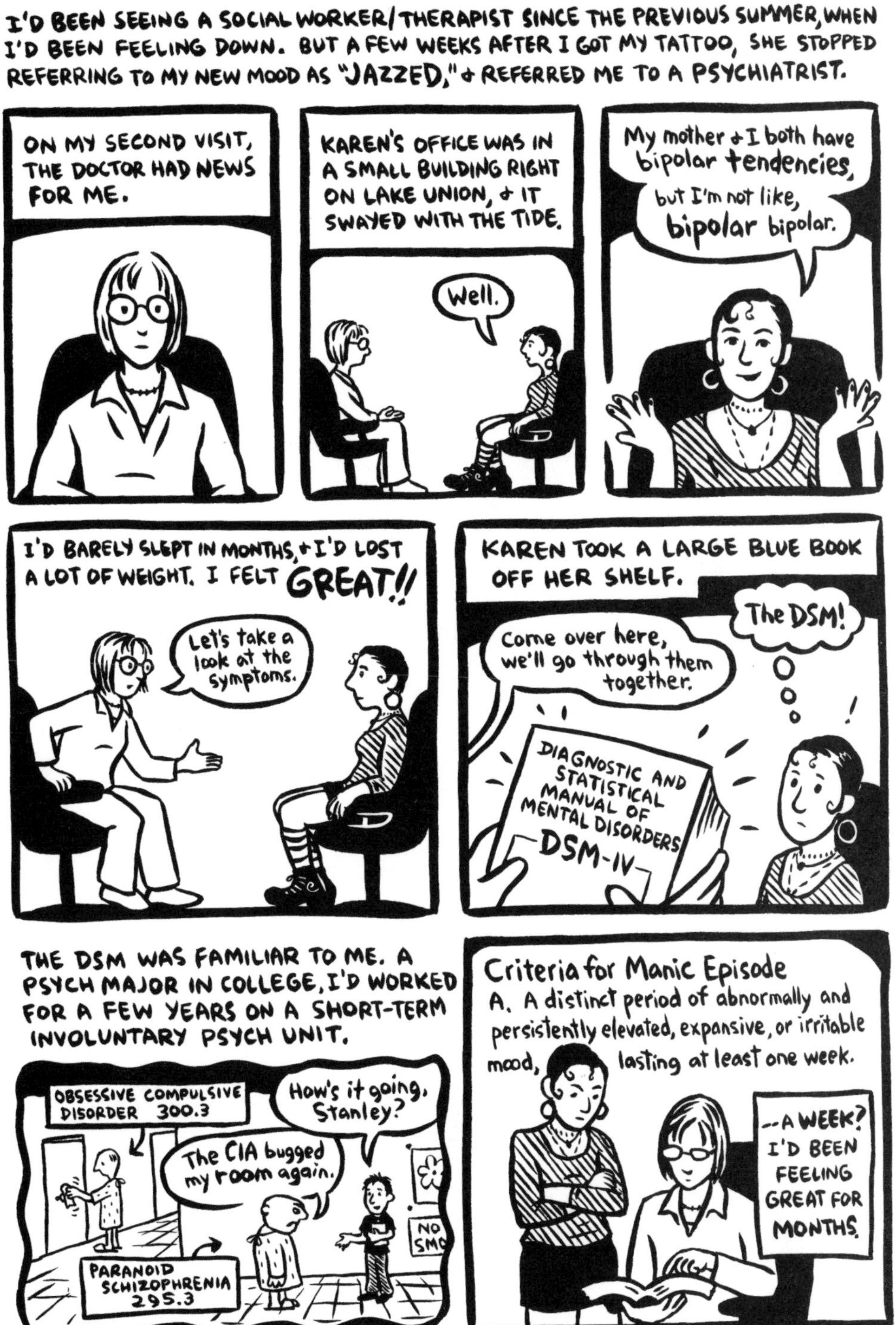
I'D BEEN SEEING A SOCIAL WORKER/THERAPIST SINCE THE PREVIOUS SUMMER, WHEN I'D BEEN FEELING DOWN. BUT A FEW WEEKS AFTER I GOT MY TATTOO, SHE STOPPED REFERRING TO MY NEW MOOD AS "JAZZED," & REFERRED ME TO A PSYCHIATRIST.
ON MY SECOND VISIT, THE DOCTOR HAD NEWS FOR ME.
KAREN'S OFFICE WAS IN A SMALL BUILDING RIGHT ON LAKE UNION, & IT SWAYED WITH THE TIDE.
Well.
My mother & I both have bipolar tendencies, but I'm not like, bipolar bipolar.
I'D BARELY SLEPT IN MONTHS, & I'D LOST A LOT OF WEIGHT. I FELT GREAT!!
Let's take a look at the symptoms.
KAREN TOOK A LARGE BLUE BOOK OFF HER SHELF.
Come over here, we'll go through them together.
The DSM!
!
DIAGNOSTIC AND STATISTICAL MANUAL OF MENTAL DISORDERS
DSM-IV
THE DSM WAS FAMILIAR TO ME. A PSYCH MAJOR IN COLLEGE, I'D WORKED FOR A FEW YEARS ON A SHORT-TERM INVOLUNTARY PSYCH UNIT.
OBSESSIVE COMPULSIVE DISORDER 300.3
How's it going, Stanley?
The CIA bugged my room again.
NO SMO
PARANOID SCHIZOPHRENIA 295.3
Criteria for Manic Episode
A. A distinct period of abnormally and persistently elevated, expansive, or irritable mood, lasting at least one week.
--A WEEK? I'D BEEN FEELING GREAT FOR MONTHS.

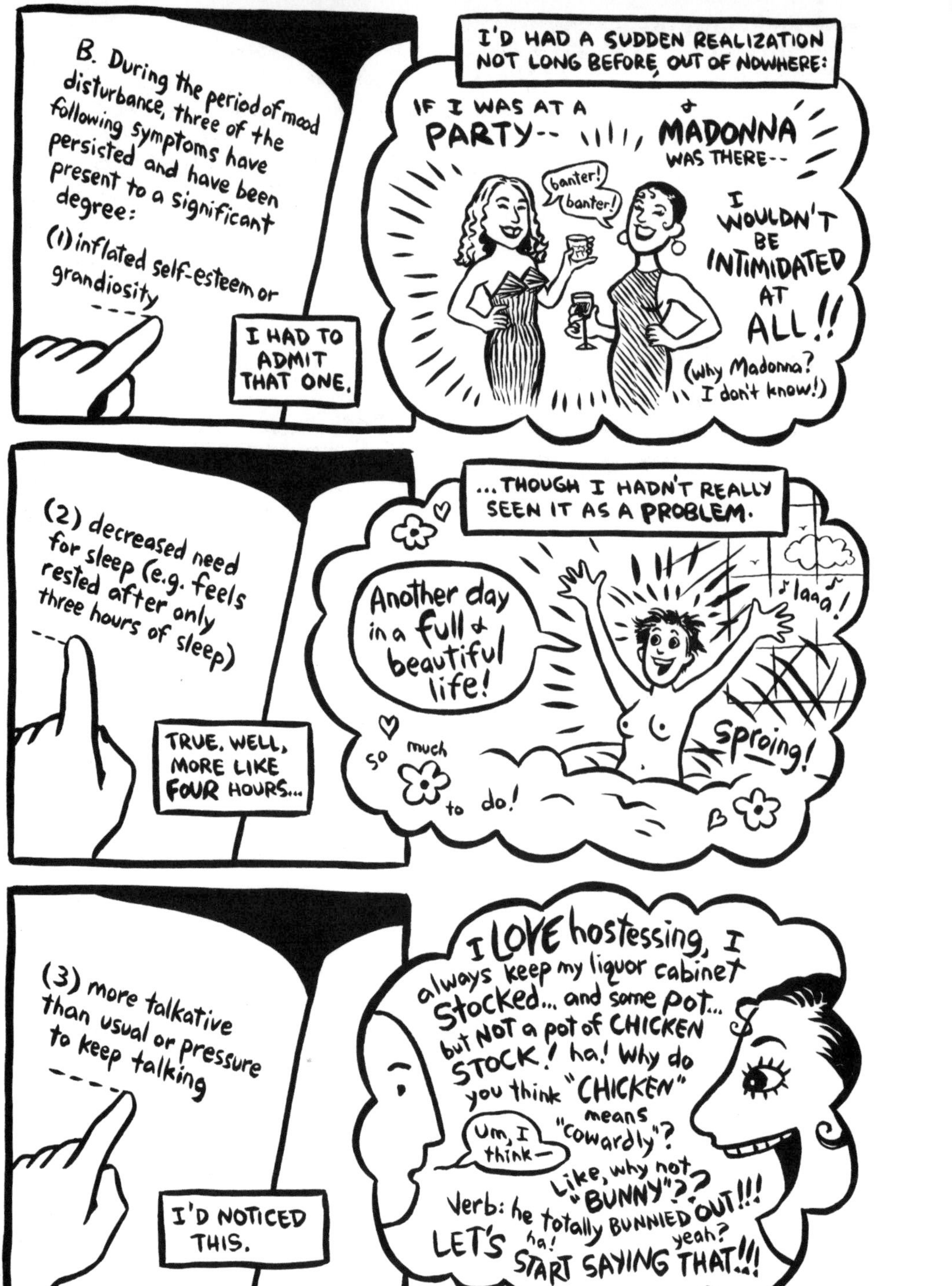
B. During the period of mood disturbance, three of the following symptoms have persisted and have been present to a significant degree:
(1) inflated self-esteem or grandiosity
I HAD TO ADMIT THAT ONE.
I'D HAD A SUDDEN REALIZATION NOT LONG BEFORE, OUT OF NOWHERE:
IF I WAS AT A PARTY-- & MADONNA WAS THERE--
banter! banter!
I WOULDN'T BE INTIMIDATED AT ALL!!
(why Madonna? I don't know!)
(2) decreased need for sleep (e.g. feels rested after only three hours of sleep)
TRUE. WELL, MORE LIKE FOUR HOURS...
...THOUGH I HADN'T REALLY SEEN IT AS A PROBLEM.
Another day in a full & beautiful life!
laaa!
Sproing!
so much to do!
(3) more talkative than usual or pressure to keep talking
I'D NOTICED THIS.
I LOVE hostessing, I always keep my liquor cabinet stocked... and some pot... but NOT a pot of CHICKEN STOCK! ha! Why do you think "CHICKEN" means "cowardly"?
Um, I think—
Like, why not "BUNNY"??
Verb: he totally BUNNIED OUT!!!
LET'S START SAYING THAT!!! ha! yeah?

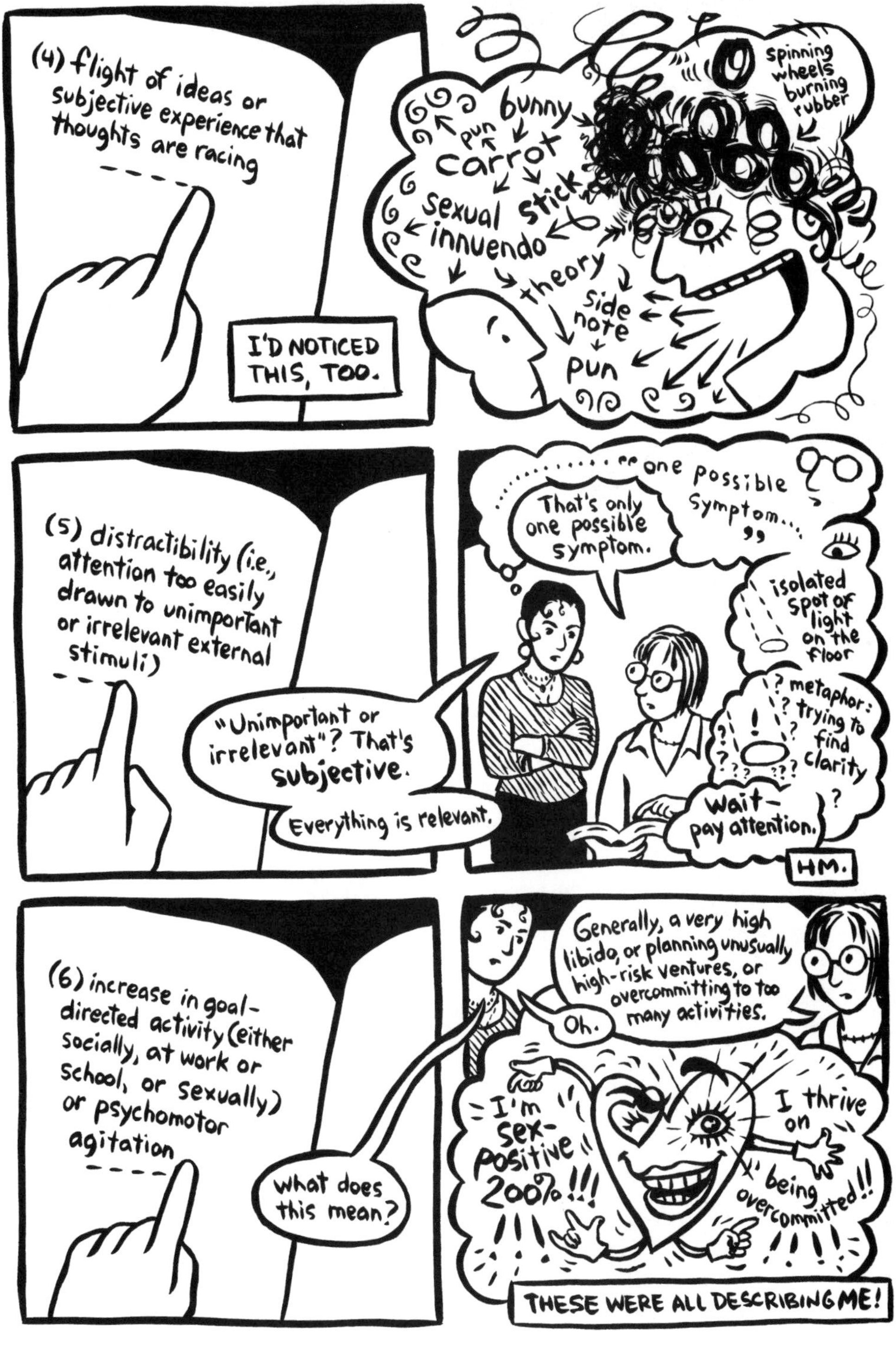
(4) flight of ideas or subjective experience that thoughts are racing
I'D NOTICED THIS, TOO.
bunny
pun
carrot
stick
sexual innuendo
theory
side note
pun
spinning wheels burning rubber
(5) distractibility (i.e., attention too easily drawn to unimportant or irrelevant external stimuli)
"Unimportant or irrelevant"? That's subjective.
Everything is relevant.
That's only one possible symptom.
"one possible symptom..."
isolated spot of light on the floor
metaphor: trying to find clarity
Wait- pay attention.
HM.
(6) increase in goal-directed activity (either socially, at work or school, or sexually) or psychomotor agitation
What does this mean?
Generally, a very high libido, or planning unusually high-risk ventures, or overcommitting to too many activities.
Oh.
I'm sex-positive 200%!!!
I thrive on being overcommitted!!
THESE WERE ALL DESCRIBING ME!

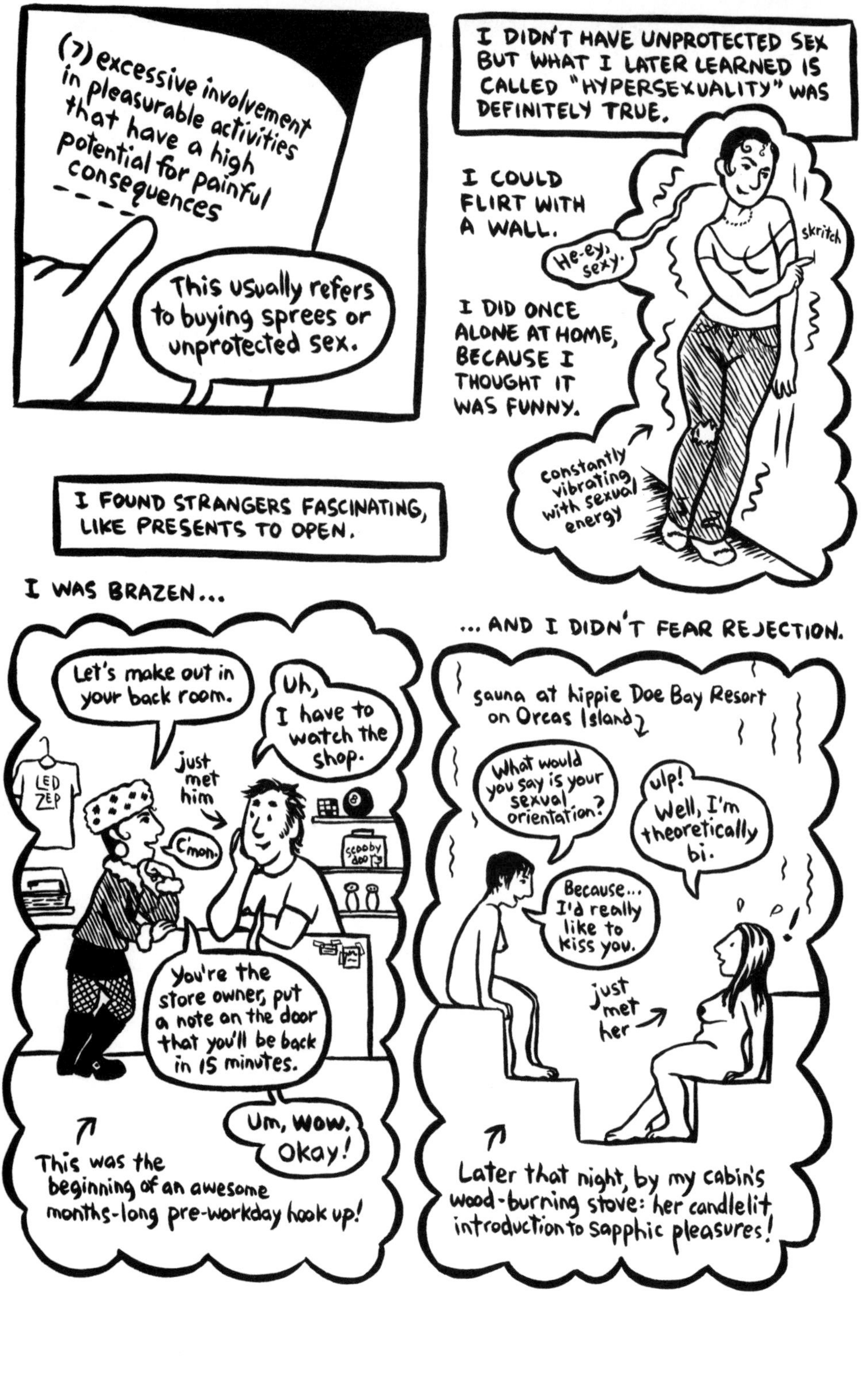

(7) excessive involvement in pleasurable activities that have a high potential for painful consequences
This usually refers to buying sprees or unprotected sex.
I DIDN'T HAVE UNPROTECTED SEX BUT WHAT I LATER LEARNED IS CALLED "HYPERSEXUALITY" WAS DEFINITELY TRUE.
I COULD FLIRT WITH A WALL.
He-ey, sexy.
skritch
I DID ONCE ALONE AT HOME, BECAUSE I THOUGHT IT WAS FUNNY.
constantly vibrating with sexual energy
I FOUND STRANGERS FASCINATING, LIKE PRESENTS TO OPEN.
I WAS BRAZEN...
Let's make out in your back room.
Uh, I have to watch the shop.
LED ZEP
just met him
C'mon.
scooby doo
You're the store owner, put a note on the door that you'll be back in 15 minutes.
Um, wow. Okay!
This was the beginning of an awesome months-long pre-workday hook up!
... AND I DIDN'T FEAR REJECTION.
sauna at hippie Doe Bay Resort on Orcas Island
What would you say is your sexual orientation?
ulp! Well, I'm theoretically bi.
Because... I'd really like to kiss you.
just met her
Later that night, by my cabin's wood-burning stove: her candlelit introduction to sapphic pleasures!

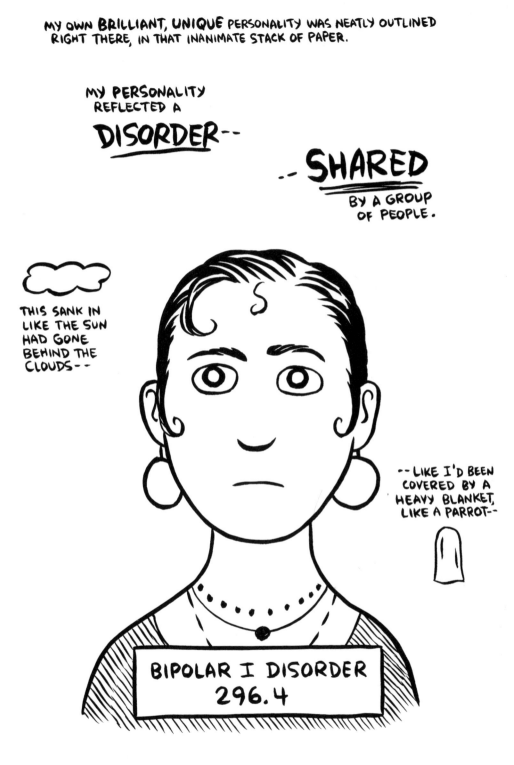

MY OWN BRILLIANT, UNIQUE PERSONALITY WAS NEATLY OUTLINED RIGHT THERE, IN THAT INANIMATE STACK OF PAPER.

MY PERSONALITY REFLECTED A

DISORDER--

-- SHARED

BY A GROUP OF PEOPLE.

THIS SANK IN LIKE THE SUN HAD GONE BEHIND THE CLOUDS--

-- LIKE I'D BEEN COVERED BY A HEAVY BLANKET, LIKE A PARROT--

BIPOLAR I DISORDER 296.4

-- LIKE A MAGIC EYE STEREOGRAM REVEALING A CLEAR, IRREFUTABLE 3-D IMAGE.

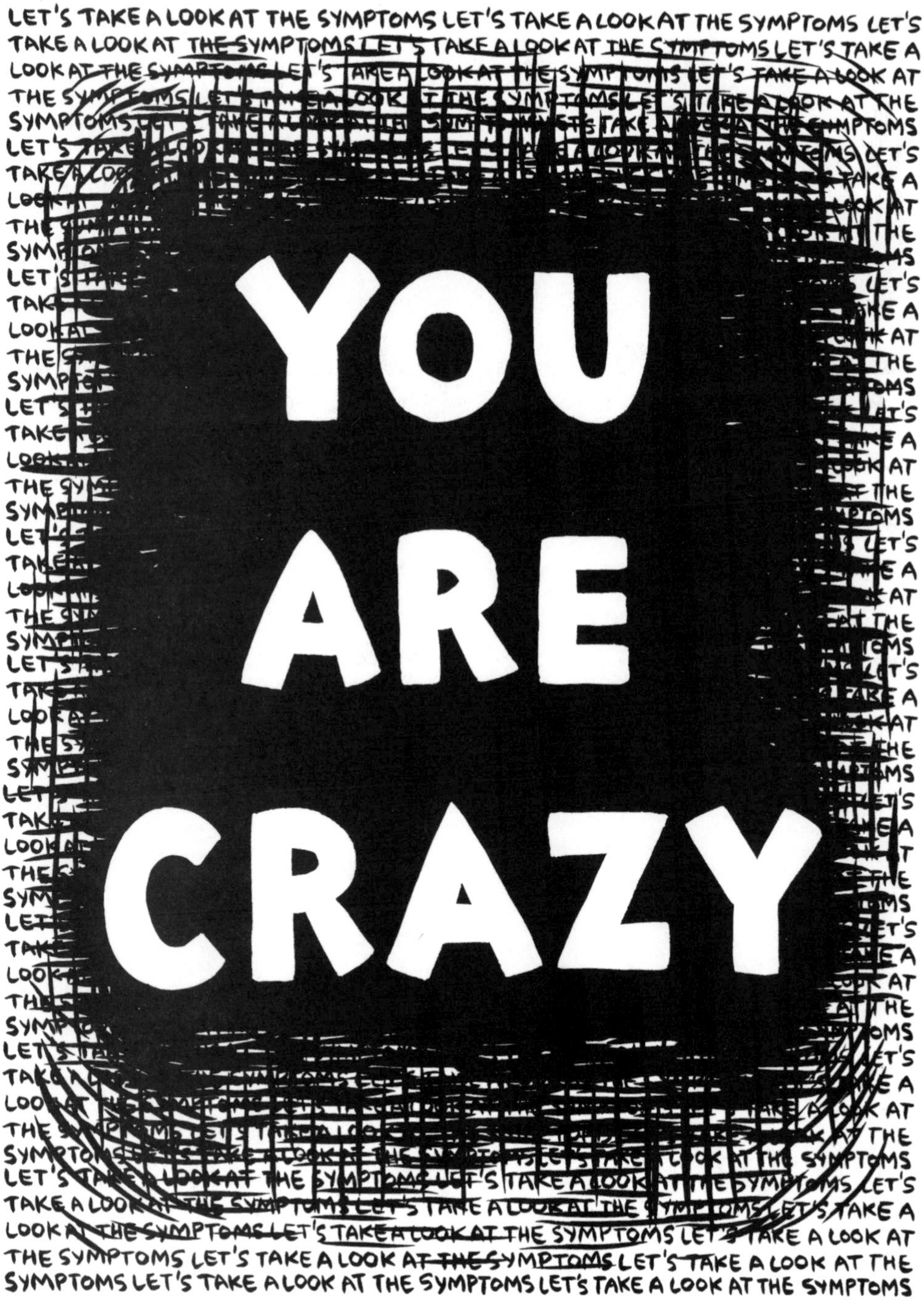
LET'S TAKE A LOOK AT THE SYMPTOMS LET'S TAKE A LOOK AT THE SYMPTOMS LET'S
YOU
ARE
CRAZY
SYMPTOMS LET'S TAKE A LOOK AT THE SYMPTOMS LET'S TAKE A LOOK AT THE SYMPTOMS

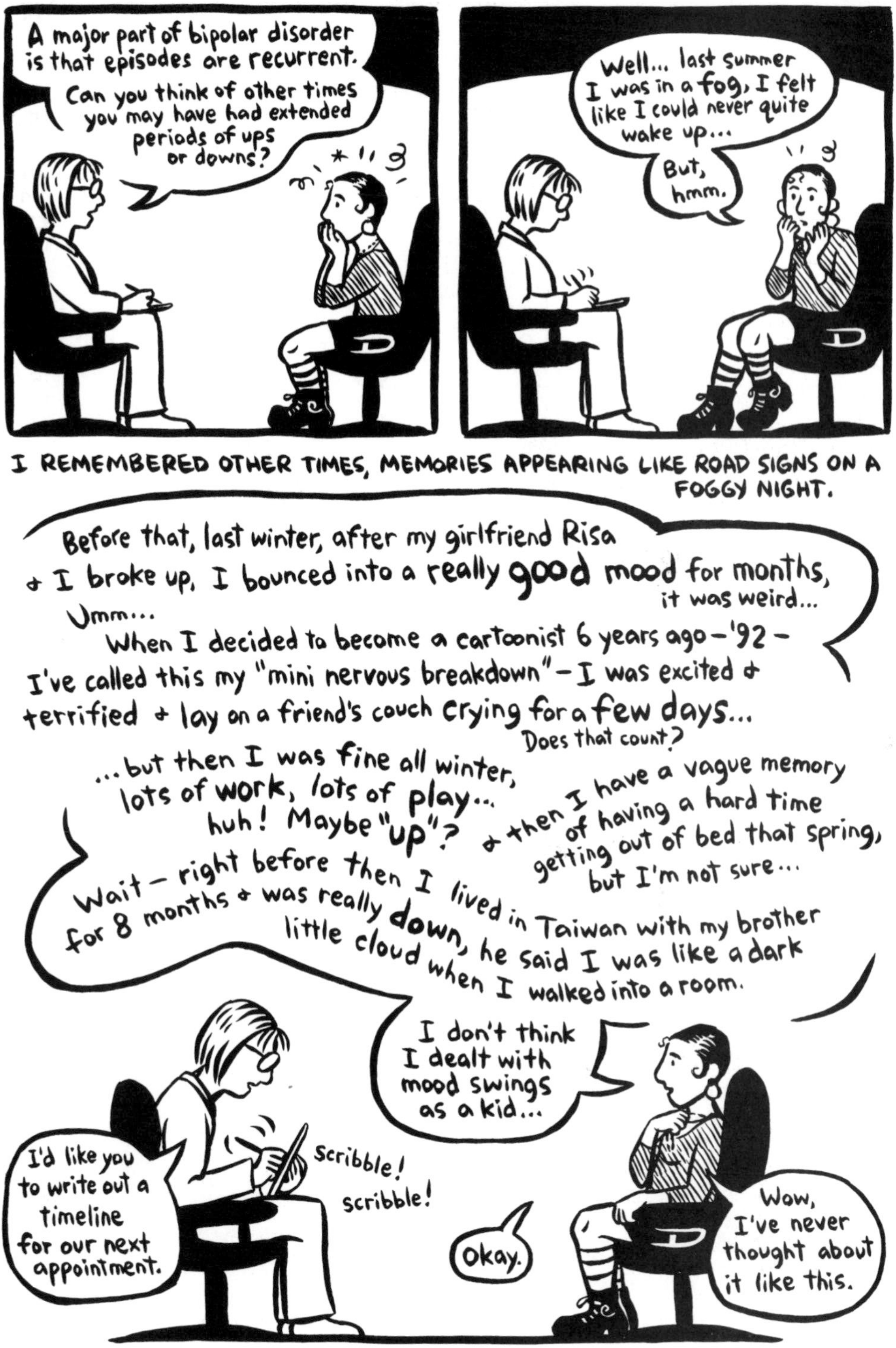
A major part of bipolar disorder is that episodes are recurrent.
Can you think of other times you may have had extended periods of ups or downs?
Well... last summer I was in a fog, I felt like I could never quite wake up...
But, hmm.
I REMEMBERED OTHER TIMES, MEMORIES APPEARING LIKE ROAD SIGNS ON A FOGGY NIGHT.
Before that, last winter, after my girlfriend Risa & I broke up, I bounced into a really good mood for months, it was weird...
Umm...
When I decided to become a cartoonist 6 years ago—'92—I've called this my "mini nervous breakdown"—I was excited & terrified & lay on a friend's couch crying for a few days... Does that count?
...but then I was fine all winter, lots of work, lots of play... huh! Maybe "up"?
& then I have a vague memory of having a hard time getting out of bed that spring, but I'm not sure...
Wait—right before then I lived in Taiwan with my brother for 8 months & was really down, he said I was like a dark little cloud when I walked into a room.
I don't think I dealt with mood swings as a kid...
I'd like you to write out a timeline for our next appointment.
scribble! scribble!
Okay.
Wow, I've never thought about it like this.

EVEN AS THE WEIGHT OF THIS NEWS SANK IN, THE SENSE OF HEAVINESS WAS ALLEVIATED BY A BACK-HANDED SENSE OF **CRED**.

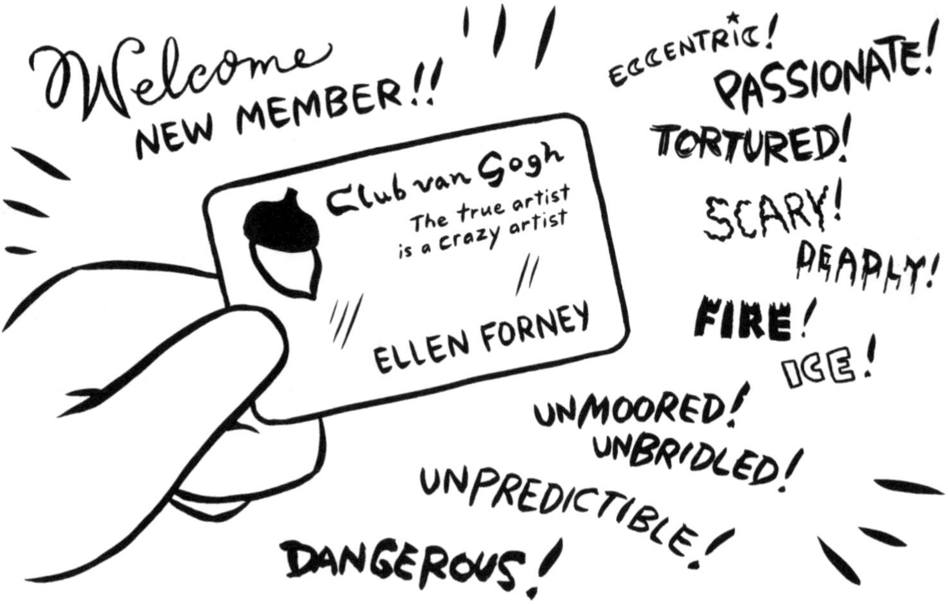

Welcome
NEW MEMBER!!
Club van Gogh
The true artist is a crazy artist
ELLEN FORNEY
ECCENTRIC!
PASSIONATE!
TORTURED!
SCARY!
DEADLY!
FIRE!
ICE!
UNMOORED!
UNBRIDLED!
UNPREDICTIBLE!
DANGEROUS!

I WAS OFFICIALLY A CRAZY ARTIST.

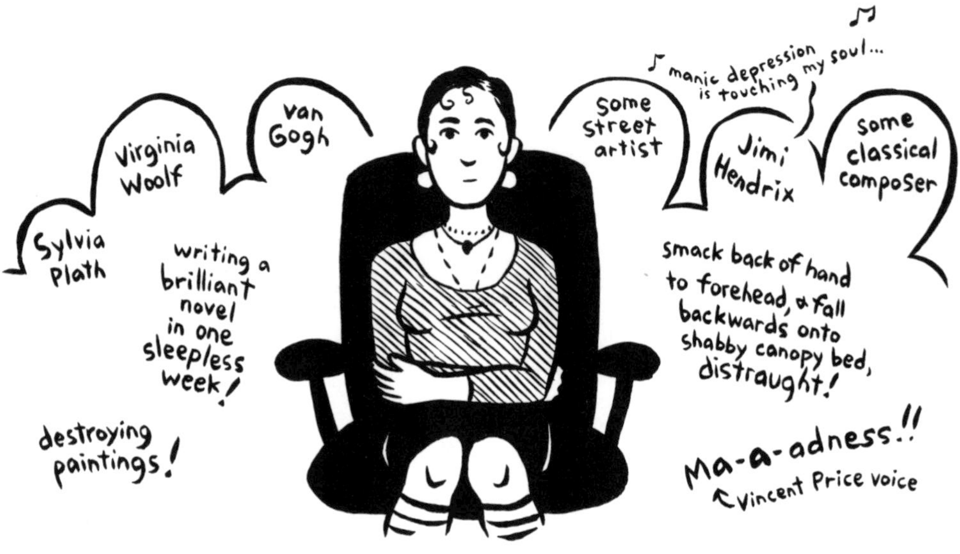

Sylvia Plath
Virginia Woolf
van Gogh
Some street artist
manic depression is touching my soul...
Jimi Hendrix
Some classical composer
writing a brilliant novel in one sleepless week!
destroying paintings!
smack back of hand to forehead, a fall backwards onto shabby canopy bed, distraught!
Ma-a-adness!!
Vincent Price voice

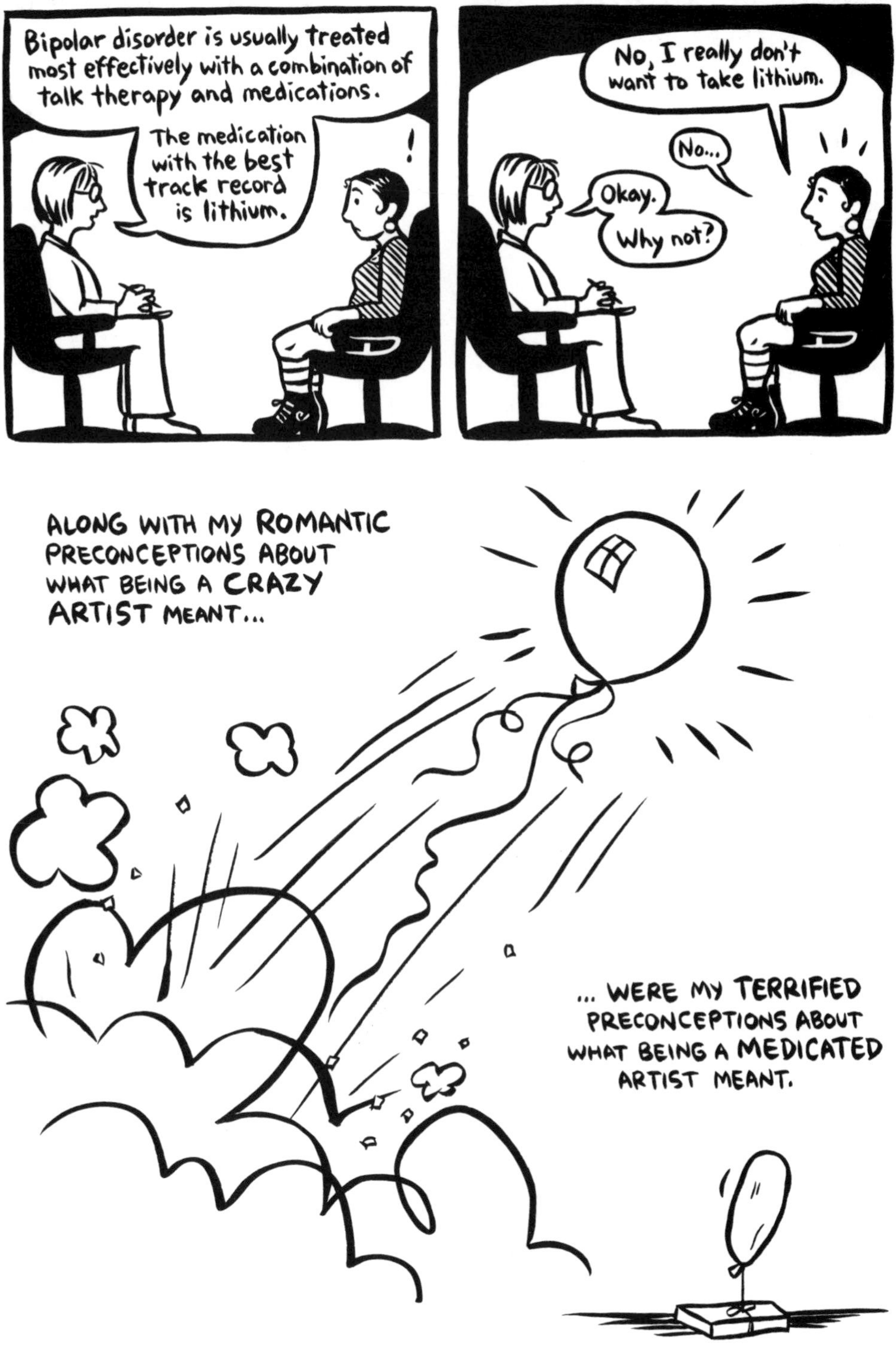
Bipolar disorder is usually treated most effectively with a combination of talk therapy and medications.
The medication with the best track record is lithium.
!
No, I really don't want to take lithium.
No...
Okay.
Why not?
ALONG WITH MY ROMANTIC PRECONCEPTIONS ABOUT WHAT BEING A CRAZY ARTIST MEANT...
... WERE MY TERRIFIED PRECONCEPTIONS ABOUT WHAT BEING A MEDICATED ARTIST MEANT.

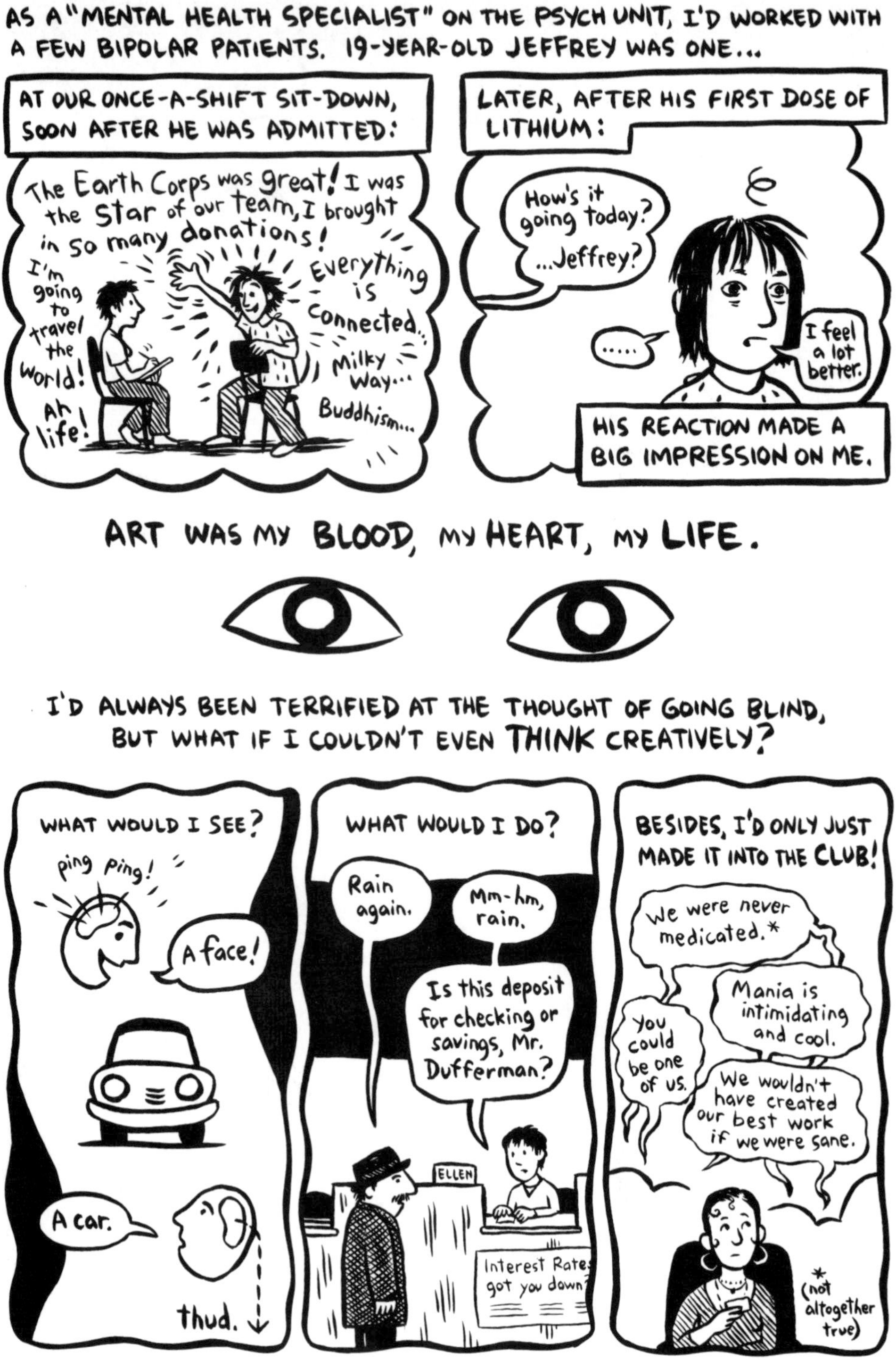

AS A "MENTAL HEALTH SPECIALIST" ON THE PSYCH UNIT, I'D WORKED WITH A FEW BIPOLAR PATIENTS. 19-YEAR-OLD JEFFREY WAS ONE...
AT OUR ONCE-A-SHIFT SIT-DOWN, SOON AFTER HE WAS ADMITTED:
The Earth Corps was great! I was the Star of our team, I brought in so many donations!
I'm going to travel the world! Ah life!
Everything is connected... Milky Way... Buddhism...
LATER, AFTER HIS FIRST DOSE OF LITHIUM:
How's it going today? ...Jeffrey?
.....
I feel a lot better.
HIS REACTION MADE A BIG IMPRESSION ON ME.
ART WAS MY BLOOD, MY HEART, MY LIFE.
I'D ALWAYS BEEN TERRIFIED AT THE THOUGHT OF GOING BLIND, BUT WHAT IF I COULDN'T EVEN THINK CREATIVELY?
WHAT WOULD I SEE?
ping ping!
A face!
A car.
thud.
WHAT WOULD I DO?
Rain again.
Mm-hm, rain.
Is this deposit for checking or savings, Mr. Dufferman?
ELLEN
Interest Rates got you down?
BESIDES, I'D ONLY JUST MADE IT INTO THE CLUB!
We were never medicated.*
Mania is intimidating and cool.
You could be one of us.
We wouldn't have created our best work if we were sane.
* (not altogether true)

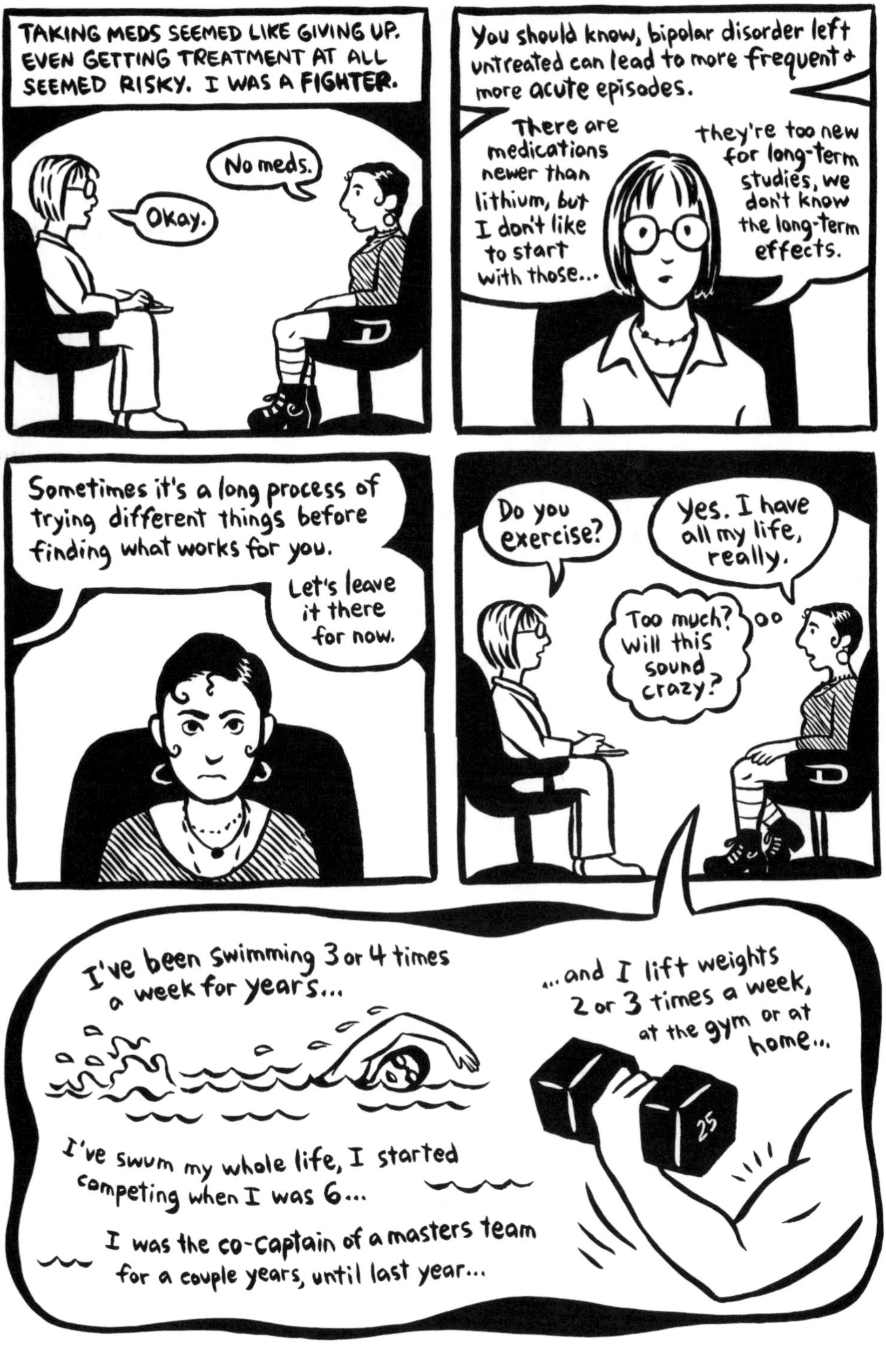
TAKING MEDS SEEMED LIKE GIVING UP. EVEN GETTING TREATMENT AT ALL SEEMED RISKY. I WAS A FIGHTER.
No meds.
Okay.
You should know, bipolar disorder left untreated can lead to more frequent & more acute episodes.
There are medications newer than lithium, but I don't like to start with those...
they're too new for long-term studies, we don't know the long-term effects.
Sometimes it's a long process of trying different things before finding what works for you.
Let's leave it there for now.
Do you exercise?
Yes. I have all my life, really.
Too much? Will this sound crazy?
I've been swimming 3 or 4 times a week for years...
...and I lift weights 2 or 3 times a week, at the gym or at home...
25
I've swum my whole life, I started competing when I was 6...
I was the co-captain of a masters team for a couple years, until last year...

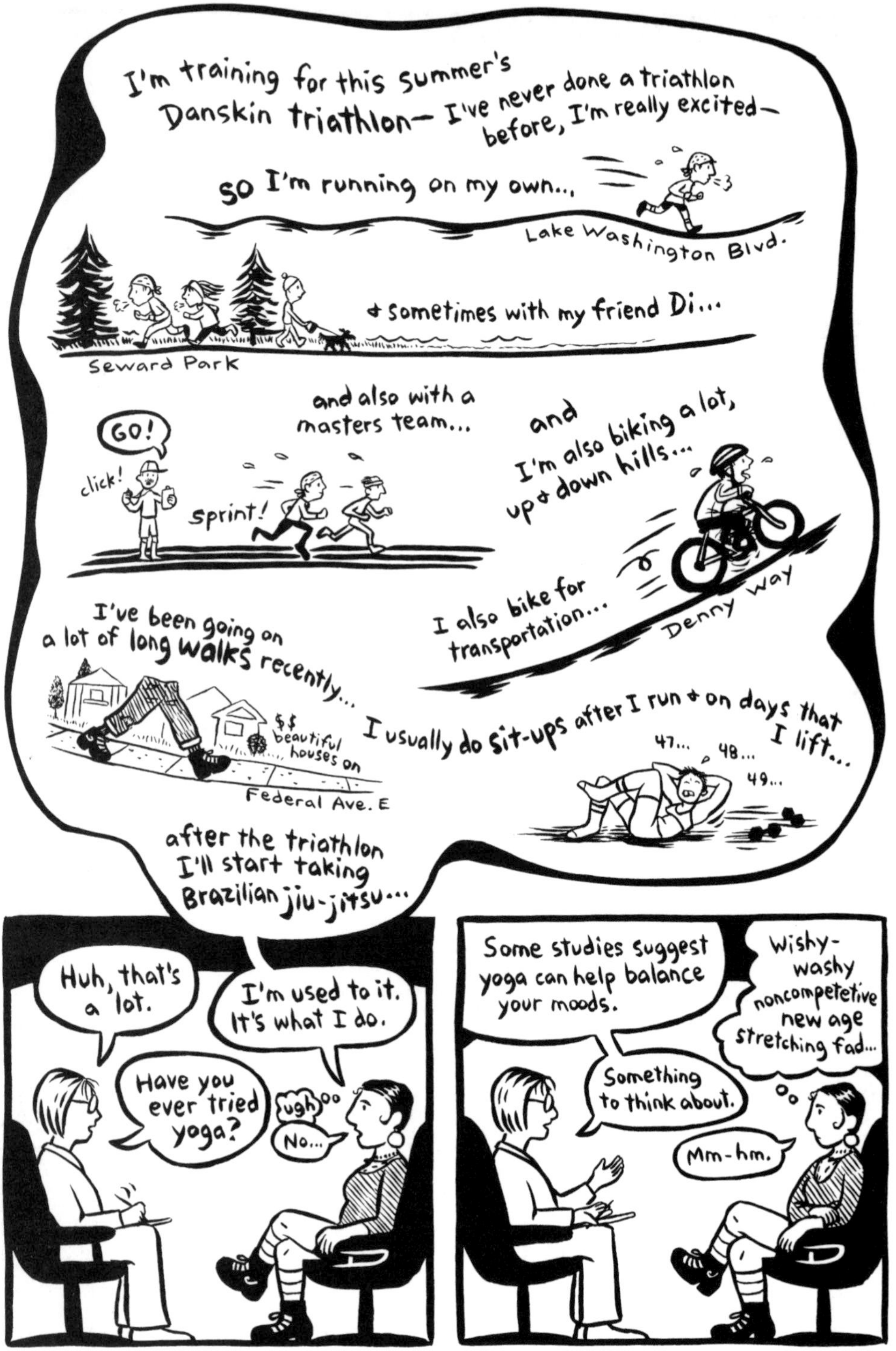
I'm training for this summer's Danskin triathlon— I've never done a triathlon before, I'm really excited—
so I'm running on my own...
Lake Washington Blvd.
+ sometimes with my friend Di...
Seward Park
and also with a masters team...
GO!
click!
sprint!
and I'm also biking a lot, up + down hills...
I also bike for transportation...
Denny Way
I've been going on a lot of long walks recently...
$$ beautiful houses on
Federal Ave. E
I usually do sit-ups after I run + on days that I lift...
47...
48...
49...
after the triathlon I'll start taking Brazilian jiu-jitsu...
Huh, that's a lot.
I'm used to it. It's what I do.
Have you ever tried yoga?
ugh
No...
Some studies suggest yoga can help balance your moods.
Wishy-washy noncompetetive new age stretching fad...
Something to think about.
Mm-hm.

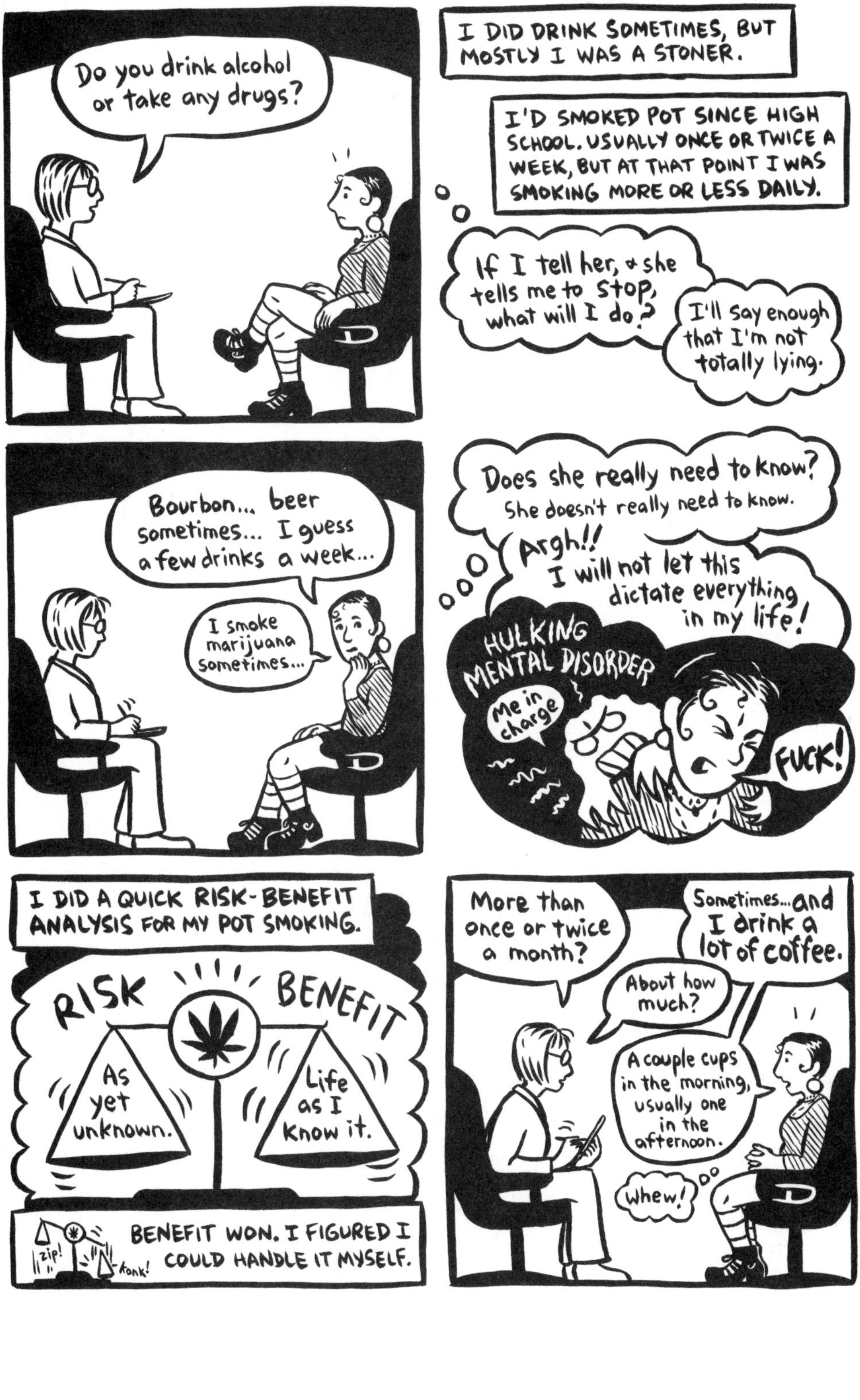

Do you drink alcohol or take any drugs?
I DID DRINK SOMETIMES, BUT MOSTLY I WAS A STONER.
I'D SMOKED POT SINCE HIGH SCHOOL. USUALLY ONCE OR TWICE A WEEK, BUT AT THAT POINT I WAS SMOKING MORE OR LESS DAILY.
If I tell her, & she tells me to stop, what will I do?
I'll say enough that I'm not totally lying.
Bourbon... beer sometimes... I guess a few drinks a week...
I smoke marijuana sometimes...
Does she really need to know?
She doesn't really need to know.
Argh!! I will not let this dictate everything in my life!
HULKING MENTAL DISORDER
Me in charge
FUCK!
I DID A QUICK RISK-BENEFIT ANALYSIS FOR MY POT SMOKING.
RISK
BENEFIT
As yet unknown.
Life as I know it.
zip!
konk!
BENEFIT WON. I FIGURED I COULD HANDLE IT MYSELF.
More than once or twice a month?
Sometimes...and I drink a lot of coffee.
About how much?
A couple cups in the morning, usually one in the afternoon.
Whew!

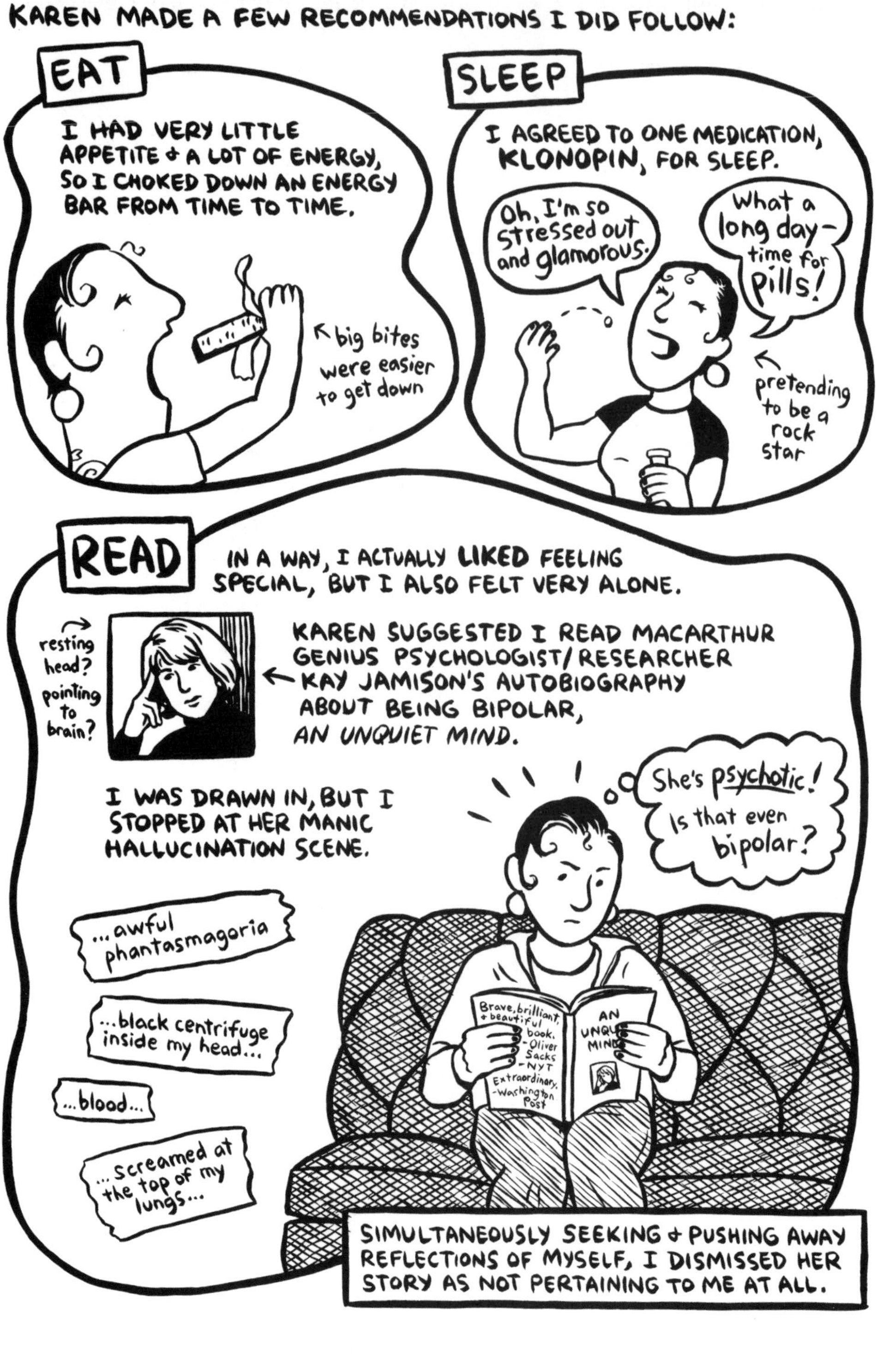
KAREN MADE A FEW RECOMMENDATIONS I DID FOLLOW:
EAT
I HAD VERY LITTLE APPETITE & A LOT OF ENERGY, SO I CHOKED DOWN AN ENERGY BAR FROM TIME TO TIME.
big bites were easier to get down
SLEEP
I AGREED TO ONE MEDICATION, KLONOPIN, FOR SLEEP.
Oh, I'm so stressed out and glamorous.
What a long day— time for pills!
pretending to be a rock star
READ
IN A WAY, I ACTUALLY LIKED FEELING SPECIAL, BUT I ALSO FELT VERY ALONE.
resting head? pointing to brain?
KAREN SUGGESTED I READ MACARTHUR GENIUS PSYCHOLOGIST/RESEARCHER KAY JAMISON'S AUTOBIOGRAPHY ABOUT BEING BIPOLAR, AN UNQUIET MIND.
I WAS DRAWN IN, BUT I STOPPED AT HER MANIC HALLUCINATION SCENE.
She's psychotic! Is that even bipolar?
...awful phantasmagoria
...black centrifuge inside my head...
...blood...
...screamed at the top of my lungs...
Brave, brilliant, & beautiful book. -Oliver Sacks -NYT
Extraordinary. -Washington Post
AN UNQU MIND
SIMULTANEOUSLY SEEKING & PUSHING AWAY REFLECTIONS OF MYSELF, I DISMISSED HER STORY AS NOT PERTAINING TO ME AT ALL.

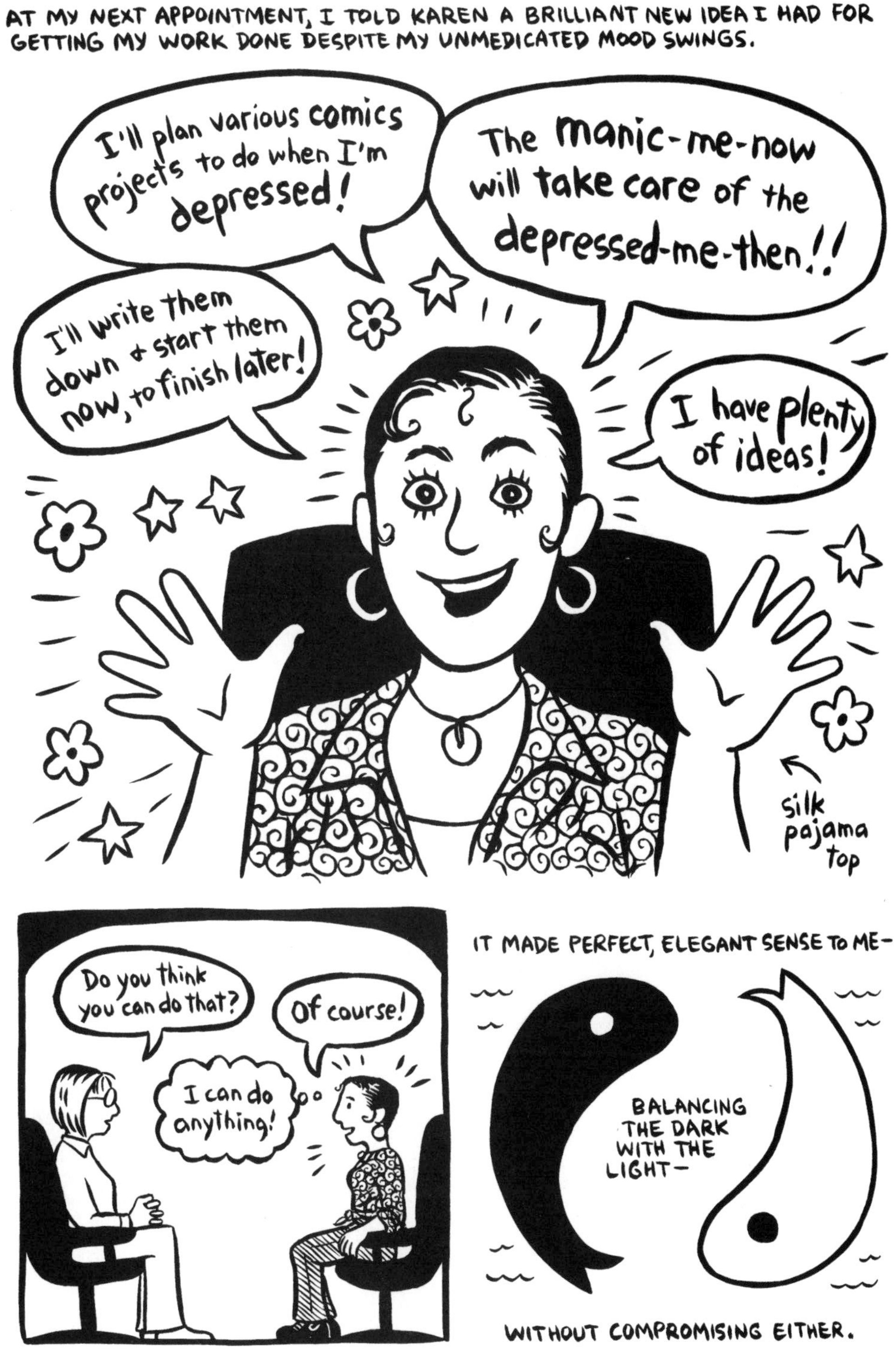
AT MY NEXT APPOINTMENT, I TOLD KAREN A BRILLIANT NEW IDEA I HAD FOR GETTING MY WORK DONE DESPITE MY UNMEDICATED MOOD SWINGS.
I'll plan various comics projects to do when I'm depressed!
The manic-me-now will take care of the depressed-me-then!!
I'll write them down & start them now, to finish later!
I have plenty of ideas!
silk pajama top
Do you think you can do that?
Of course!
I can do anything!
IT MADE PERFECT, ELEGANT SENSE TO ME–
BALANCING THE DARK WITH THE LIGHT–
WITHOUT COMPROMISING EITHER.

BUT MY MEMORY OF WHAT IT WAS LIKE TO BE DEPRESSED WAS FUZZY, & HEAVILY-INFLUENCED BY MY MANIA. KAREN WOULD LATER TELL ME,

"Memory is mood-specific."

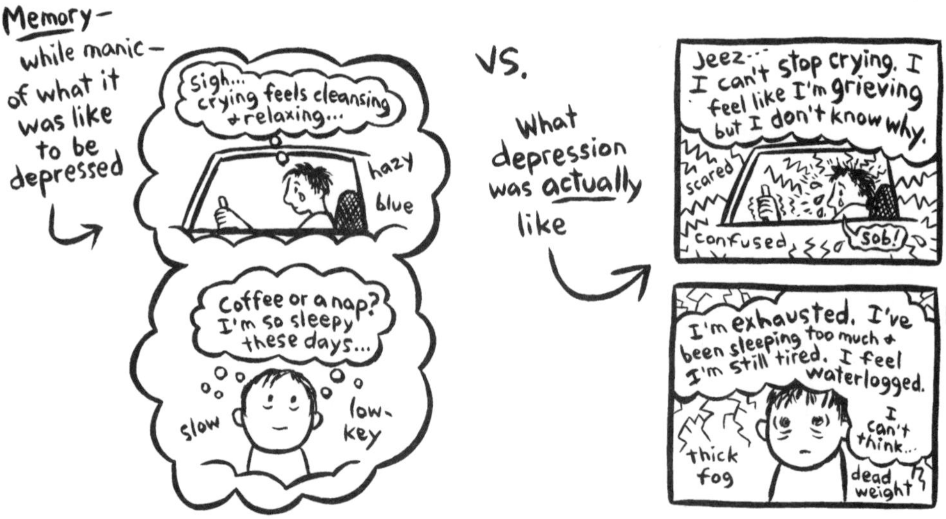

Memory— while manic— of what it was like to be depressed
Sigh... crying feels cleansing & relaxing...
hazy
blue
Coffee or a nap? I'm so sleepy these days...
slow
low-key
VS.
What depression was actually like
Jeez... stop crying. I can't feel like I'm grieving but I don't know why.
scared
confused
Sob!
I'm exhausted. I've been sleeping too much & I'm still tired. I feel waterlogged.
I can't think...
thick fog
dead weight

MY EUPHORIC MIND JUST COULDN'T CONJURE UP THAT DRAMATIC SHIFT WITHIN ITSELF.

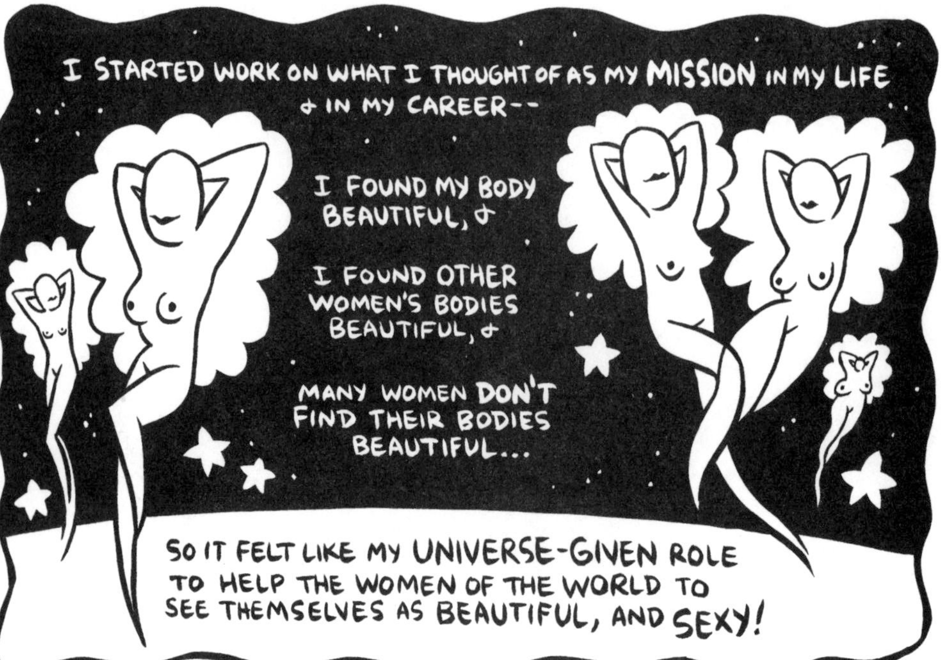

I STARTED WORK ON WHAT I THOUGHT OF AS MY MISSION IN MY LIFE & IN MY CAREER--
I FOUND MY BODY BEAUTIFUL, &
I FOUND OTHER WOMEN'S BODIES BEAUTIFUL, &
MANY WOMEN DON'T FIND THEIR BODIES BEAUTIFUL...
SO IT FELT LIKE MY UNIVERSE-GIVEN ROLE TO HELP THE WOMEN OF THE WORLD TO SEE THEMSELVES AS BEAUTIFUL, AND SEXY!

MY PROJECT-PLANNING CONSISTED ALMOST ENTIRELY OF ORGANIZING PHOTO SHOOTS, AS REFERENCE MATERIAL FOR FUTURE COMICS.

THE MORNING SWIMMERS, A VARIETY OF AGES & BODY TYPES, WERE **PERFECT!**

I SUGGESTED WE TAKE PHOTOS AFTER SWIMMING SOMETIME, & THEY WERE GAME.

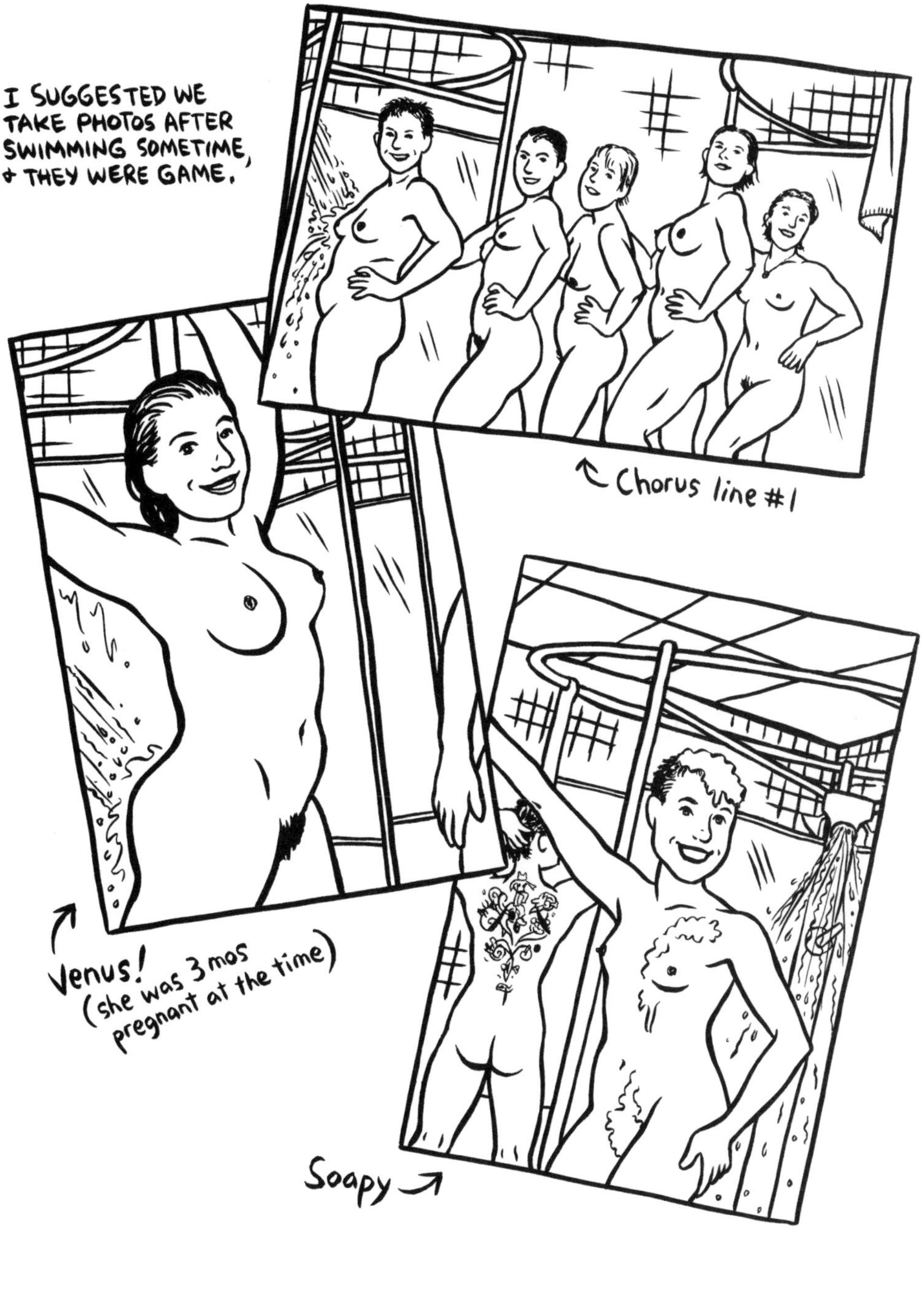

← Chorus line #1

Venus! (she was 3 mos pregnant at the time)

Soapy →

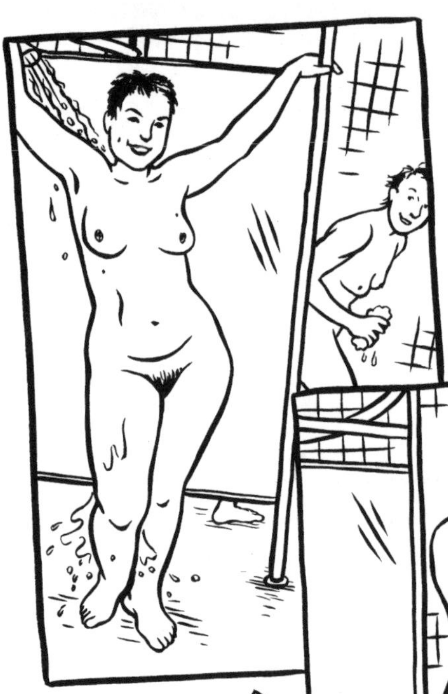

S. HAD BOUGHT THE DISPOSABLE WATERPROOF CAMERA, & GOT THE PHOTOS DEVELOPED. SHE WAS AN OIL PAINTER AND HAD DECIDED TO TRY PAINTING US, TOO.

The 3 Graces

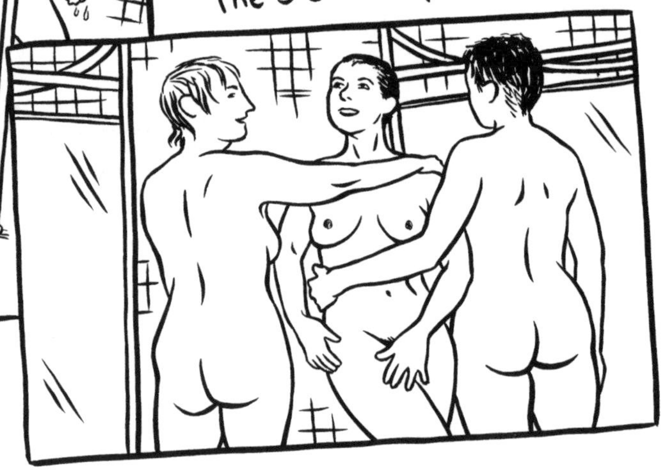

A first for C.

Chorus line #2

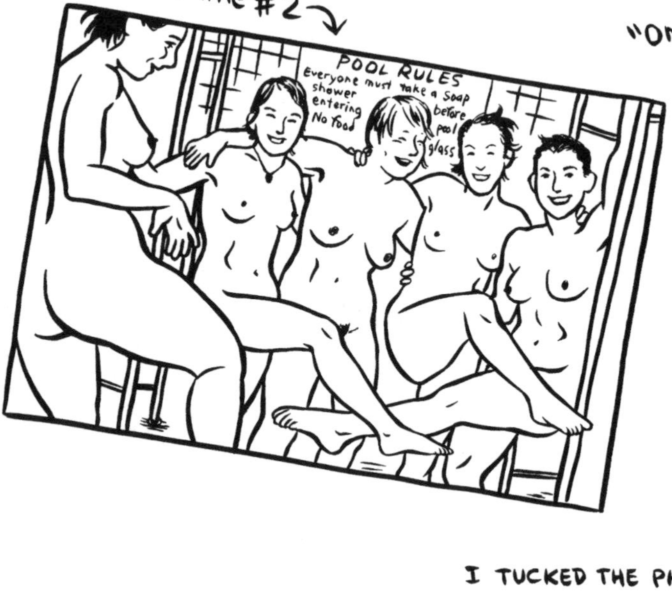
POOL RULES
Everyone must take a Soap shower before entering pool
No food
glass

"Only you, Ellen!"

THEY SAID MY ENERGY WAS INFECTIOUS.

WE GIGGLED ABOUT OUR PHOTO SHOOT FOR WEEKS.

I TUCKED THE PHOTOS AWAY FOR LATER.

I WASN'T GOING TO MISS THE OPPORTUNITY FOR DOCUMENTATION WHEN I HAD MY SECOND TATTOO SESSION, WHEN OWEN FINISHED THE LINEWORK.

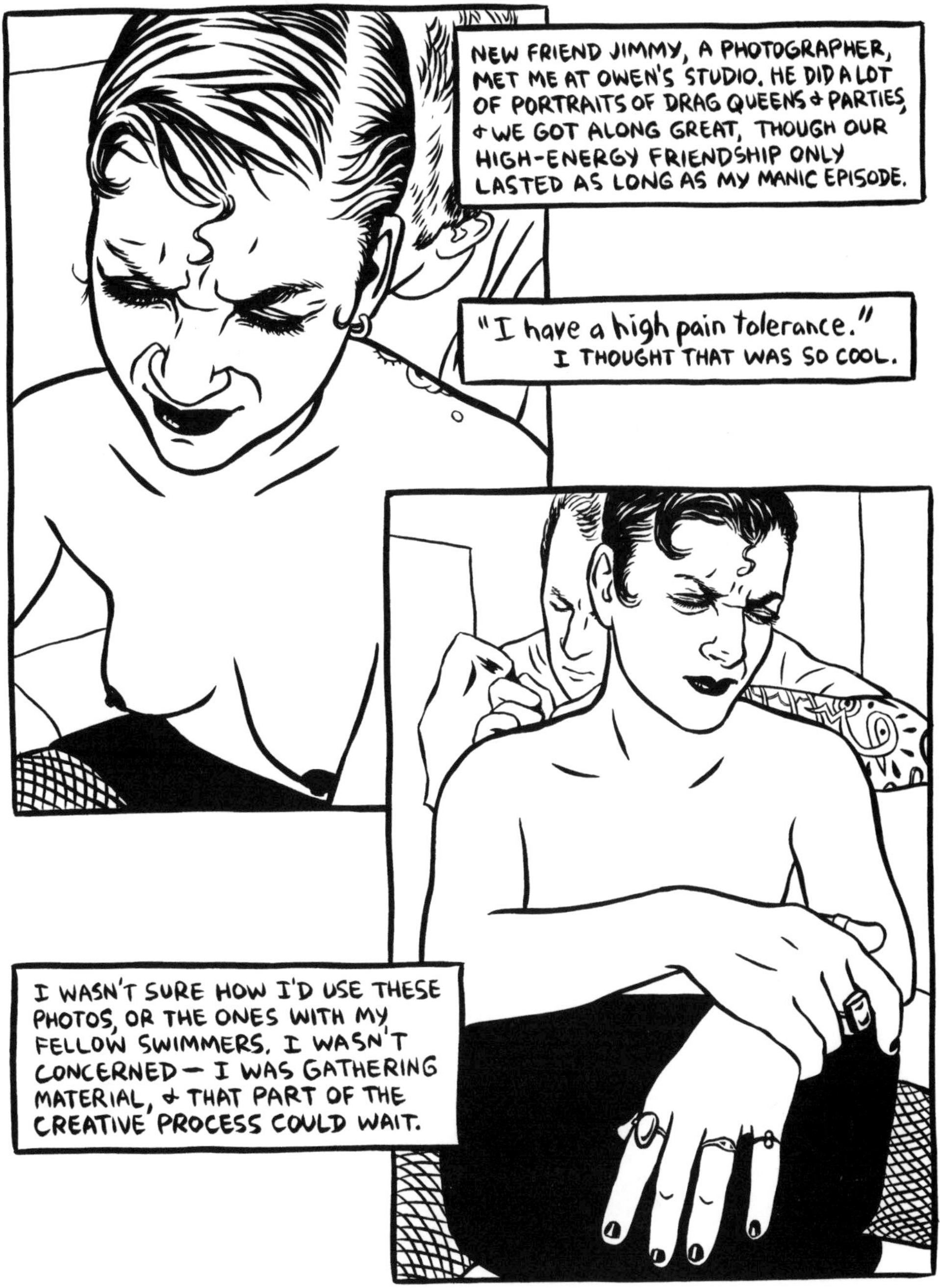
NEW FRIEND JIMMY, A PHOTOGRAPHER, MET ME AT OWEN'S STUDIO. HE DID A LOT OF PORTRAITS OF DRAG QUEENS & PARTIES, & WE GOT ALONG GREAT, THOUGH OUR HIGH-ENERGY FRIENDSHIP ONLY LASTED AS LONG AS MY MANIC EPISODE.
"I have a high pain tolerance." I THOUGHT THAT WAS SO COOL.
I WASN'T SURE HOW I'D USE THESE PHOTOS, OR THE ONES WITH MY FELLOW SWIMMERS. I WASN'T CONCERNED — I WAS GATHERING MATERIAL, & THAT PART OF THE CREATIVE PROCESS COULD WAIT.

I TUCKED THESE PHOTOS AWAY FOR LATER, TOO.

MY BIGGEST SHOOT
WAS FOR A PORN COMIC
FOR EROS COMIX,
AN IMPRINT OF
FANTAGRAPHICS.

THE PUBLISHER, GARY,
GAVE AN ENTHUSIASTIC
THUMBS-UP TO MY
PROPOSAL.

"S'about time, Forney!"

← folding chairs =
"car"

Trader Joe's ↑
baguette =
"steering wheel"

I ROUGHED OUT THE
WHOLE COMIC IN ONE
SITTING— A GRRL ROCK
BAND, ON THE WAY HOME
FROM PRACTICE, STOP
INTO A DEPARTMENT
STORE, TRY ON
LINGERIE, & HAVE
SEX IN THE FITTING
ROOM.

← "lingerie
department"

"fitting
room"
↙

MY GORGEOUS FRIENDS
MOLLY & ANITA,
PSYCHED TO BE IN AN
ART PROJECT, AGREED
TO POSE AS MY
BANDMATES.

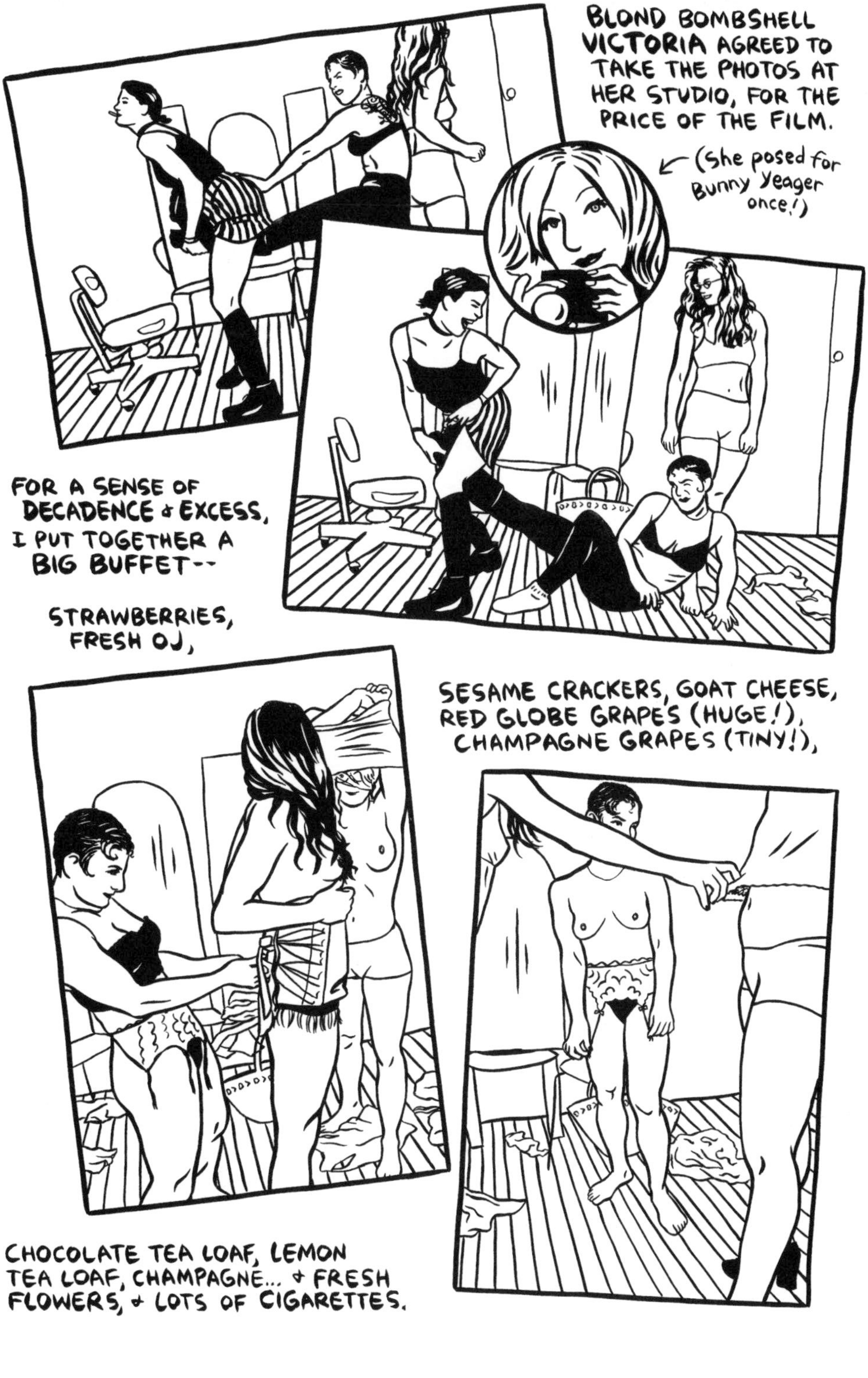
BLOND BOMBSHELL VICTORIA AGREED TO TAKE THE PHOTOS AT HER STUDIO, FOR THE PRICE OF THE FILM.
(She posed for Bunny Yeager once!)
FOR A SENSE OF DECADENCE & EXCESS, I PUT TOGETHER A BIG BUFFET--
STRAWBERRIES, FRESH OJ,
SESAME CRACKERS, GOAT CHEESE, RED GLOBE GRAPES (HUGE!), CHAMPAGNE GRAPES (TINY!),
CHOCOLATE TEA LOAF, LEMON TEA LOAF, CHAMPAGNE... & FRESH FLOWERS, & LOTS OF CIGARETTES.

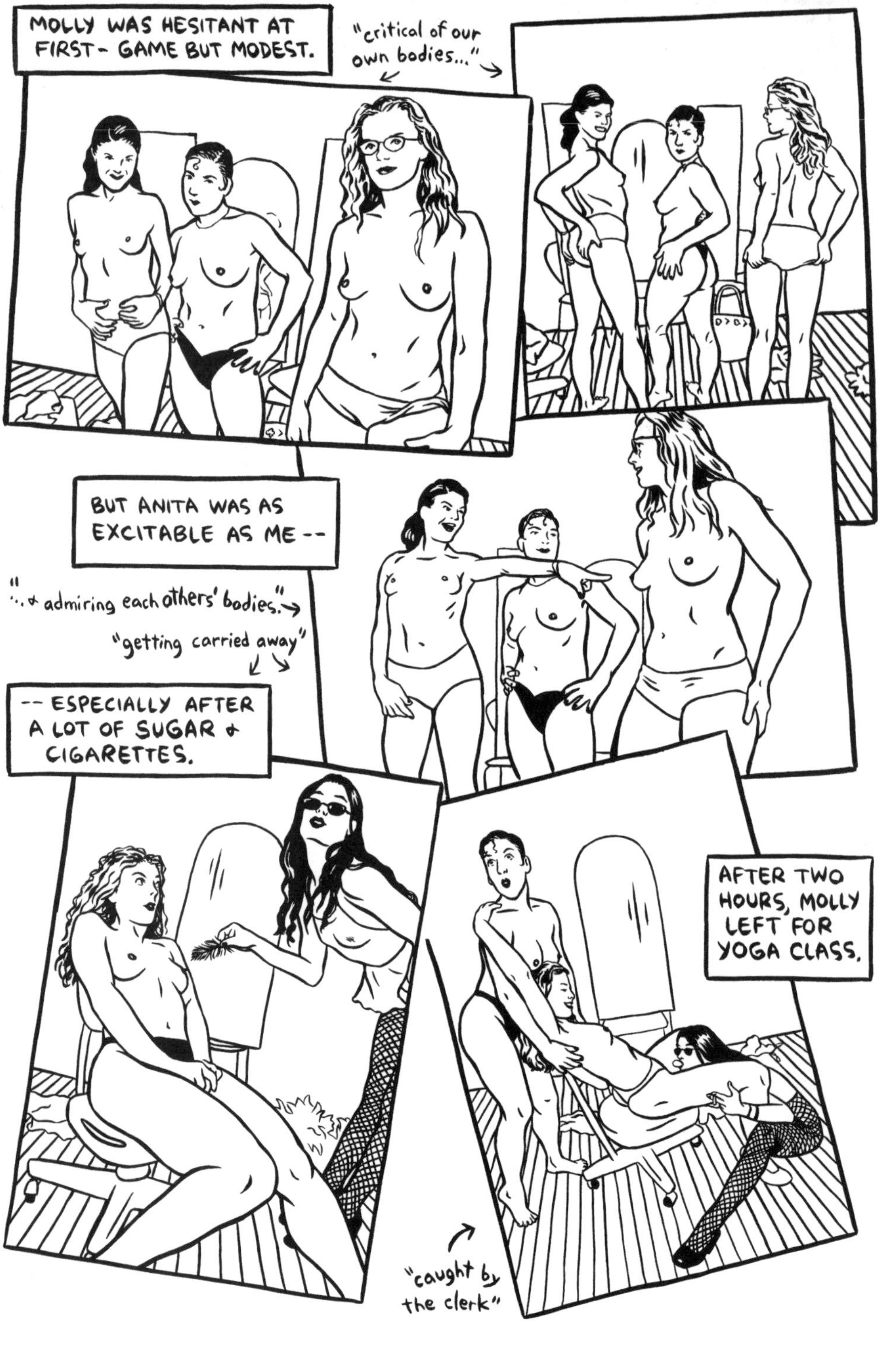
MOLLY WAS HESITANT AT FIRST - GAME BUT MODEST.
"critical of our own bodies..."
BUT ANITA WAS AS EXCITABLE AS ME --
"...& admiring each others' bodies."
"getting carried away"
-- ESPECIALLY AFTER A LOT OF SUGAR & CIGARETTES.
AFTER TWO HOURS, MOLLY LEFT FOR YOGA CLASS.
"caught by the clerk"

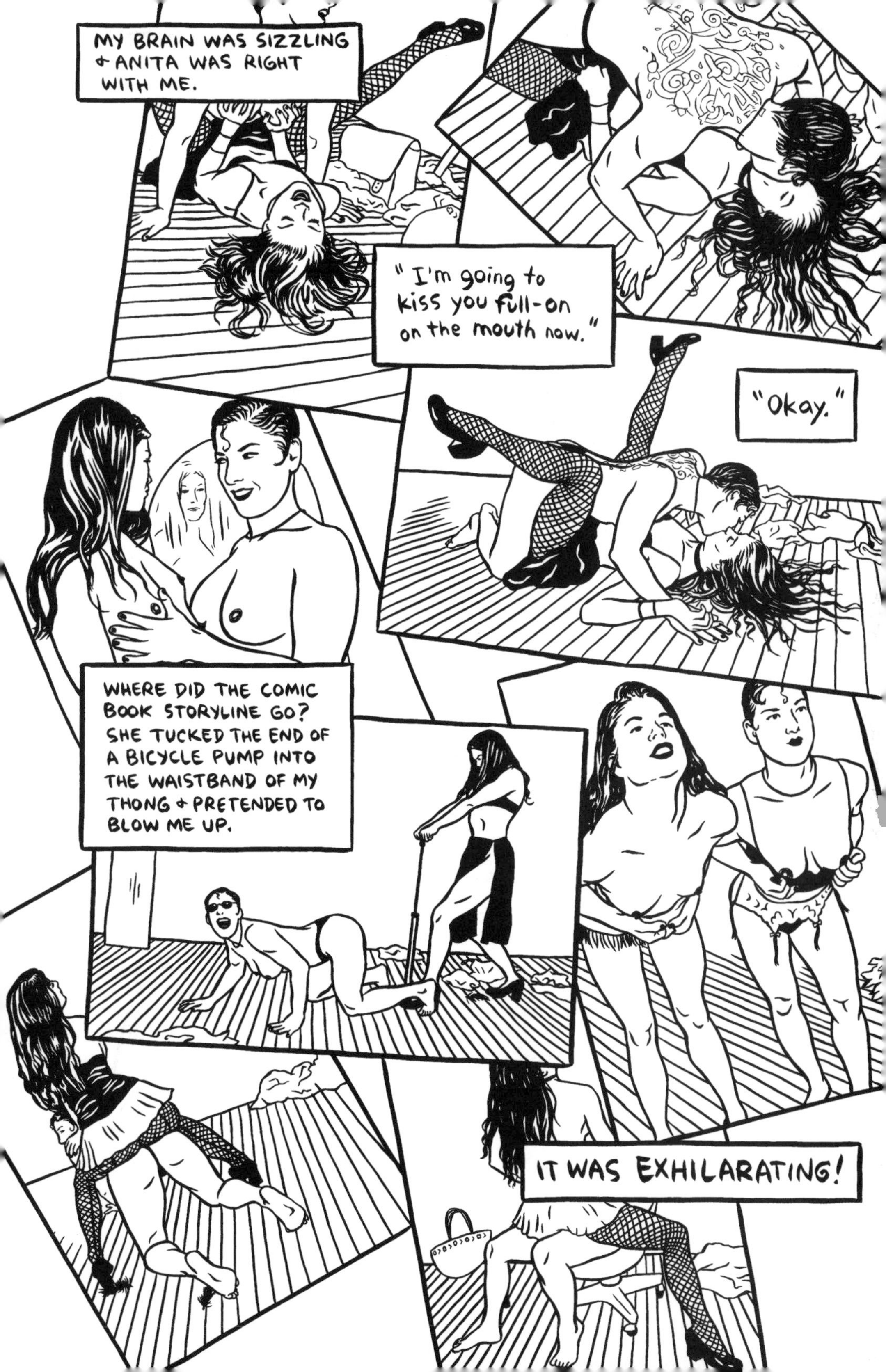
MY BRAIN WAS SIZZLING & ANITA WAS RIGHT WITH ME.
" I'm going to kiss you full-on on the mouth now."
"Okay."
WHERE DID THE COMIC BOOK STORYLINE GO? SHE TUCKED THE END OF A BICYCLE PUMP INTO THE WAISTBAND OF MY THONG & PRETENDED TO BLOW ME UP.
IT WAS EXHILARATING!

WALKING OUT OF VICTORIA'S STUDIO, ANITA & I AGREED IT FELT LIKE WE'D JUST FUCKED FOR HOURS.

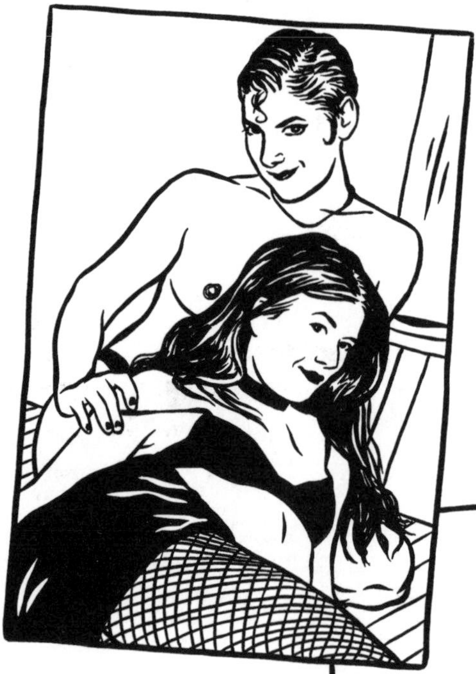

I TUCKED THESE PHOTOS AWAY WITH THE OTHERS.

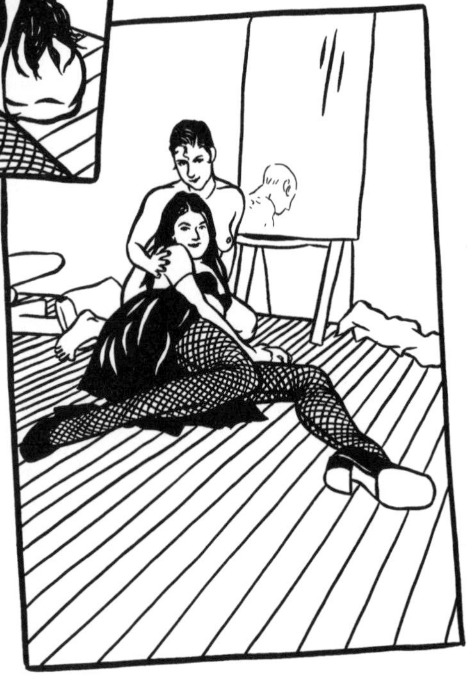

THE PHOTOS FROM THESE SHOOTS WOULD REMAIN TUCKED AWAY FOR YEARS.

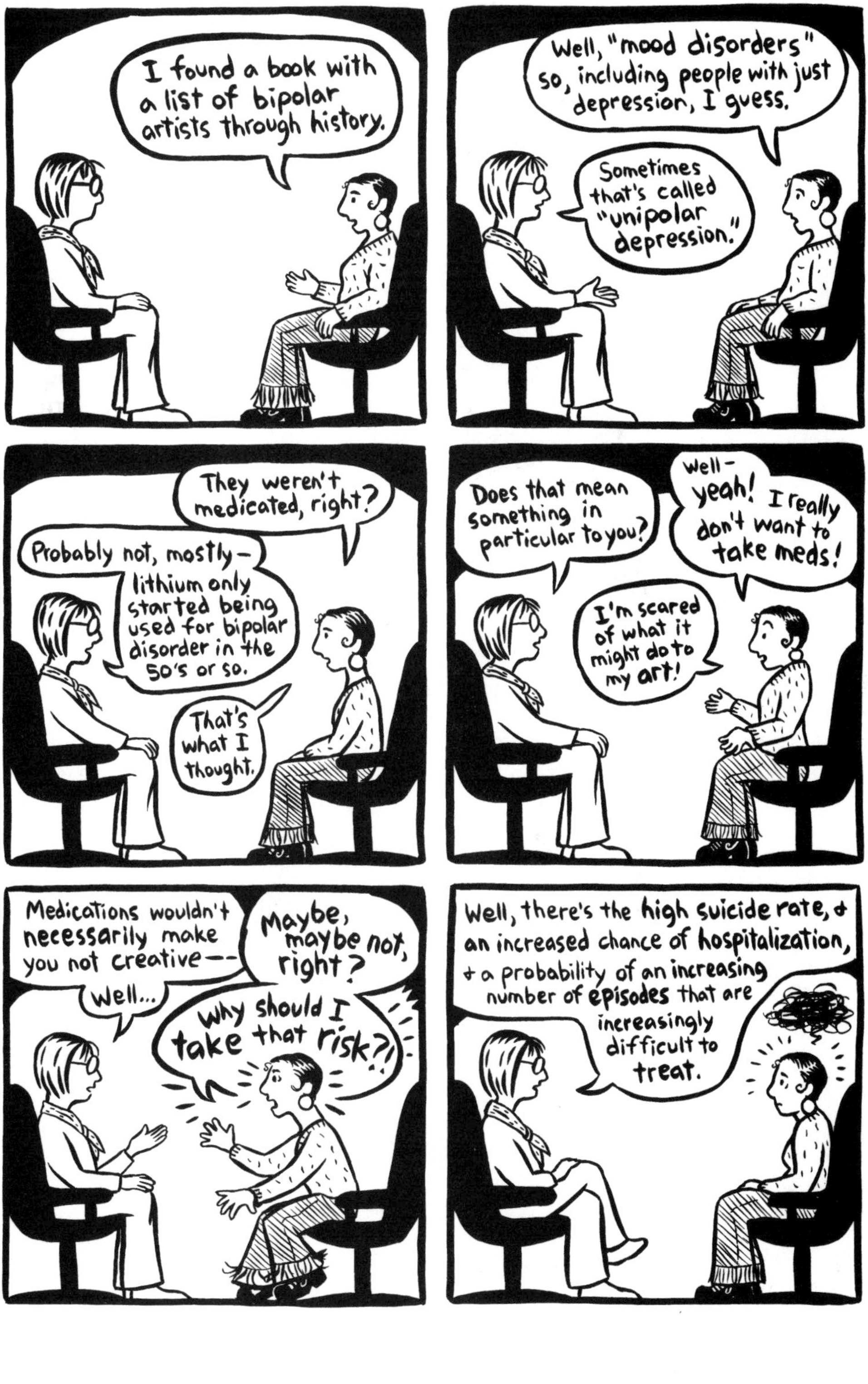
I found a book with a list of bipolar artists through history.
Well, "mood disorders" so, including people with just depression, I guess.
Sometimes that's called "unipolar depression."
They weren't medicated, right?
Probably not, mostly— lithium only started being used for bipolar disorder in the 50's or so.
That's what I thought.
Does that mean something in particular to you?
Well— yeah! I really don't want to take meds!
I'm scared of what it might do to my art!
Medications wouldn't necessarily make you not creative——
Maybe, maybe not, right?
Well...
Why should I take that risk?!
Well, there's the high suicide rate, & an increased chance of hospitalization, & a probability of an increasing number of episodes that are increasingly difficult to treat.

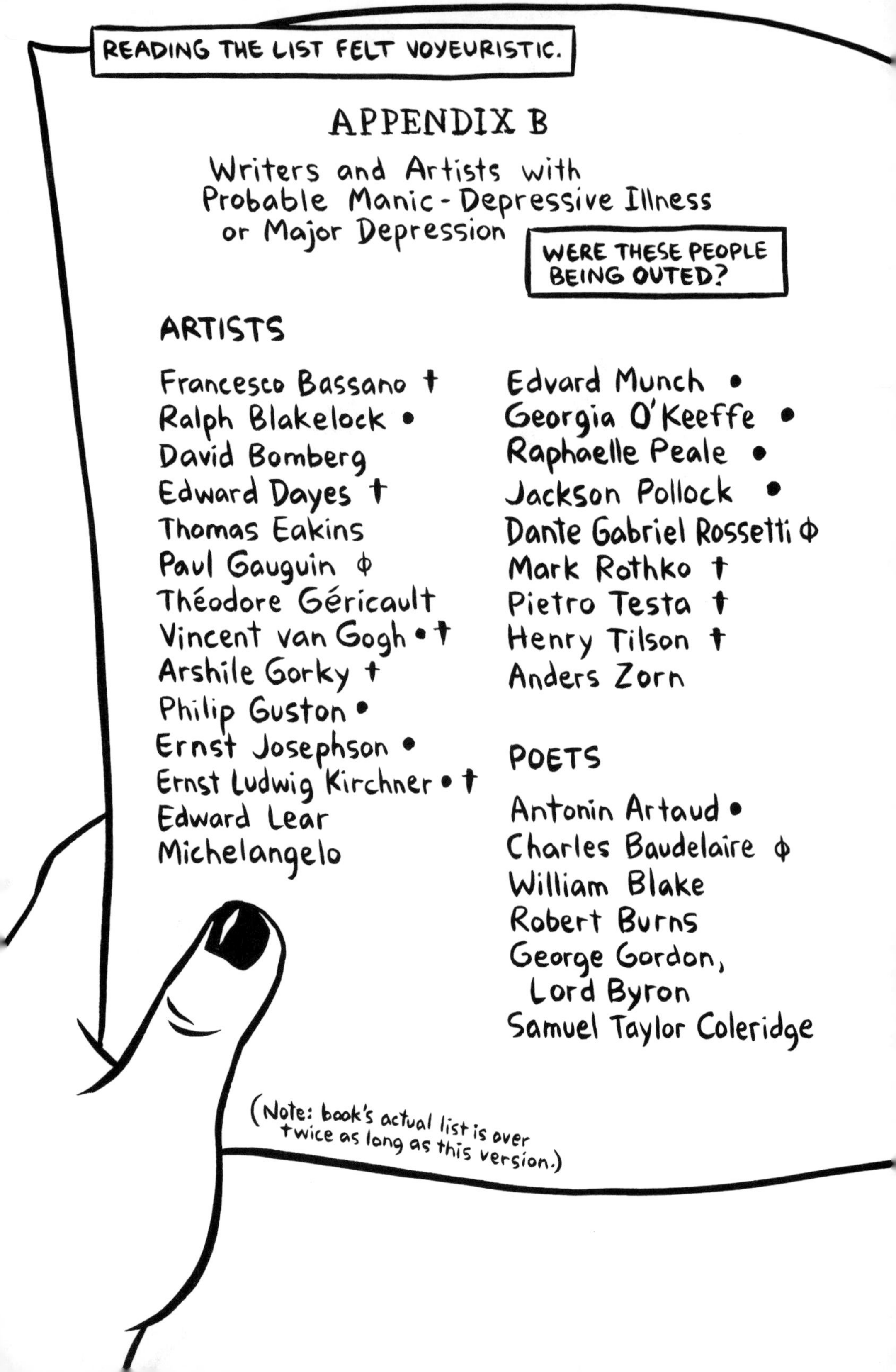
READING THE LIST FELT VOYEURISTIC.
APPENDIX B
Writers and Artists with
Probable Manic-Depressive Illness
or Major Depression
WERE THESE PEOPLE BEING OUTED?
ARTISTS
Francesco Bassano †
Ralph Blakelock •
David Bomberg
Edward Dayes †
Thomas Eakins
Paul Gauguin ϕ
Théodore Géricault
Vincent van Gogh • †
Arshile Gorky †
Philip Guston •
Ernst Josephson •
Ernst Ludwig Kirchner • †
Edward Lear
Michelangelo
Edvard Munch •
Georgia O'Keeffe •
Raphaelle Peale •
Jackson Pollock •
Dante Gabriel Rossetti ϕ
Mark Rothko †
Pietro Testa †
Henry Tilson †
Anders Zorn
POETS
Antonin Artaud •
Charles Baudelaire ϕ
William Blake
Robert Burns
George Gordon,
Lord Byron
Samuel Taylor Coleridge
(Note: book's actual list is over twice as long as this version.)

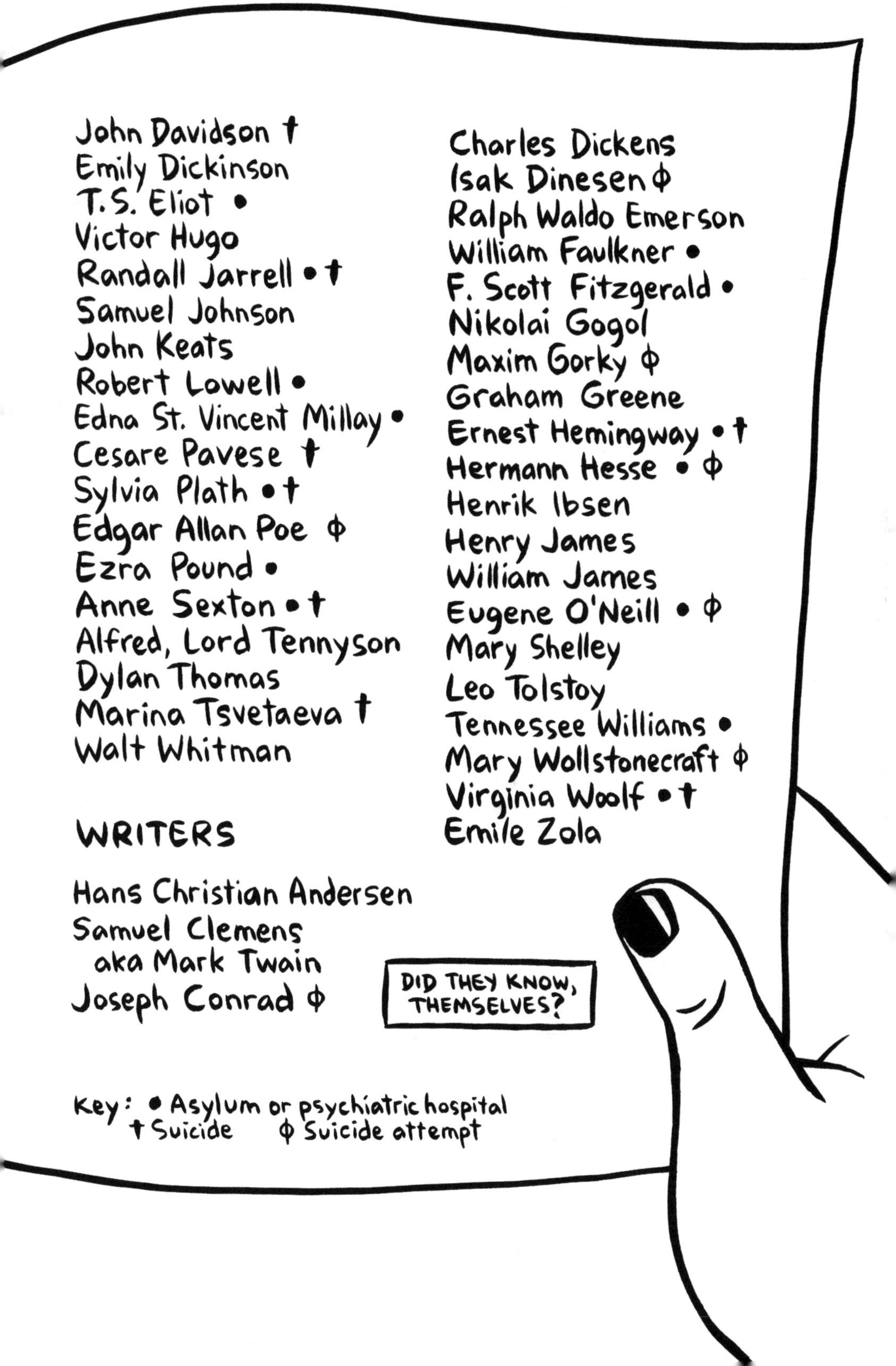
John Davidson †
Emily Dickinson
T.S. Eliot •
Victor Hugo
Randall Jarrell • †
Samuel Johnson
John Keats
Robert Lowell •
Edna St. Vincent Millay •
Cesare Pavese †
Sylvia Plath • †
Edgar Allan Poe ϕ
Ezra Pound •
Anne Sexton • †
Alfred, Lord Tennyson
Dylan Thomas
Marina Tsvetaeva †
Walt Whitman
WRITERS
Hans Christian Andersen
Samuel Clemens aka Mark Twain
Joseph Conrad ϕ
Charles Dickens
Isak Dinesen ϕ
Ralph Waldo Emerson
William Faulkner •
F. Scott Fitzgerald •
Nikolai Gogol
Maxim Gorky ϕ
Graham Greene
Ernest Hemingway • †
Hermann Hesse • ϕ
Henrik Ibsen
Henry James
William James
Eugene O'Neill • ϕ
Mary Shelley
Leo Tolstoy
Tennessee Williams •
Mary Wollstonecraft ϕ
Virginia Woolf • †
Emile Zola
DID THEY KNOW, THEMSELVES?
Key: • Asylum or psychiatric hospital
† Suicide ϕ Suicide attempt

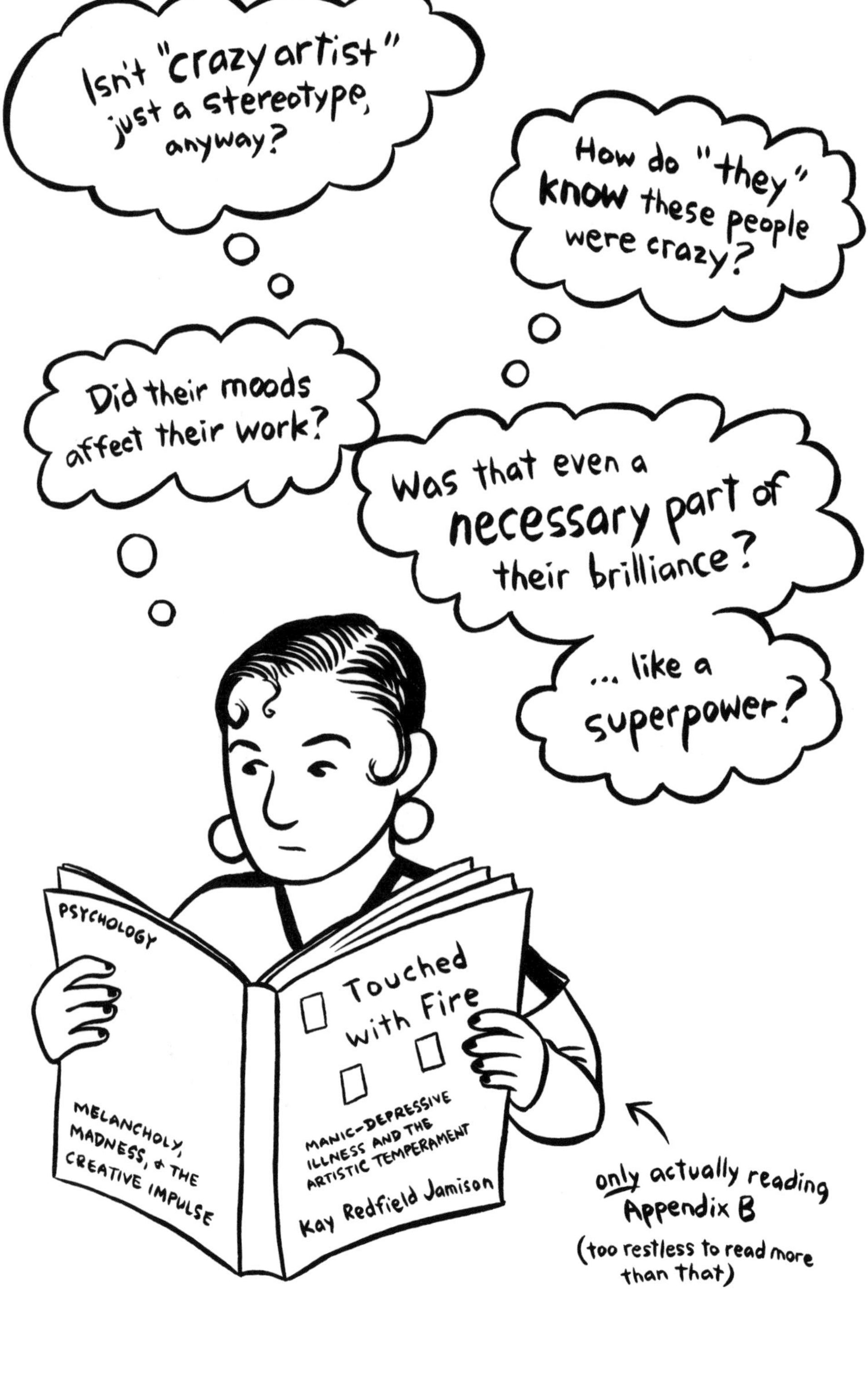
Isn't "crazy artist" just a stereotype, anyway?
How do "they" know these people were crazy?
Did their moods affect their work?
Was that even a necessary part of their brilliance?
... like a superpower?
PSYCHOLOGY
MELANCHOLY, MADNESS, & THE CREATIVE IMPULSE
Touched with Fire
MANIC-DEPRESSIVE ILLNESS AND THE ARTISTIC TEMPERAMENT
Kay Redfield Jamison
only actually reading Appendix B
(too restless to read more than that)

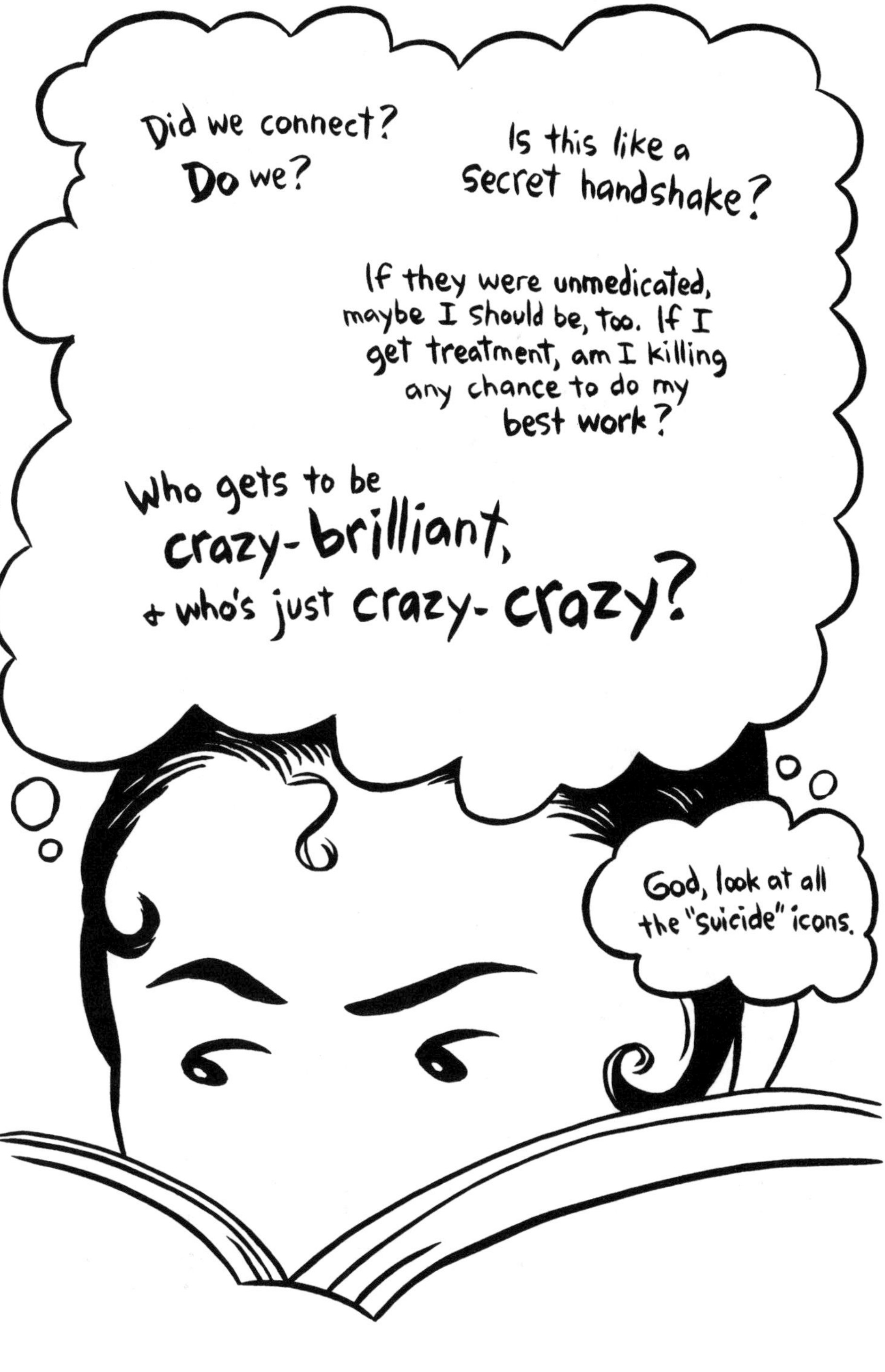
Did we connect? Do we?
Is this like a secret handshake?
If they were unmedicated, maybe I should be, too. If I get treatment, am I killing any chance to do my best work?
Who gets to be crazy-brilliant, & who's just crazy-crazy?
God, look at all the "suicide" icons.

BIPOLAR DISORDER IS INFAMOUS FOR ITS SUICIDE RATE. TO CLARIFY, HERE ARE...

SOME SUICIDE STATS

SUICIDE DEATHS IN OVERALL POPULATION:
11.5 per 100,000 people

SUICIDE ATTEMPTS IN OVERALL POPULATION:
estimated 8 - 25 per every suicide death

SUICIDE ATTEMPTS IN BIPOLAR POPULATION:
estimated 25% — 50% ← 1 out of 2!
↑ 1 out of 4!

SUICIDE DEATHS IN BIPOLAR POPULATION:
3 out of 100 → 3% - 20% ← 1 out of 5!!

SUICIDE DEATH RATE FOR BIPOLARS IS USUALLY CITED AS **15%** BUT THE FIGURES VARY DEPENDING ON MANY FACTORS (ON THE **LOW** END FOR NEVER-HOSPITALIZED GROUPS, ON THE **HIGH** END WHEN ILLNESS IS COMBINED WITH ALCOHOL ABUSE, **LOW** END FOR LITHIUM-TAKERS, **HIGH** END SHORTLY AFTER ONSET OF ILLNESS, ETC.).

REGARDLESS,
EVEN THE **LOW** END IS HIGH.

I FILED THIS INFORMATION AWAY IN MY HEAD.

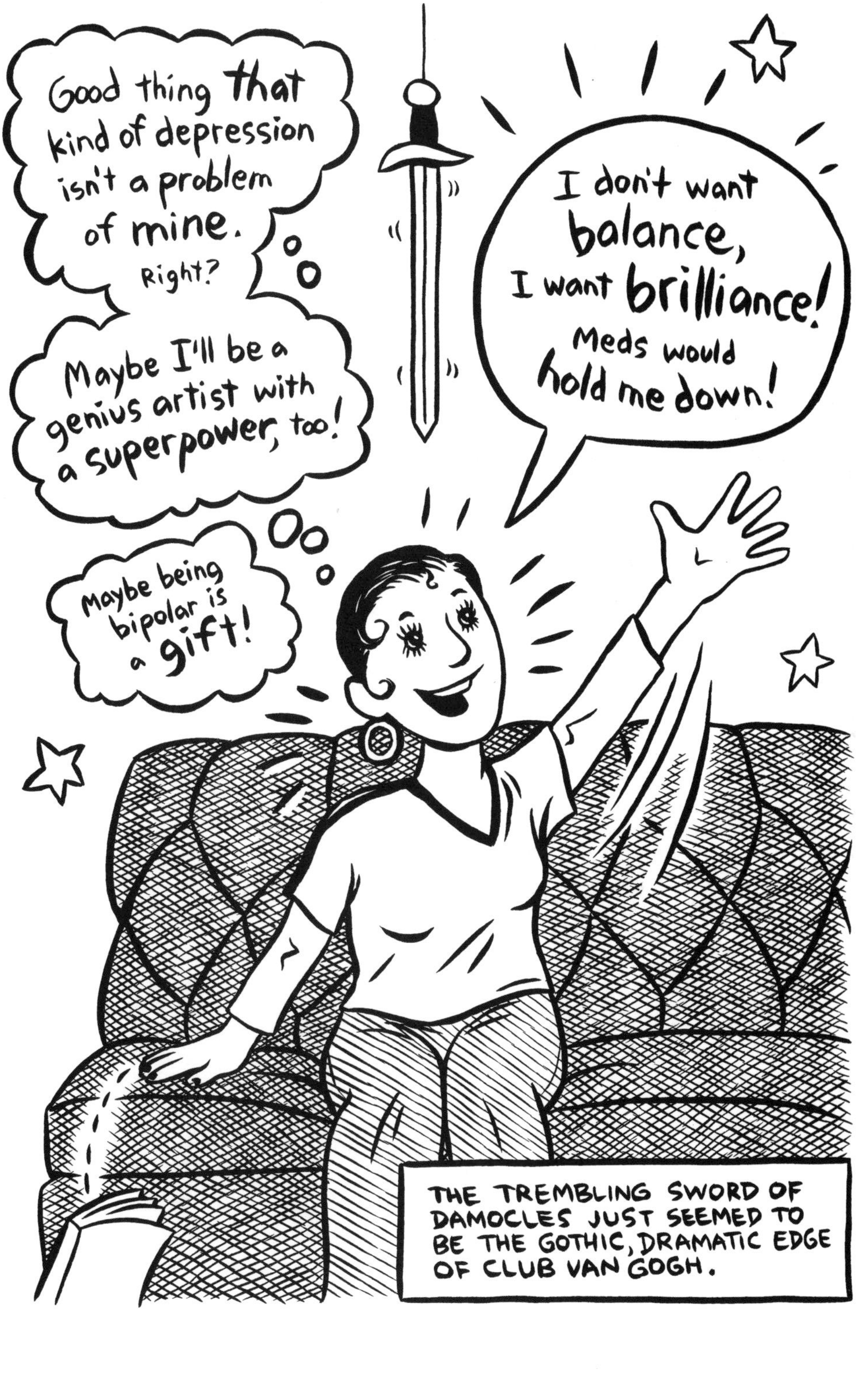
Good thing that kind of depression isn't a problem of mine. Right?
Maybe I'll be a genius artist with a superpower, too!
Maybe being bipolar is a gift!
I don't want balance, I want brilliance! Meds would hold me down!
THE TREMBLING SWORD OF DAMOCLES JUST SEEMED TO BE THE GOTHIC, DRAMATIC EDGE OF CLUB VAN GOGH.

CHAPTER 3

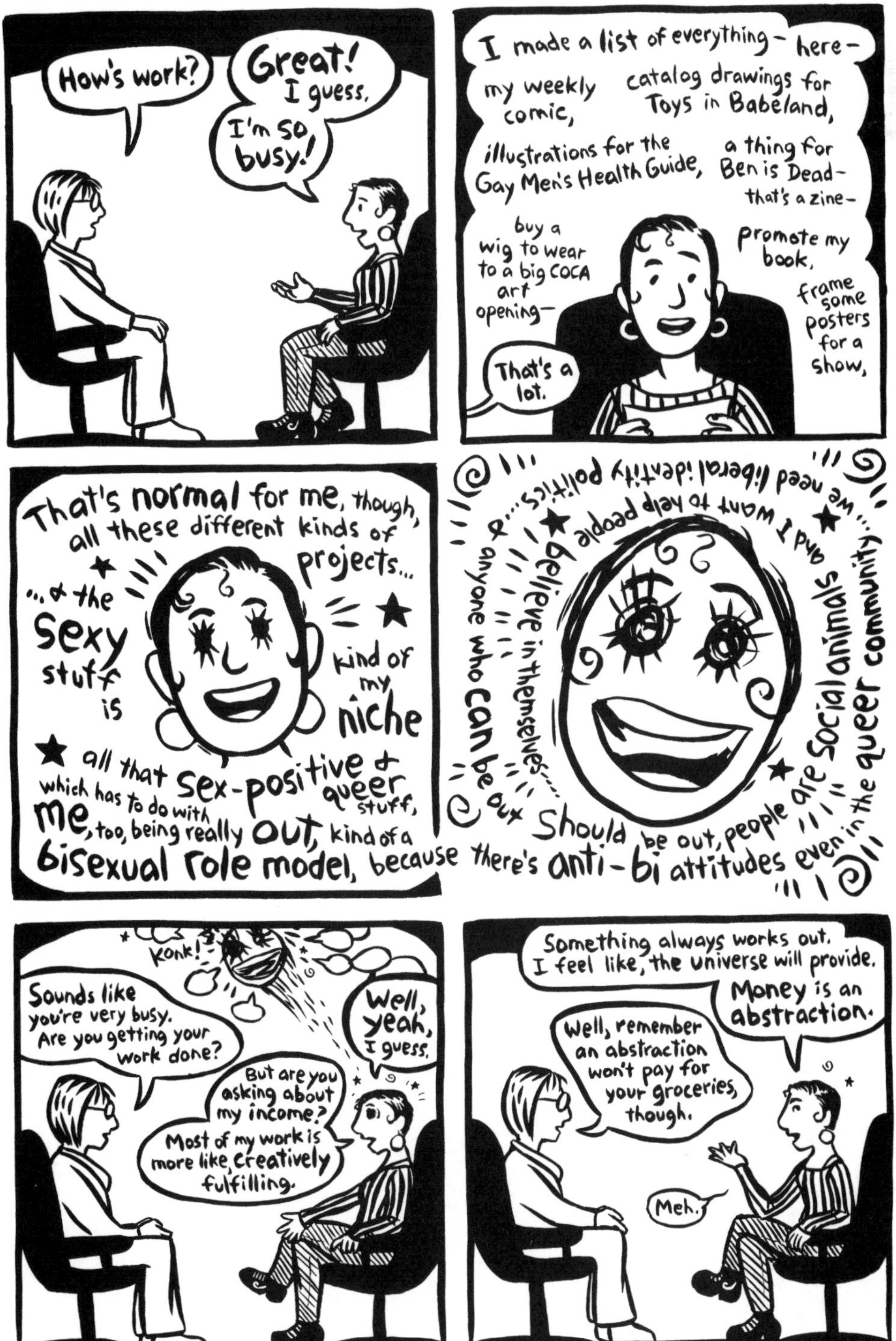
How's work?
Great! I guess, I'm so busy!
I made a list of everything - here -
my weekly comic,
catalog drawings for Toys in Babeland,
illustrations for the Gay Men's Health Guide,
a thing for Ben is Dead - that's a zine -
buy a wig to wear to a big COCA art opening -
promote my book,
frame some posters for a show,
That's a lot.
That's normal for me, though, all these different kinds of projects...
...& the sexy stuff is kind of my niche
all that sex-positive & queer stuff, which has to do with me, too, being really out, kind of a bisexual role model, because there's anti-bi attitudes even in the queer community...
we need liberal identity politics... & anyone who can be out should be out, people are social animals
and I want to help people believe in themselves...
Konk!
Sounds like you're very busy. Are you getting your work done?
Well, yeah, I guess.
But are you asking about my income? Most of my work is more like, creatively fulfilling.
Something always works out. I feel like, the universe will provide.
Money is an abstraction.
Well, remember an abstraction won't pay for your groceries, though.
Meh.

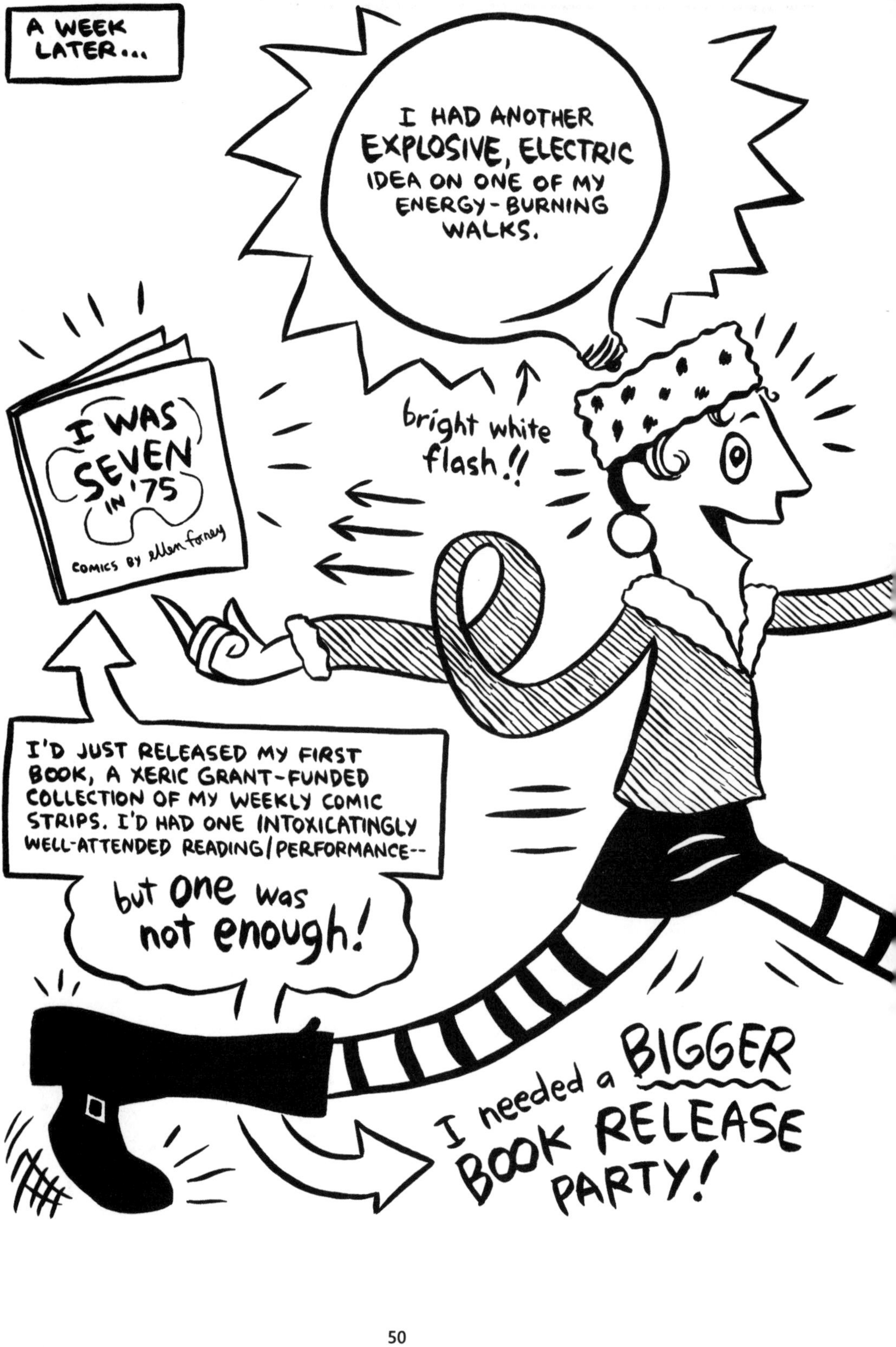
A WEEK LATER...
I HAD ANOTHER EXPLOSIVE, ELECTRIC IDEA ON ONE OF MY ENERGY-BURNING WALKS.
bright white flash!!
I WAS SEVEN IN '75
COMICS BY ellen forney
I'D JUST RELEASED MY FIRST BOOK, A XERIC GRANT-FUNDED COLLECTION OF MY WEEKLY COMIC STRIPS. I'D HAD ONE INTOXICATINGLY WELL-ATTENDED READING/PERFORMANCE--
but one was not enough!
I needed a BIGGER BOOK RELEASE PARTY!

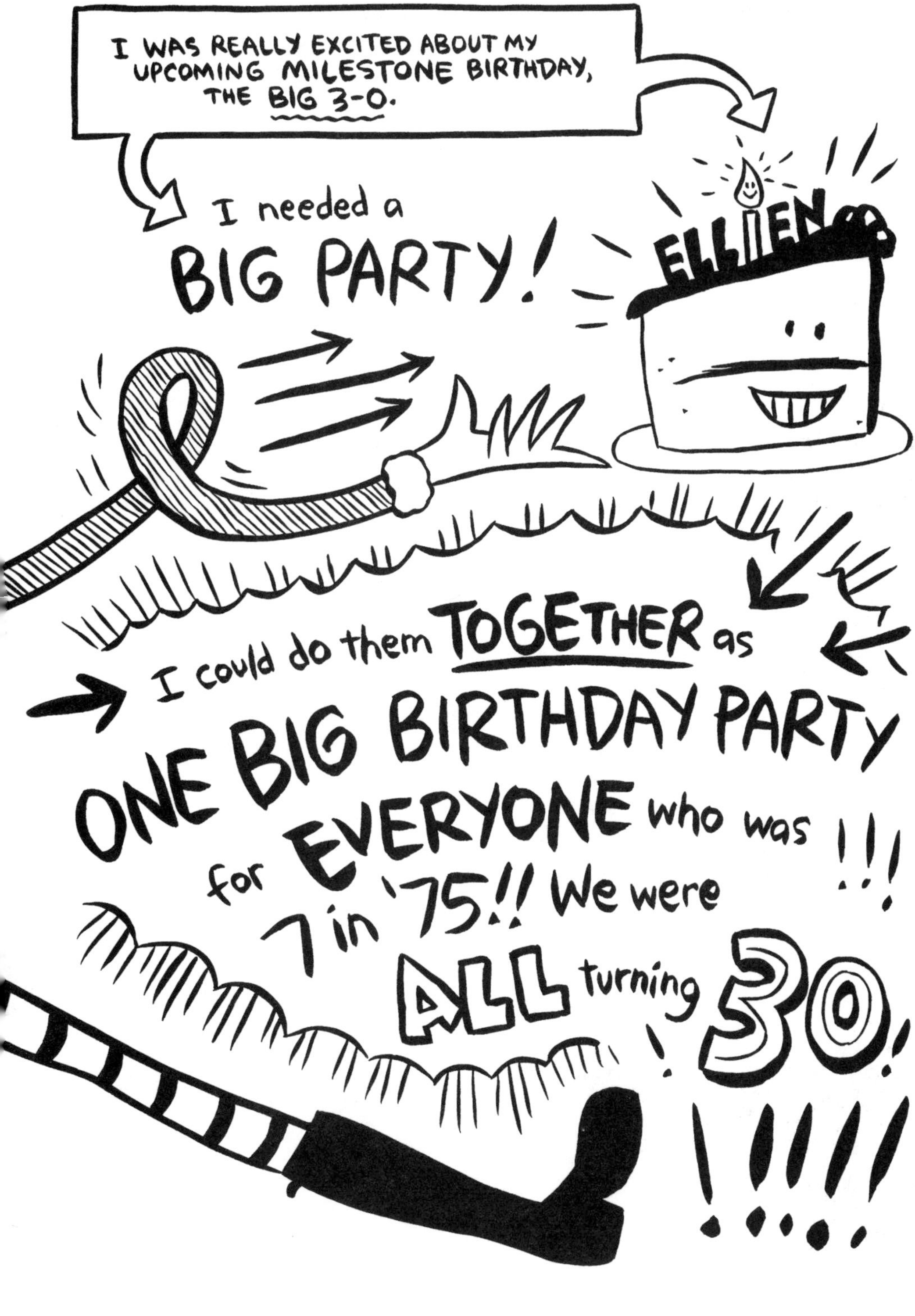
I WAS REALLY EXCITED ABOUT MY UPCOMING MILESTONE BIRTHDAY, THE BIG 3-O.
I needed a BIG PARTY!
ELLIEN
I could do them TOGETHER as ONE BIG BIRTHDAY PARTY for EVERYONE who was 7 in '75!! We were ALL turning 30!

I ROPED IN MY FRIENDS & MADE THE MOST OF MY CONNECTIONS.

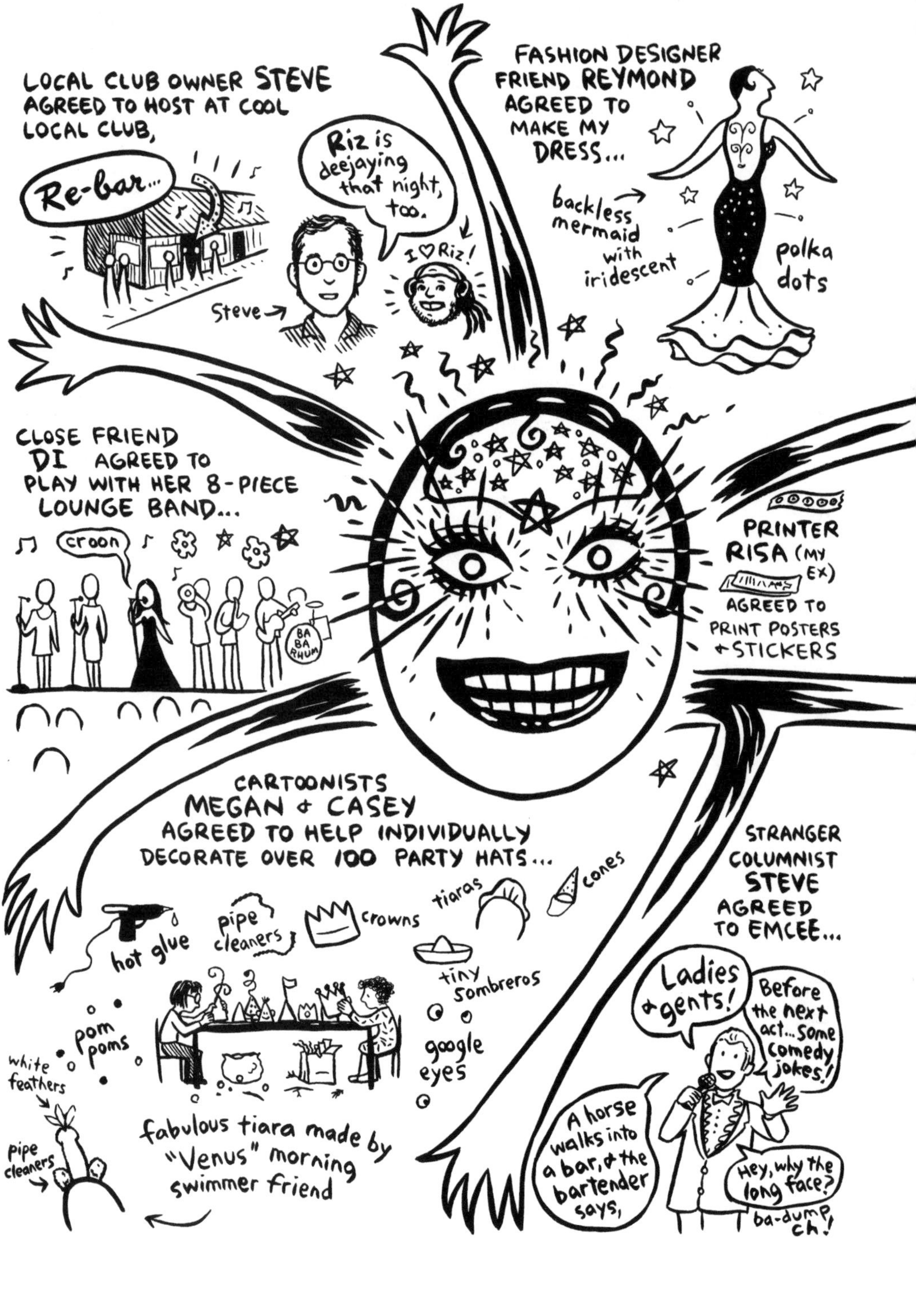
LOCAL CLUB OWNER STEVE AGREED TO HOST AT COOL LOCAL CLUB,
Re-bar...
Riz is deejaying that night, too.
Steve
I ♡ Riz!
FASHION DESIGNER FRIEND REYMOND AGREED TO MAKE MY DRESS...
backless mermaid with iridescent
polka dots
CLOSE FRIEND DI AGREED TO PLAY WITH HER 8-PIECE LOUNGE BAND...
croon
BA BA RHUM
PRINTER RISA (MY EX) AGREED TO PRINT POSTERS & STICKERS
CARTOONISTS MEGAN & CASEY AGREED TO HELP INDIVIDUALLY DECORATE OVER 100 PARTY HATS...
hot glue
pipe cleaners
crowns
tiaras
cones
tiny sombreros
pom poms
google eyes
white feathers
pipe cleaners
fabulous tiara made by "Venus" morning swimmer friend
STRANGER COLUMNIST STEVE AGREED TO EMCEE...
Ladies & gents!
Before the next act... some comedy jokes!
A horse walks into a bar, & the bartender says,
Hey, why the long face?
ba-dump ch!

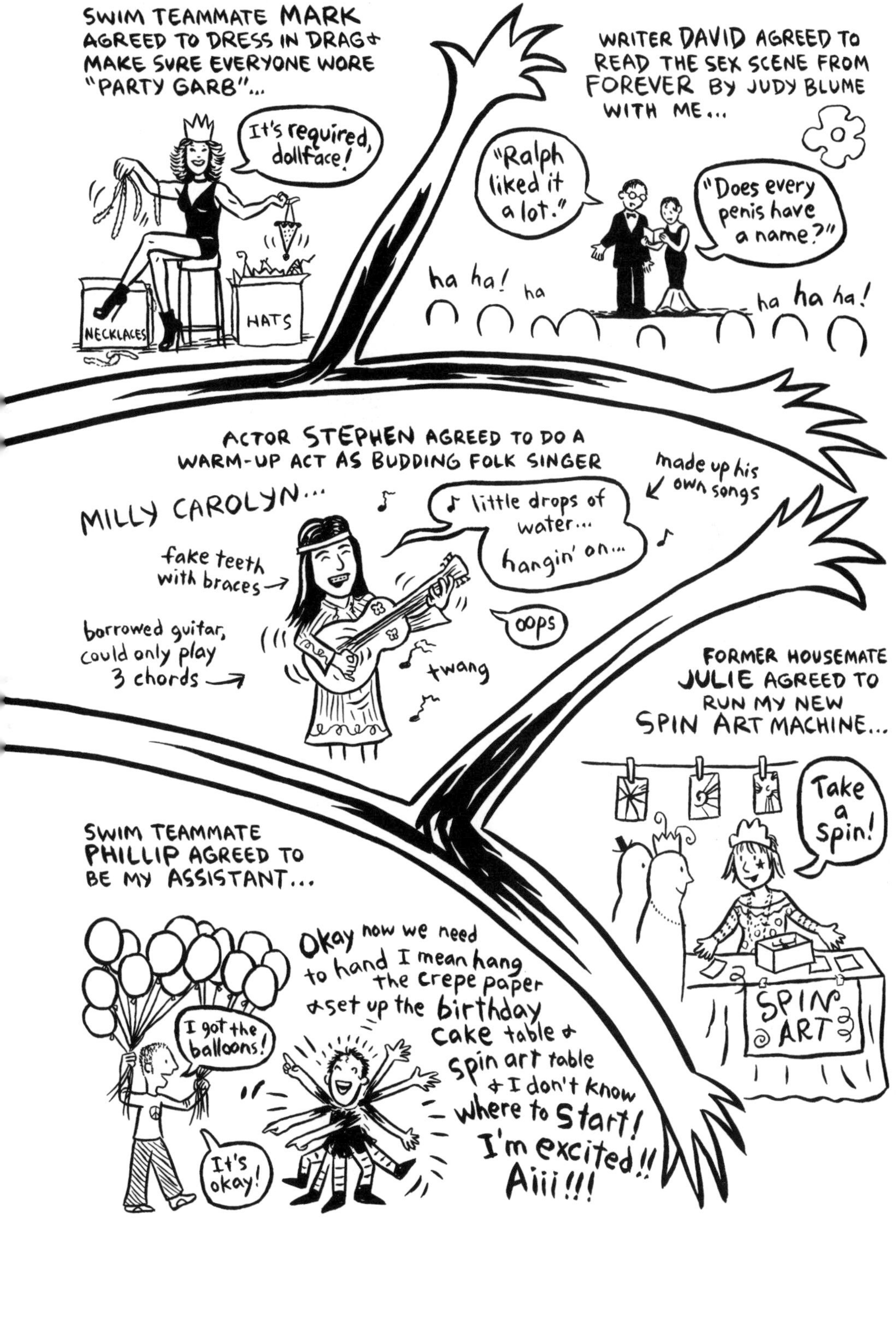
SWIM TEAMMATE MARK AGREED TO DRESS IN DRAG & MAKE SURE EVERYONE WORE "PARTY GARB"...
It's required, dollface!
NECKLACES
HATS
WRITER DAVID AGREED TO READ THE SEX SCENE FROM FOREVER BY JUDY BLUME WITH ME...
"Ralph liked it a lot."
"Does every penis have a name?"
ha ha! ha
ha ha ha!
ACTOR STEPHEN AGREED TO DO A WARM-UP ACT AS BUDDING FOLK SINGER
MILLY CAROLYN...
made up his own songs
little drops of water... hangin' on...
fake teeth with braces
borrowed guitar, could only play 3 chords
oops
twang
FORMER HOUSEMATE JULIE AGREED TO RUN MY NEW SPIN ART MACHINE...
Take a spin!
SPIN ART
SWIM TEAMMATE PHILLIP AGREED TO BE MY ASSISTANT...
I got the balloons!
It's okay!
Okay now we need to hand I mean hang the crepe paper & set up the birthday cake table & spin art table & I don't know where to start! I'm excited!! Aiii!!!

...AND SHAWN AGREED TO DESIGN THE POSTER. HE URGED ME TO EDIT DOWN THE WORD COUNT* BUT I COULDN'T – IT WAS ALL TOO IMPORTANT.

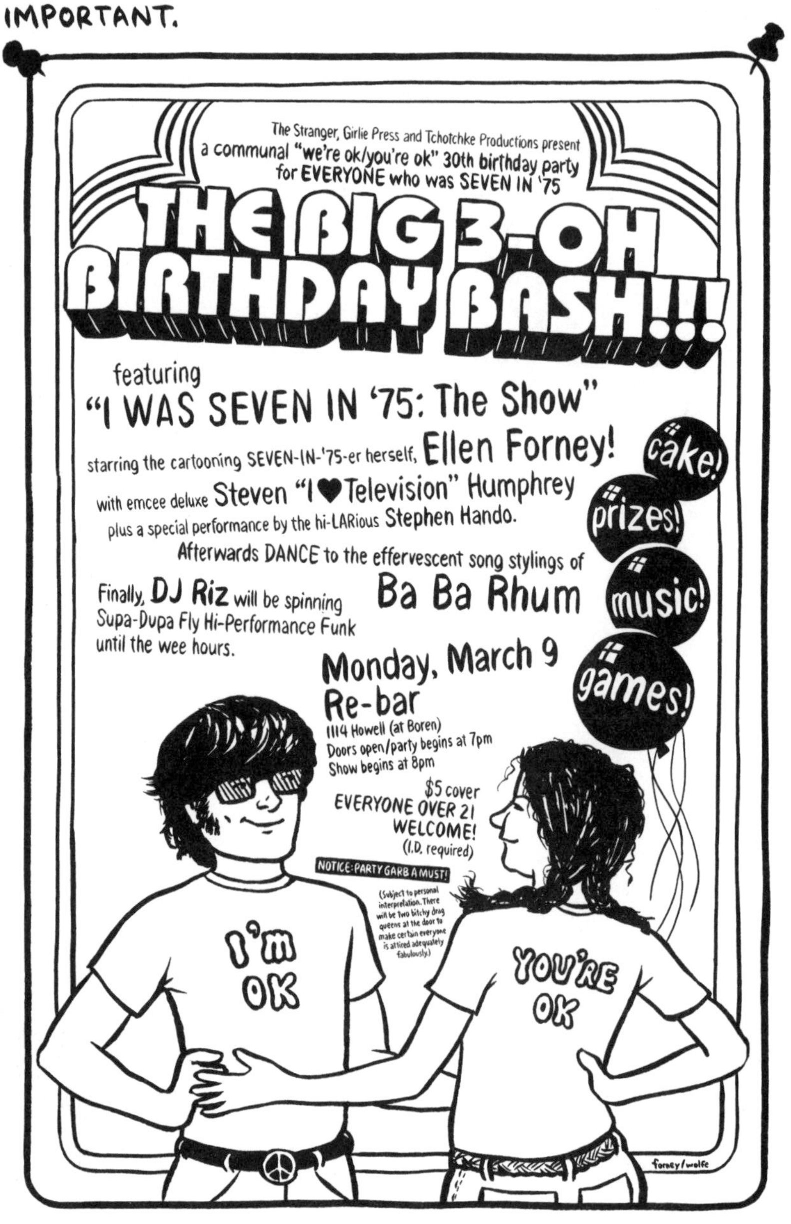

The Stranger, Girlie Press and Tchotchke Productions present
a communal "we're ok/you're ok" 30th birthday party
for EVERYONE who was SEVEN IN '75
THE BIG 3-OH BIRTHDAY BASH!!!
featuring
"I WAS SEVEN IN '75: The Show"
starring the cartooning SEVEN-IN-'75-er herself, Ellen Forney!
with emcee deluxe Steven "I ♥ Television" Humphrey
plus a special performance by the hi-LARious Stephen Hando.
Afterwards DANCE to the effervescent song stylings of
Ba Ba Rhum
Finally, DJ Riz will be spinning Supa-Dupa Fly Hi-Performance Funk until the wee hours.
cake!
prizes!
music!
games!
Monday, March 9
Re-bar
1114 Howell (at Boren)
Doors open/party begins at 7pm
Show begins at 8pm
$5 cover
EVERYONE OVER 21 WELCOME!
(I.D. required)
NOTICE: PARTY GARB A MUST!
(Subject to personal interpretation. There will be two bitchy drag queens at the door to make certain everyone is atticed adequately fabulously.)
I'M OK
YOU'RE OK
forney/wolfe

I COULDN'T STOP – EVERY TIME I HAD AN IDEA, I WAS COMPELLED TO PURSUE IT.

*DESIGNERS, MYSELF INCLUDED, HATE WORKING WITH LOTS OF CLUTTERING TEXT.

I CONVINCED MY FAMILY TO COME.

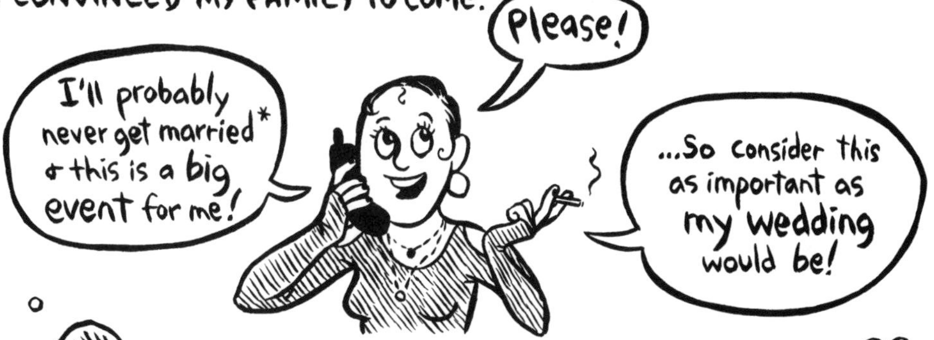
Please!
I'll probably never get married* & this is a big event for me!
...So consider this as important as my wedding would be!

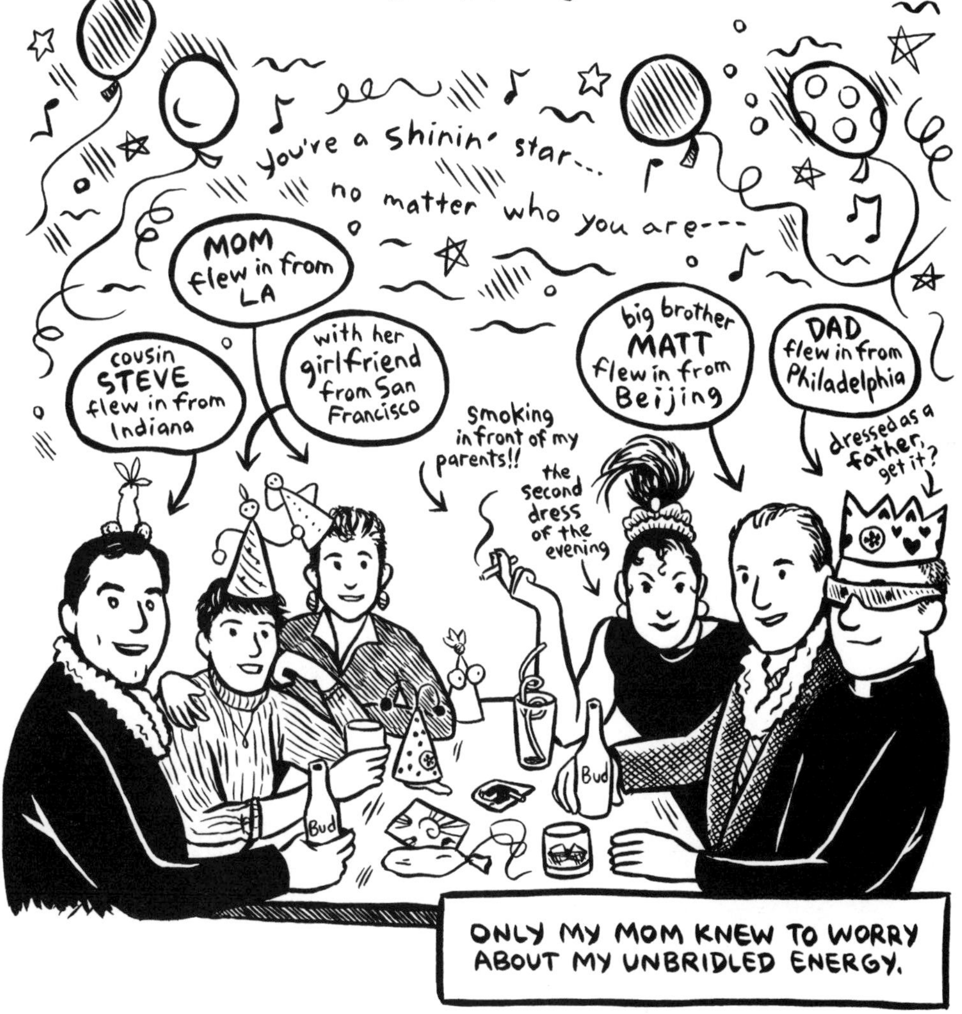
you're a shinin' star...
no matter who you are---
MOM flew in from LA
with her girlfriend from San Francisco
cousin STEVE flew in from Indiana
smoking in front of my parents!!
the second dress of the evening
big brother MATT flew in from Beijing
DAD flew in from Philadelphia
dressed as a father, get it?
Bud
Bud
ONLY MY MOM KNEW TO WORRY ABOUT MY UNBRIDLED ENERGY.

* I BELIEVED MARRIAGE WAS AN OBSOLETE INSTITUTION THAT INEVITABLY LEADS TO DIVORCE (COINCIDENTALLY... LIKE **MY PARENTS'** DIVORCE).

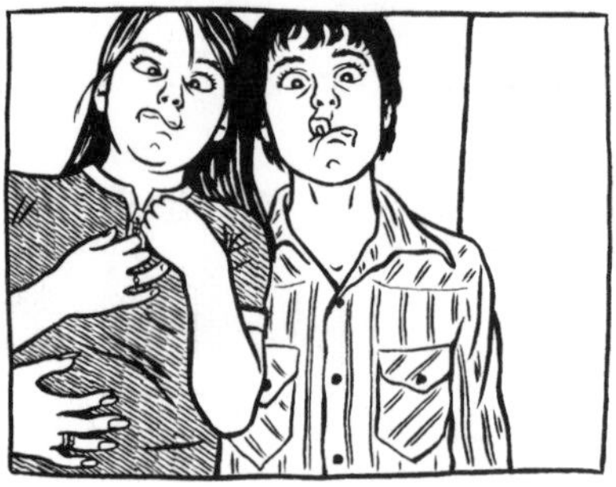

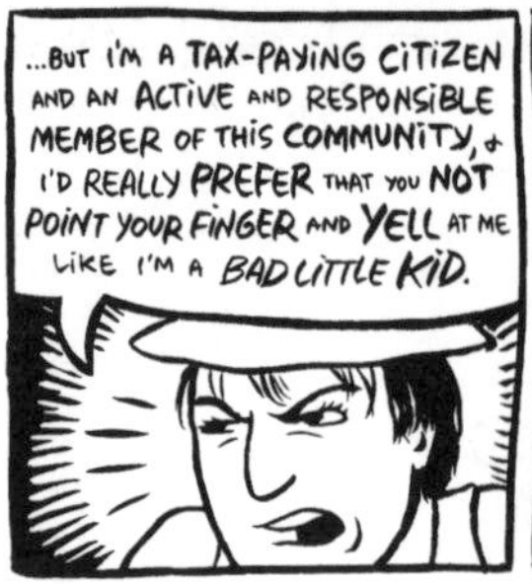
...BUT I'M A TAX-PAYING CITIZEN AND AN ACTIVE AND RESPONSIBLE MEMBER OF THIS COMMUNITY, & I'D REALLY PREFER THAT YOU NOT POINT YOUR FINGER AND YELL AT ME LIKE I'M A BAD LITTLE KID.

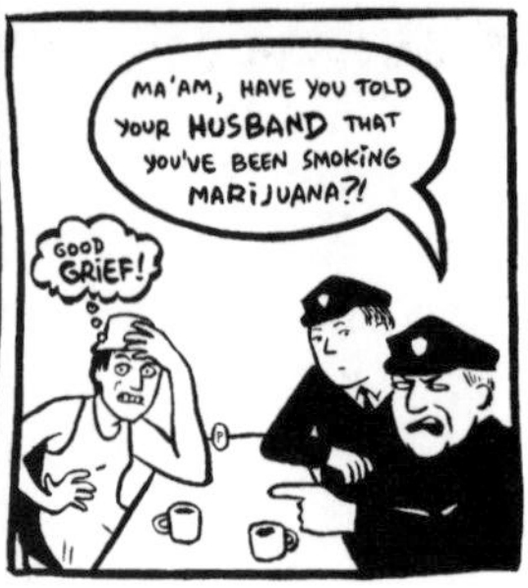
MA'AM, HAVE YOU TOLD YOUR HUSBAND THAT YOU'VE BEEN SMOKING MARIJUANA?!
GOOD GRIEF!

MOM & I HAVE ALWAYS BEEN CLOSE.

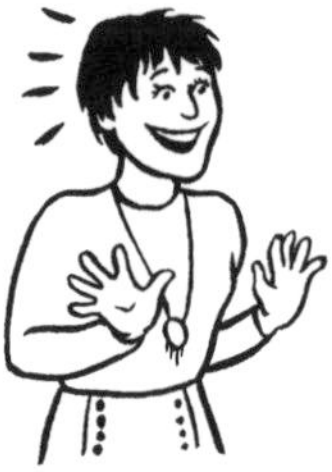

SHE APPEARED AS A LOVING, HEROIC FORCE IN MY 7 IN '75 COMICS.

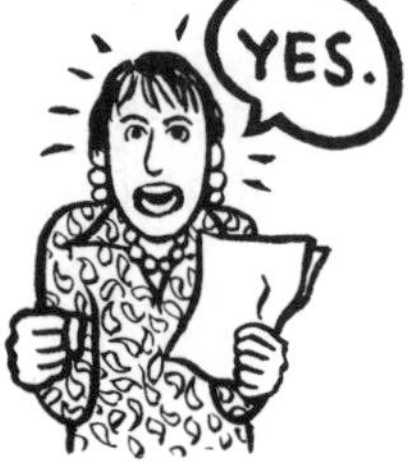
YES.

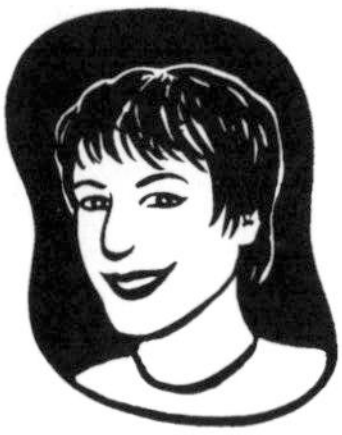

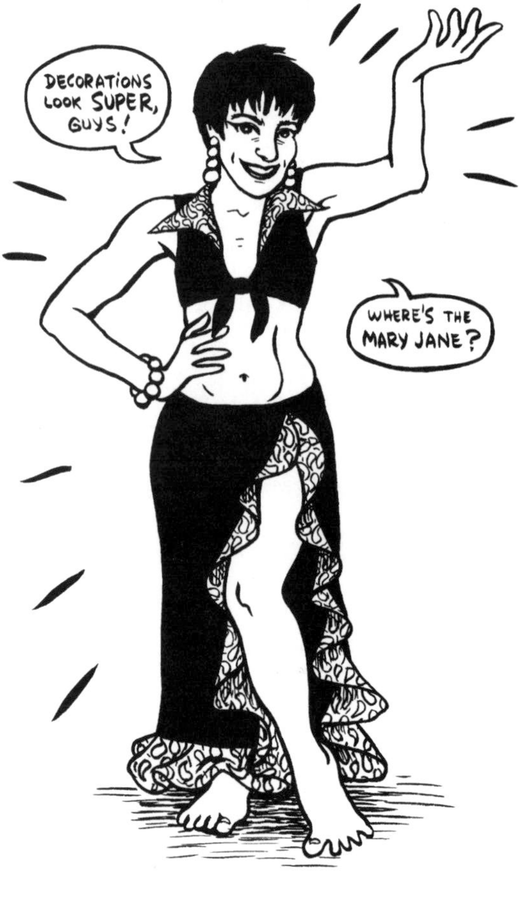
DECORATIONS LOOK SUPER, GUYS!
WHERE'S THE MARY JANE?

A LOT OF PEOPLE THOUGHT I WAS DRAWING MYSELF, WHICH PLEASED ME.

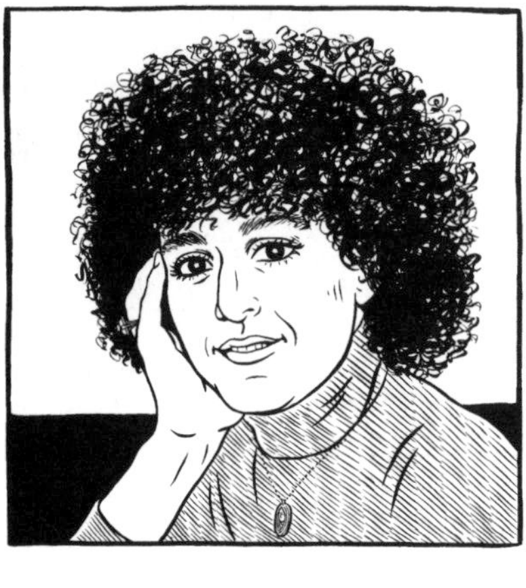

I HAD TOLD MY MOM (A DOCTOR) THAT I WAS BIPOLAR A FEW DAYS AFTER MY DIAGNOSIS. SHE LISTENED TO THE REST OF MY PART OF THE CONVERSATION AS A PARADE OF SYMPTOMS.

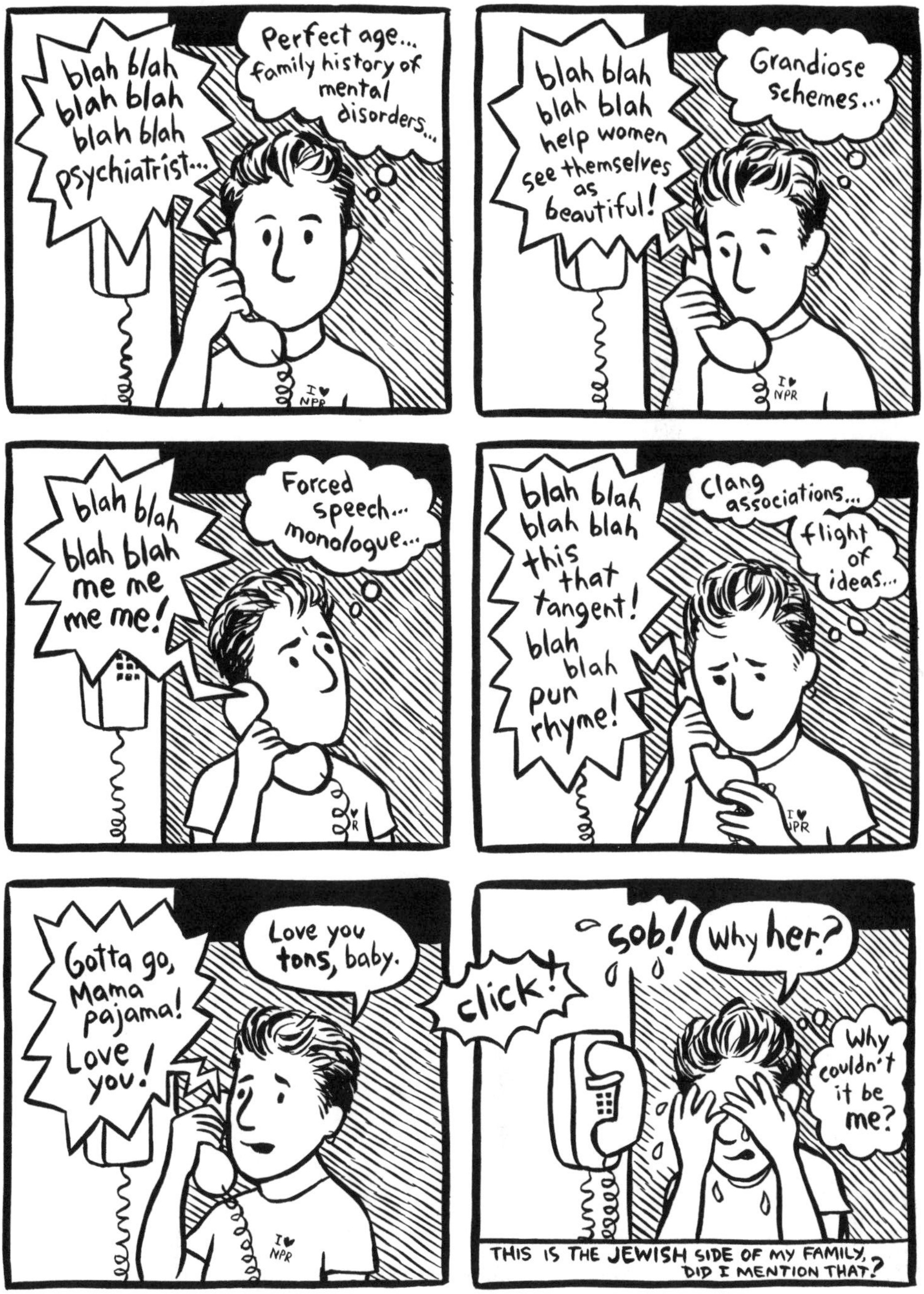
blah blah blah blah blah blah psychiatrist...
Perfect age... family history of mental disorders...
I ♥ NPR
blah blah blah blah help women see themselves as beautiful!
Grandiose schemes...
I ♥ NPR
blah blah blah blah me me me me!
Forced speech... monologue...
blah blah blah blah this that tangent! blah blah pun rhyme!
Clang associations... flight of ideas...
Gotta go, Mama pajama! Love you!
Love you tons, baby.
I ♥ NPR
click!
sob!
Why her?
Why couldn't it be me?
THIS IS THE JEWISH SIDE OF MY FAMILY, DID I MENTION THAT?

IT WAS MOM'S SIDE OF THE FAMILY WITH THE MOOD DISORDERS.

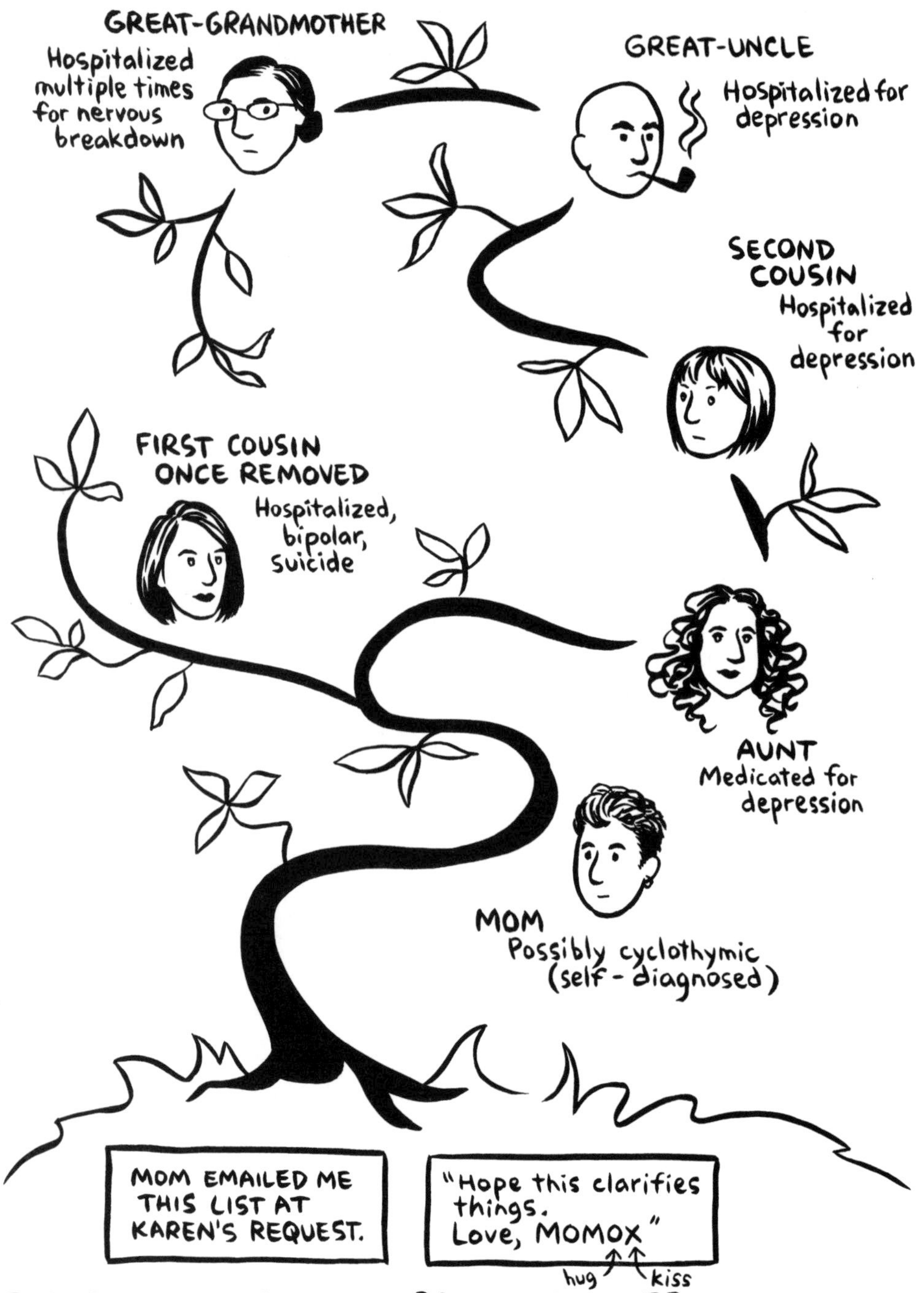
GREAT-GRANDMOTHER
Hospitalized multiple times for nervous breakdown
GREAT-UNCLE
Hospitalized for depression
SECOND COUSIN
Hospitalized for depression
FIRST COUSIN ONCE REMOVED
Hospitalized, bipolar, suicide
AUNT
Medicated for depression
MOM
Possibly cyclothymic (self-diagnosed)
MOM EMAILED ME THIS LIST AT KAREN'S REQUEST.
"Hope this clarifies things.
Love, MOMOX"
hug
kiss

DEPRESSION, NERVOUS BREAKDOWN? BIPOLAR, SUICIDE?? I'D HAD NO IDEA.

What is a "MOOD DISORDER" anyway?

BASICALLY, IT'S A CONDITION WHERE EMOTIONS ARE DERAILED FOR AN EXTENDED PERIOD OF TIME. **THE MAIN TYPES ARE:**

⭐ **BIPOLAR I:** ←(that's me)
ALTERNATING MANIC & DEPRESSIVE EPISODES

⭐ **BIPOLAR II:**
ALTERNATING HYPOMANIC & DEPRESSIVE EPISODES
↖ "HYPOMANIA" = MILD MANIA

⭐ **CYCLOTHYMIA:**
ALTERNATING HYPOMANIC & MILD DEPRESSIVE EPISODES

⭐ **UNIPOLAR DEPRESSION:**
SINGLE OR RECURRENT EPISODES WITH NO MANIA

⭐ **DYSTHYMIA:**
CHRONIC, LOW-GRADE DEPRESSION

...WHICH REFER TO THESE MOOD STATES:

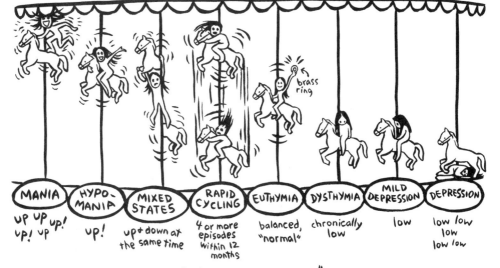

MANIA	HYPO-MANIA	MIXED STATES	RAPID CYCLING	EUTHYMIA	DYSTHYMIA	MILD DEPRESSION	DEPRESSION
UP UP up! UP! UP	UP!	up & down at the same time	4 or more episodes within 12 months	balanced, "normal"	chronically low	low	low low low low low

NOTE: "BIPOLAR DISORDER" & "MANIC DEPRESSION" ARE THE **SAME THING.**

I TURNED 30! LOTS OF OTHER 7-IN-'75-ERS WERE THERE, TOO, ALSO TURNING 30! I WAS ON TOP OF THE WORLD.

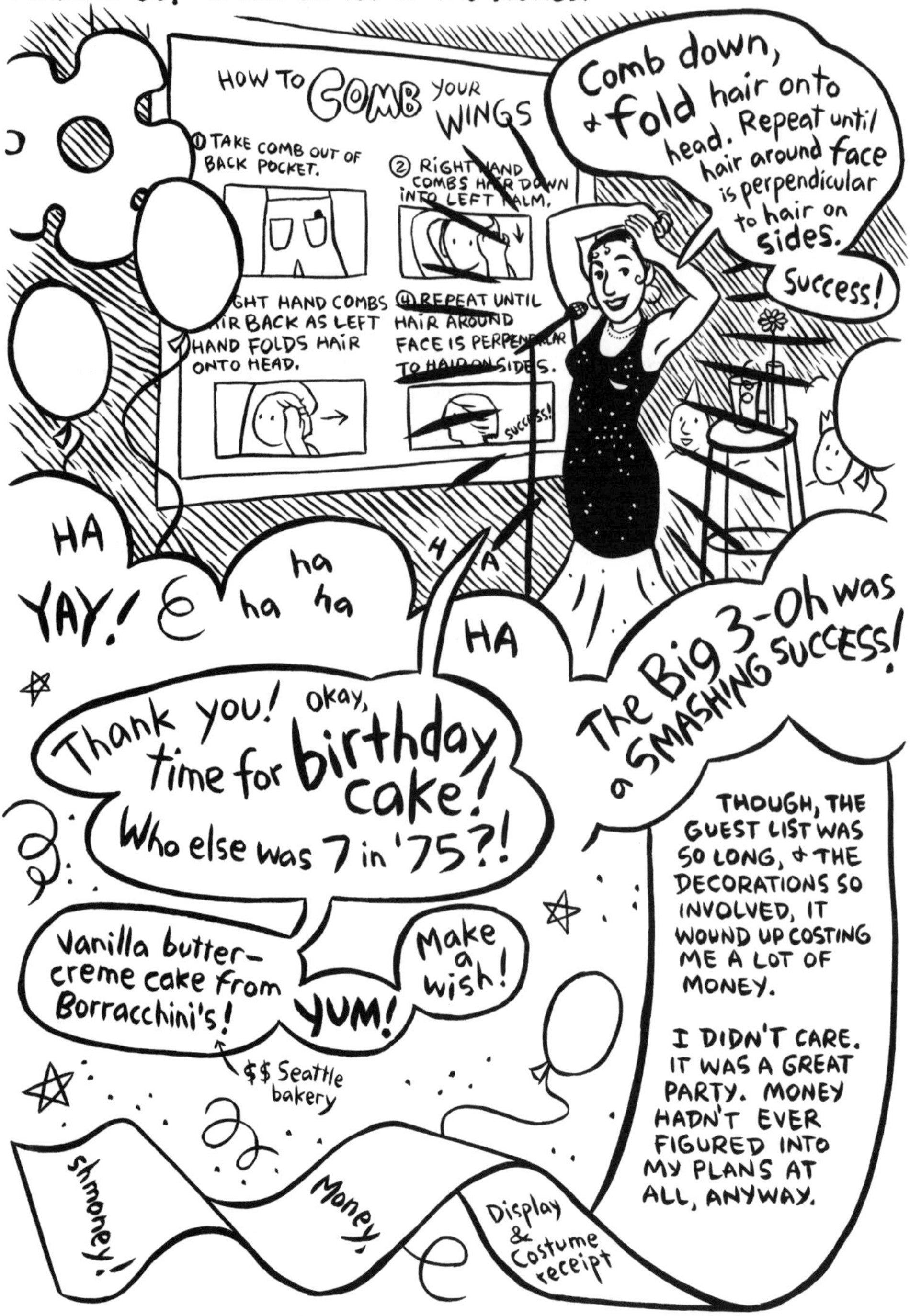

HOW TO COMB YOUR WINGS
1 TAKE COMB OUT OF BACK POCKET.
2 RIGHT HAND COMBS HAIR DOWN INTO LEFT PALM.
GHT HAND COMBS AIR BACK AS LEFT HAND FOLDS HAIR ONTO HEAD.
4 REPEAT UNTIL HAIR AROUND FACE IS PERPEN LAR TO HAIR ON SIDES.
SUCCESS!
Comb down, & fold hair onto head. Repeat until hair around face is perpendicular to hair on sides.
Success!
HA
YAY!
ha ha ha
HA
The Big 3-Oh was a SMASHING SUCCESS!
Thank you! Okay, time for birthday cake! Who else was 7 in '75?!
Vanilla butter-creme cake from Borracchini's!
$$ Seattle bakery
YUM!
Make a wish!
THOUGH, THE GUEST LIST WAS SO LONG, & THE DECORATIONS SO INVOLVED, IT WOUND UP COSTING ME A LOT OF MONEY.
I DIDN'T CARE. IT WAS A GREAT PARTY. MONEY HADN'T EVER FIGURED INTO MY PLANS AT ALL, ANYWAY.
shmoney!
Money.
Display & Costume receipt

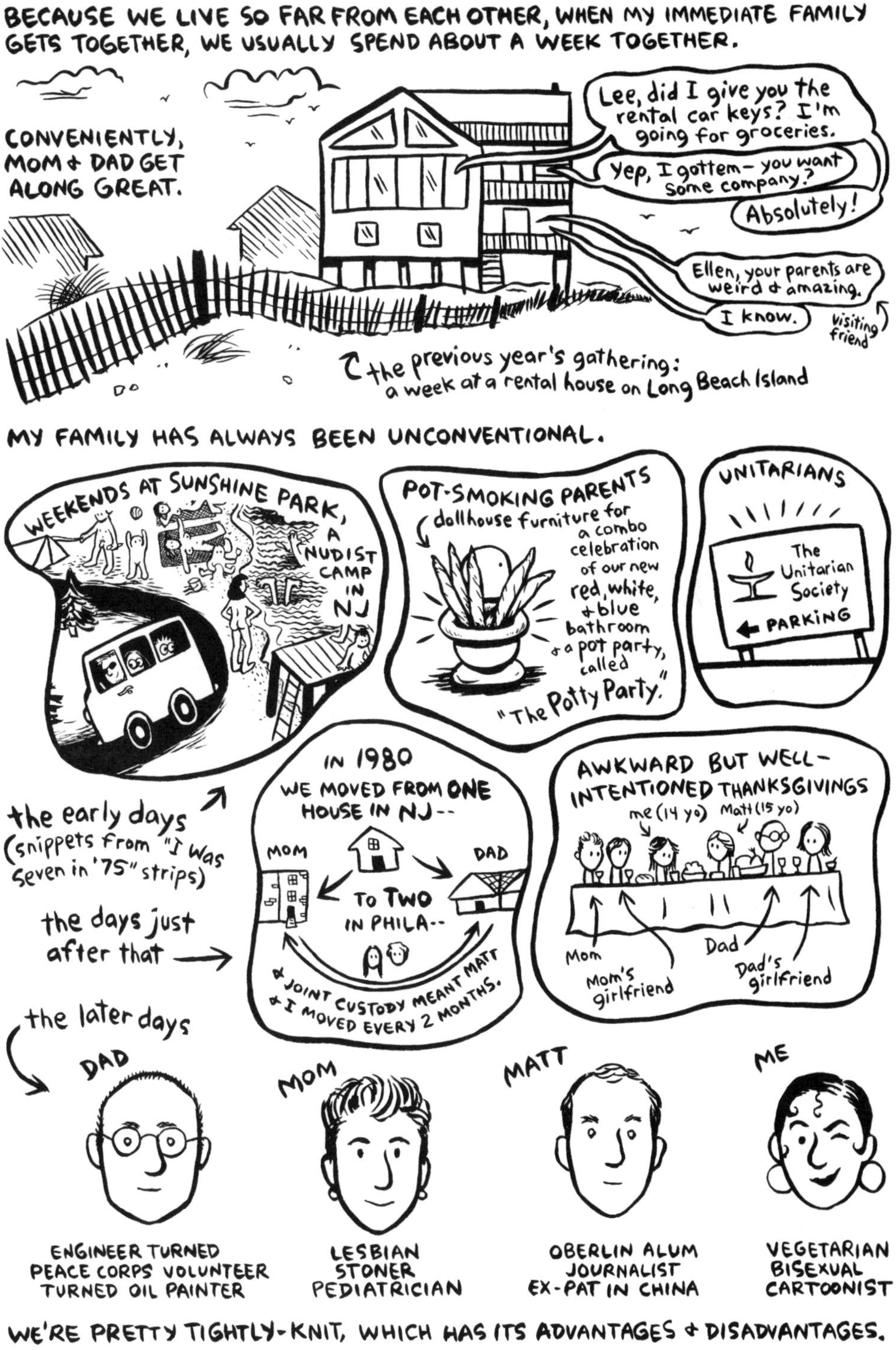
BECAUSE WE LIVE SO FAR FROM EACH OTHER, WHEN MY IMMEDIATE FAMILY GETS TOGETHER, WE USUALLY SPEND ABOUT A WEEK TOGETHER.
CONVENIENTLY, MOM & DAD GET ALONG GREAT.
Lee, did I give you the rental car keys? I'm going for groceries.
Yep, I gottem - you want some company?
Absolutely!
Ellen, your parents are weird & amazing.
I know.
visiting friend
the previous year's gathering: a week at a rental house on Long Beach Island
MY FAMILY HAS ALWAYS BEEN UNCONVENTIONAL.
WEEKENDS AT SUNSHINE PARK, A NUDIST CAMP IN NJ
POT-SMOKING PARENTS
dollhouse furniture for a combo celebration of our new red, white, & blue bathroom & a pot party, called "The Potty Party."
UNITARIANS
The Unitarian Society
PARKING
the early days (snippets from "I Was Seven in '75" strips)
IN 1980 WE MOVED FROM ONE HOUSE IN NJ--
MOM
DAD
TO TWO IN PHILA--
& JOINT CUSTODY MEANT MATT & I MOVED EVERY 2 MONTHS.
the days just after that
AWKWARD BUT WELL-INTENTIONED THANKSGIVINGS
me (14 yo)
Matt (15 yo)
Mom
Mom's girlfriend
Dad
Dad's girlfriend
the later days
DAD
ENGINEER TURNED PEACE CORPS VOLUNTEER TURNED OIL PAINTER
MOM
LESBIAN STONER PEDIATRICIAN
MATT
OBERLIN ALUM JOURNALIST EX-PAT IN CHINA
ME
VEGETARIAN BISEXUAL CARTOONIST
WE'RE PRETTY TIGHTLY-KNIT, WHICH HAS ITS ADVANTAGES & DISADVANTAGES.

AS PART OF MY FAMILY'S EXTENDED VISIT, I PLANNED A 3-DAY STAY FOR US AT DOE BAY, A SEMI-RUNDOWN HIPPIE RESORT ON ORCAS ISLAND.

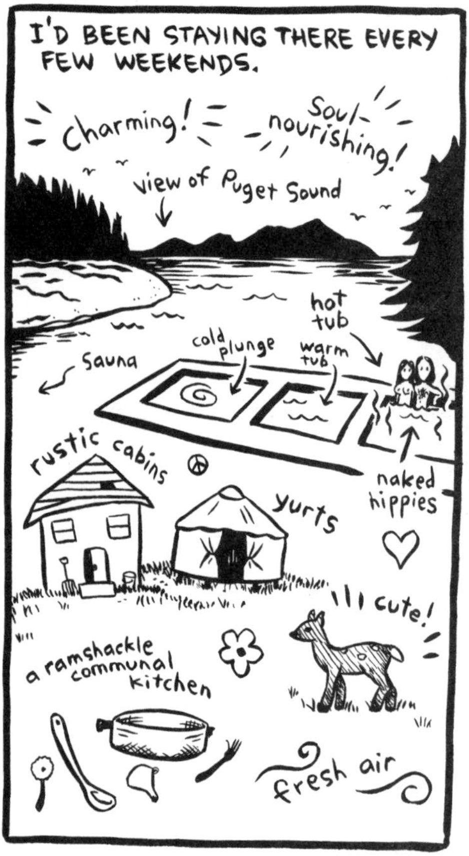
I'D BEEN STAYING THERE EVERY FEW WEEKENDS.
Charming!
Soul-nourishing!
view of Puget Sound
hot tub
cold plunge
warm tub
Sauna
naked hippies
rustic cabins
yurts
cute!
a ramshackle communal kitchen
fresh air

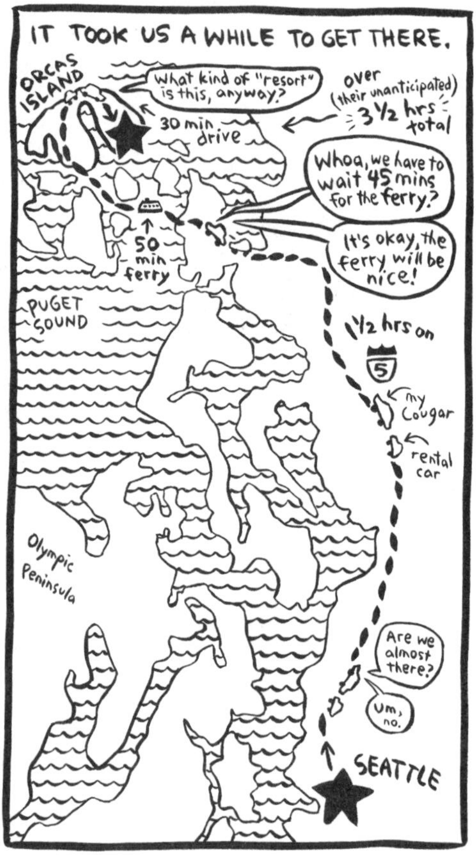
IT TOOK US A WHILE TO GET THERE.
ORCAS ISLAND
What kind of "resort" is this, anyway?
over (their unanticipated) 3 1/2 hrs total
30 min drive
Whoa, we have to wait 45 mins for the ferry?
It's okay, the ferry will be nice!
50 min ferry
PUGET SOUND
1/2 hrs on
5
my Cougar
rental car
Olympic Peninsula
Are we almost there?
Um, no.
SEATTLE

IT WAS IMMEDIATELY CLEAR THAT THIS HAD NOT BEEN A GOOD IDEA.

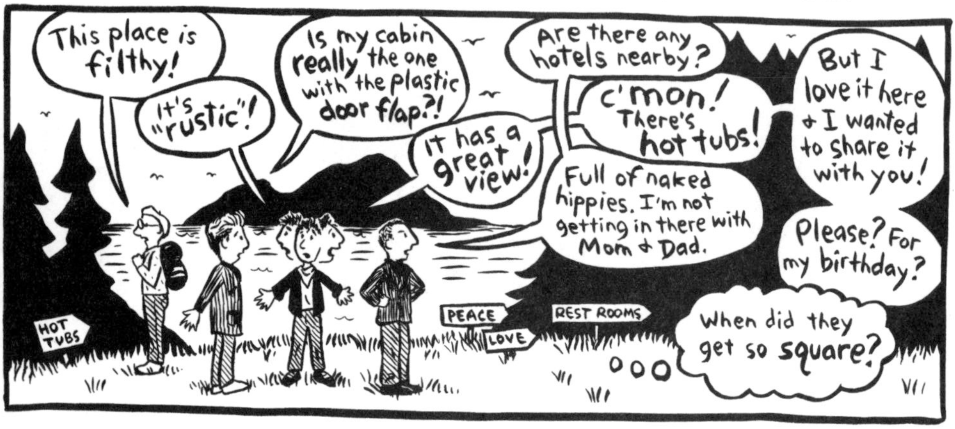
This place is filthy!
It's "rustic"!
Is my cabin really the one with the plastic door flap?!
It has a great view!
Are there any hotels nearby?
C'mon! There's hot tubs!
Full of naked hippies. I'm not getting in there with Mom & Dad.
But I love it here & I wanted to share it with you!
Please? For my birthday?
When did they get so square?
HOT TUBS
PEACE
LOVE
REST ROOMS

WE STAYED ANYWAY, DESPITE THE NAKED HIPPIES & PLASTIC DOOR FLAPS.

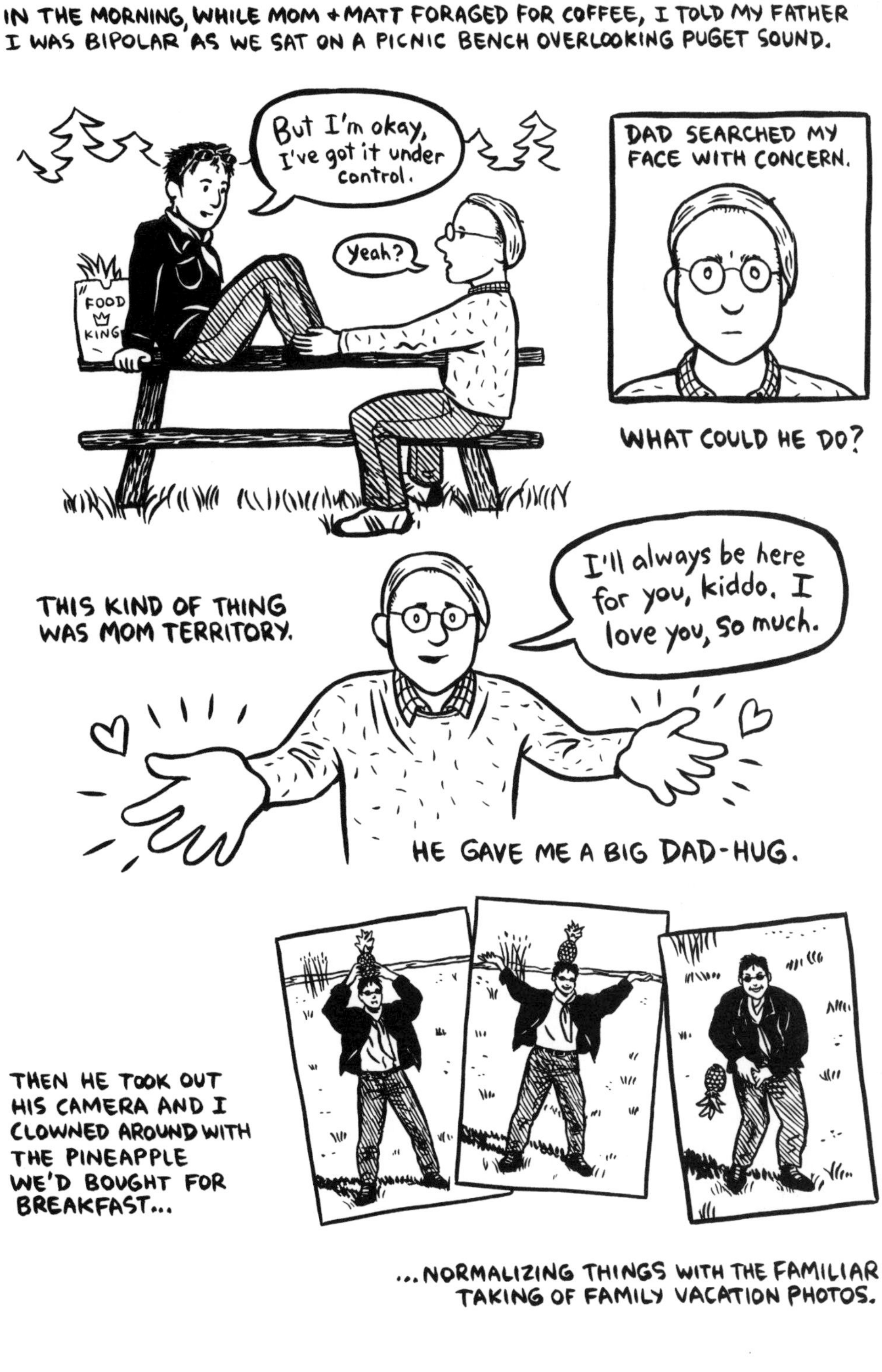
IN THE MORNING, WHILE MOM + MATT FORAGED FOR COFFEE, I TOLD MY FATHER I WAS BIPOLAR AS WE SAT ON A PICNIC BENCH OVERLOOKING PUGET SOUND.
But I'm okay, I've got it under control.
Yeah?
FOOD KING
DAD SEARCHED MY FACE WITH CONCERN.
WHAT COULD HE DO?
THIS KIND OF THING WAS MOM TERRITORY.
I'll always be here for you, kiddo. I love you, so much.
HE GAVE ME A BIG DAD-HUG.
THEN HE TOOK OUT HIS CAMERA AND I CLOWNED AROUND WITH THE PINEAPPLE WE'D BOUGHT FOR BREAKFAST...
...NORMALIZING THINGS WITH THE FAMILIAR TAKING OF FAMILY VACATION PHOTOS.

I TOLD MY BROTHER LATER, WHEN WE WERE HIKING ON THE TENDED PATHS OF MOUNT CONSTITUTION.

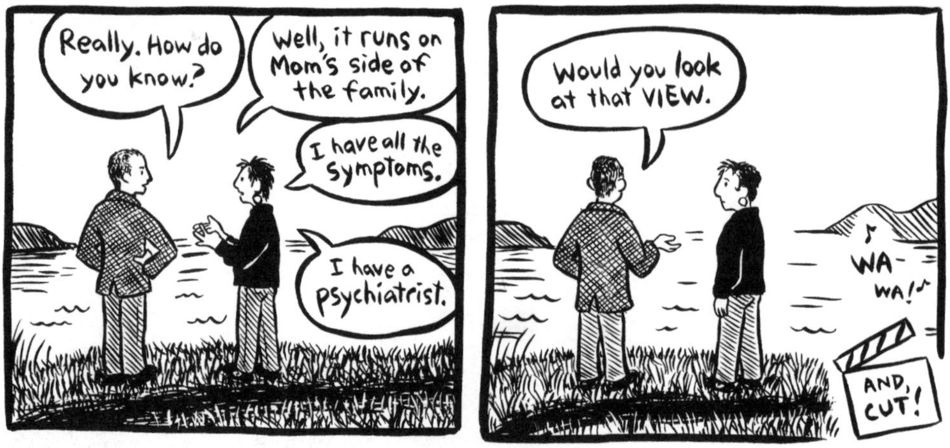
Really. How do you know?
Well, it runs on Mom's side of the family.
I have all the symptoms.
I have a psychiatrist.
Would you look at that VIEW.
WA-WA!
AND, CUT!

BUT LATER, ON THE WAY BACK TO DOE BAY:

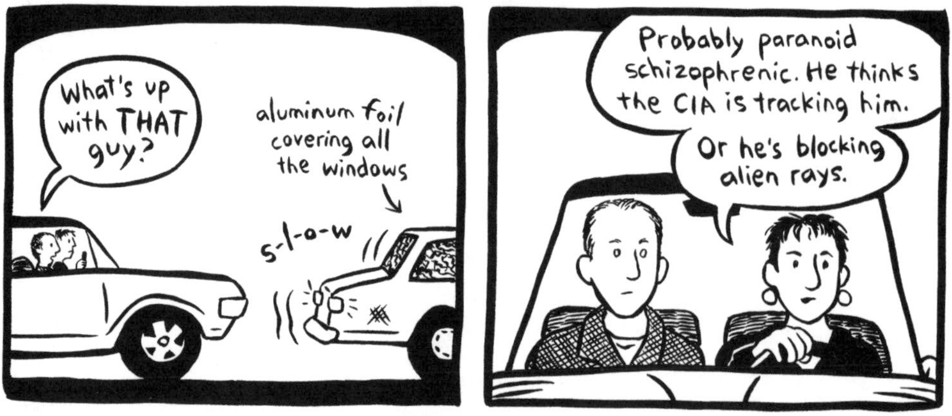
What's up with THAT guy?
aluminum foil covering all the windows
s-l-o-w
Probably paranoid schizophrenic. He thinks the CIA is tracking him.
Or he's blocking alien rays.

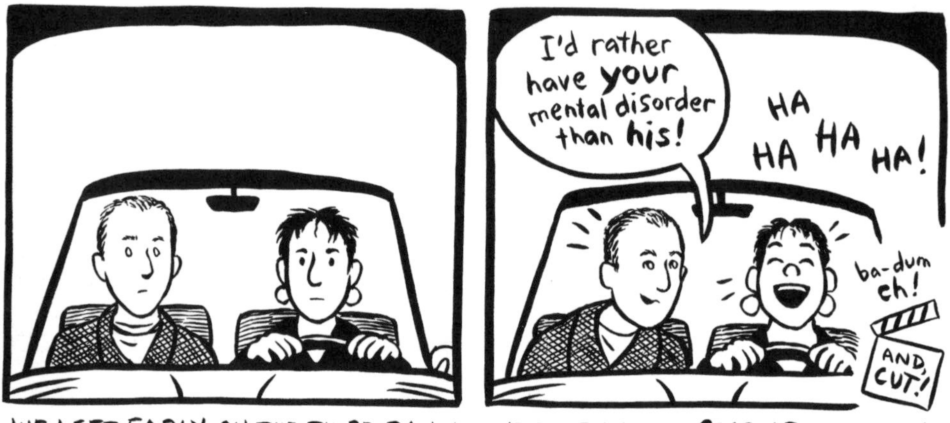
I'd rather have your mental disorder than his!
HA HA HA HA!
ba-dum ch!
AND, CUT!

WE LEFT EARLY ON THE THIRD DAY & HEADED BACK TO SEATTLE. AND THEN, WITH LOVE & RELIEF, BACK TO OUR SEPARATE PARTS OF THE WORLD.

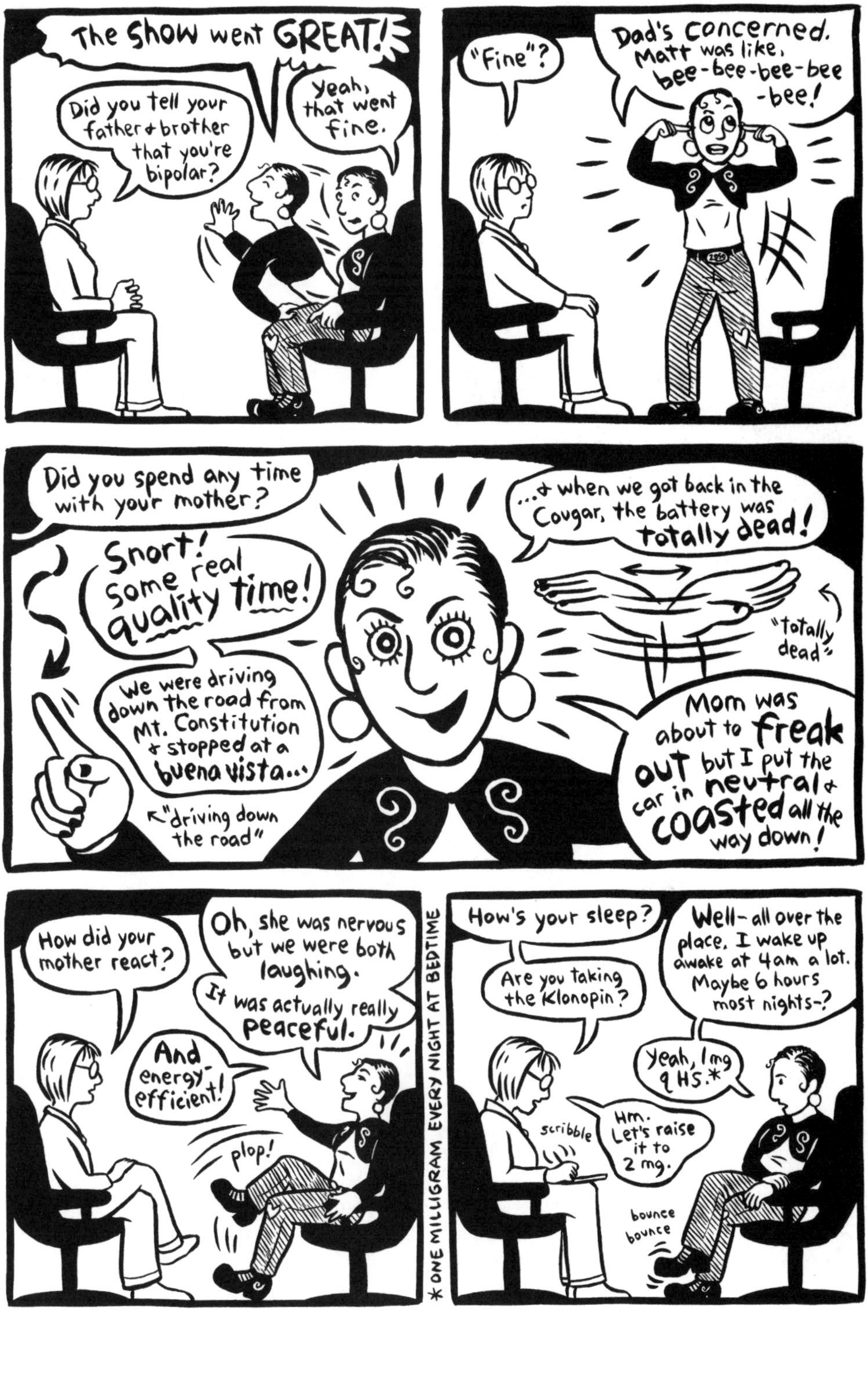
Did you tell your father & brother that you're bipolar?
Yeah, that went fine.
The show went GREAT!
"Fine"?
Dad's concerned. Matt was like, bee-bee-bee-bee-bee!
Did you spend any time with your mother?
Snort! Some real quality time!
We were driving down the road from Mt. Constitution & stopped at a buena vista...
"driving down the road"
...& when we got back in the Cougar, the battery was totally dead!
"totally dead"
Mom was about to freak out but I put the car in neutral & coasted all the way down!
How did your mother react?
Oh, she was nervous but we were both laughing.
It was actually really peaceful.
And energy-efficient!
plop!
How's your sleep?
Are you taking the Klonopin?
Well- all over the place. I wake up awake at 4am a lot. Maybe 6 hours most nights-?
Yeah, 1mg q HS.*
Hm. Let's raise it to 2 mg.
scribble
bounce bounce
* ONE MILLIGRAM EVERY NIGHT AT BEDTIME

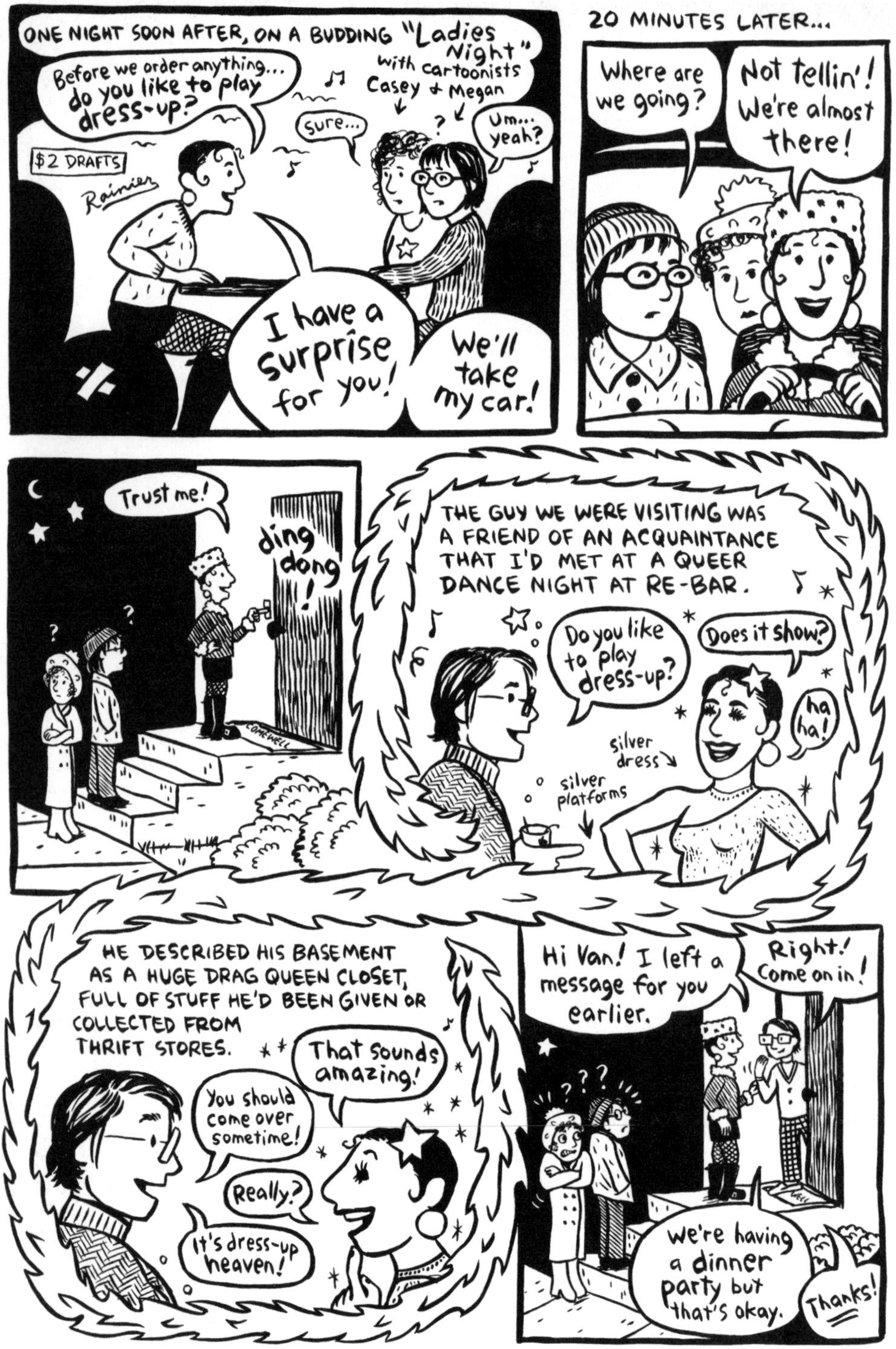
ONE NIGHT SOON AFTER, ON A BUDDING "Ladies Night" with cartoonists Casey & Megan
Before we order anything... do you like to play dress-up?
Sure...
Um... yeah?
$2 DRAFTS
Rainier
I have a surprise for you!
We'll take my car!
20 MINUTES LATER...
Where are we going?
Not tellin'! We're almost there!
Trust me!
ding dong!
COME WELL
THE GUY WE WERE VISITING WAS A FRIEND OF AN ACQUAINTANCE THAT I'D MET AT A QUEER DANCE NIGHT AT RE-BAR.
Do you like to play dress-up?
Does it show?
ha ha!
silver dress
silver platforms
HE DESCRIBED HIS BASEMENT AS A HUGE DRAG QUEEN CLOSET, FULL OF STUFF HE'D BEEN GIVEN OR COLLECTED FROM THRIFT STORES.
That sounds amazing!
You should come over sometime!
Really?
It's dress-up heaven!
Hi Van! I left a message for you earlier.
Right! Come on in!
We're having a dinner party but that's okay.
Thanks!

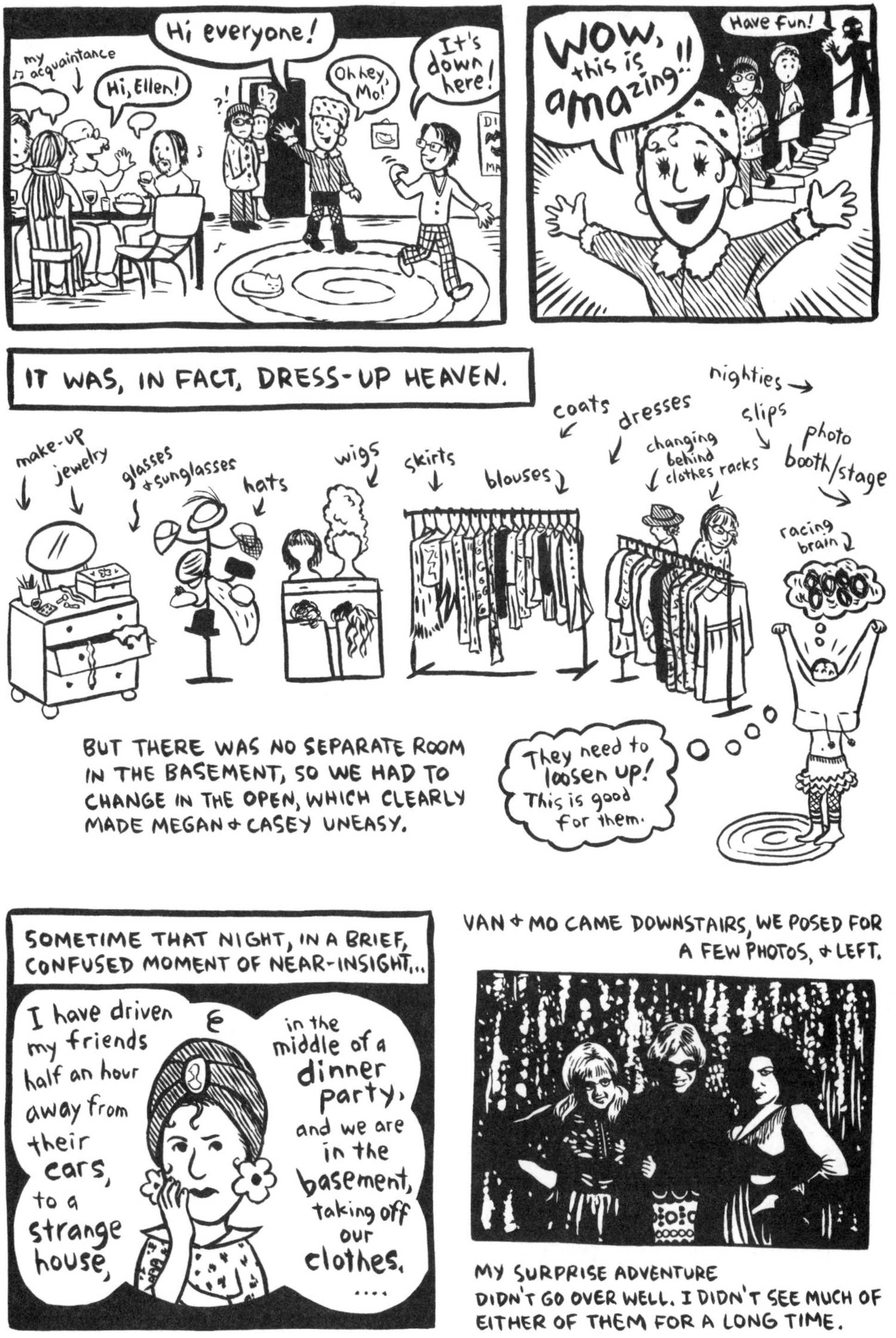
Hi everyone!
my acquaintance
Hi, Ellen!
?!
!?
Oh hey, Mo!
It's down here!
WOW, this is amazing!!
Have fun!
IT WAS, IN FACT, DRESS-UP HEAVEN.
make-up
jewelry
glasses & sunglasses
hats
wigs
skirts
blouses
coats
dresses
nighties
slips
changing behind clothes racks
photo booth/stage
racing brain
BUT THERE WAS NO SEPARATE ROOM IN THE BASEMENT, SO WE HAD TO CHANGE IN THE OPEN, WHICH CLEARLY MADE MEGAN & CASEY UNEASY.
They need to loosen up! This is good for them.
SOMETIME THAT NIGHT, IN A BRIEF, CONFUSED MOMENT OF NEAR-INSIGHT...
I have driven my friends half an hour away from their cars, to a strange house,
in the middle of a dinner party, and we are in the basement, taking off our clothes, ...
VAN & MO CAME DOWNSTAIRS, WE POSED FOR A FEW PHOTOS, & LEFT.
MY SURPRISE ADVENTURE DIDN'T GO OVER WELL. I DIDN'T SEE MUCH OF EITHER OF THEM FOR A LONG TIME.

AFTER A FEW WEEKS, I SENSED THAT I HAD LANDED, A FAMILIAR FEELING I'D FORGOTTEN.

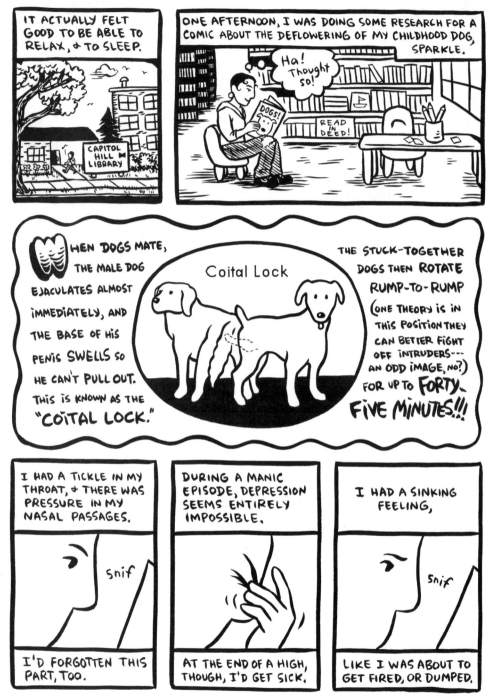

IT ACTUALLY FELT GOOD TO BE ABLE TO RELAX, & TO SLEEP.

CAPITOL HILL LIBRARY

ONE AFTERNOON, I WAS DOING SOME RESEARCH FOR A COMIC ABOUT THE DEFLOWERING OF MY CHILDHOOD DOG, SPARKLE.

Ha! Thought so!

DOGS!

READ IN DEED!

HEN DOGS MATE, THE MALE DOG EJACULATES ALMOST IMMEDIATELY, AND THE BASE OF HIS PENIS SWELLS SO HE CAN'T PULL OUT. THIS IS KNOWN AS THE "COÏTAL LOCK."

Coital Lock

THE STUCK-TOGETHER DOGS THEN ROTATE RUMP-TO-RUMP (ONE THEORY IS IN THIS POSITION THEY CAN BETTER FIGHT OFF INTRUDERS--- AN ODD IMAGE, NO?) FOR UP TO FORTY-FIVE MINUTES!!!

I HAD A TICKLE IN MY THROAT, & THERE WAS PRESSURE IN MY NASAL PASSAGES.

Snif

I'D FORGOTTEN THIS PART, TOO.

DURING A MANIC EPISODE, DEPRESSION SEEMS ENTIRELY IMPOSSIBLE.

AT THE END OF A HIGH, THOUGH, I'D GET SICK.

I HAD A SINKING FEELING,

Snif

LIKE I WAS ABOUT TO GET FIRED, OR DUMPED.

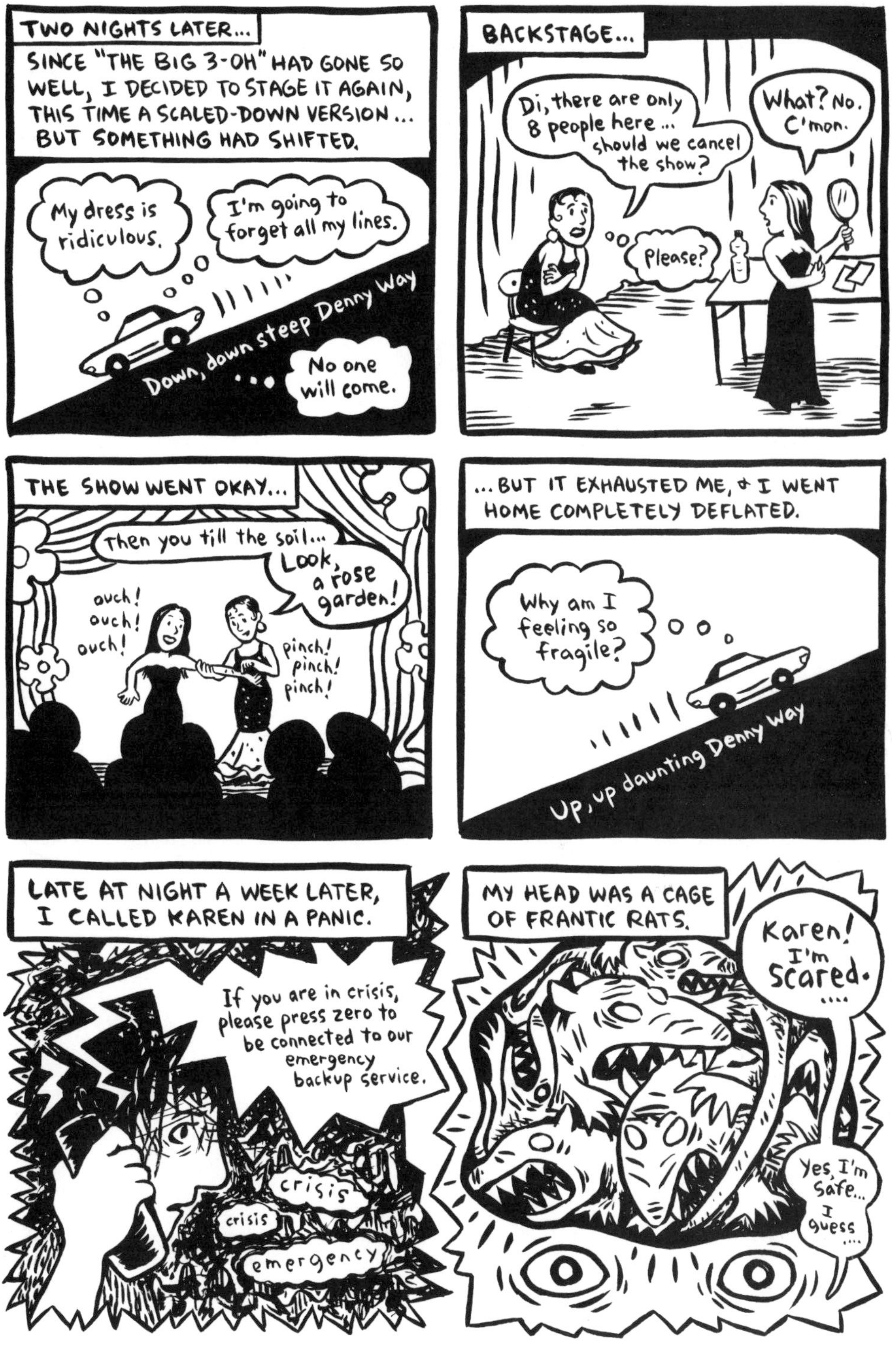
TWO NIGHTS LATER...
SINCE "THE BIG 3-OH" HAD GONE SO WELL, I DECIDED TO STAGE IT AGAIN, THIS TIME A SCALED-DOWN VERSION... BUT SOMETHING HAD SHIFTED.
My dress is ridiculous.
I'm going to forget all my lines.
Down, down steep Denny Way
No one will come.
BACKSTAGE...
Di, there are only 8 people here... should we cancel the show?
What? No. C'mon.
Please?
THE SHOW WENT OKAY...
Then you till the soil...
Look, a rose garden!
ouch! ouch! ouch!
pinch! pinch! pinch!
...BUT IT EXHAUSTED ME, & I WENT HOME COMPLETELY DEFLATED.
Why am I feeling so fragile?
Up, up daunting Denny Way
LATE AT NIGHT A WEEK LATER, I CALLED KAREN IN A PANIC.
If you are in crisis, please press zero to be connected to our emergency backup service.
crisis
crisis
emergency
MY HEAD WAS A CAGE OF FRANTIC RATS.
Karen! I'm Scared....
Yes, I'm Safe... I guess....

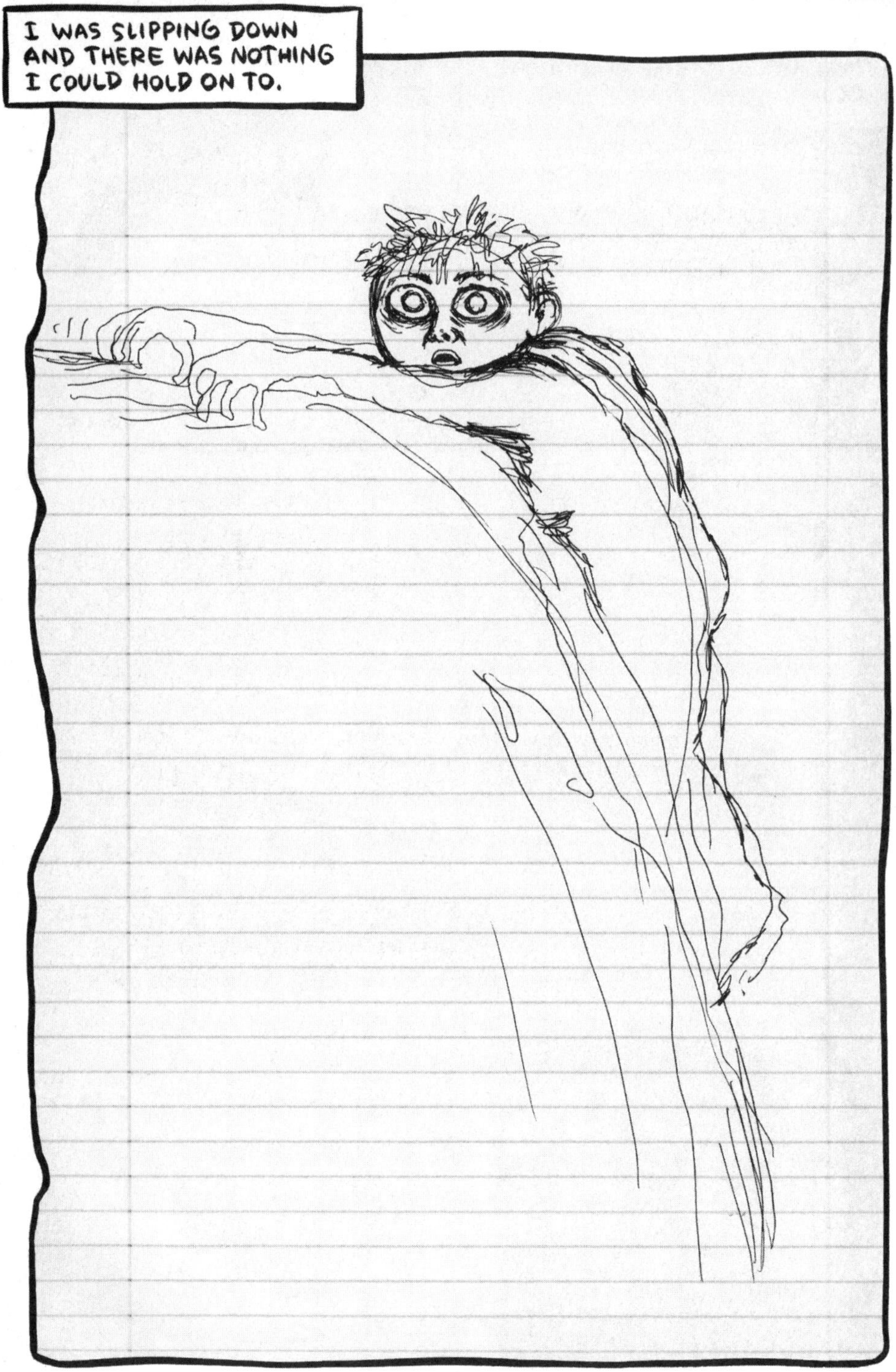
I WAS SLIPPING DOWN AND THERE WAS NOTHING I COULD HOLD ON TO.

I'D BEEN SO SURE I COULD MANAGE WITHOUT MEDS, THAT I COULD TAKE CARE OF MYSELF.

THAT CONVICTION DISAPPEARED ALL AT ONCE.

IN COLLEGE, I WAS A LIFEGUARD FOR A SUMMER, AND WE WERE TRAINED TO STAY BACK FROM A PERSON WHO WAS DROWNING & IN A PANIC. CHANCES WERE GOOD THEY'D CLIMB ON TOP OF YOU IN AN INSTINCTUAL DRIVE TO GET TO THE SURFACE, & YOU'D BOTH GO UNDER.

YOU TOSS THEM A LIFE PRESERVER.

FLAILING, TUMBLING OVER MYSELF & DESPERATE, I DIDN'T KNOW WHAT TO DO BUT PUT ALL MY TRUST IN KAREN.

SHE PUT ME ON LITHIUM & I NO LONGER RESISTED.

LITHIUM MADE IT OFFICIAL: I WAS

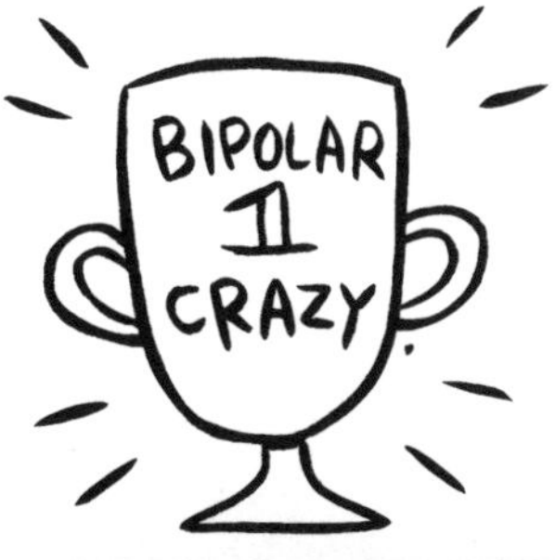
BIPOLAR
I
CRAZY.

THE LIST OF POTENTIAL
SIDE EFFECTS WAS LONG.

Lithium also Eskalith Lithobid

weight gain
hand tremor
blurred vision
confusion
mental
    slowness
poor concentration
impaired memory
skin problems
    (acne, hair loss)
thirst
polyuria
    (peeing a lot)
renal problems
    (kidneys)
liver problems
thyroid problems
cognitive
    problems
cognitive
    dulling
loss of
    coordination

    etc.

plus:
wrong
blood levels
can cause
dangerous
lithium toxicity
so drink
3 liters water
every day
+
expect lots of
blood draws.

MY HANDS &
EYES WERE
TWO OF MY
ESSENTIAL
WORK TOOLS.

AS IF
I DIDN'T
ALREADY HAVE
ENOUGH SKIN
PROBLEMS!

HOW COULD
I WORK WITH
"COGNITIVE
DULLING"?

WHAT CHOICE
DID I HAVE?

I WAS
LOST.

BUT LITHIUM IS
A MOOD STABILIZER
AND DOESN'T USUALLY
LIFT A DEPRESSION
THAT'S ALREADY
BEGUN...

...SO I FELL INTO THE
HOLE ANYWAY.

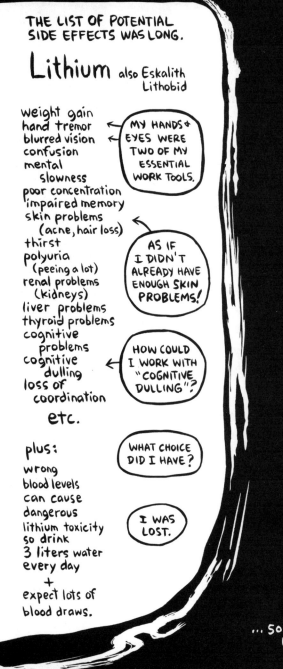

I COULD BARELY DRAG MYSELF OUT OF BED & TO THE COUCH.

IT WAS CLEAR: THERE WAS NO WAY I'D BE ABLE TO DREDGE UP THE ENERGY OR SASS TO DO THE COMICS I'D PLANNED -- *HALF*-PLANNED.

THE MANIC-ME-THEN HAD NO POWER TO TAKE CARE OF THE DEPRESSED-ME-NOW.

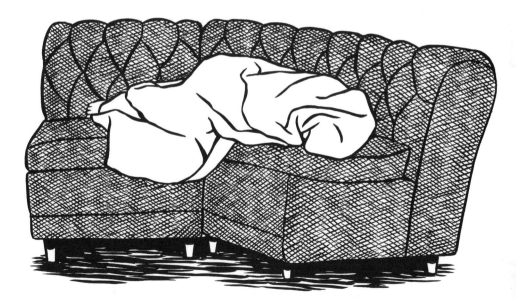

CHAPTER 4

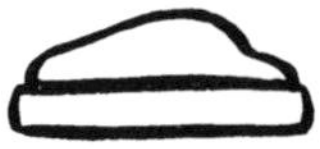

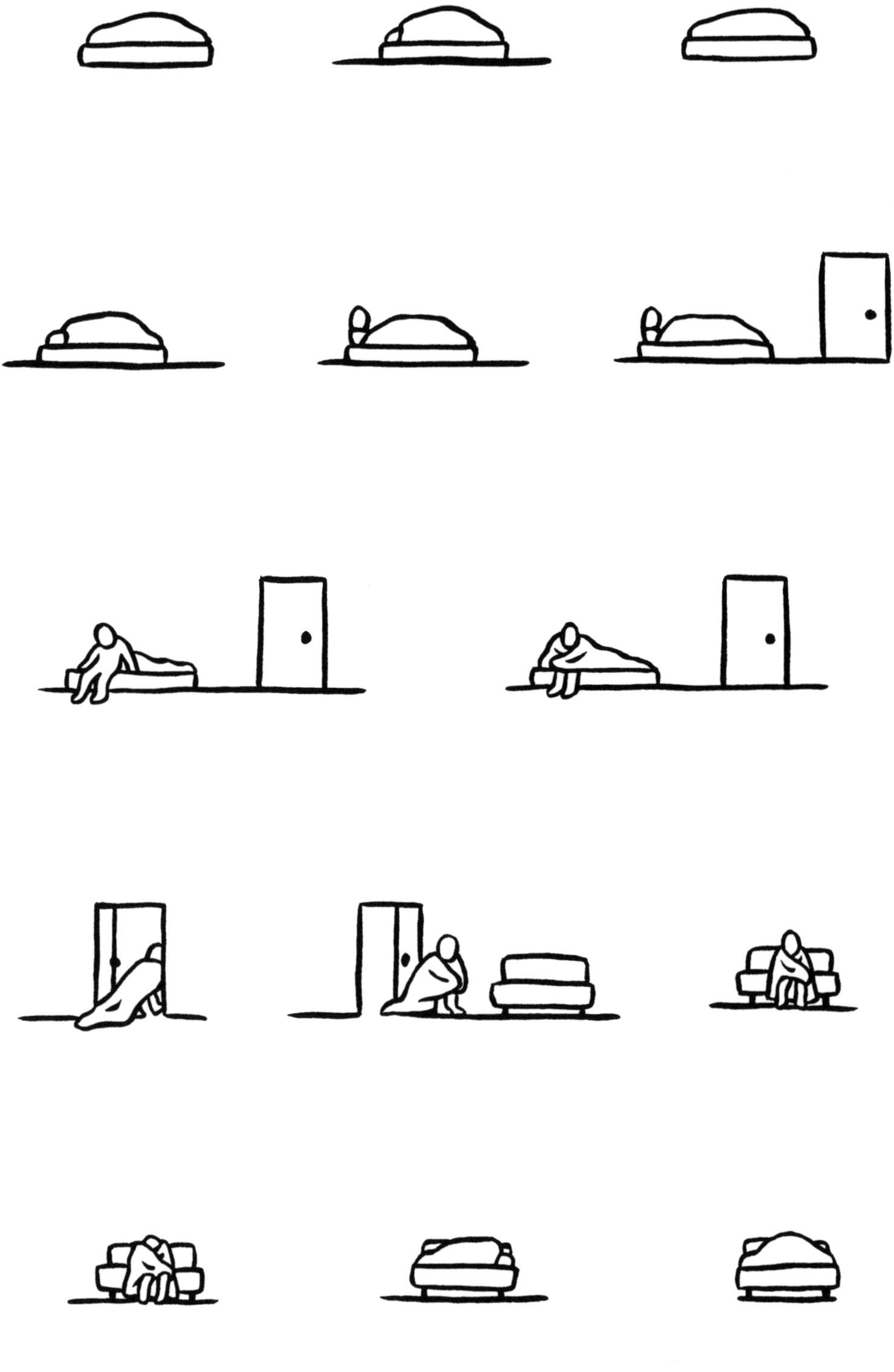

MANIC, I KNEW THE "UP" ME WAS THE TRUE ME ("I'm exponentially me!"); DEPRESSED, I KNEW THE "LOW" ME WAS THE TRUE ME (A WASTE OF SPACE).

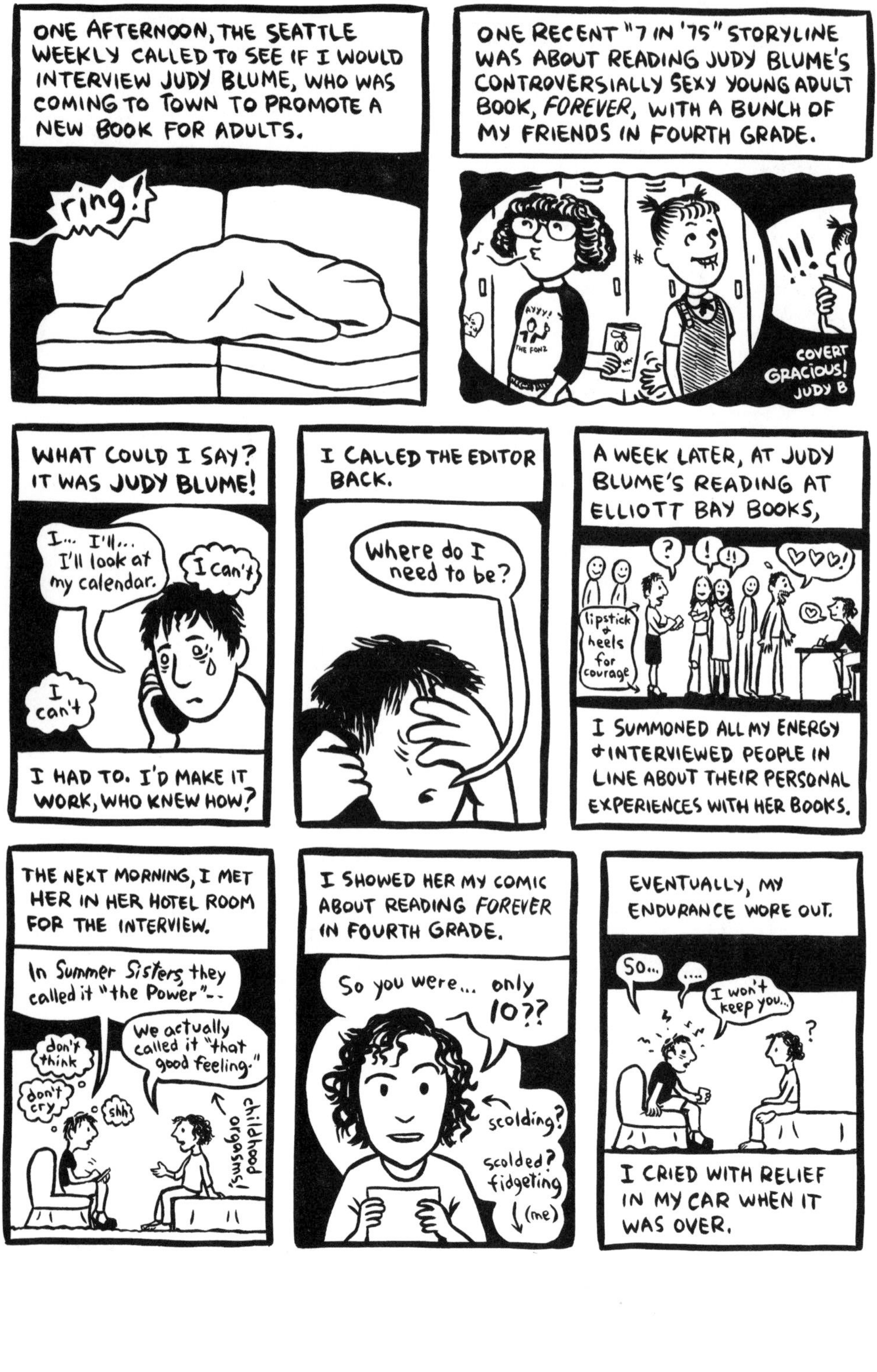

ONE AFTERNOON, THE SEATTLE WEEKLY CALLED TO SEE IF I WOULD INTERVIEW JUDY BLUME, WHO WAS COMING TO TOWN TO PROMOTE A NEW BOOK FOR ADULTS.
ring!
ONE RECENT "7 IN '75" STORYLINE WAS ABOUT READING JUDY BLUME'S CONTROVERSIALLY SEXY YOUNG ADULT BOOK, FOREVER, WITH A BUNCH OF MY FRIENDS IN FOURTH GRADE.
AYYY! THE FONZ
!!!
COVERT GRACIOUS! JUDY B
WHAT COULD I SAY? IT WAS JUDY BLUME!
I... I'll... I'll look at my calendar.
I can't
I can't
I HAD TO. I'D MAKE IT WORK, WHO KNEW HOW?
I CALLED THE EDITOR BACK.
Where do I need to be?
A WEEK LATER, AT JUDY BLUME'S READING AT ELLIOTT BAY BOOKS,
?
!
!!
♡♡♡!
lipstick & heels for courage
I SUMMONED ALL MY ENERGY & INTERVIEWED PEOPLE IN LINE ABOUT THEIR PERSONAL EXPERIENCES WITH HER BOOKS.
THE NEXT MORNING, I MET HER IN HER HOTEL ROOM FOR THE INTERVIEW.
In Summer Sisters, they called it "the Power"--
We actually called it "that good feeling."
don't think
don't cry
shh
childhood orgasms!
I SHOWED HER MY COMIC ABOUT READING FOREVER IN FOURTH GRADE.
So you were... only 10??
scolding?
scolded? fidgeting
(me)
EVENTUALLY, MY ENDURANCE WORE OUT.
So...
....
I won't keep you...
?
I CRIED WITH RELIEF IN MY CAR WHEN IT WAS OVER.

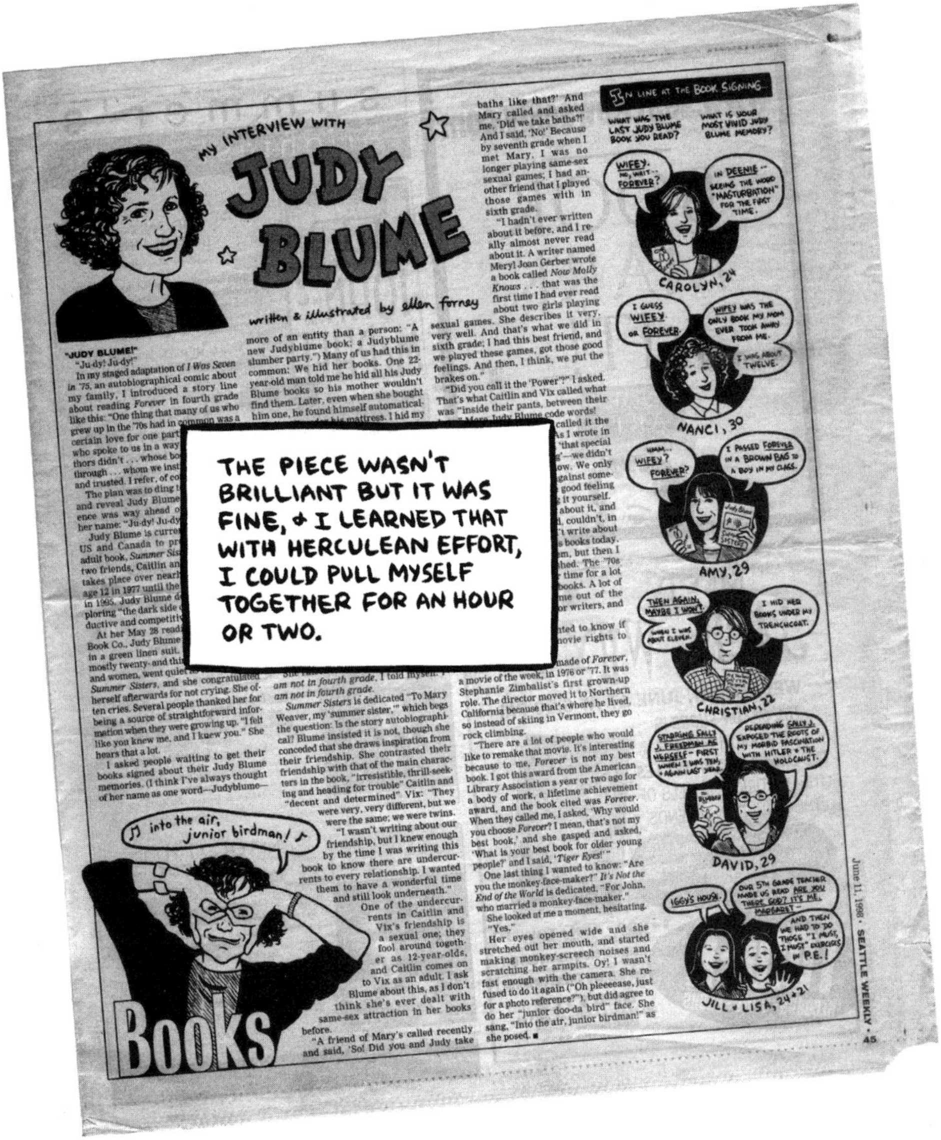

MY INTERVIEW WITH

JUDY BLUME

written & illustrated by ellen forney

"JUDY BLUME!"

"Ju-dy! Ju-dy!"

In my staged adaptation of *I Was Seven in '75*, an autobiographical comic about my family, I introduced a story line about reading *Forever* in fourth grade like this: "One thing that many of us who grew up in the '70s had in common was a
certain love for one part
who spoke to us in a way
thors didn't . . . whose bo
through . . . whom we inst
and trusted. I refer, of co

The plan was to ding t
and reveal Judy Blume
ence was way ahead o
her name: "Ju-dy! Ju-dy

Judy Blume is curre
US and Canada to pr
adult book, *Summer Sis*
two friends, Caitlin an
takes place over near
age 12 in 1977 until the
in 1995. Judy Blume d
ploring "the dark side
ductive and competiti

At her May 28 read
Book Co., Judy Blume
in a green linen suit.
mostly twenty- and thi
and women, went quiet
Summer Sisters, and she congratulated herself afterwards for not crying. She often cries. Several people thanked her for being a source of straightforward information when they were growing up. "I felt like you knew me, and I knew you." She hears that a lot.

I asked people waiting to get their books signed about their Judy Blume memories. (I think I've always thought of her name as one word—Judyblume—more of an entity than a person: "A new Judyblume book; a Judyblume slumber party.") Many of us had this in common: We hid her books. One 22-year-old man told me he hid all his Judy Blume books so his mother wouldn't find them. Later, even when she bought him one, he found himself automatically
his mattress. I hid my

am not in fourth grade, I told myself. *I am not in fourth grade.*

Summer Sisters is dedicated "To Mary Weaver, my 'summer sister,'" which begs the question: Is the story autobiographical? Blume insisted it is not, though she conceded that she draws inspiration from their friendship. She contrasted their friendship with that of the main characters in the book, "irresistible, thrill-seeking and heading for trouble" Caitlin and "decent and determined" Vix: "They were very, very different, but we were the same; we were twins.

"I wasn't writing about our friendship, but I knew enough by the time I was writing this book to know there are undercurrents to every relationship. I wanted them to have a wonderful time and still look underneath."

One of the undercurrents in Caitlin and Vix's friendship is a sexual one; they fool around together as 12-year-olds, and Caitlin comes on to Vix as an adult. I ask Blume about this, as I don't think she's ever dealt with same-sex attraction in her books before.

"A friend of Mary's called recently and said, 'So! Did you and Judy take baths like that?' And Mary called and asked me, 'Did we take baths?!' And I said, 'No!' Because by seventh grade when I met Mary, I was no longer playing same-sex sexual games; I had another friend that I played those games with in sixth grade.

"I hadn't ever written about it before, and I really almost never read about it. A writer named Meryl Joan Gerber wrote a book called *Now Molly Knows* . . . that was the first time I had ever read about two girls playing sexual games. She describes it very, very well. And that's what we did in sixth grade; I had this best friend, and we played these games, got those good feelings. And then, I think, we put the brakes on."

"Did you call it the 'Power'?" I asked. That's what Caitlin and Vix called what was "inside their pants, between their
Blume code words!
called it the
As I wrote in
'that special
g'—we didn't
ow. We only
gainst some-
good feeling
it yourself.
about it, and
couldn't, in
't write about
s books today.
m, but then I
shed. The '70s
time for a lot
books. A lot of
me out of the
or writers, and

nted to know if
movie rights to

made of *Forever*, a movie of the week, in 1976 or '77. It was Stephanie Zimbalist's first grown-up role. The director moved it to Northern California because that's where he lived, so instead of skiing in Vermont, they go rock climbing.

"There are a lot of people who would like to remake that movie. It's interesting because to me, *Forever* is not my best book. I got this award from the American Library Association a year or two ago for a body of work, a lifetime achievement award, and the book cited was *Forever*. When they called me, I asked, 'Why would you choose *Forever*? I mean, that's not my best book,' and she gasped and asked, 'What is your best book for older young people?' and I said, '*Tiger Eyes*!'"

One last thing I wanted to know: "Are you the monkey-face-maker?" *It's Not the End of the World* is dedicated, "For John, who married a monkey-face-maker."

She looked at me a moment, hesitating. "Yes."

Her eyes opened wide and she stretched out her mouth, and started making monkey-screech noises and scratching her armpits. Oy! I wasn't fast enough with the camera. She refused to do it again ("Oh pleeeease, just for a photo reference?"), but did agree to do her "junior doo-da bird" face. She sang, "Into the air, junior birdman!" as she posed. ■

♪ into the air, junior birdman! ♪
Books
IN LINE AT THE BOOK SIGNING...
WHAT WAS THE LAST JUDY BLUME BOOK YOU READ?
WHAT IS YOUR MOST VIVID JUDY BLUME MEMORY?
WIFEY. NO, WAIT-- FOREVER?
IN DEENIE -- SEEING THE WORD "MASTURBATION" FOR THE FIRST TIME.
CAROLYN, 24
I GUESS WIFEY. OR FOREVER.
WIFEY WAS THE ONLY BOOK MY MOM EVER TOOK AWAY FROM ME.
I WAS ABOUT TWELVE.
NANCI, 30
HMM... WIFEY? FOREVER?
I PASSED FOREVER IN A BROWN BAG TO A BOY IN MY CLASS.
AMY, 29
THEN AGAIN, MAYBE I WON'T.
WHEN I WAS ABOUT ELEVEN.
I HID HER BOOKS UNDER MY TRENCHCOAT.
CHRISTIAN, 22
STARRING SALLY J. FREEDMAN AS HERSELF - FIRST WHEN I WAS TEN, + AGAIN LAST YEAR.
REREADING SALLY J. EXPOSED THE ROOTS OF MY MORBID FASCINATION WITH HITLER + THE HOLOCAUST.
DAVID, 29
IGGY'S HOUSE.
OUR 5TH GRADE TEACHER MADE US READ ARE YOU THERE GOD? IT'S ME, MARGARET -
AND THEN WE HAD TO DO THOSE "I MUST, I MUST" EXERCISES IN P.E.!
JILL + LISA, 24 + 21
June 11, 1998 • SEATTLE WEEKLY • 45
THE PIECE WASN'T BRILLIANT BUT IT WAS FINE, & I LEARNED THAT WITH HERCULEAN EFFORT, I COULD PULL MYSELF TOGETHER FOR AN HOUR OR TWO.

WITH A SIMILAR SUMMONING OF ENERGY, I MANAGED TO EKE OUT A "7 IN '75" STRIP EACH WEEK.

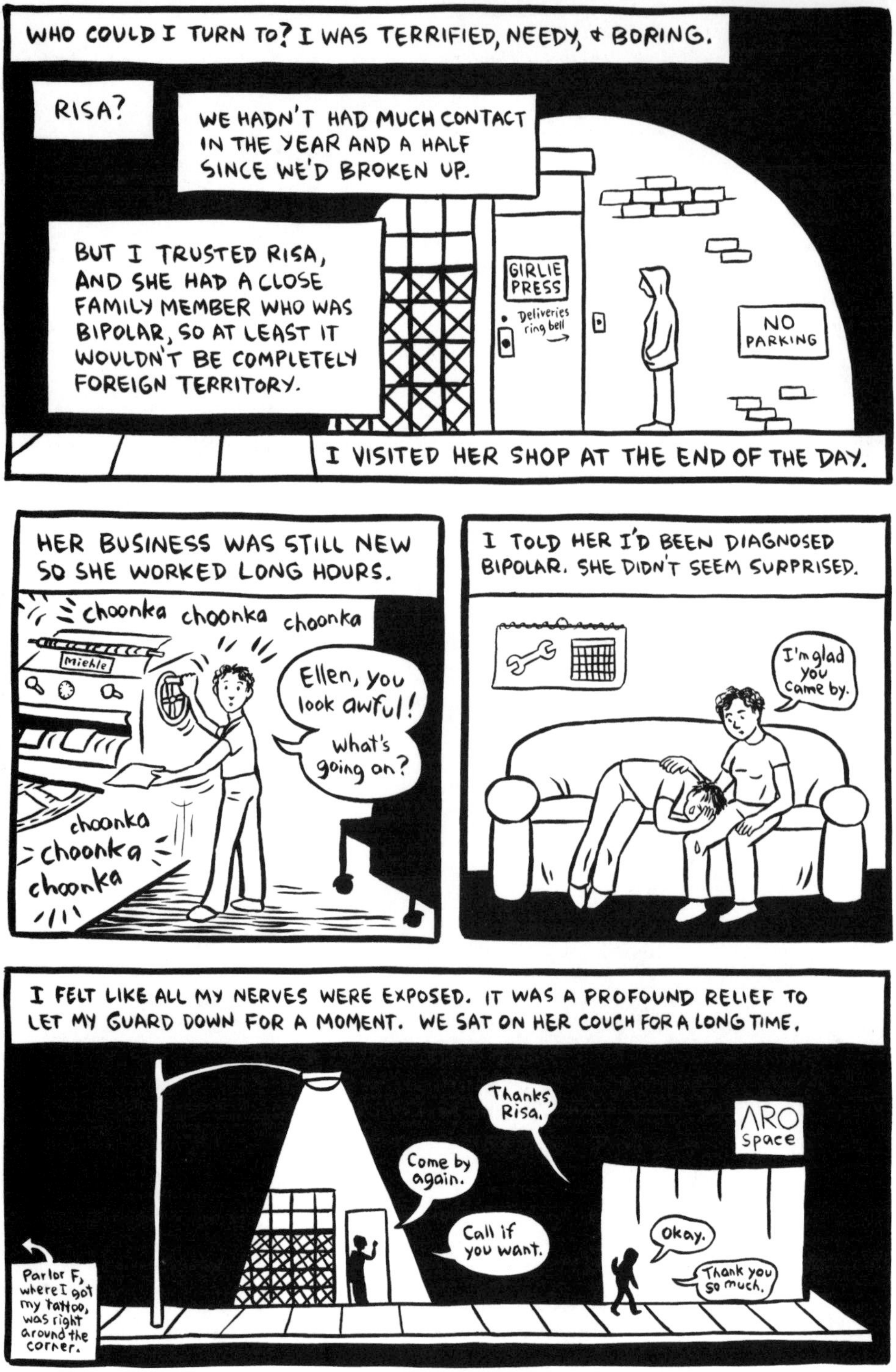
WHO COULD I TURN TO? I WAS TERRIFIED, NEEDY, & BORING.
RISA?
WE HADN'T HAD MUCH CONTACT IN THE YEAR AND A HALF SINCE WE'D BROKEN UP.
BUT I TRUSTED RISA, AND SHE HAD A CLOSE FAMILY MEMBER WHO WAS BIPOLAR, SO AT LEAST IT WOULDN'T BE COMPLETELY FOREIGN TERRITORY.
GIRLIE PRESS
Deliveries ring bell
NO PARKING
I VISITED HER SHOP AT THE END OF THE DAY.
HER BUSINESS WAS STILL NEW SO SHE WORKED LONG HOURS.
choonka choonka choonka
Miehle
Ellen, you look awful!
What's going on?
choonka choonka choonka
I TOLD HER I'D BEEN DIAGNOSED BIPOLAR. SHE DIDN'T SEEM SURPRISED.
I'm glad you came by.
I FELT LIKE ALL MY NERVES WERE EXPOSED. IT WAS A PROFOUND RELIEF TO LET MY GUARD DOWN FOR A MOMENT. WE SAT ON HER COUCH FOR A LONG TIME.
Thanks, Risa.
ARO space
Come by again.
Call if you want.
Okay.
Thank you so much.
Parlor F, where I got my tattoo, was right around the corner.

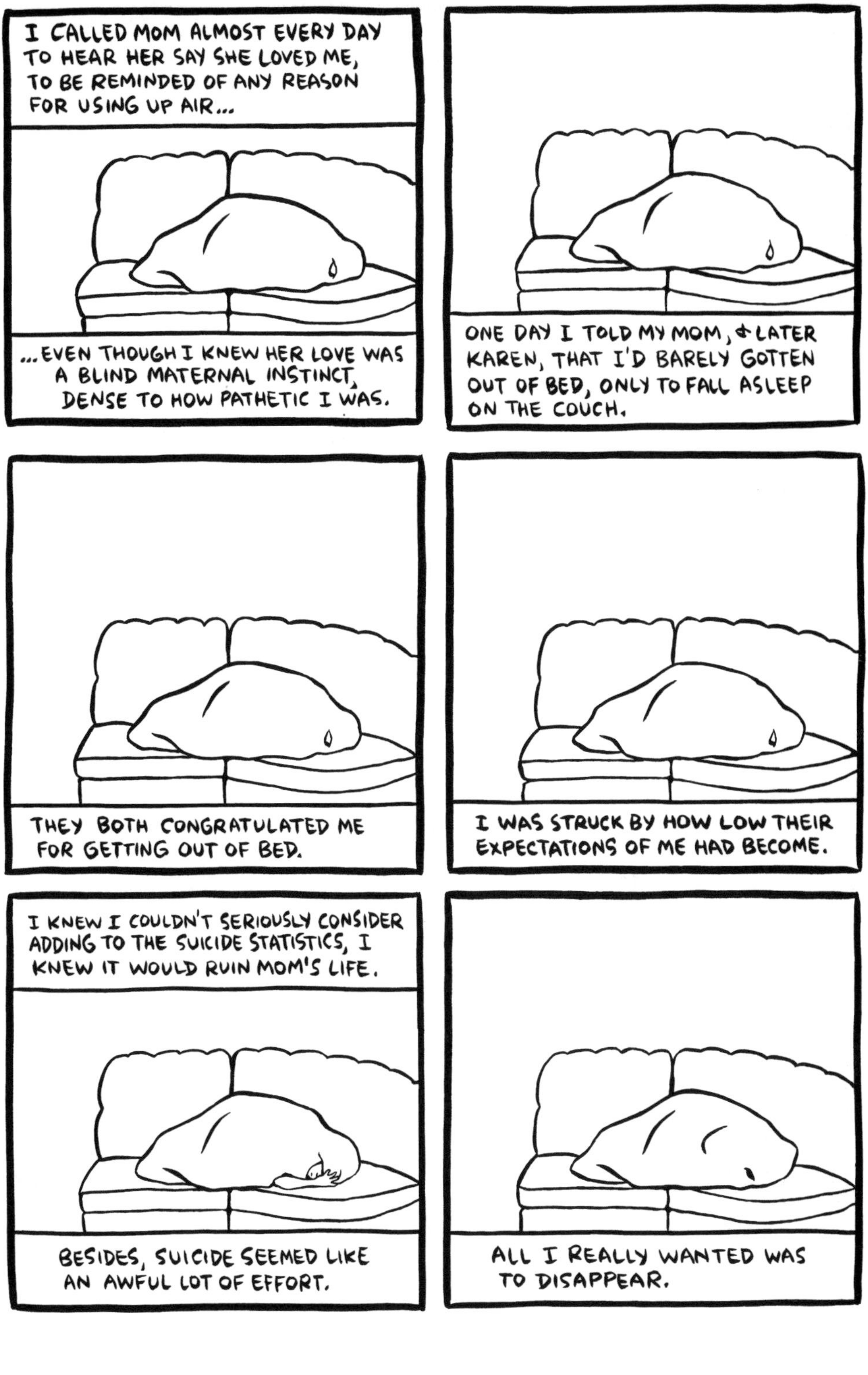
I CALLED MOM ALMOST EVERY DAY TO HEAR HER SAY SHE LOVED ME, TO BE REMINDED OF ANY REASON FOR USING UP AIR...
...EVEN THOUGH I KNEW HER LOVE WAS A BLIND MATERNAL INSTINCT, DENSE TO HOW PATHETIC I WAS.
ONE DAY I TOLD MY MOM, & LATER KAREN, THAT I'D BARELY GOTTEN OUT OF BED, ONLY TO FALL ASLEEP ON THE COUCH.
THEY BOTH CONGRATULATED ME FOR GETTING OUT OF BED.
I WAS STRUCK BY HOW LOW THEIR EXPECTATIONS OF ME HAD BECOME.
I KNEW I COULDN'T SERIOUSLY CONSIDER ADDING TO THE SUICIDE STATISTICS, I KNEW IT WOULD RUIN MOM'S LIFE.
BESIDES, SUICIDE SEEMED LIKE AN AWFUL LOT OF EFFORT.
ALL I REALLY WANTED WAS TO DISAPPEAR.

I WAS HAVING A TOUGH TIME WITH THE LITHIUM.

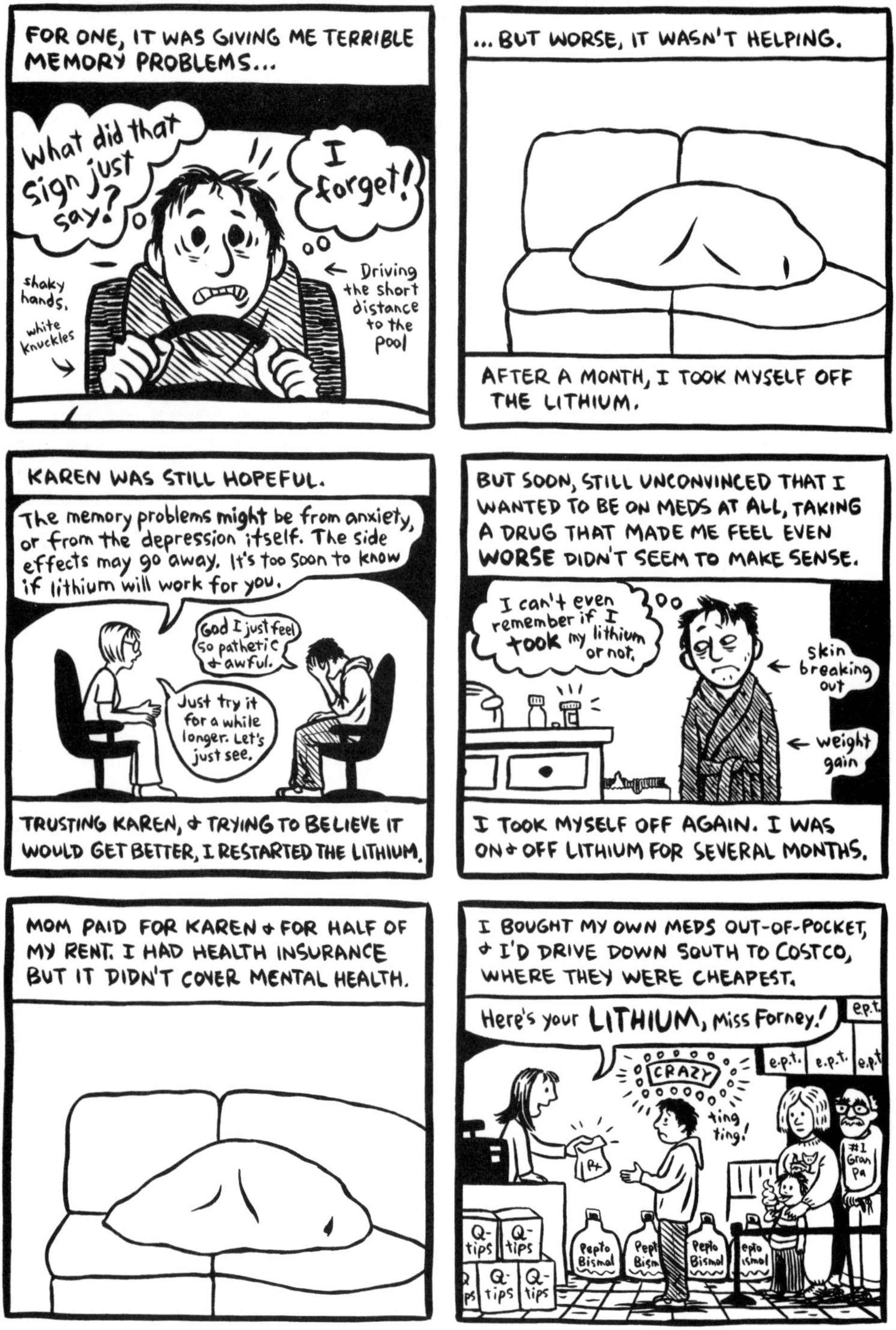
FOR ONE, IT WAS GIVING ME TERRIBLE MEMORY PROBLEMS...
What did that sign just say?
I forget!
shaky hands,
white knuckles
Driving the short distance to the pool
... BUT WORSE, IT WASN'T HELPING.
AFTER A MONTH, I TOOK MYSELF OFF THE LITHIUM.
KAREN WAS STILL HOPEFUL.
The memory problems might be from anxiety, or from the depression itself. The side effects may go away. It's too soon to know if lithium will work for you.
God I just feel so pathetic & awful.
Just try it for a while longer. Let's just see.
TRUSTING KAREN, & TRYING TO BELIEVE IT WOULD GET BETTER, I RESTARTED THE LITHIUM.
BUT SOON, STILL UNCONVINCED THAT I WANTED TO BE ON MEDS AT ALL, TAKING A DRUG THAT MADE ME FEEL EVEN WORSE DIDN'T SEEM TO MAKE SENSE.
I can't even remember if I took my lithium or not.
skin breaking out
weight gain
I TOOK MYSELF OFF AGAIN. I WAS ON & OFF LITHIUM FOR SEVERAL MONTHS.
MOM PAID FOR KAREN & FOR HALF OF MY RENT. I HAD HEALTH INSURANCE BUT IT DIDN'T COVER MENTAL HEALTH.
I BOUGHT MY OWN MEDS OUT-OF-POCKET, & I'D DRIVE DOWN SOUTH TO COSTCO, WHERE THEY WERE CHEAPEST.
Here's your LITHIUM, Miss Forney!
CRAZY
ting ting!
e.p.t.
#1 Gran Pa
Q-tips
Pepto Bismol

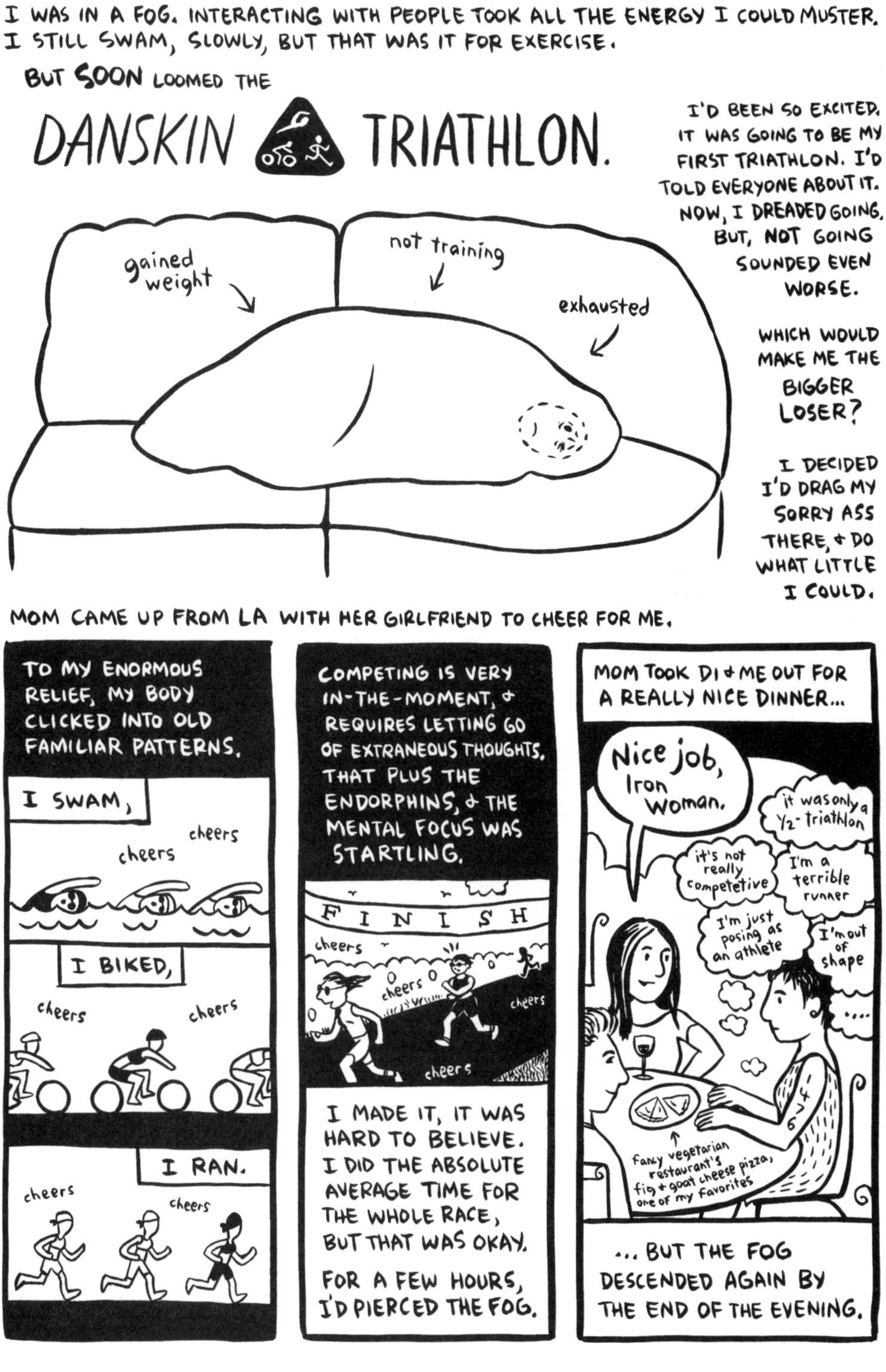
I WAS IN A FOG. INTERACTING WITH PEOPLE TOOK ALL THE ENERGY I COULD MUSTER. I STILL SWAM, SLOWLY, BUT THAT WAS IT FOR EXERCISE.
BUT SOON LOOMED THE
DANSKIN TRIATHLON.
I'D BEEN SO EXCITED. IT WAS GOING TO BE MY FIRST TRIATHLON. I'D TOLD EVERYONE ABOUT IT. NOW, I DREADED GOING. BUT, NOT GOING SOUNDED EVEN WORSE.
WHICH WOULD MAKE ME THE BIGGER LOSER?
I DECIDED I'D DRAG MY SORRY ASS THERE, & DO WHAT LITTLE I COULD.
gained weight
not training
exhausted
MOM CAME UP FROM LA WITH HER GIRLFRIEND TO CHEER FOR ME.
TO MY ENORMOUS RELIEF, MY BODY CLICKED INTO OLD FAMILIAR PATTERNS.
I SWAM,
cheers
cheers
I BIKED,
cheers
cheers
I RAN.
cheers
cheers
COMPETING IS VERY IN-THE-MOMENT, & REQUIRES LETTING GO OF EXTRANEOUS THOUGHTS. THAT PLUS THE ENDORPHINS, & THE MENTAL FOCUS WAS STARTLING.
FINISH
cheers
cheers
cheers
cheers
I MADE IT, IT WAS HARD TO BELIEVE. I DID THE ABSOLUTE AVERAGE TIME FOR THE WHOLE RACE, BUT THAT WAS OKAY.
FOR A FEW HOURS, I'D PIERCED THE FOG.
MOM TOOK DI & ME OUT FOR A REALLY NICE DINNER...
Nice job, Iron Woman.
it was only a 1/2-triathlon
it's not really competetive
I'm a terrible runner
I'm just posing as an athlete
I'm out of shape
....
fancy vegetarian restaurant's fig & goat cheese pizza, one of my favorites
... BUT THE FOG DESCENDED AGAIN BY THE END OF THE EVENING.

I HAD NO SENSE OF PURPOSE. I FELT LIKE I WAS MISSING MY SKIN.

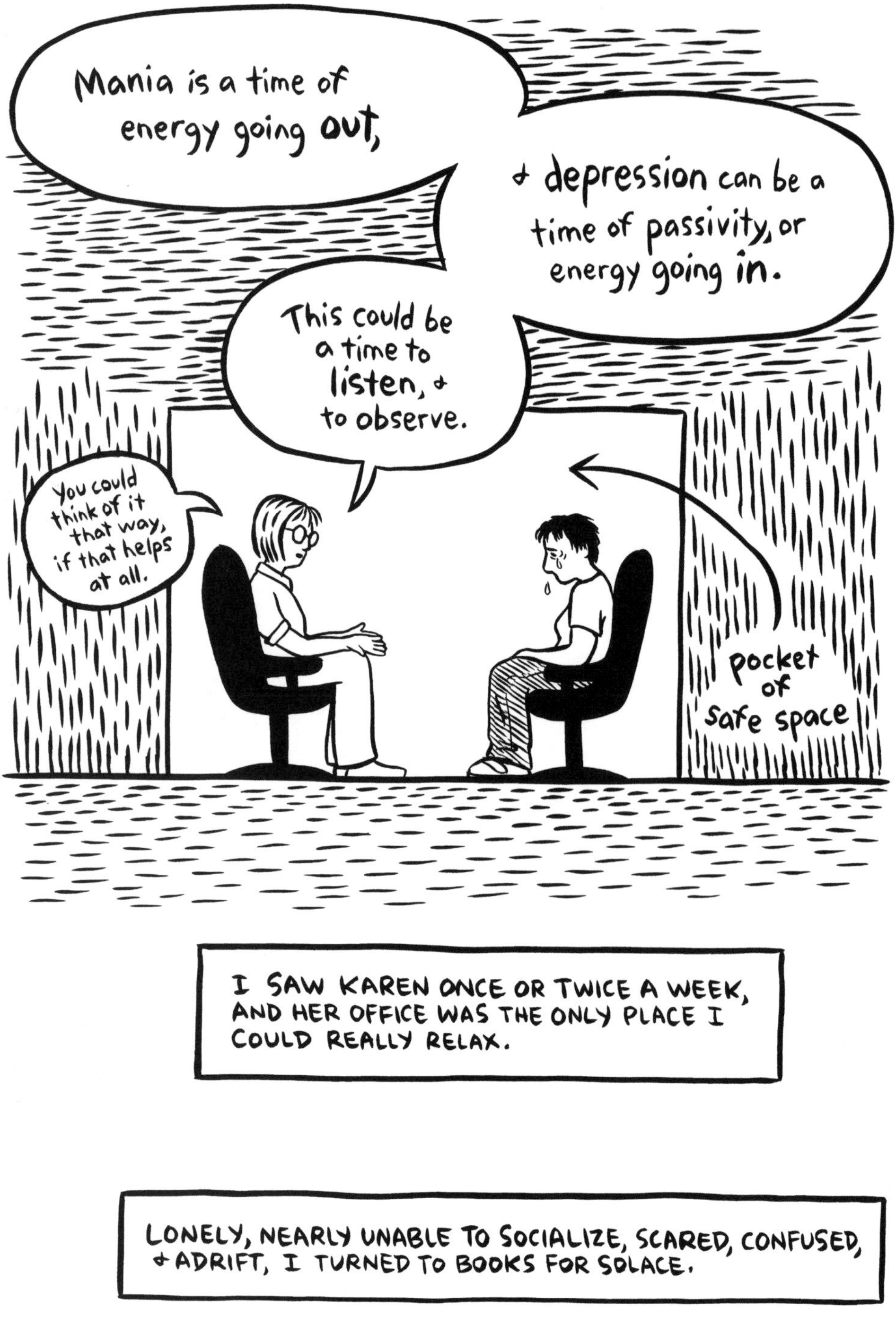
Mania is a time of energy going out,
& depression can be a time of passivity, or energy going in.
This could be a time to listen, & to observe.
You could think of it that way, if that helps at all.
pocket of safe space

I SAW KAREN ONCE OR TWICE A WEEK, AND HER OFFICE WAS THE ONLY PLACE I COULD REALLY RELAX.

LONELY, NEARLY UNABLE TO SOCIALIZE, SCARED, CONFUSED, & ADRIFT, I TURNED TO BOOKS FOR SOLACE.

THERE WERE A FEW BOOKS IN PARTICULAR THAT PLAYED AN IMPORTANT ROLE FOR ME.

THERE WAS THE FAMILIAR

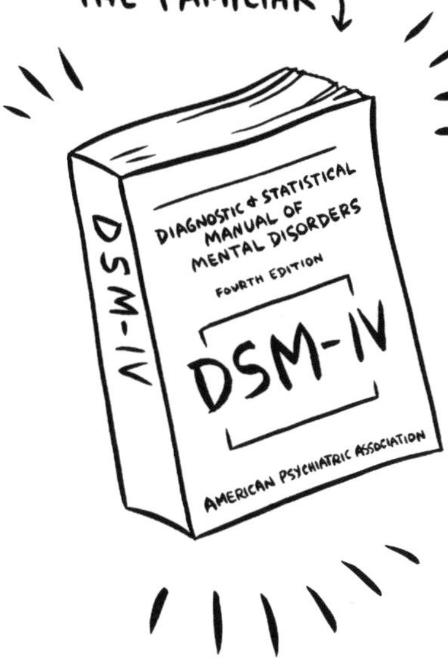
DSM-IV
DIAGNOSTIC & STATISTICAL MANUAL OF MENTAL DISORDERS
FOURTH EDITION
DSM-IV
AMERICAN PSYCHIATRIC ASSOCIATION

I DIDN'T FIND THE KEY TO RELIEF IN MY LOCAL BOOKSTORE, BUT I GOT TO READ THE LIST OF DSM-IV SYMPTOMS CITED OVER & OVER.

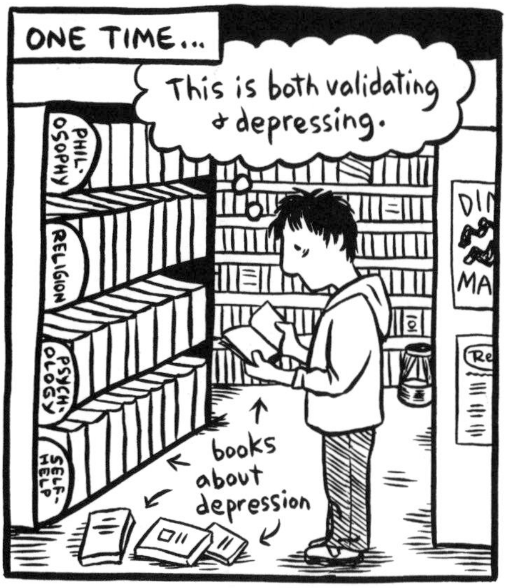
ONE TIME...
This is both validating & depressing.
PHIL-OSOPHY
RELIGION
PSYCH-OLOGY
SELF-HELP
books about depression

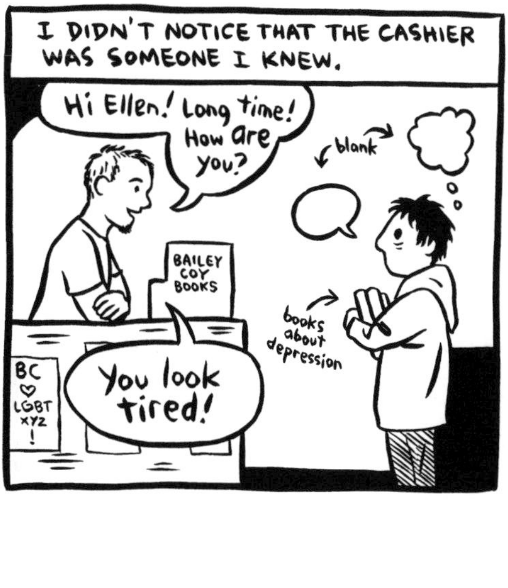
I DIDN'T NOTICE THAT THE CASHIER WAS SOMEONE I KNEW.
Hi Ellen! Long time! How are you?
blank
BAILEY COY BOOKS
books about depression
BC ♡ LGBT XYZ !
You look tired!

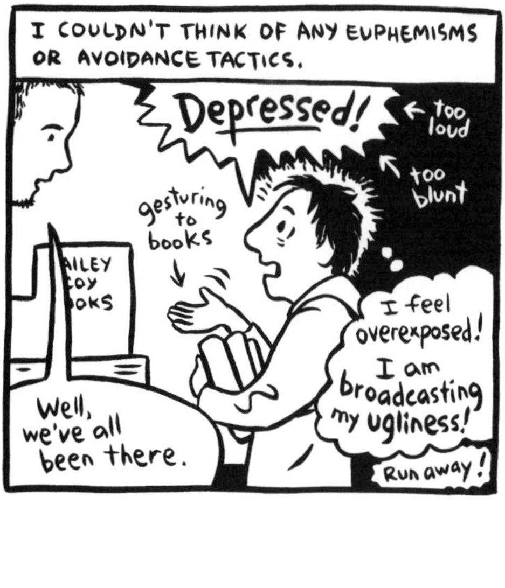
I COULDN'T THINK OF ANY EUPHEMISMS OR AVOIDANCE TACTICS.
Depressed!
too loud
too blunt
gesturing to books
AILEY COY OKS
I feel overexposed! I am broadcasting my ugliness!
Run away!
Well, we've all been there.

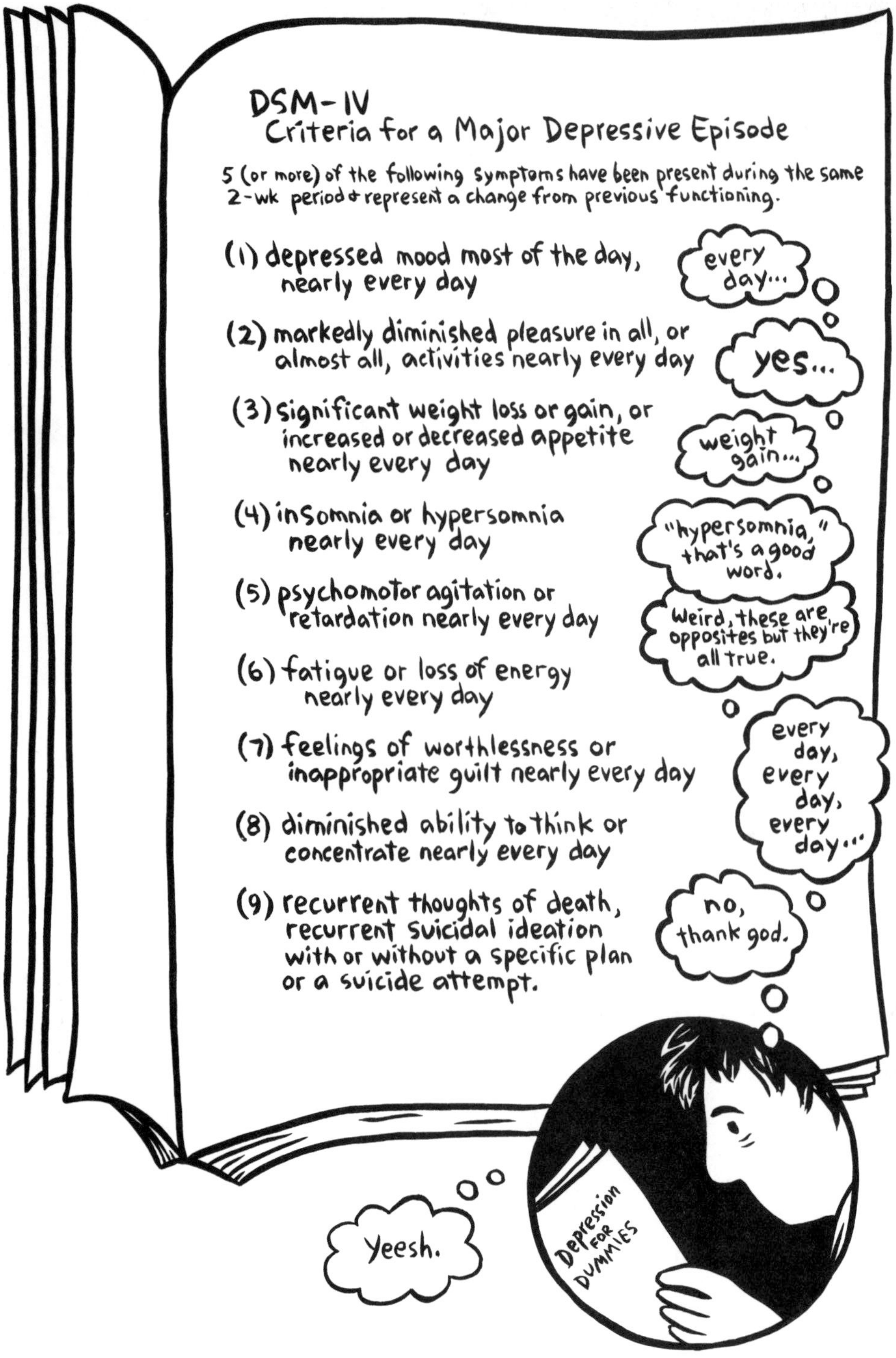
DSM-IV
Criteria for a Major Depressive Episode
5 (or more) of the following symptoms have been present during the same 2-wk period & represent a change from previous functioning.
(1) depressed mood most of the day, nearly every day
every day...
(2) markedly diminished pleasure in all, or almost all, activities nearly every day
yes...
(3) significant weight loss or gain, or increased or decreased appetite nearly every day
weight gain...
(4) insomnia or hypersomnia nearly every day
"hypersomnia," that's a good word.
(5) psychomotor agitation or retardation nearly every day
Weird, these are opposites but they're all true.
(6) fatigue or loss of energy nearly every day
(7) feelings of worthlessness or inappropriate guilt nearly every day
every day, every day, every day...
(8) diminished ability to think or concentrate nearly every day
(9) recurrent thoughts of death, recurrent suicidal ideation with or without a specific plan or a suicide attempt.
no, thank god.
Yeesh.
Depression FOR DUMMIES

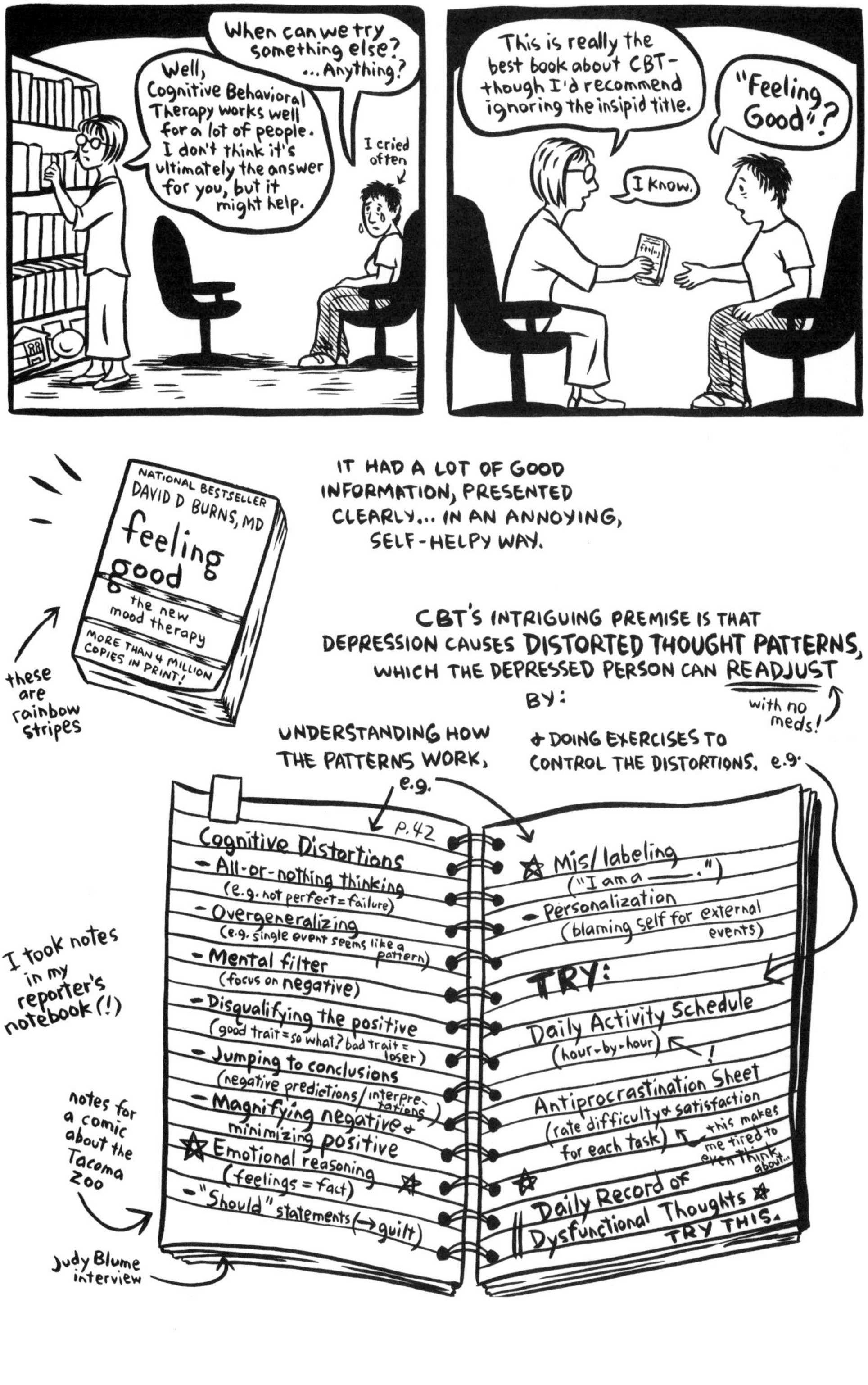
When can we try something else? ...Anything?
Well, Cognitive Behavioral Therapy works well for a lot of people. I don't think it's ultimately the answer for you, but it might help.
I cried often
This is really the best book about CBT- though I'd recommend ignoring the insipid title.
"Feeling Good"?
I know.
NATIONAL BESTSELLER
DAVID D BURNS, MD
feeling good
the new mood therapy
MORE THAN 4 MILLION COPIES IN PRINT!
these are rainbow stripes
IT HAD A LOT OF GOOD INFORMATION, PRESENTED CLEARLY... IN AN ANNOYING, SELF-HELPY WAY.
CBT'S INTRIGUING PREMISE IS THAT DEPRESSION CAUSES DISTORTED THOUGHT PATTERNS, WHICH THE DEPRESSED PERSON CAN READJUST BY:
with no meds!
UNDERSTANDING HOW THE PATTERNS WORK, e.g.
& DOING EXERCISES TO CONTROL THE DISTORTIONS. e.g.
p.42
Cognitive Distortions
- All-or-nothing thinking (e.g. not perfect = failure)
- Overgeneralizing (e.g. single event seems like a pattern)
- Mental filter (focus on negative)
- Disqualifying the positive (good trait = so what? bad trait = loser)
- Jumping to conclusions (negative predictions/interpretations)
- Magnifying negative & minimizing positive
Emotional reasoning (feelings = fact)
- "Should" statements (→ guilt)
Mis/labeling ("I am a ____.")
- Personalization (blaming self for external events)
TRY:
Daily Activity Schedule (hour-by-hour) !
Antiprocrastination Sheet (rate difficulty & satisfaction for each task)
this makes me tired to even think about...
Daily Record of Dysfunctional Thoughts
TRY THIS.
I took notes in my reporter's notebook (!)
notes for a comic about the Tacoma Zoo
Judy Blume interview

THE EXERCISE I FOUND MOST USEFUL WAS CALLED

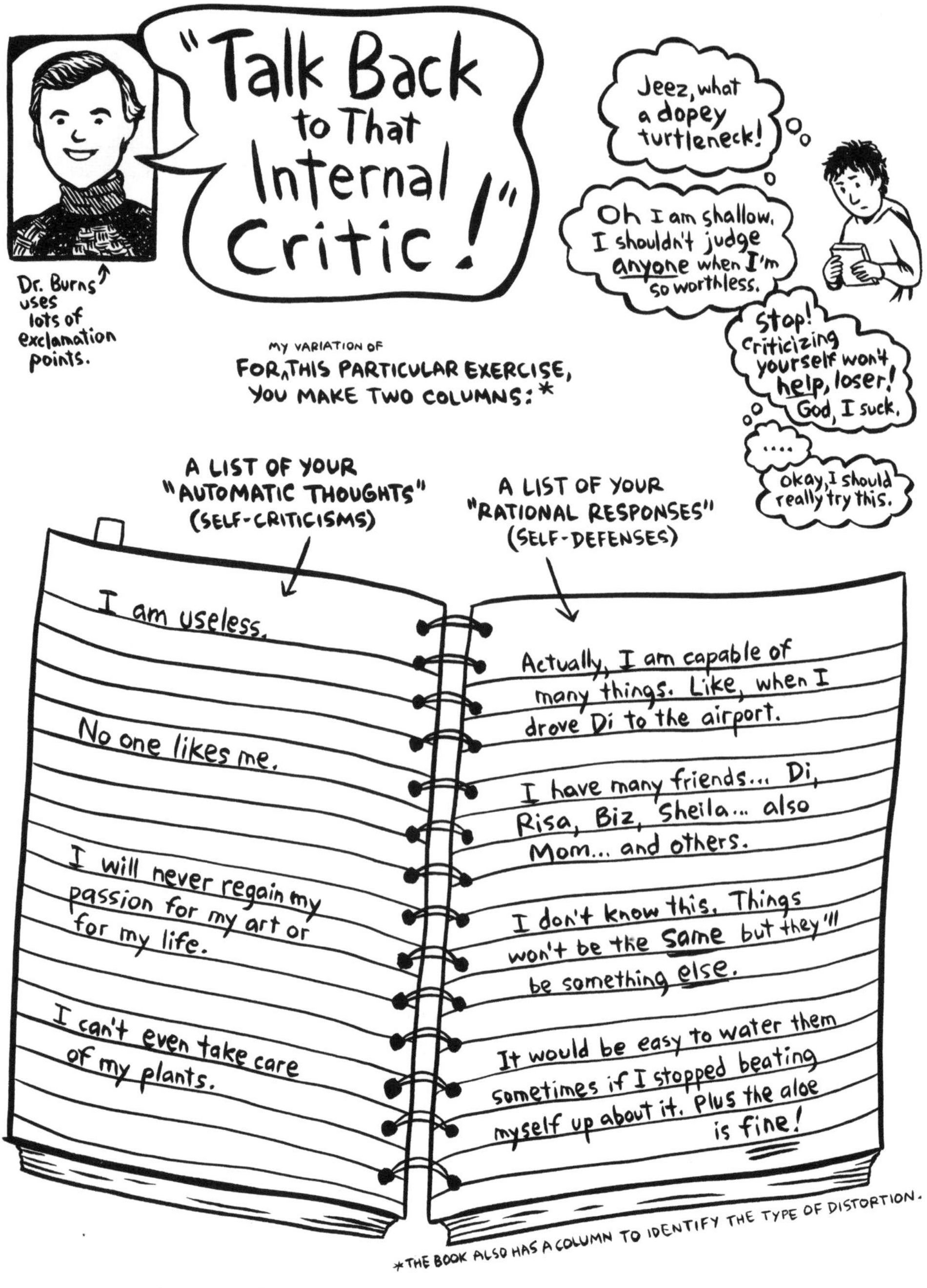
"Talk Back to That Internal Critic!"
Dr. Burns uses lots of exclamation points.
Jeez, what a dopey turtleneck!
Oh I am shallow. I shouldn't judge anyone when I'm so worthless.
Stop! Criticizing yourself won't help, loser! God, I suck.
....
Okay, I should really try this.
FOR MY VARIATION OF THIS PARTICULAR EXERCISE, YOU MAKE TWO COLUMNS: *
A LIST OF YOUR "AUTOMATIC THOUGHTS" (SELF-CRITICISMS)
A LIST OF YOUR "RATIONAL RESPONSES" (SELF-DEFENSES)
I am useless.
Actually, I am capable of many things. Like, when I drove Di to the airport.
No one likes me.
I have many friends... Di, Risa, Biz, Sheila... also Mom... and others.
I will never regain my passion for my art or for my life.
I don't know this. Things won't be the same but they'll be something else.
I can't even take care of my plants.
It would be easy to water them sometimes if I stopped beating myself up about it. Plus the aloe is fine!
* THE BOOK ALSO HAS A COLUMN TO IDENTIFY THE TYPE OF DISTORTION.

EVEN MY TEPID "RESPONSE" COLUMN WAS A HUGE EFFORT TO GENERATE, BUT IT HELPED A LOT. I DID THIS EXERCISE NUMEROUS TIMES, BUT DIDN'T CONNECT WITH THE MORE REGIMENTED ONES. KAREN WAS RIGHT– COGNITIVE BEHAVIORAL THERAPY WAS HELPFUL FOR ME, BUT ONLY SO MUCH.

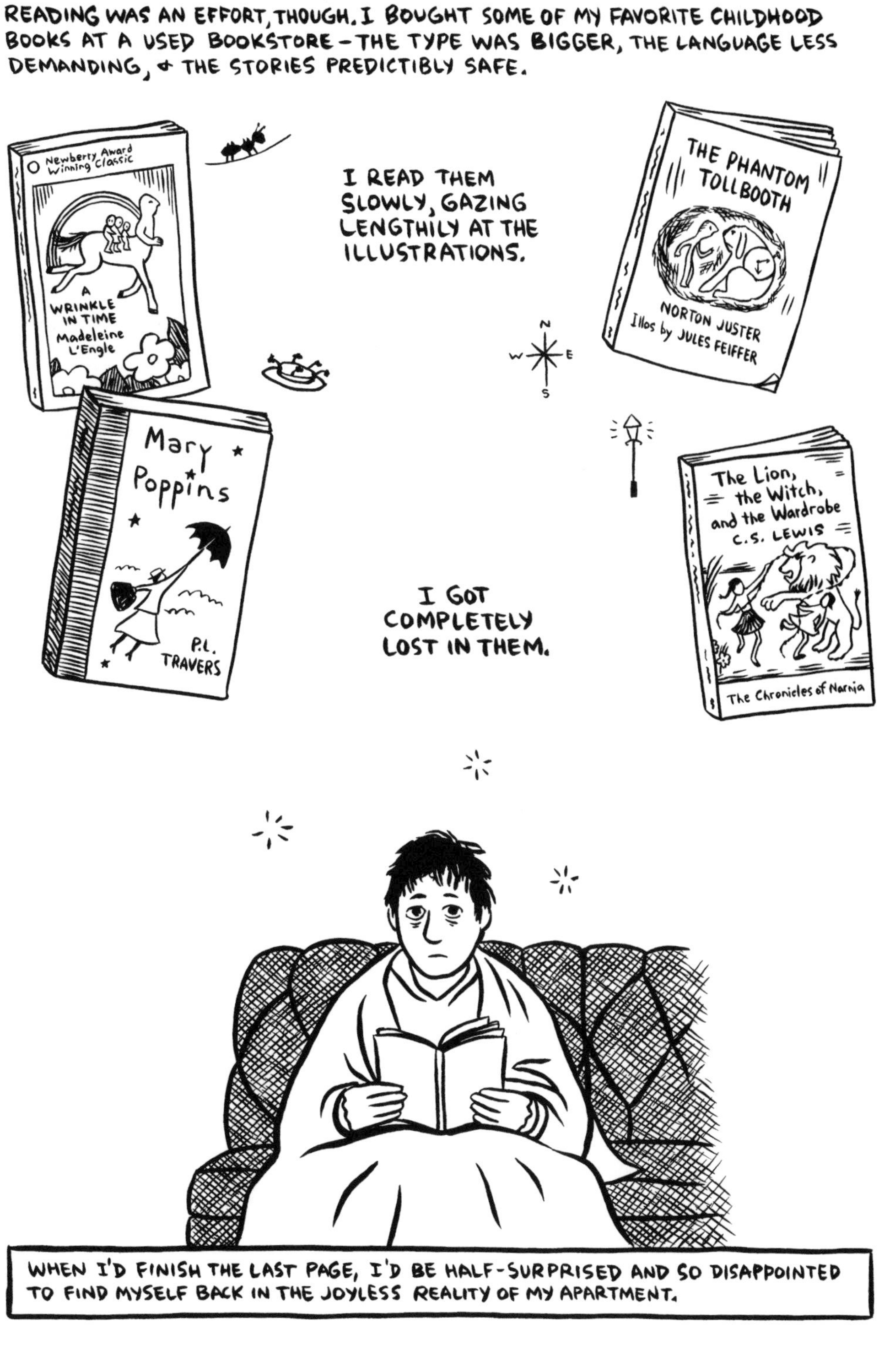
READING WAS AN EFFORT, THOUGH. I BOUGHT SOME OF MY FAVORITE CHILDHOOD BOOKS AT A USED BOOKSTORE – THE TYPE WAS BIGGER, THE LANGUAGE LESS DEMANDING, & THE STORIES PREDICTIBLY SAFE.
Newberry Award Winning Classic
A WRINKLE IN TIME
Madeleine L'Engle
I READ THEM SLOWLY, GAZING LENGTHILY AT THE ILLUSTRATIONS.
THE PHANTOM TOLLBOOTH
NORTON JUSTER
Illos by JULES FEIFFER
N
W
E
S
Mary Poppins
P.L. TRAVERS
The Lion, the Witch, and the Wardrobe
C.S. LEWIS
The Chronicles of Narnia
I GOT COMPLETELY LOST IN THEM.
WHEN I'D FINISH THE LAST PAGE, I'D BE HALF-SURPRISED AND SO DISAPPOINTED TO FIND MYSELF BACK IN THE JOYLESS REALITY OF MY APARTMENT.

TWO AUTOBIOGRAPHIES BECAME HUGELY IMPORTANT TO ME.

HAVING DISMISSED ANY RELEVANCE TO ME WHEN I'D READ IT A FEW MONTHS EARLIER, I READ THIS AGAIN:

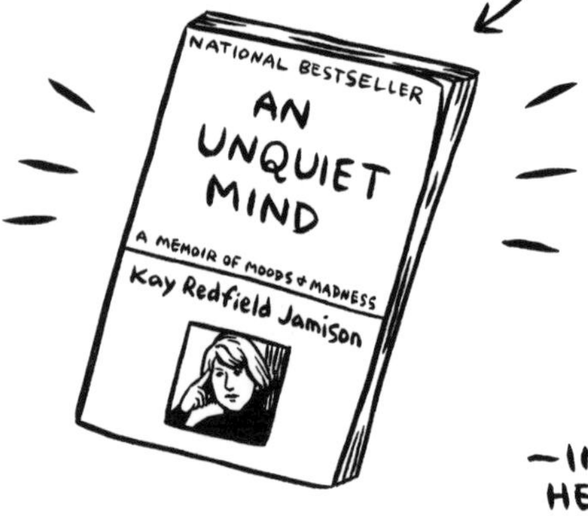
NATIONAL BESTSELLER
AN UNQUIET MIND
A MEMOIR OF MOODS & MADNESS
Kay Redfield Jamison

THIS TIME, I DIDN'T PUSH HER STORY AWAY JUST BECAUSE IT DIDN'T LINE UP EXACTLY WITH MINE.

WE WERE DIFFERENT, BUT WE SHARED SOMETHING IMPORTANT—

—IMPORTANT ENOUGH FOR HER TO WRITE A BOOK ABOUT.

SHE WAS **COMPANY.**

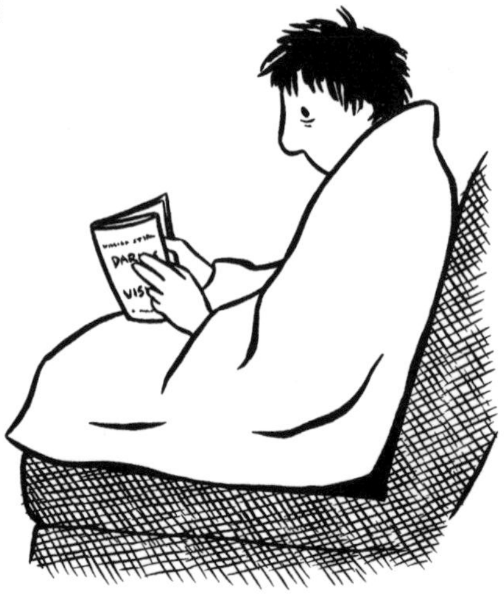

WILLIAM STYRON DESCRIBES THE PAIN OF HIS OWN EXPERIENCE OF DEPRESSION SO ELOQUENTLY, & SO VIVIDLY, IN HIS MEMOIR:

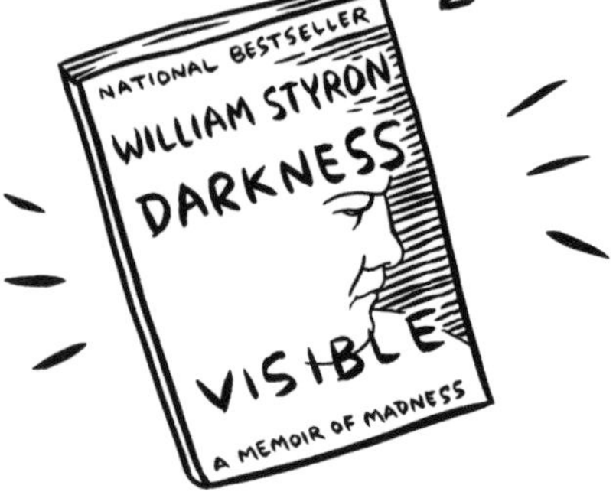
NATIONAL BESTSELLER
WILLIAM STYRON
DARKNESS VISIBLE
A MEMOIR OF MADNESS

HE POINTS OUT THAT ARTISTS & WRITERS, "CHRONICLERS OF THE HUMAN SPIRIT," OFTEN STRUGGLE WITH DEPRESSION IN THEIR LIVES & THEIR WORK. (Club Van Gogh!)

IT WAS STUNNING TO SEE MY OWN
DEMONS NAILED SO EFFECTIVELY.

...self-hatred...

...fragility...

...hopelessness...

...dank
joylessness...

...unrelenting...

...loss.

...diabolical discomfort of
being imprisoned in a
fiercely overheated room.

...smothering confinement...

...infantile dread...

...an immense and
aching solitude.

...howling tempest...
a storm of murk.

HE WAS COMPANY.

THE BOOK WAS ALSO EVIDENCE
THAT DEPRESSION MIGHT GO AWAY,
& CREATIVITY MIGHT COME BACK.

BUT IT WAS REALLY MY SKETCHBOOK WHERE I COULD FACE MY
EMOTIONAL DEMONS IN A WHOLLY PERSONAL WAY.

I DIDN'T HAVE THE ENERGY TO DRAW VERY OFTEN,
BUT I STARTED CARRYING MY SKETCHBOOK WITH ME—

A COMBINATION OF CARRYING A TEDDY BEAR
& CARRYING A CAN OF MACE.

THE DRAWINGS BOTH
SCARED ME & GAVE ME COMFORT.

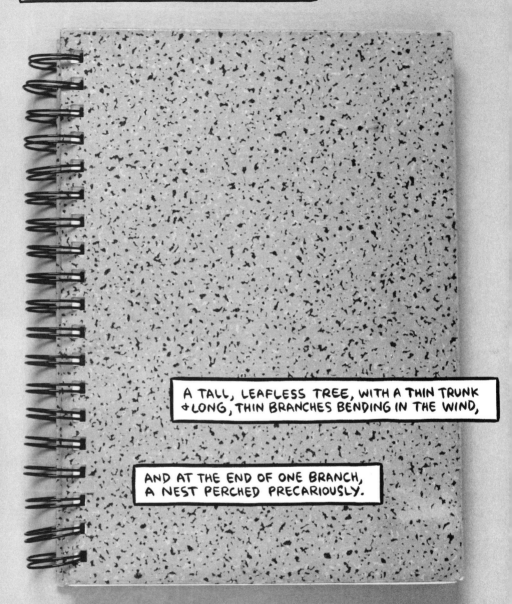

I'D INITIALLY TAKEN THE SKETCHBOOK OFF MY SHELF BECAUSE I WANTED TO DRAW A MENTAL IMAGE I'D BEEN HAVING —

A TALL, LEAFLESS TREE, WITH A THIN TRUNK & LONG, THIN BRANCHES BENDING IN THE WIND,

AND AT THE END OF ONE BRANCH, A NEST PERCHED PRECARIOUSLY.

I SHOWED THE DRAWING TO KAREN & SHE SAID IT DIDN'T LOOK SO PRECARIOUS, BUT I ALREADY KNEW I HADN'T DRAWN IT RIGHT.

MY MENTAL IMAGE WAS MORE LIKE THIS:

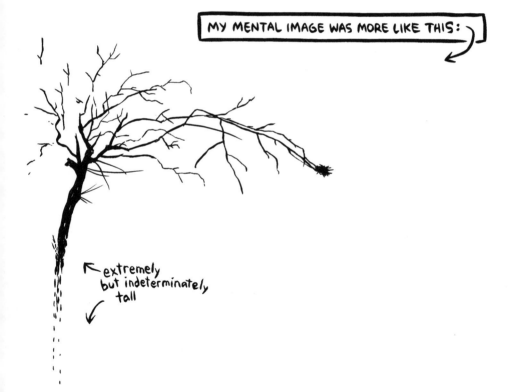

extremely but indeterminately tall

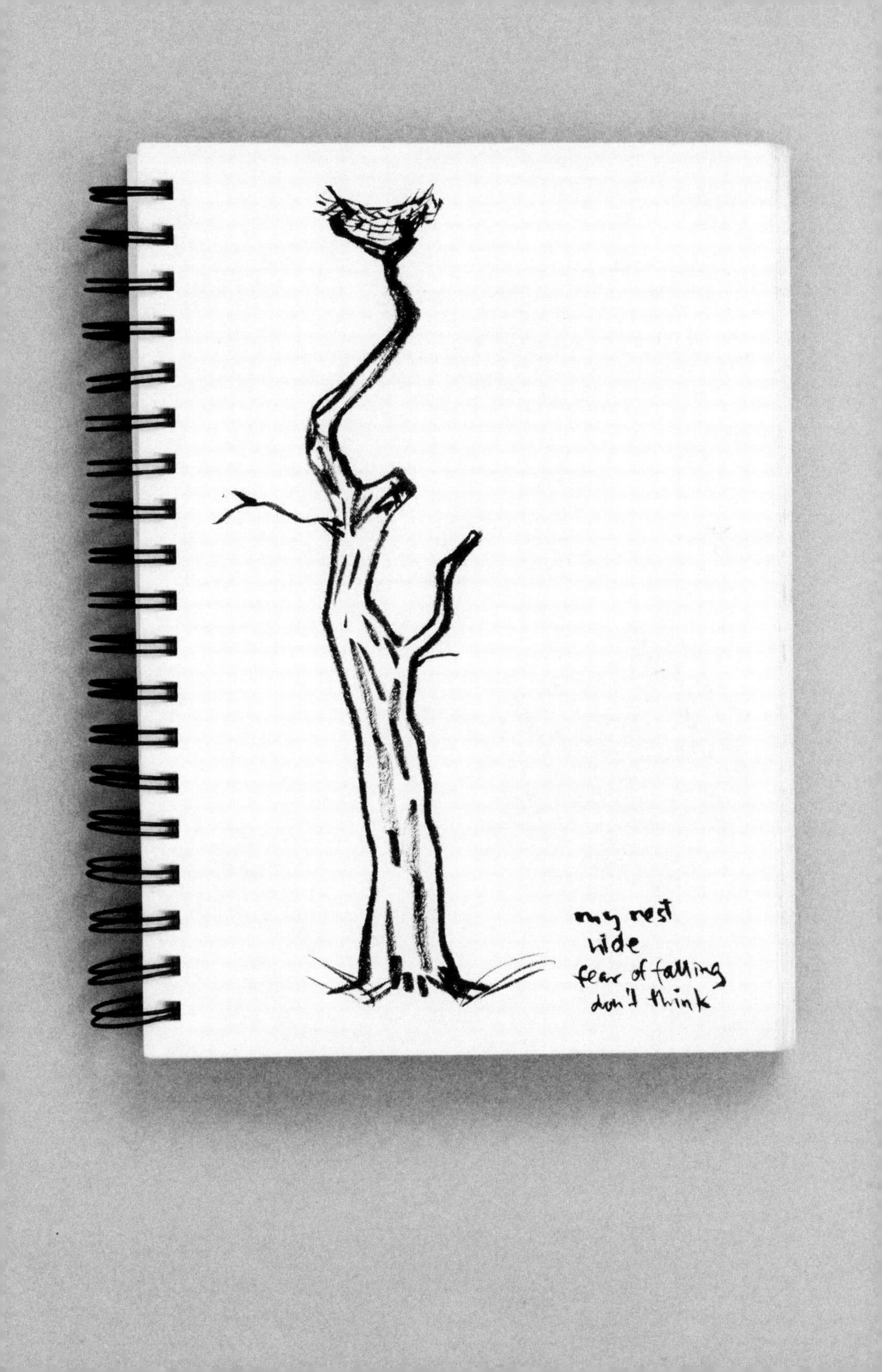
my nest
hide
fear of falling
don't think

MY NEXT DRAWING CAUGHT IT BETTER, THOUGH THE NEST SHOULD HAVE BEEN TWIGGIER, WITH POINTY THINGS STICKING OUT & STICKING IN.

I SOON LEARNED TO KEEP DRAWING UNTIL I REALLY NAILED MY FEELINGS DOWN. I DIDN'T GET NEARLY THE SAME RELIEF IF I ONLY CAME CLOSE.

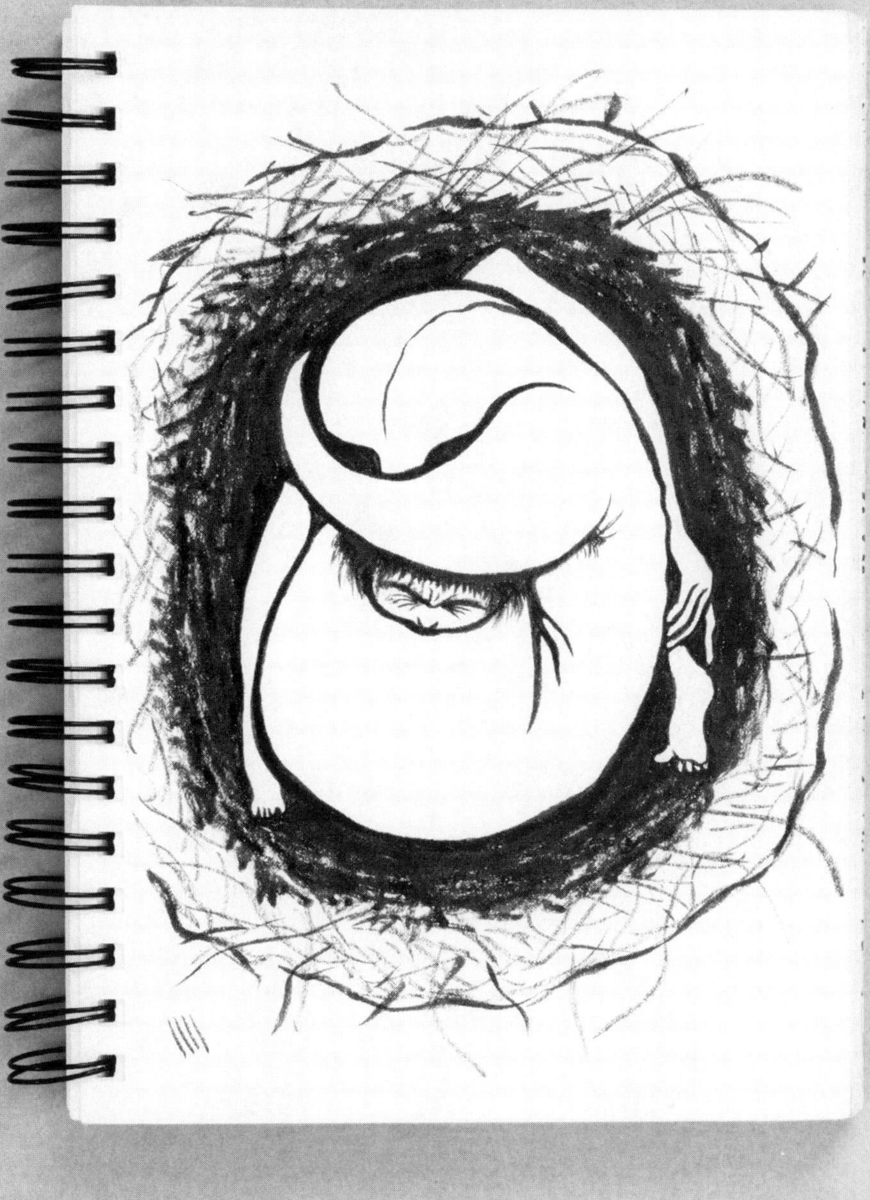

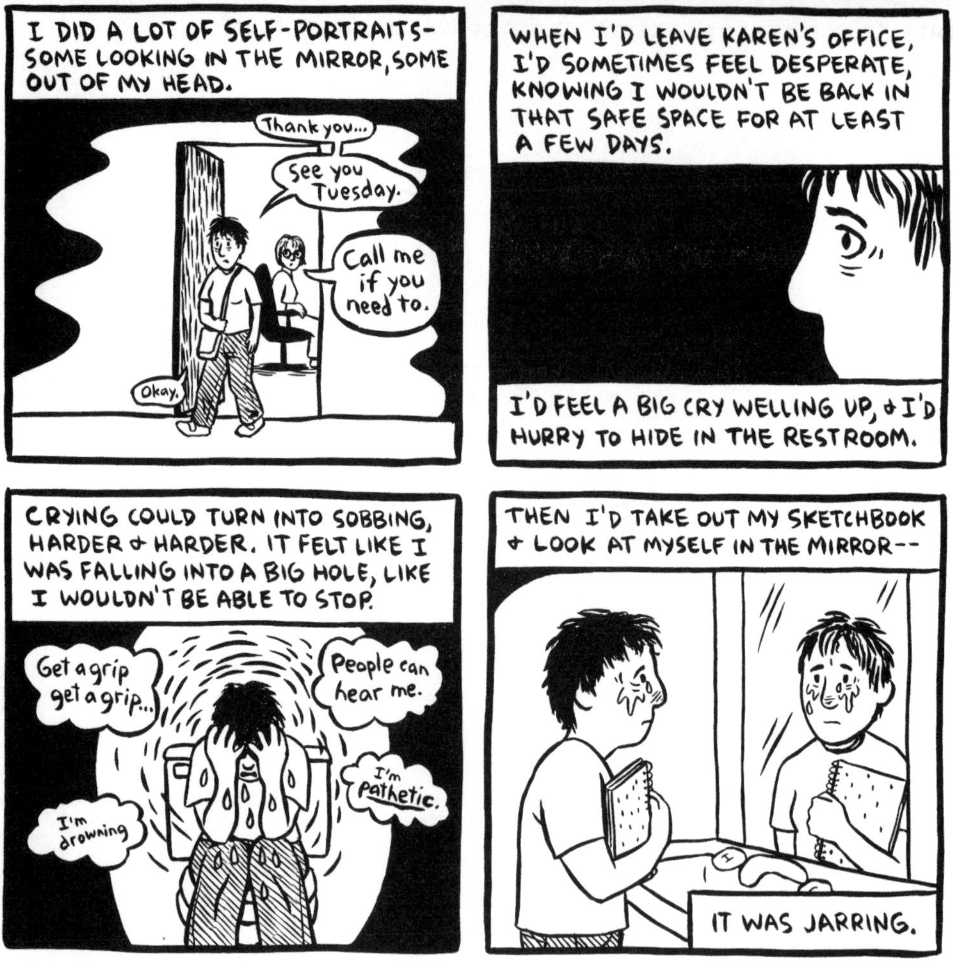
I DID A LOT OF SELF-PORTRAITS- SOME LOOKING IN THE MIRROR, SOME OUT OF MY HEAD.
Thank you...
See you Tuesday.
Call me if you need to.
Okay.
WHEN I'D LEAVE KAREN'S OFFICE, I'D SOMETIMES FEEL DESPERATE, KNOWING I WOULDN'T BE BACK IN THAT SAFE SPACE FOR AT LEAST A FEW DAYS.
I'D FEEL A BIG CRY WELLING UP, & I'D HURRY TO HIDE IN THE RESTROOM.
CRYING COULD TURN INTO SOBBING, HARDER & HARDER. IT FELT LIKE I WAS FALLING INTO A BIG HOLE, LIKE I WOULDN'T BE ABLE TO STOP.
Get a grip get a grip...
People can hear me.
I'm pathetic.
I'm drowning
THEN I'D TAKE OUT MY SKETCHBOOK & LOOK AT MYSELF IN THE MIRROR--
IT WAS JARRING.

I LOOKED SO SMALL, AND SO HUMAN - A SAD HUMAN - NOT LIKE THE HORRIBLE MONSTER I HALF-EXPECTED TO SEE.

IN MY SKETCHBOOK, I'D TRACE THE FAMILIAR LINES OF MY FACE, & I'D CALM DOWN & COME BACK INTO MYSELF.

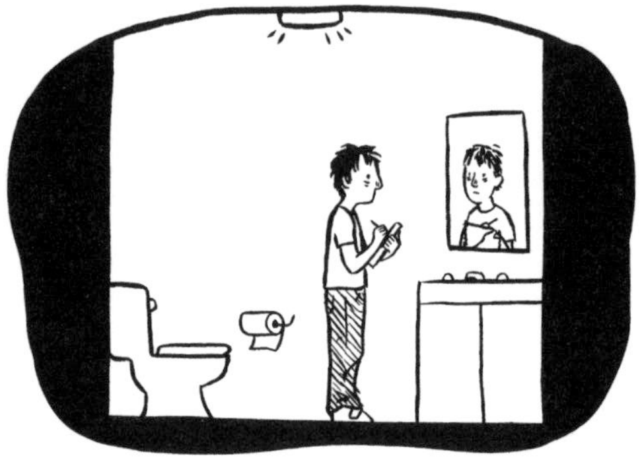

INERT ON A PIECE OF PAPER, THE DEMONS WERE MORE HANDLEABLE.

OTHER SELF-PORTRAITS WERE DEPICTIONS OF HOW I WAS <u>FEELING</u>.

I OFTEN KNEW WHAT I WAS AIMING TO DRAW —
SOME MENTAL IMAGE THAT I NEEDED TO GET
OUTSIDE OF ME.

SOMETIMES I WOULD HAVE TO DRAW
IT SEVERAL TIMES BEFORE I WAS
SATISFIED I HAD CAUGHT IT.

OTHER TIMES I DIDN'T KNOW WHAT I WOULD DRAW,
& JUST LET THE IMAGES POUR OUT OF MY PEN.

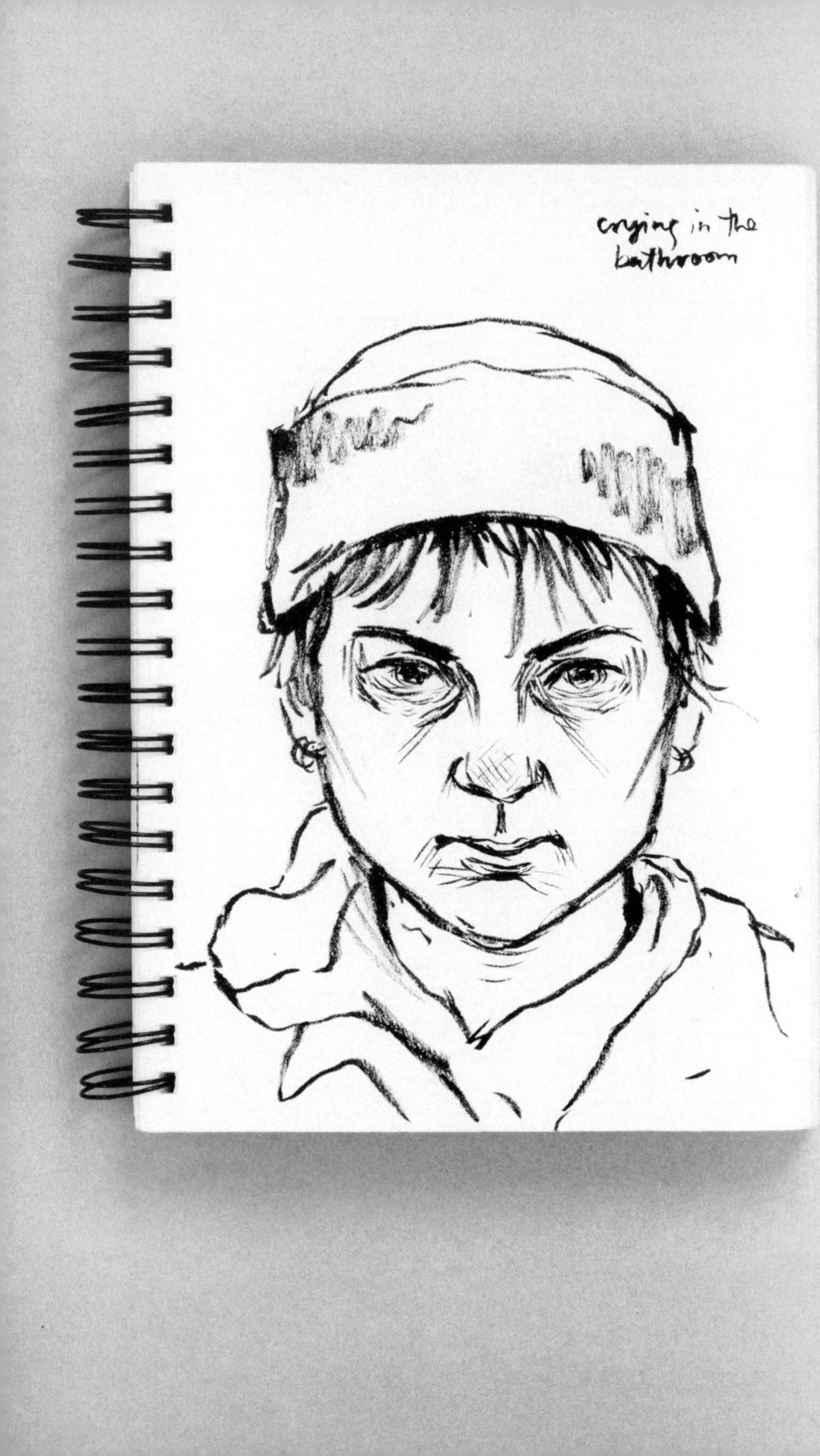
crying in the
bathroom

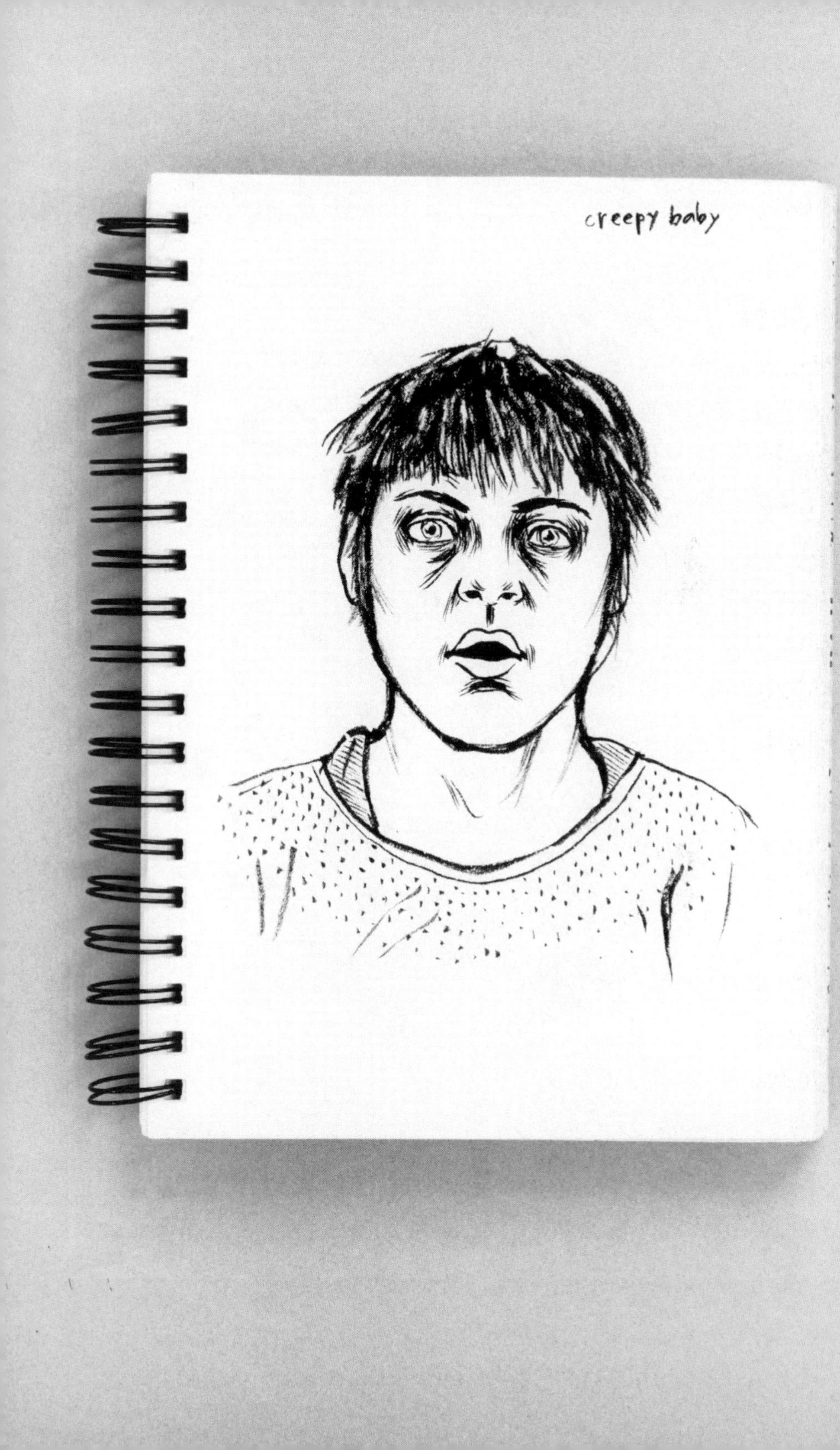
creepy baby

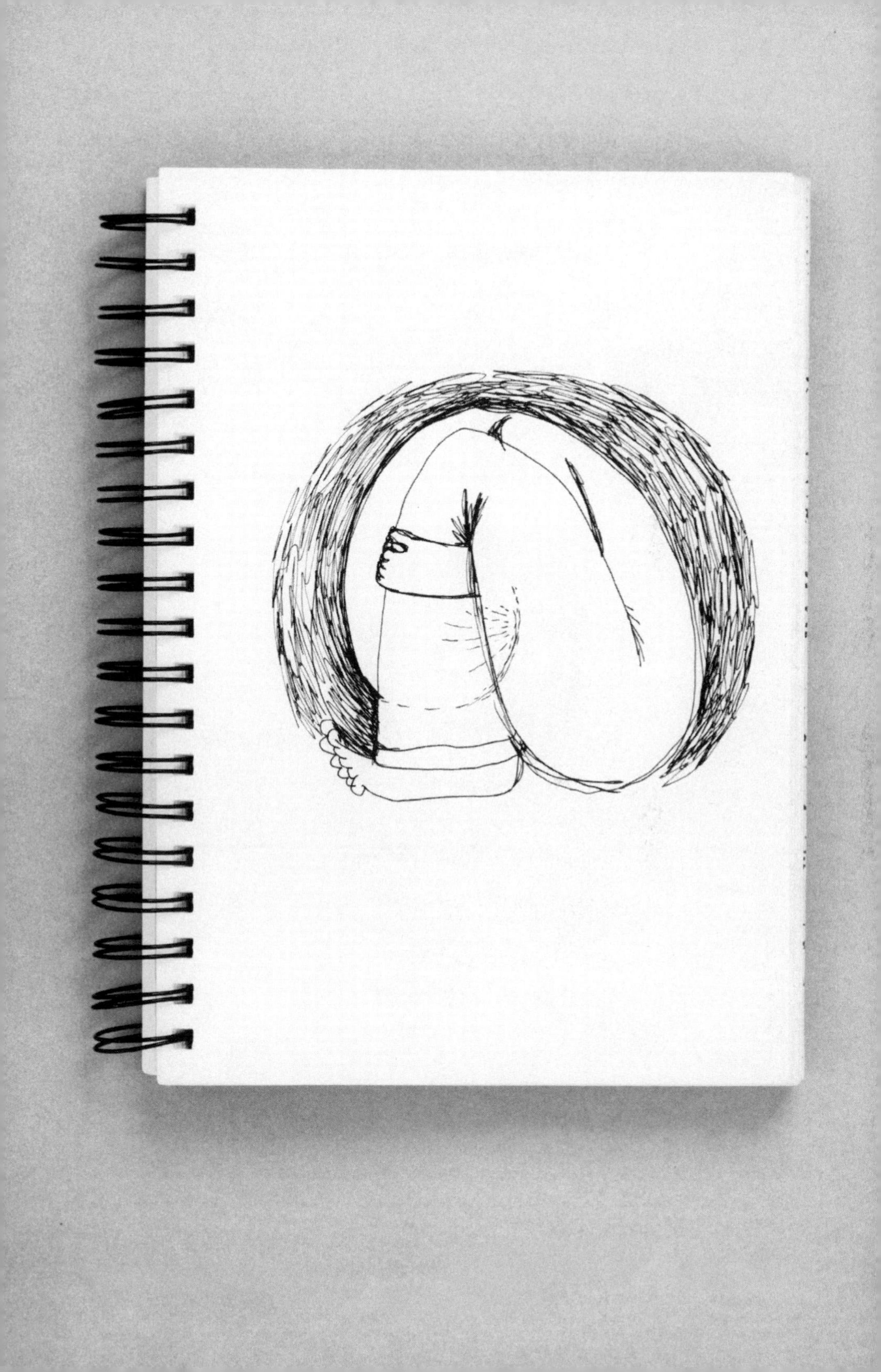

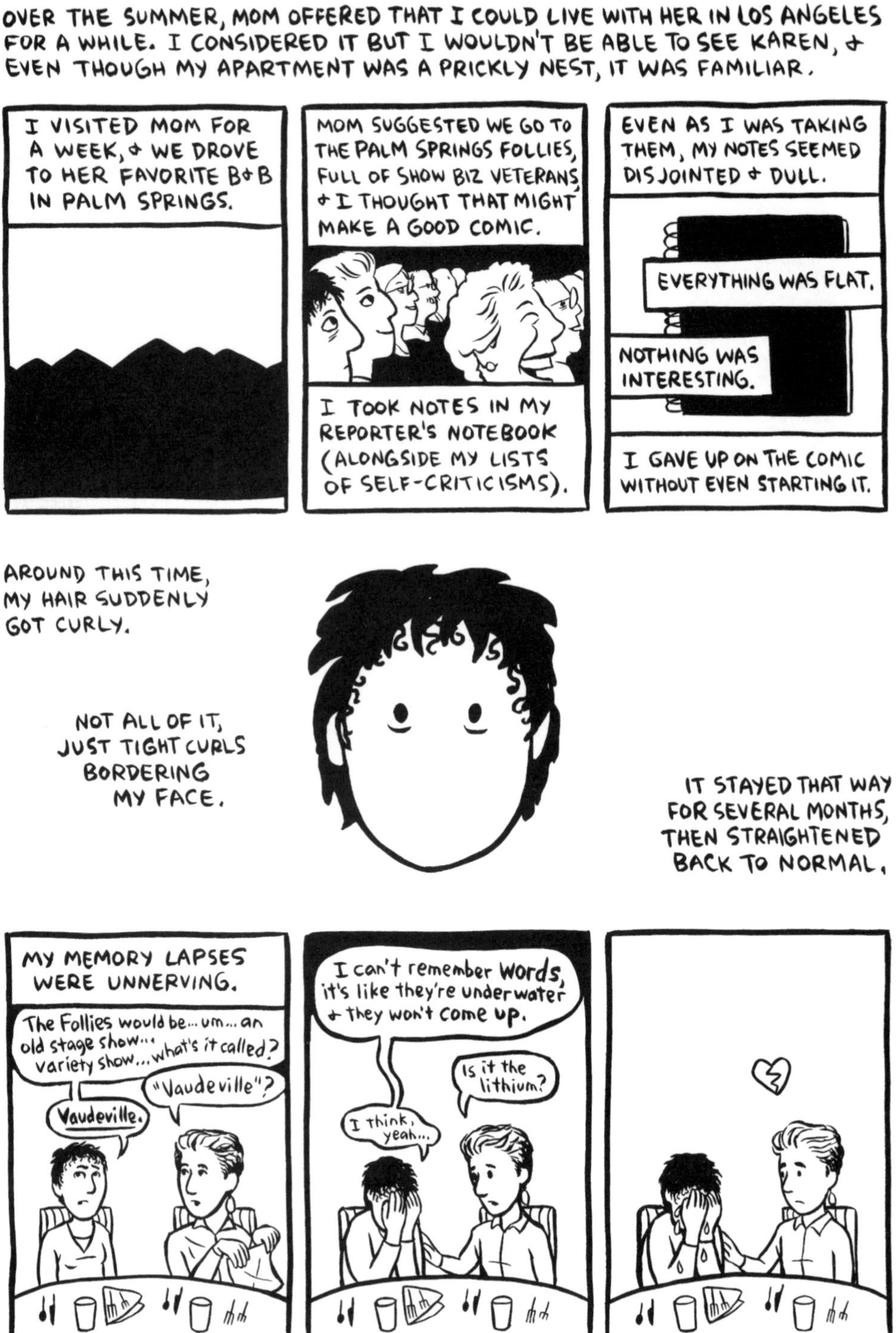
OVER THE SUMMER, MOM OFFERED THAT I COULD LIVE WITH HER IN LOS ANGELES FOR A WHILE. I CONSIDERED IT BUT I WOULDN'T BE ABLE TO SEE KAREN, & EVEN THOUGH MY APARTMENT WAS A PRICKLY NEST, IT WAS FAMILIAR.
I VISITED MOM FOR A WEEK, & WE DROVE TO HER FAVORITE B&B IN PALM SPRINGS.
MOM SUGGESTED WE GO TO THE PALM SPRINGS FOLLIES, FULL OF SHOW BIZ VETERANS, & I THOUGHT THAT MIGHT MAKE A GOOD COMIC.
I TOOK NOTES IN MY REPORTER'S NOTEBOOK (ALONGSIDE MY LISTS OF SELF-CRITICISMS).
EVEN AS I WAS TAKING THEM, MY NOTES SEEMED DISJOINTED & DULL.
EVERYTHING WAS FLAT.
NOTHING WAS INTERESTING.
I GAVE UP ON THE COMIC WITHOUT EVEN STARTING IT.
AROUND THIS TIME, MY HAIR SUDDENLY GOT CURLY.
NOT ALL OF IT, JUST TIGHT CURLS BORDERING MY FACE.
IT STAYED THAT WAY FOR SEVERAL MONTHS, THEN STRAIGHTENED BACK TO NORMAL.
MY MEMORY LAPSES WERE UNNERVING.
The Follies would be... um... an old stage show... variety show... what's it called?
Vaudeville.
"Vaudeville"?
I can't remember words, it's like they're underwater & they won't come up.
Is it the lithium?
I think, yeah...

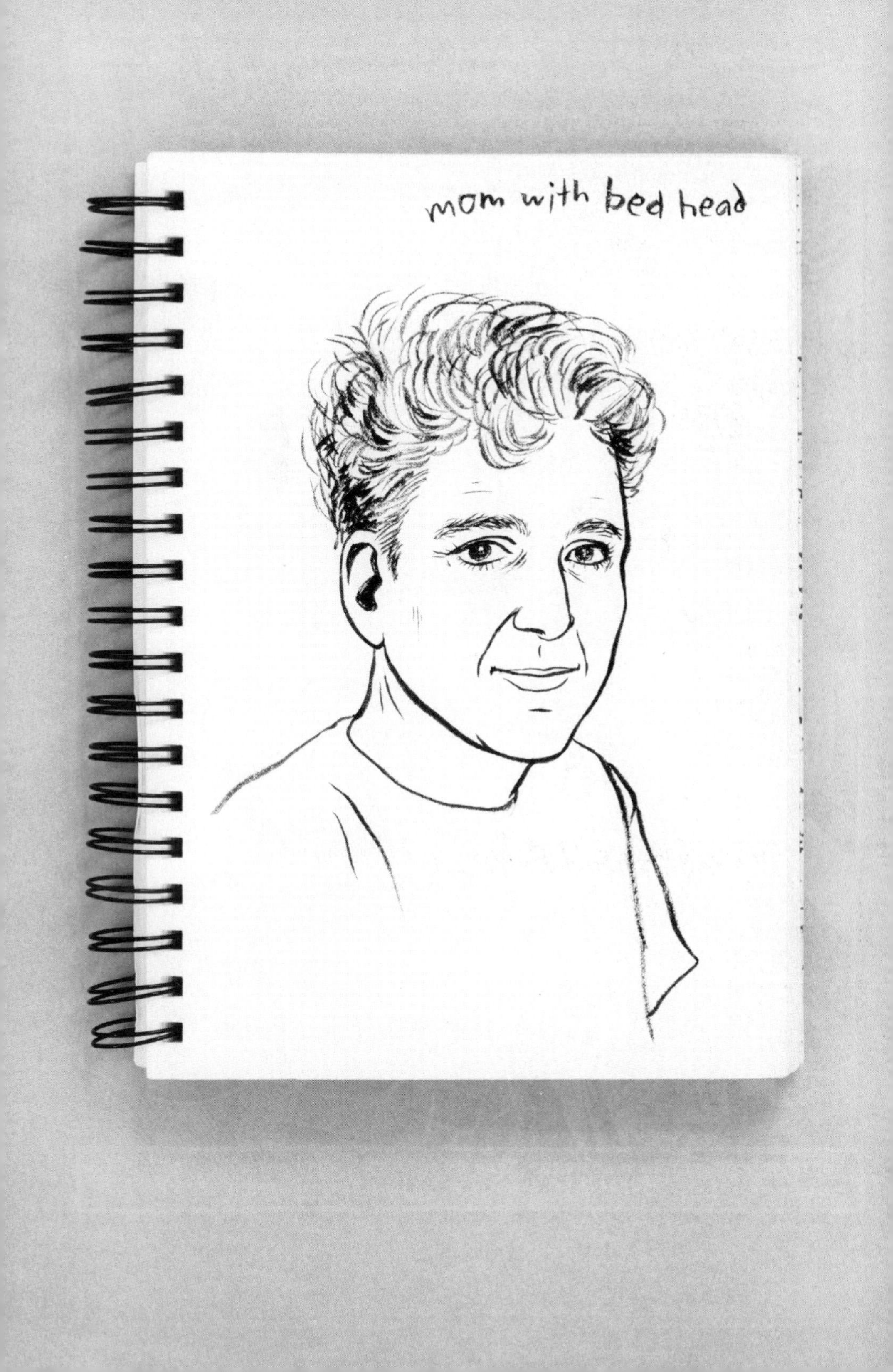
mom with bed head

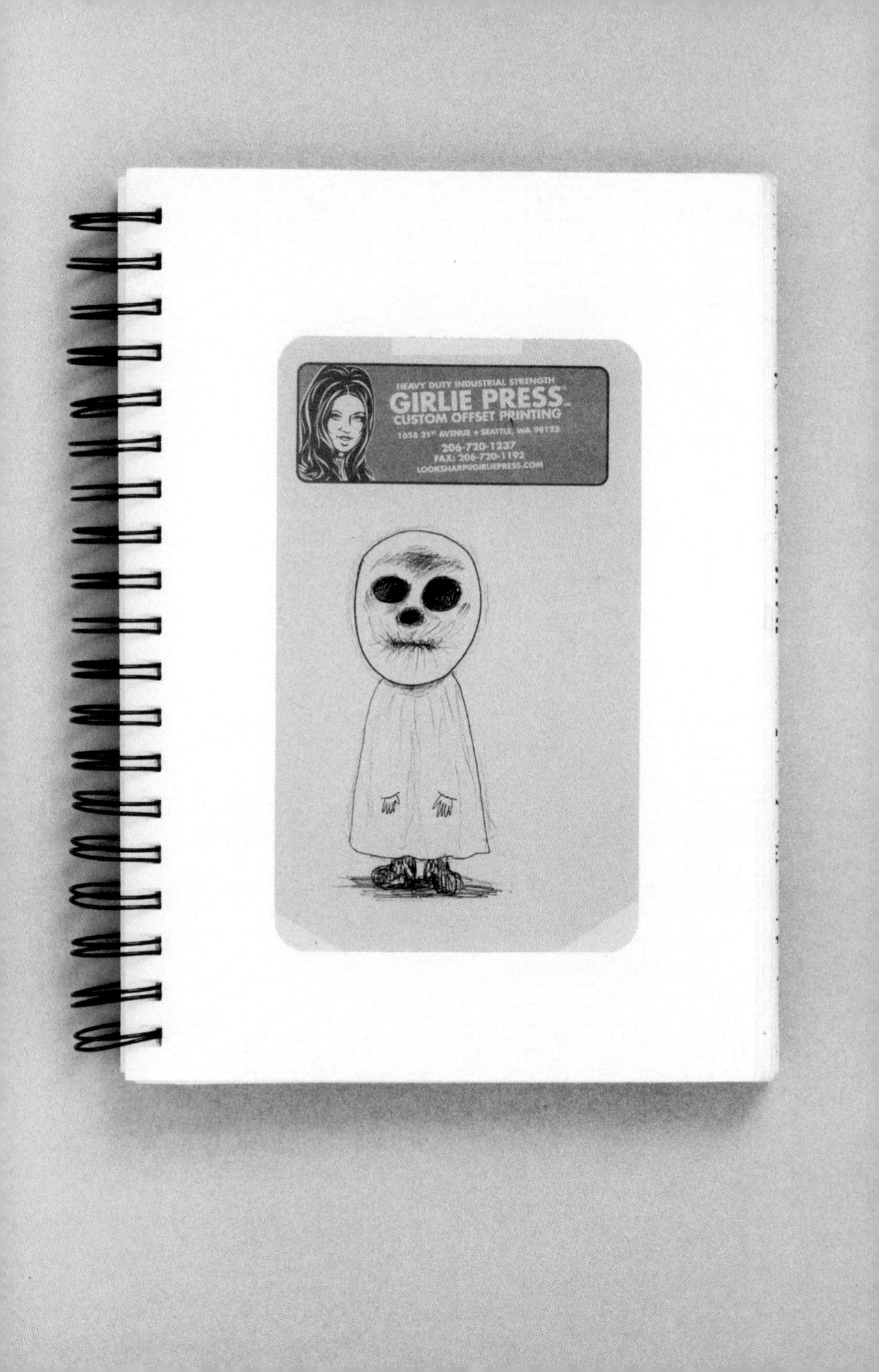
HEAVY DUTY INDUSTRIAL STRENGTH
GIRLIE PRESS
CUSTOM OFFSET PRINTING
1658 21ST AVENUE ★ SEATTLE, WA 98122
206-720-1237
FAX: 206-720-1192
LOOKSHARP@GIRLIEPRESS.COM

DI WAS ONE OF MY ONLY FRIENDS I COULD GO OUT & DO STUFF WITH. SHE WOULD LET ME JUST BE QUIET. ONE DAY SHE TOOK ME TO SEE A MATINEE OF "THE WEDDING SINGER" AT AN ENORMOUS, MOSTLY-EMPTY CINEMA DOWNTOWN.

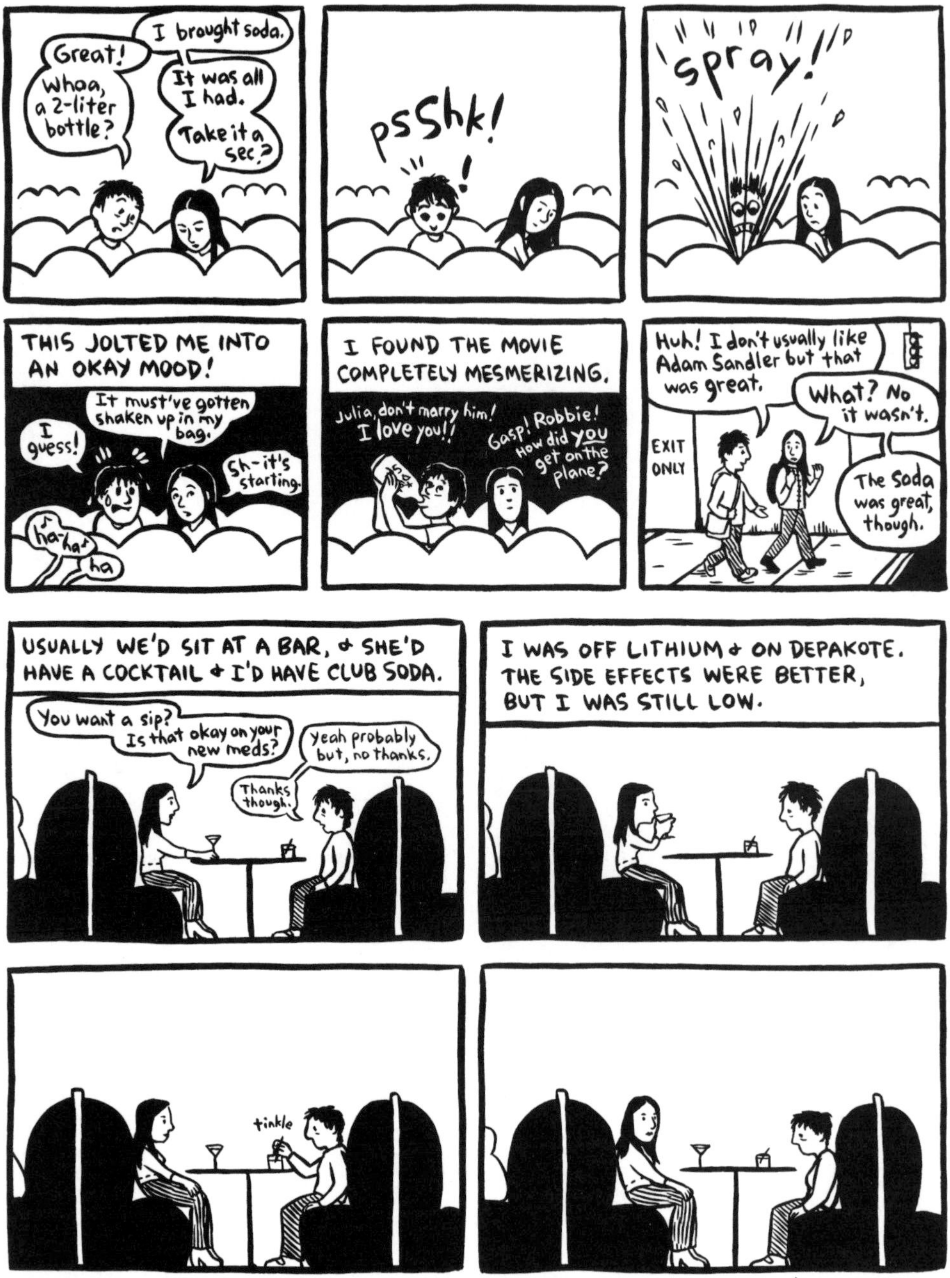

I brought soda.
Great! Whoa, a 2-liter bottle?
It was all I had.
Take it a sec.?
psShk!
spray!
THIS JOLTED ME INTO AN OKAY MOOD!
It must've gotten shaken up in my bag.
I guess!
Sh-it's starting.
ha-ha-ha
I FOUND THE MOVIE COMPLETELY MESMERIZING.
Julia, don't marry him! I love you!!
Gasp! Robbie! How did YOU get on the plane?
Huh! I don't usually like Adam Sandler but that was great.
What? No it wasn't.
EXIT ONLY
The Soda was great, though.
USUALLY WE'D SIT AT A BAR, & SHE'D HAVE A COCKTAIL & I'D HAVE CLUB SODA.
You want a sip? Is that okay on your new meds?
Yeah probably but, no thanks.
Thanks though.
I WAS OFF LITHIUM & ON DEPAKOTE. THE SIDE EFFECTS WERE BETTER, BUT I WAS STILL LOW.
tinkle

MY SKETCHBOOK WAS PRIVATE, BUT I GAVE DI A COPY OF MY "PHOENIXLIKE" DRAWING ↗ & SHE LOVED IT. (SHE HAS A DARK SENSE OF HUMOR, TOO.)

PHOENIX-LIKE ELLEN 1999 RISES FROM THE ASHES OF ELLEN 1998...?

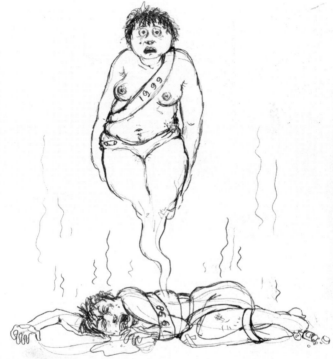

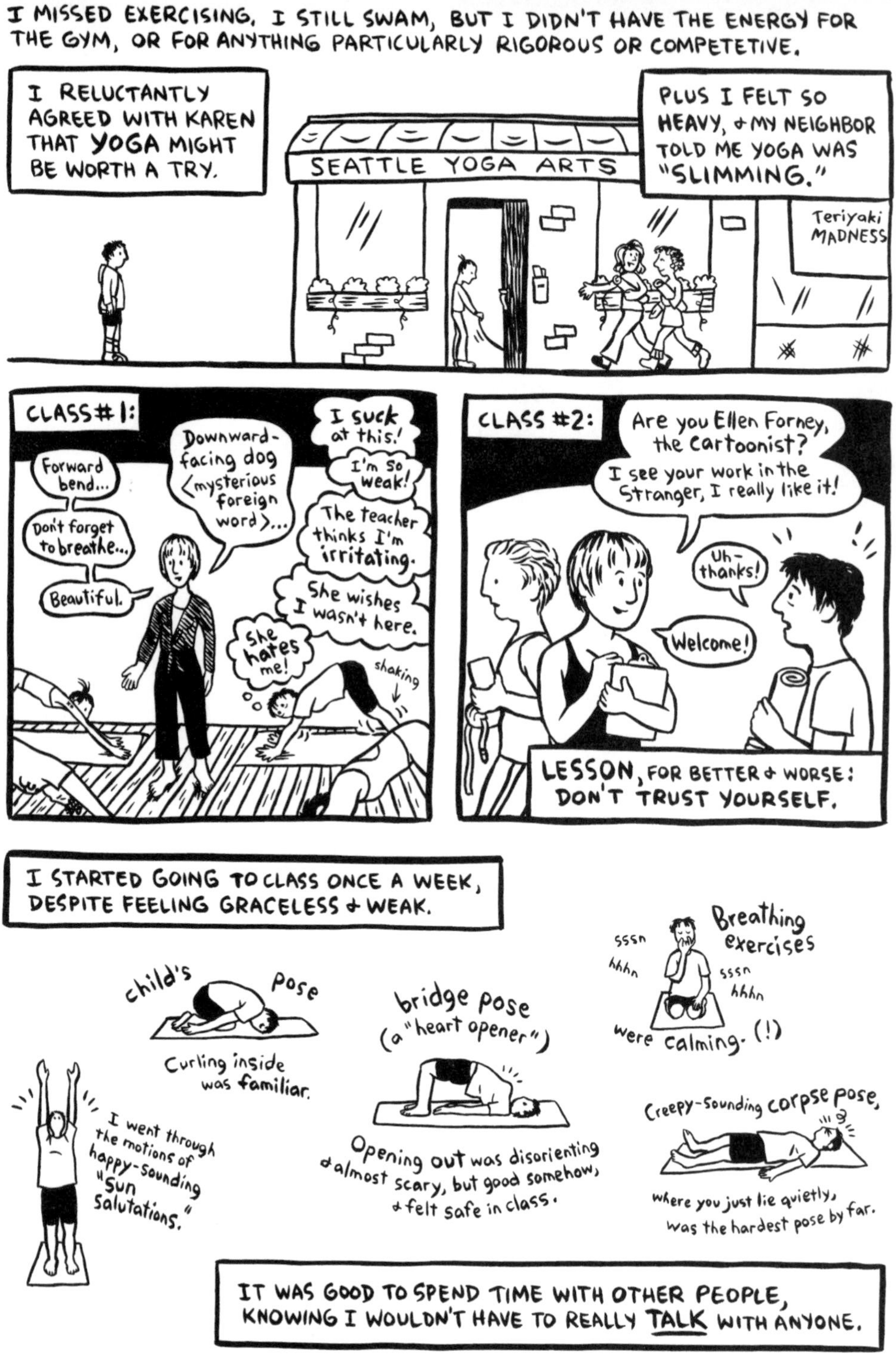
I MISSED EXERCISING. I STILL SWAM, BUT I DIDN'T HAVE THE ENERGY FOR THE GYM, OR FOR ANYTHING PARTICULARLY RIGOROUS OR COMPETETIVE.
I RELUCTANTLY AGREED WITH KAREN THAT YOGA MIGHT BE WORTH A TRY.
SEATTLE YOGA ARTS
PLUS I FELT SO HEAVY, & MY NEIGHBOR TOLD ME YOGA WAS "SLIMMING."
Teriyaki MADNESS
CLASS #1:
Forward bend...
Don't forget to breathe...
Beautiful.
Downward-facing dog <mysterious foreign word>...
I suck at this!
I'm so weak!
The teacher thinks I'm irritating.
She wishes I wasn't here.
She hates me!
shaking
CLASS #2:
Are you Ellen Forney, the cartoonist? I see your work in the Stranger, I really like it!
Uh-thanks!
Welcome!
LESSON, FOR BETTER & WORSE: DON'T TRUST YOURSELF.
I STARTED GOING TO CLASS ONCE A WEEK, DESPITE FEELING GRACELESS & WEAK.
child's pose
Curling inside was familiar.
bridge pose (a "heart opener")
Opening out was disorienting & almost scary, but good somehow, & felt safe in class.
Breathing exercises
sssn hhhn sssn hhhn
were calming. (!)
I went through the motions of happy-sounding "Sun Salutations."
Creepy-sounding corpse pose,
where you just lie quietly, was the hardest pose by far.
IT WAS GOOD TO SPEND TIME WITH OTHER PEOPLE, KNOWING I WOULDN'T HAVE TO REALLY TALK WITH ANYONE.

peace mission

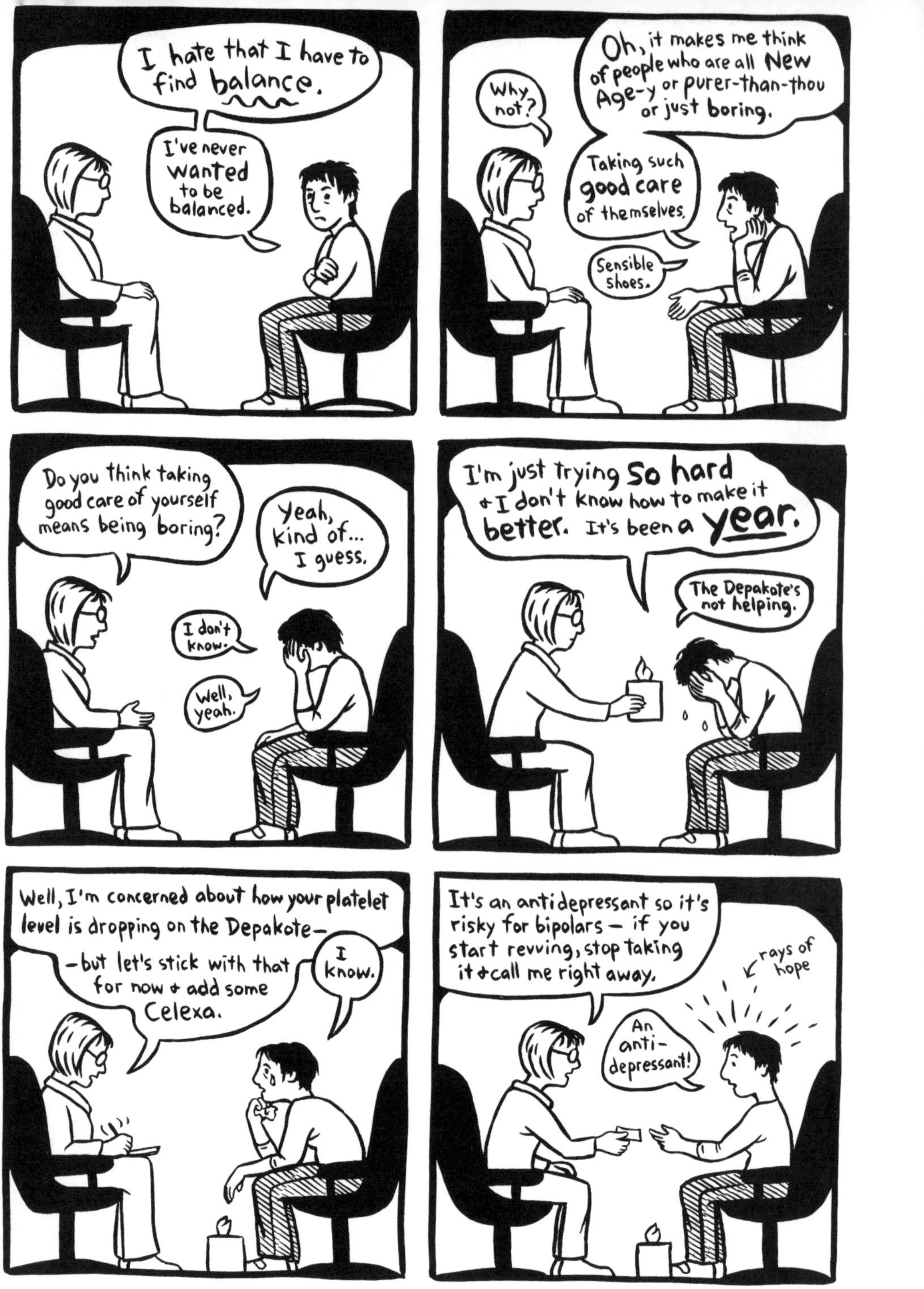
I hate that I have to find balance.
I've never wanted to be balanced.
Why not?
Oh, it makes me think of people who are all New Age-y or purer-than-thou or just boring.
Taking such good care of themselves.
Sensible shoes.
Do you think taking good care of yourself means being boring?
Yeah, kind of... I guess.
I don't know.
Well, yeah.
I'm just trying so hard & I don't know how to make it better. It's been a year.
The Depakote's not helping.
Well, I'm concerned about how your platelet level is dropping on the Depakote—
—but let's stick with that for now & add some Celexa.
I know.
It's an antidepressant so it's risky for bipolars — if you start revving, stop taking it & call me right away.
An anti-depressant!
rays of hope

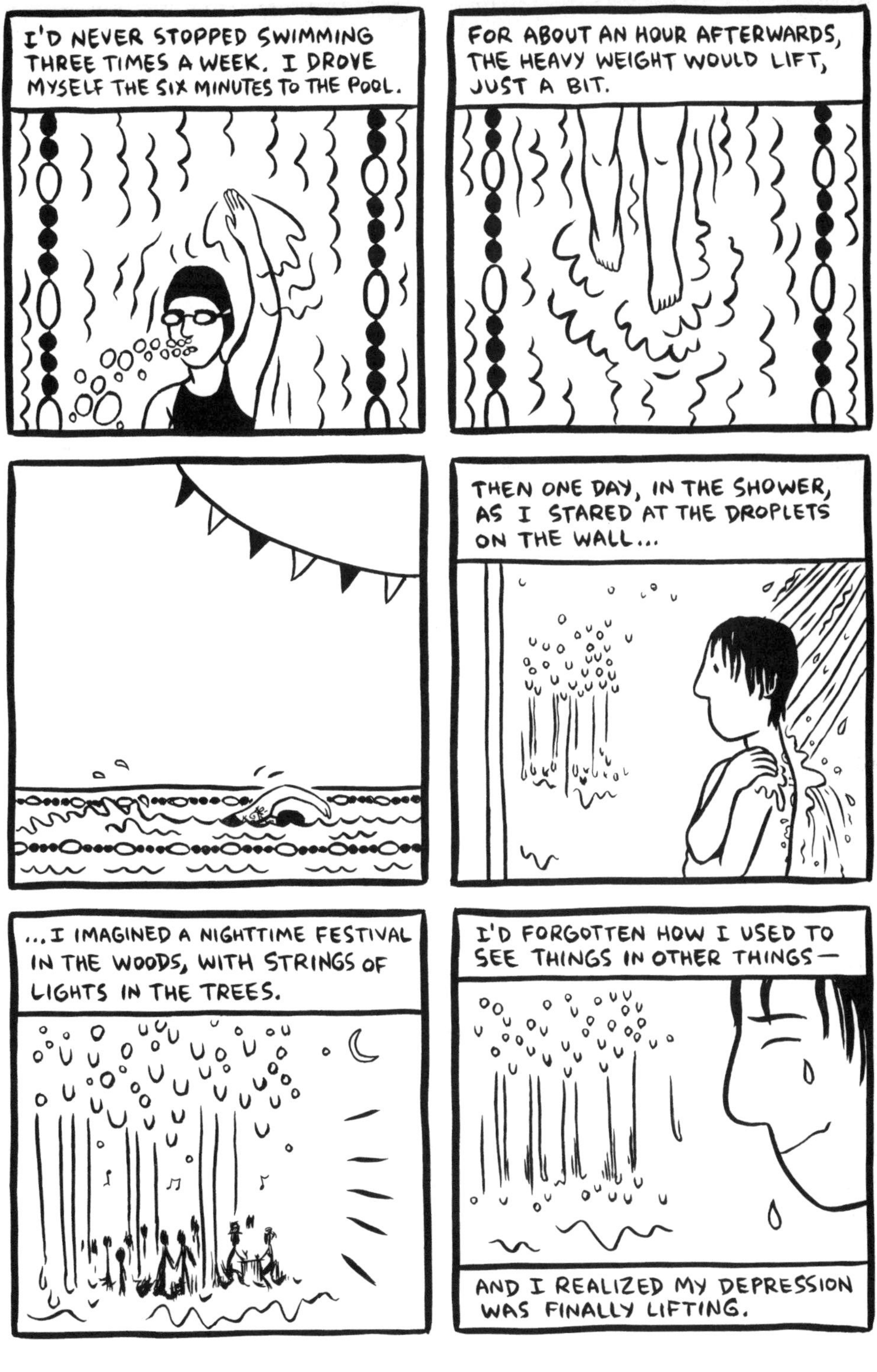
I'D NEVER STOPPED SWIMMING THREE TIMES A WEEK. I DROVE MYSELF THE SIX MINUTES TO THE POOL.
FOR ABOUT AN HOUR AFTERWARDS, THE HEAVY WEIGHT WOULD LIFT, JUST A BIT.
THEN ONE DAY, IN THE SHOWER, AS I STARED AT THE DROPLETS ON THE WALL...
...I IMAGINED A NIGHTTIME FESTIVAL IN THE WOODS, WITH STRINGS OF LIGHTS IN THE TREES.
I'D FORGOTTEN HOW I USED TO SEE THINGS IN OTHER THINGS—
AND I REALIZED MY DEPRESSION WAS FINALLY LIFTING.

CHAPTER 5

MY DAD SENT ME A LOT OF ART BOOKS OVER THE YEARS, & ONCE EVERY SO OFTEN I'D LOOK THROUGH THEM-- KIND OF A WEEKEND-LATE-MORNING THING TO DO.

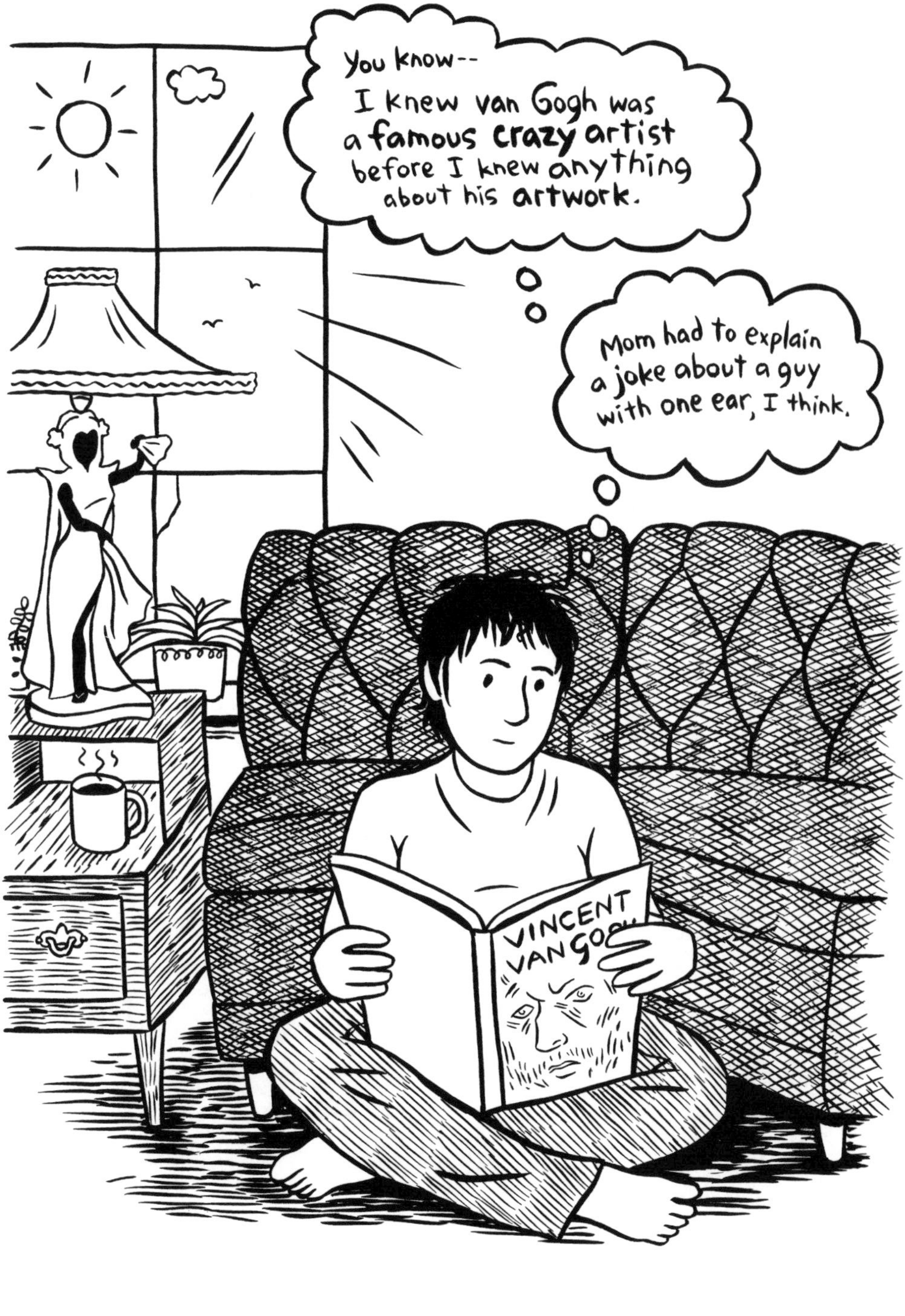
You know--
I knew van Gogh was a famous crazy artist before I knew anything about his artwork.
Mom had to explain a joke about a guy with one ear, I think.
VINCENT VAN GO

VAN GOGH WAS TRULY THE ULTIMATE CRAZY TORTURED GENIUS ARTIST.

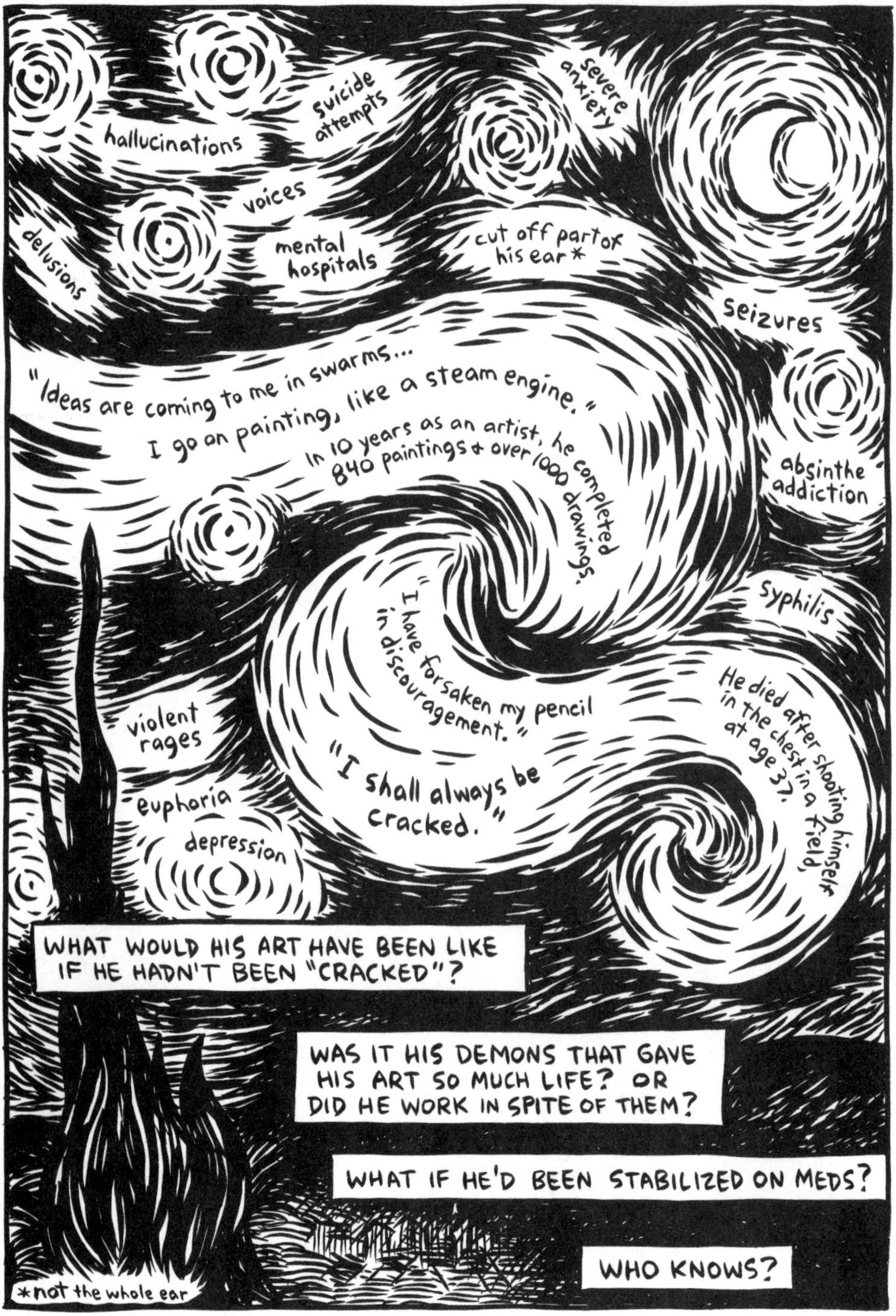
hallucinations
suicide attempts
severe anxiety
voices
delusions
mental hospitals
cut off part of his ear*
seizures
"Ideas are coming to me in swarms... I go on painting, like a steam engine."
In 10 years as an artist, he completed 840 paintings & over 1000 drawings.
absinthe addiction
syphilis
"I have forsaken my pencil in discouragement."
He died after shooting himself in the chest in a field, at age 37.
violent rages
euphoria
depression
"I shall always be cracked."
WHAT WOULD HIS ART HAVE BEEN LIKE IF HE HADN'T BEEN "CRACKED"?
WAS IT HIS DEMONS THAT GAVE HIS ART SO MUCH LIFE? OR DID HE WORK IN SPITE OF THEM?
WHAT IF HE'D BEEN STABILIZED ON MEDS?
WHO KNOWS?
*not the whole ear

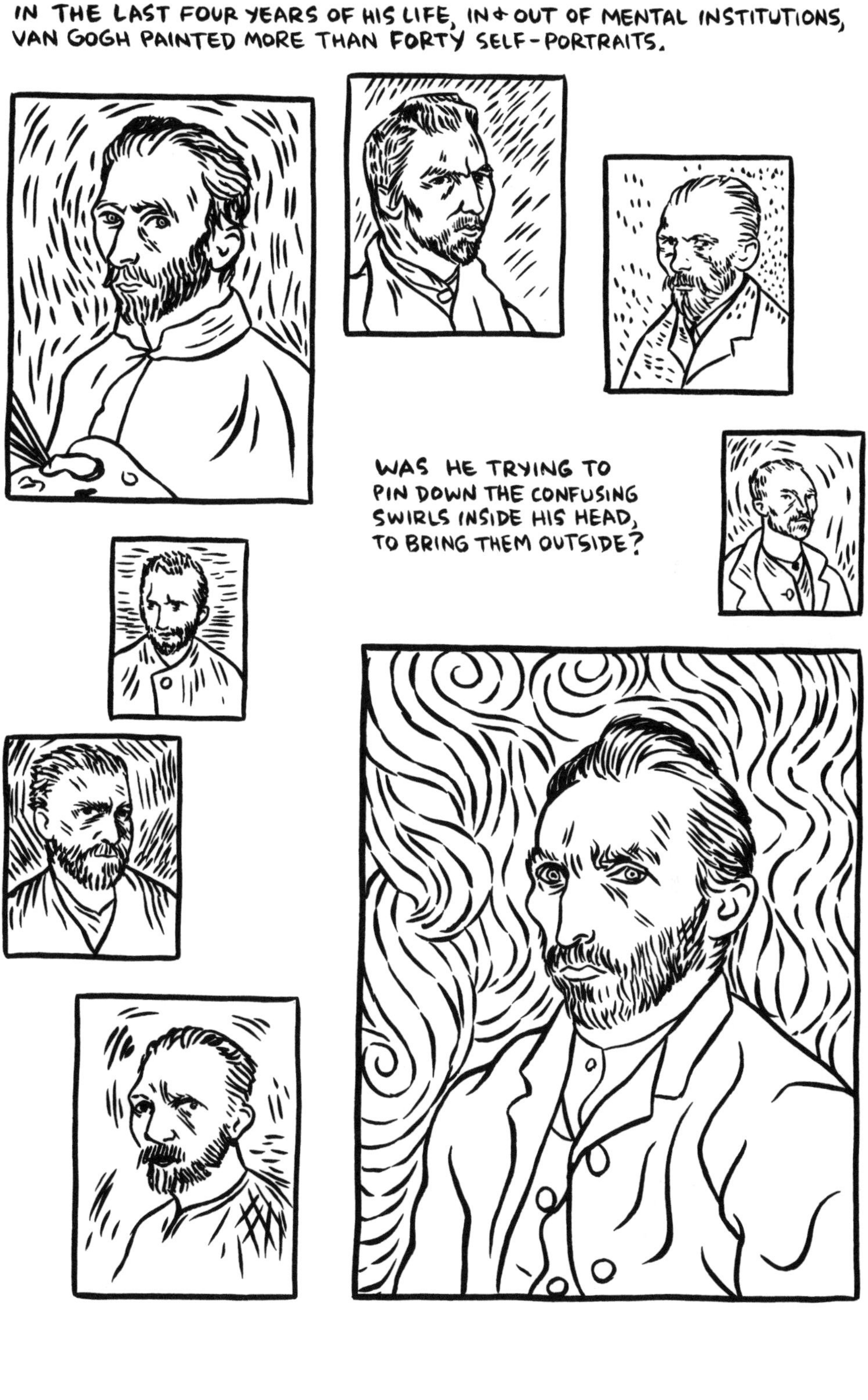
IN THE LAST FOUR YEARS OF HIS LIFE, IN & OUT OF MENTAL INSTITUTIONS, VAN GOGH PAINTED MORE THAN FORTY SELF-PORTRAITS.
WAS HE TRYING TO PIN DOWN THE CONFUSING SWIRLS INSIDE HIS HEAD, TO BRING THEM OUTSIDE?

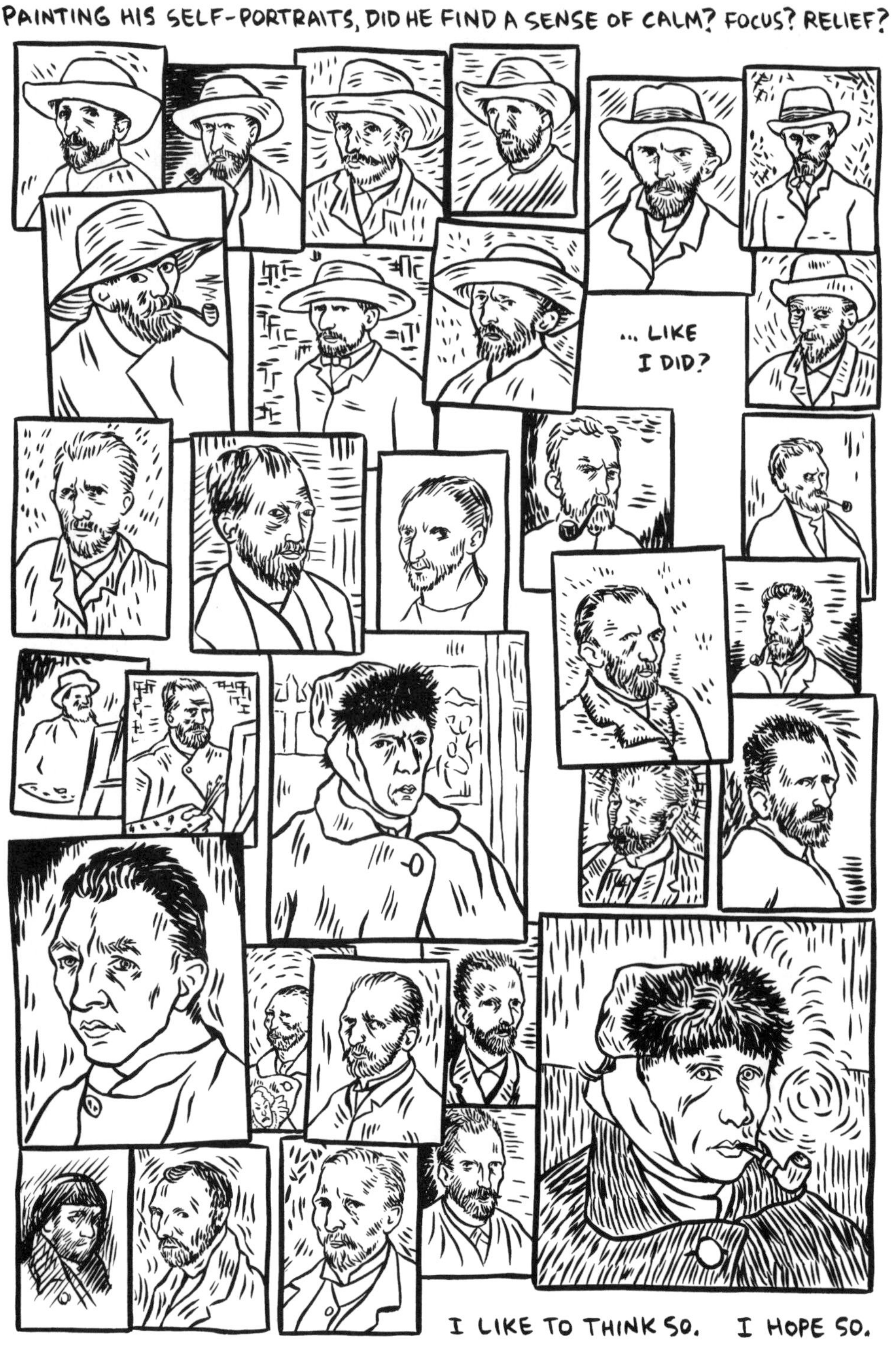
PAINTING HIS SELF-PORTRAITS, DID HE FIND A SENSE OF CALM? FOCUS? RELIEF?
... LIKE I DID?
I LIKE TO THINK SO. I HOPE SO.

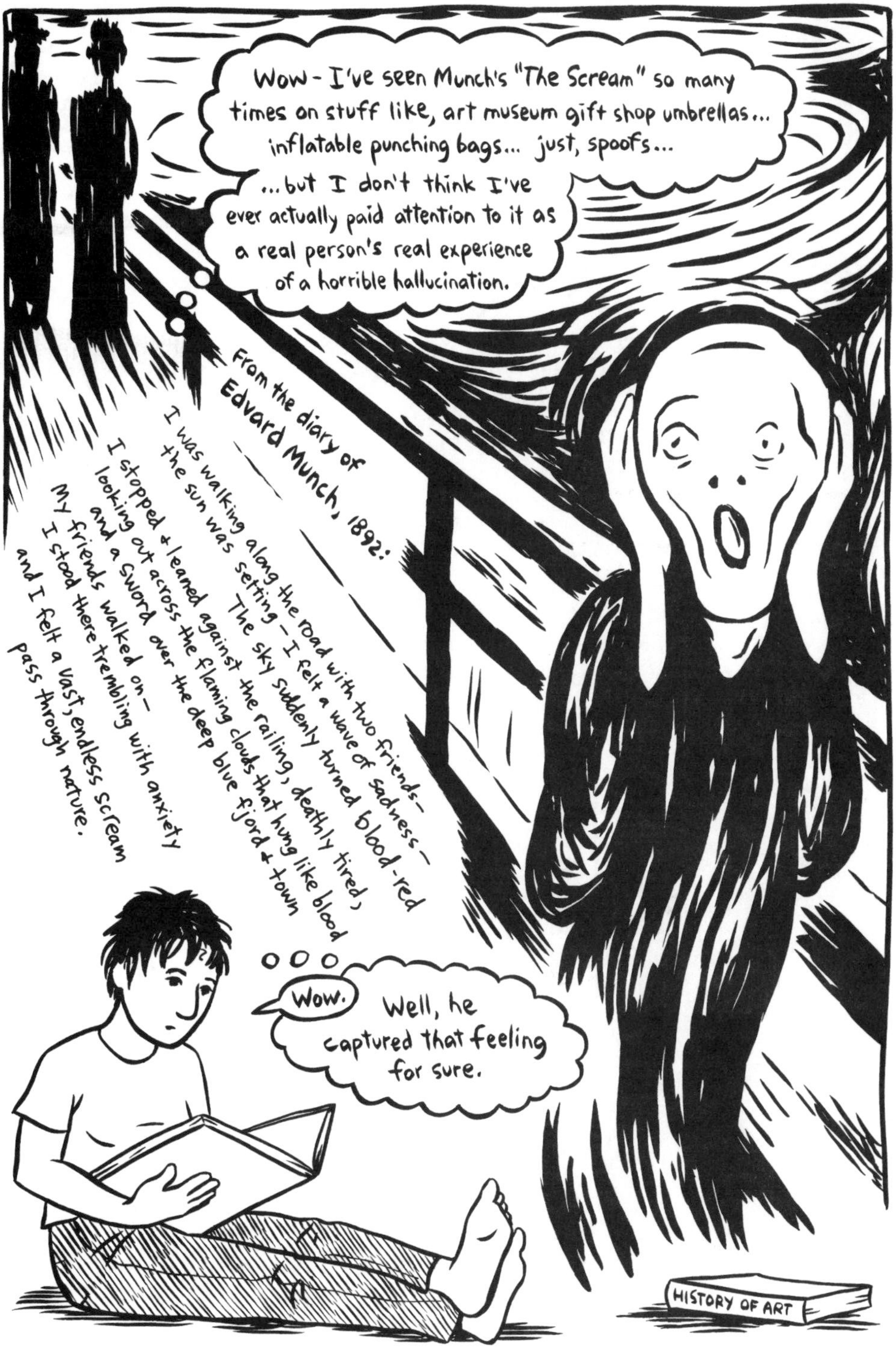
Wow - I've seen Munch's "The Scream" so many times on stuff like, art museum gift shop umbrellas... inflatable punching bags... just, spoofs...
...but I don't think I've ever actually paid attention to it as a real person's real experience of a horrible hallucination.
From the diary of Edvard Munch, 1892:
I was walking along the road with two friends—
the sun was setting — I felt a wave of sadness—
The sky suddenly turned blood-red
I stopped + leaned against the railing, deathly tired,
looking out across the flaming clouds that hung like blood
and a sword over the deep blue fjord + town
My friends walked on—
I stood there trembling with anxiety
and I felt a vast, endless scream
pass through nature.
Wow.
Well, he captured that feeling for sure.
HISTORY OF ART

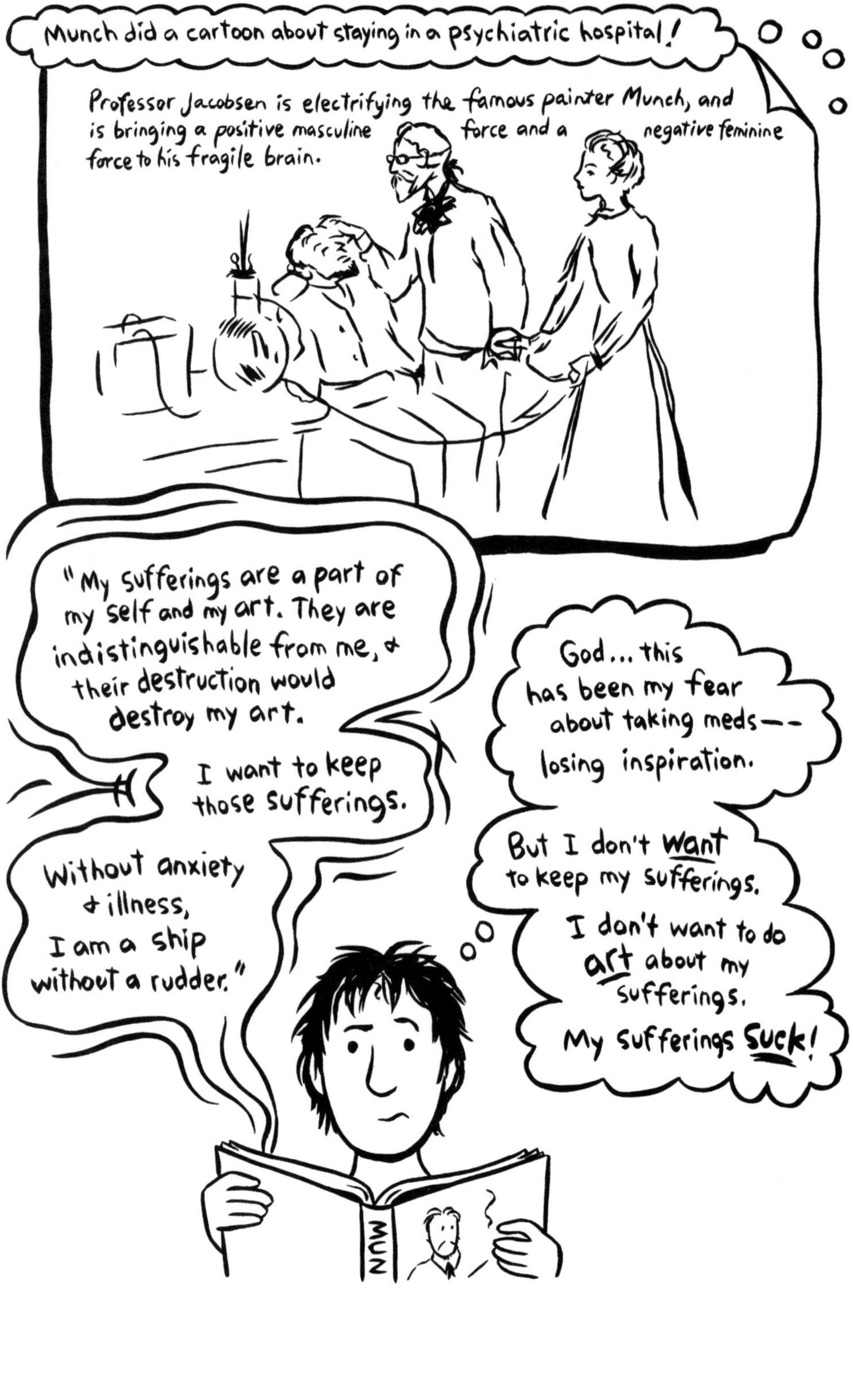
Munch did a cartoon about staying in a psychiatric hospital!
Professor Jacobsen is electrifying the famous painter Munch, and is bringing a positive masculine force and a negative feminine force to his fragile brain.
"My sufferings are a part of my self and my art. They are indistinguishable from me, & their destruction would destroy my art.
I want to keep those sufferings.
Without anxiety & illness, I am a ship without a rudder."
God... this has been my fear about taking meds-- losing inspiration.
But I don't WANT to keep my sufferings.
I don't want to do art about my sufferings.
My sufferings SUCK!
MUN

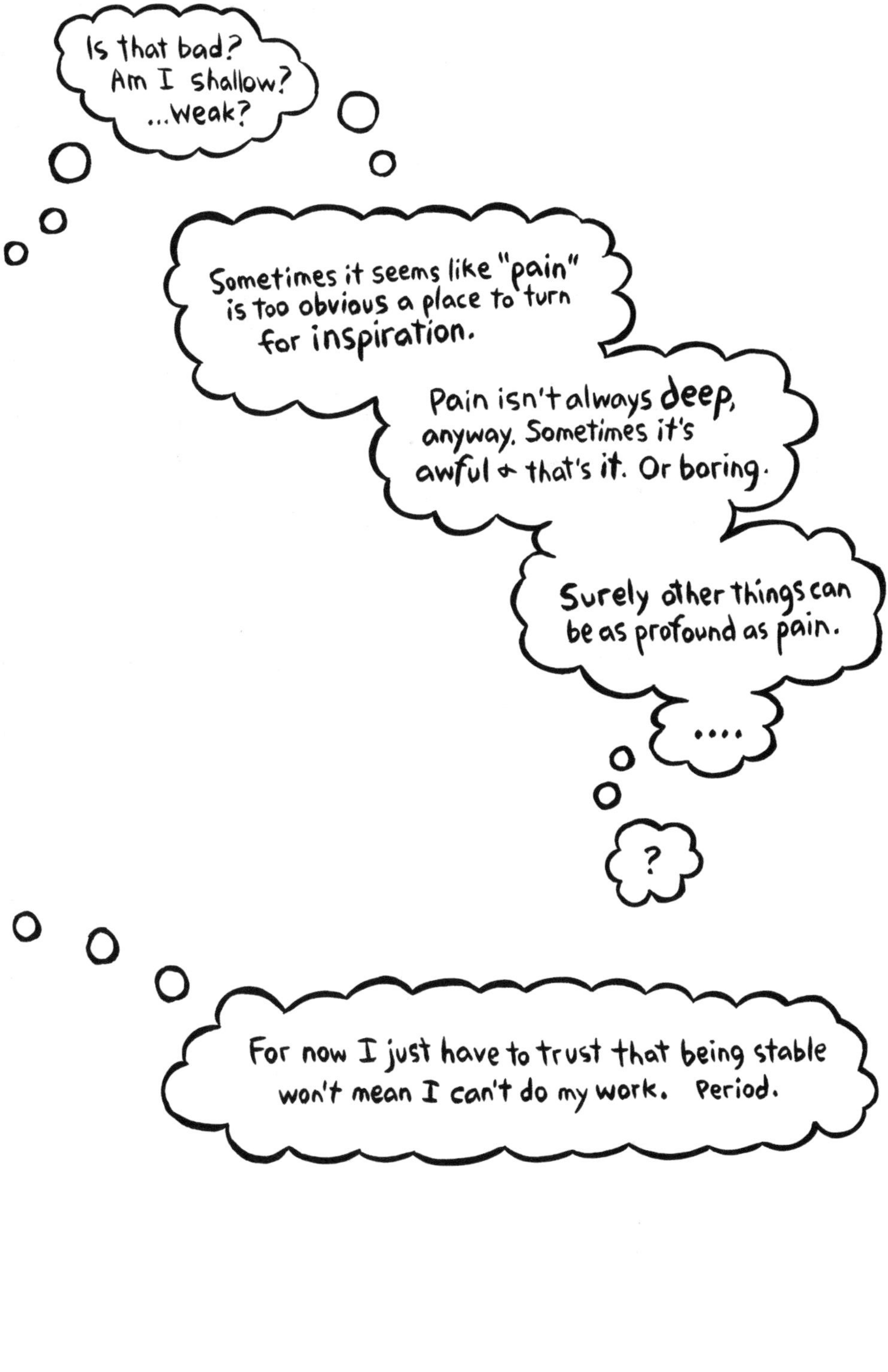
Is that bad? Am I shallow? ...weak?
Sometimes it seems like "pain" is too obvious a place to turn for inspiration.
Pain isn't always deep, anyway. Sometimes it's awful & that's it. Or boring.
Surely other things can be as profound as pain.
....
?
For now I just have to trust that being stable won't mean I can't do my work. Period.

EVENTUALLY, I DID USE ONE "DEPRESSION DRAWING" IN MY WORK, IN A PANEL WHERE I WANTED TO DEPICT FLOATING, RUMBLING ANXIETIES. (panel 7) →

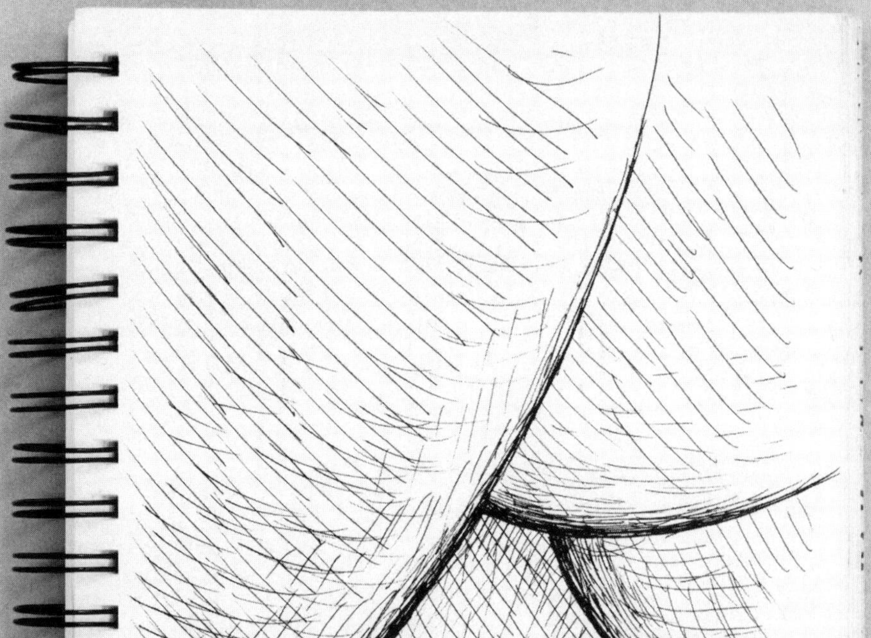

USING THE DRAWING FELT STRANGE, LIKE I WAS SECRETLY REVEALING MY INSIDES, BUT CRYING QUIETLY IN YOGA CLASS FELT THAT WAY, TOO (AND I DID A LOT OF CRYING QUIETLY IN YOGA CLASS). SO, IT SEEMED TO MAKE SENSE.

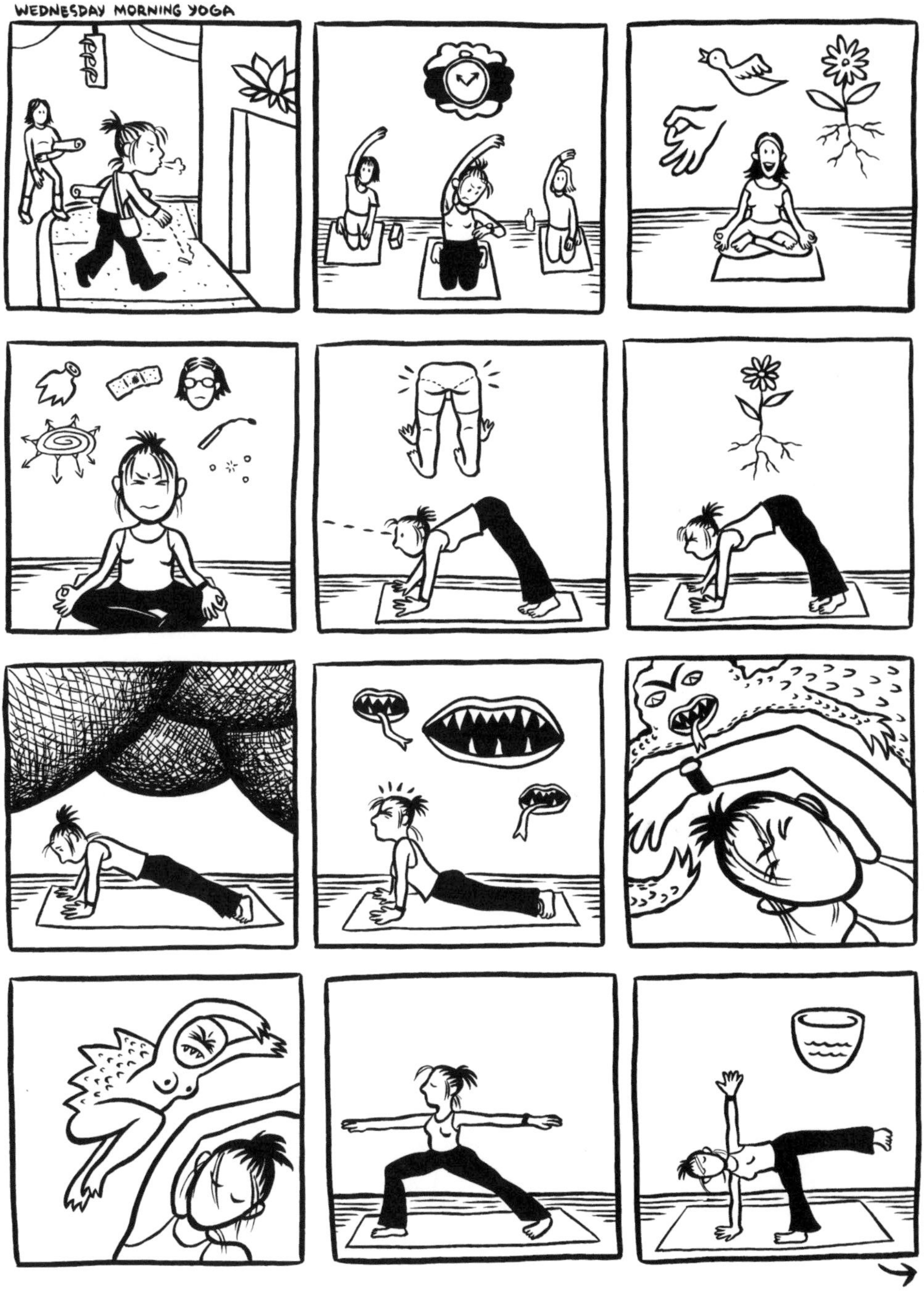
WEDNESDAY MORNING YOGA

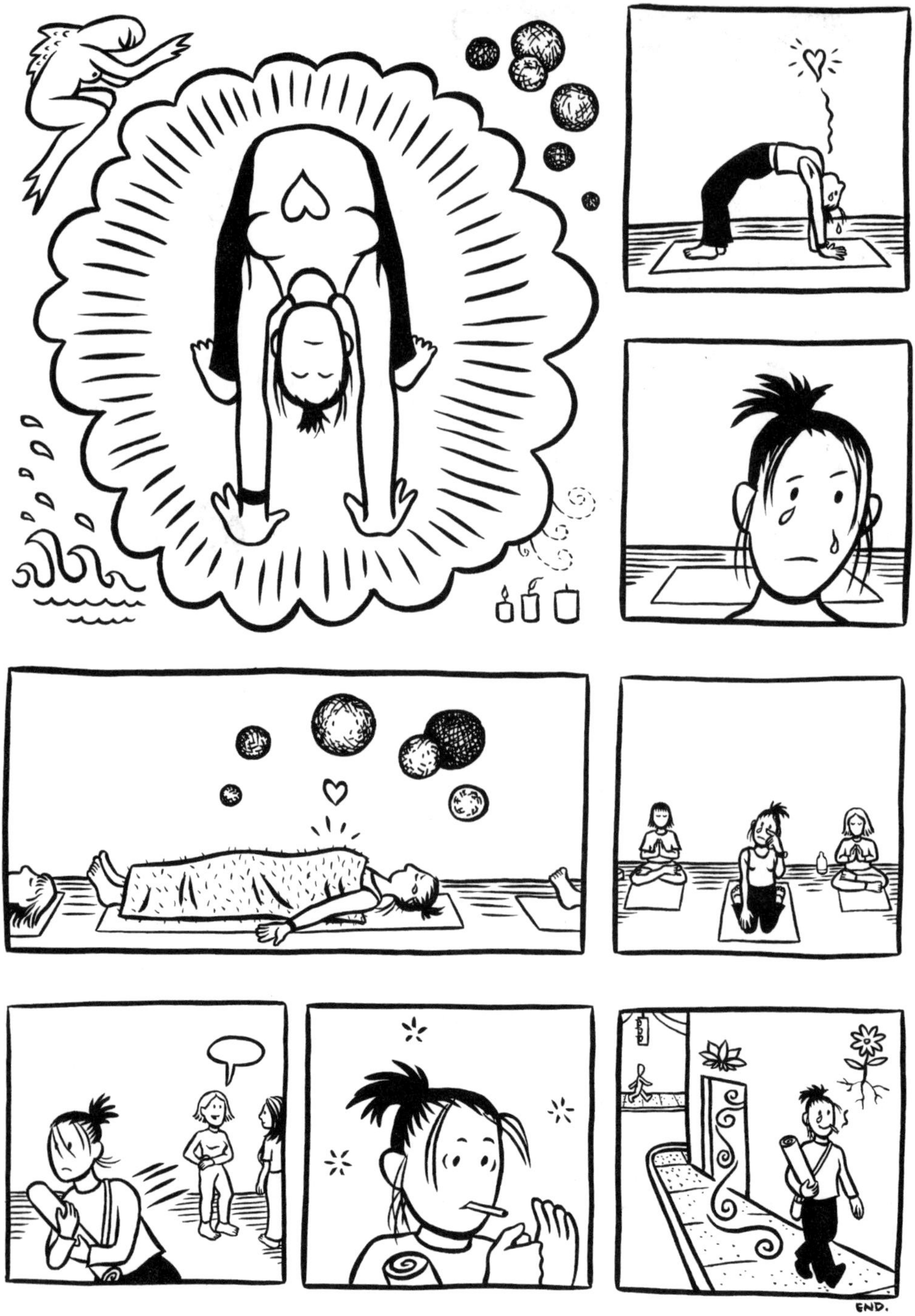
END.

BUT FOR THE MOST PART, I DIDN'T FIND INSPIRATION FROM MY DEPRESSION, AND MY PRODUCTIVITY IN THE MIDST OF IT WAS VERY LOW.

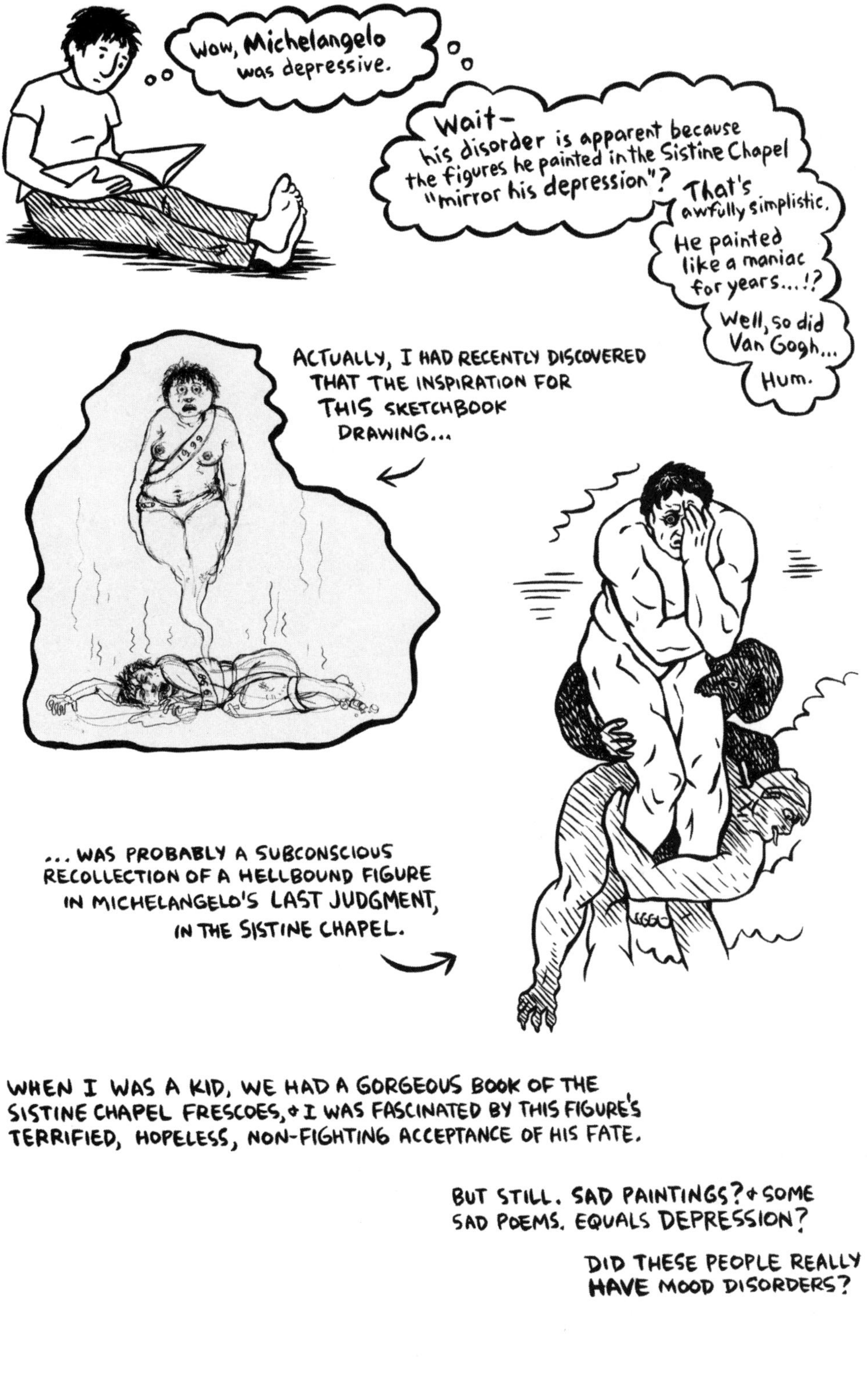

Wow, Michelangelo was depressive.
Wait- his disorder is apparent because the figures he painted in the Sistine Chapel "mirror his depression"?
That's awfully simplistic.
He painted like a maniac for years...!?
Well, so did Van Gogh...
Hum.
ACTUALLY, I HAD RECENTLY DISCOVERED THAT THE INSPIRATION FOR THIS SKETCHBOOK DRAWING...
1999
...WAS PROBABLY A SUBCONSCIOUS RECOLLECTION OF A HELLBOUND FIGURE IN MICHELANGELO'S LAST JUDGMENT, IN THE SISTINE CHAPEL.
WHEN I WAS A KID, WE HAD A GORGEOUS BOOK OF THE SISTINE CHAPEL FRESCOES, & I WAS FASCINATED BY THIS FIGURE'S TERRIFIED, HOPELESS, NON-FIGHTING ACCEPTANCE OF HIS FATE.
BUT STILL. SAD PAINTINGS? & SOME SAD POEMS. EQUALS DEPRESSION?
DID THESE PEOPLE REALLY HAVE MOOD DISORDERS?

IT'S NOT LIKE RESEARCHERS CAN SIT DOWN WITH MICHELANGELO TO EVALUATE HIS SYMPTOMS. I FOUND I WAS GETTING DEFENSIVE FOR ALL THE "PROBABLY CRAZY" PEOPLE ON THE LIST.

HOW CAN THE LISTMAKERS SO CAVALIERLY LEVEL SUCH ACCUSATIONS?

HOW DO "THEY" KNOW?!

THE ANSWER IS: A LOT OF RESEARCH.

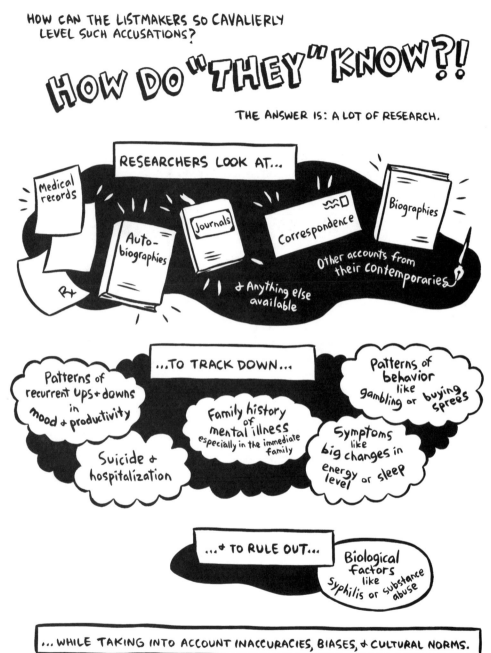

RESEARCHERS LOOK AT...

Medical records

Auto-biographies

Journals

Correspondence

Biographies

Other accounts from their contemporaries

& Anything else available

...TO TRACK DOWN...

Patterns of recurrent ups + downs in mood + productivity

Patterns of behavior like gambling or buying sprees

Family history of mental illness especially in the immediate family

Symptoms like big changes in energy level or sleep

Suicide & hospitalization

...& TO RULE OUT...

Biological factors like syphilis or substance abuse

...WHILE TAKING INTO ACCOUNT INACCURACIES, BIASES, & CULTURAL NORMS.

QUITE THE TASK — BUT THAT WAS GOOD ENOUGH FOR ME.

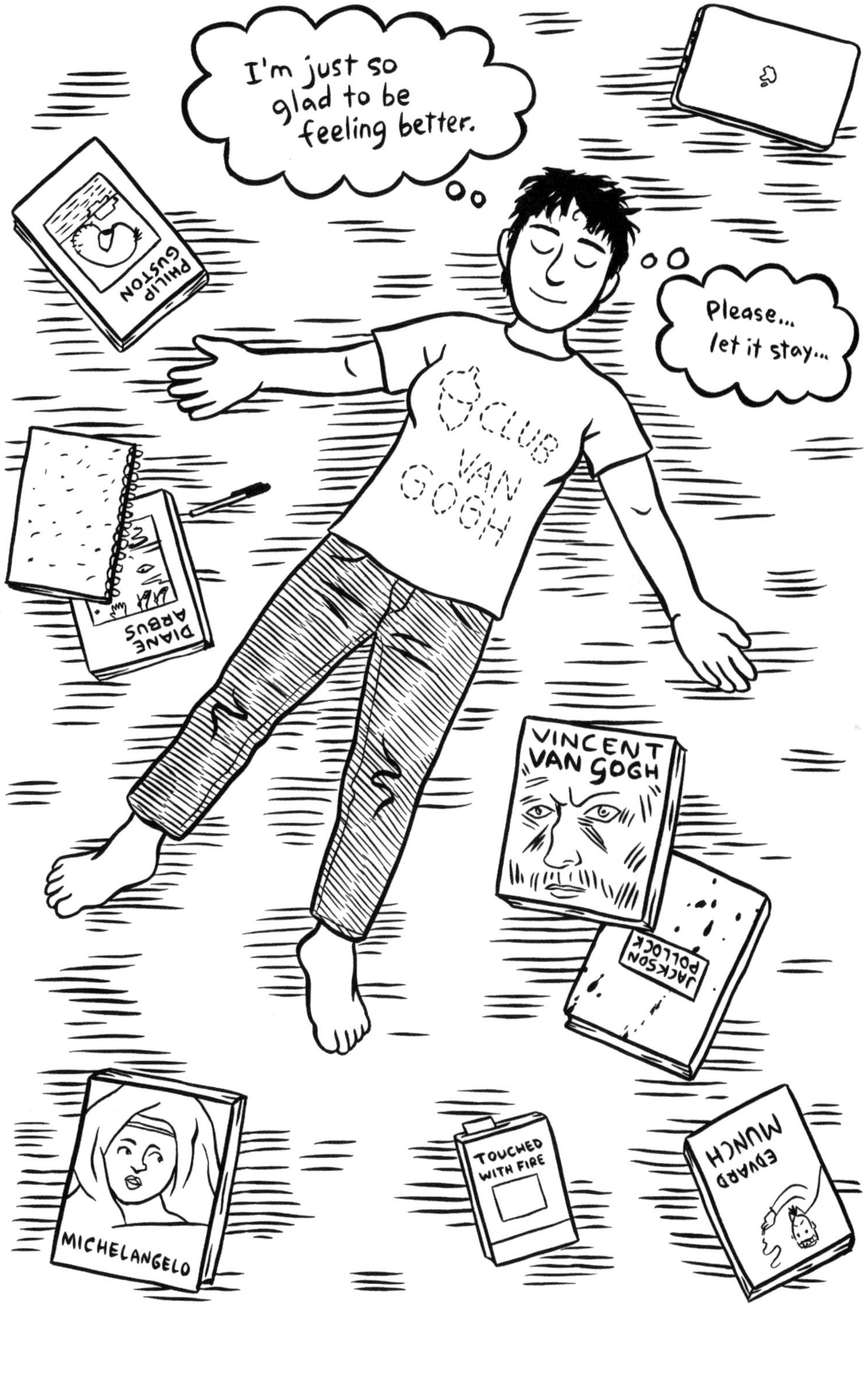
I'm just so glad to be feeling better.
Please... let it stay...
PHILIP GUSTON
CLUB VAN GOGH
DIANE ARBUS
VINCENT VAN GOGH
JACKSON POLLOCK
MICHELANGELO
TOUCHED WITH FIRE
EDVARD MUNCH

CHAPTER 6

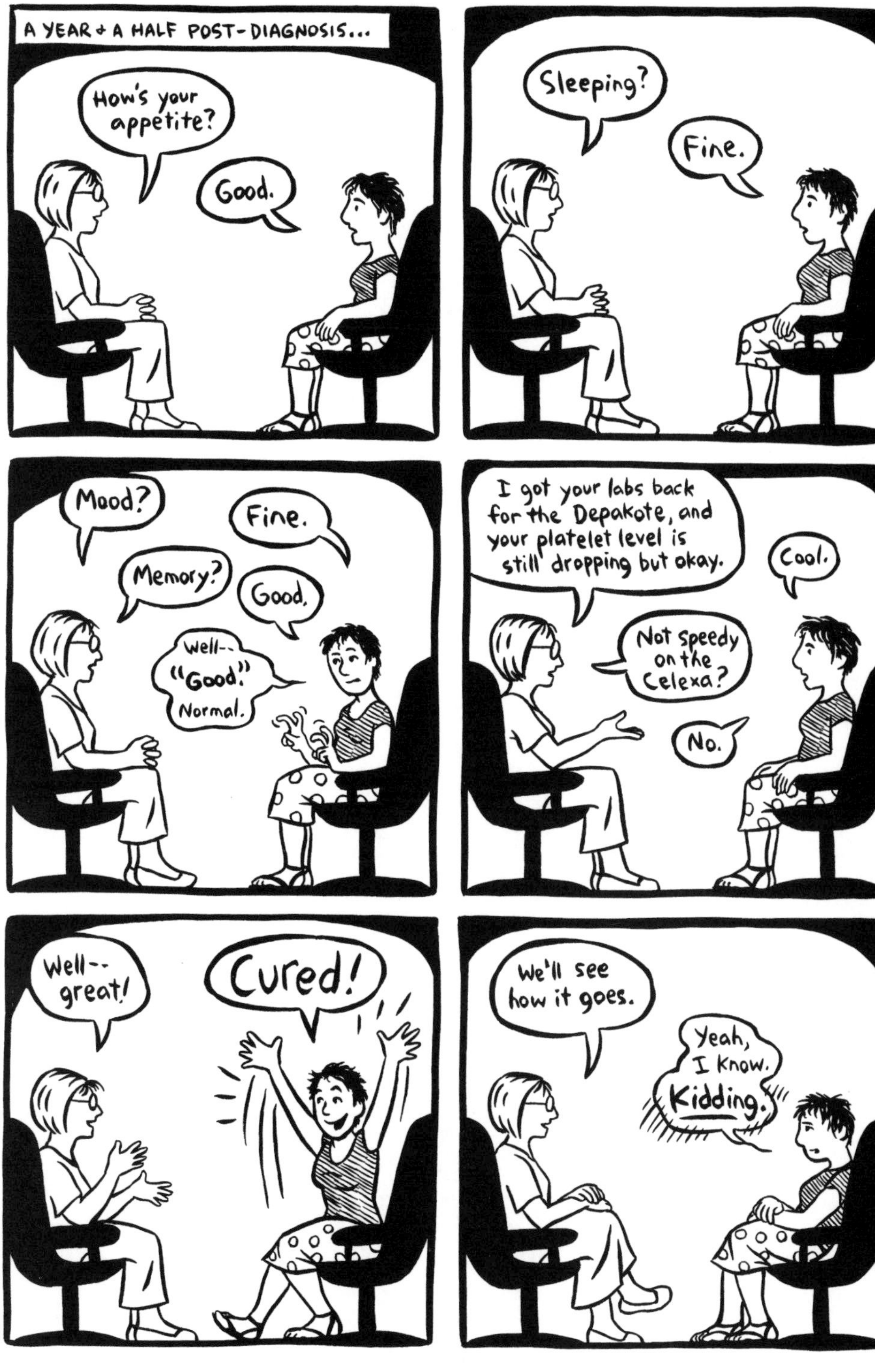
A YEAR & A HALF POST-DIAGNOSIS...
How's your appetite?
Good.
Sleeping?
Fine.
Mood?
Fine.
Memory?
Good.
Well-- "Good." Normal.
I got your labs back for the Depakote, and your platelet level is still dropping but okay.
Cool.
Not speedy on the Celexa?
No.
Well-- great!
Cured!
We'll see how it goes.
Yeah, I know. Kidding.

BUT MY PLATELET LEVEL DID KEEP DROPPING.
LESS THAN A MONTH AFTER FINALLY – FINALLY –
FEELING LIKE I'D SURFACED, I HAD TO
SWITCH TO A NEW MEDICATION, NEURONTIN.

MY MOOD LIFTED...

AND LIFTED...

AND DIDN'T STOP LIFTING.

I COULD FEEL MYSELF
GETTING SWEPT AWAY.

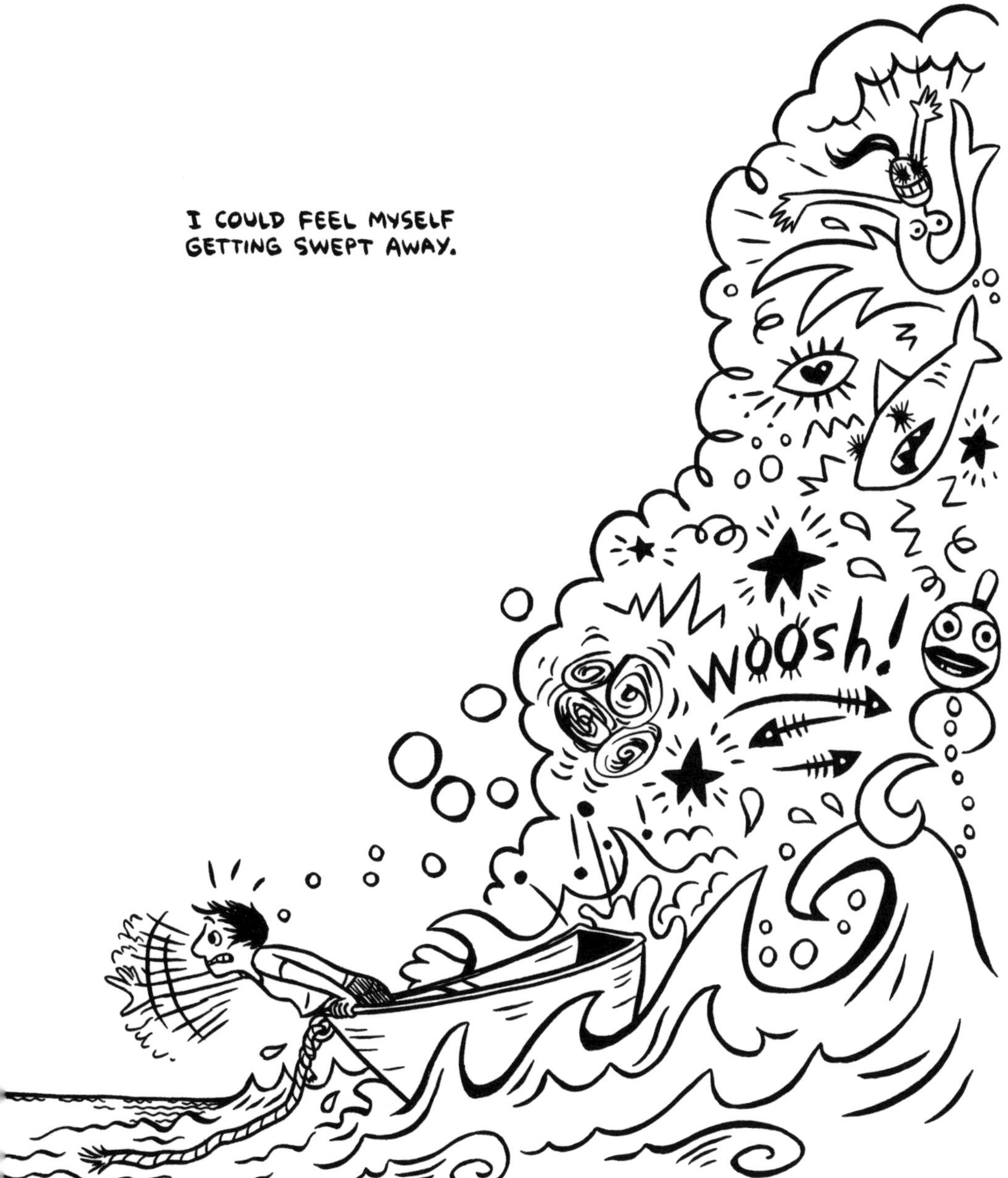
WOOSH!

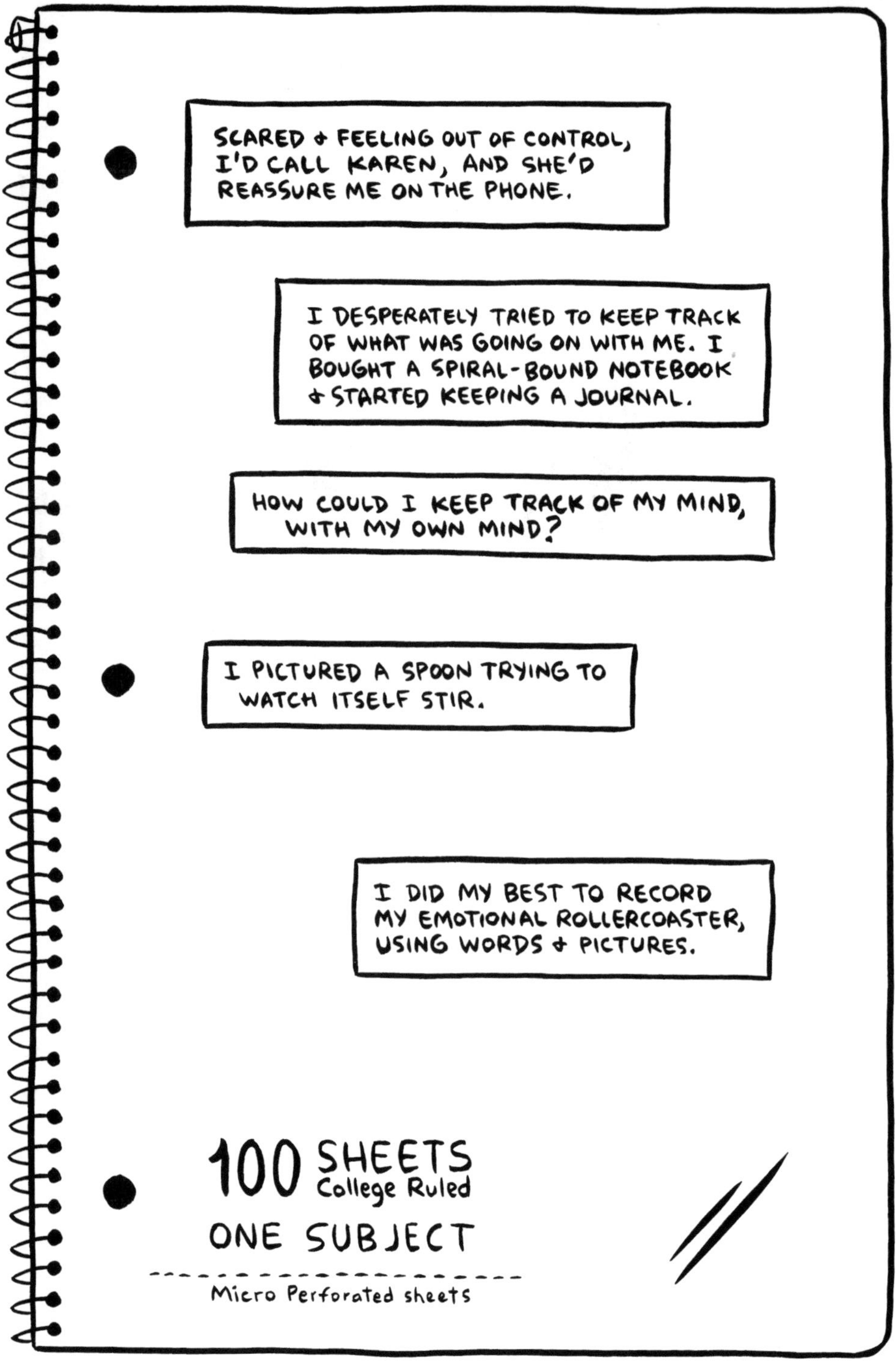
SCARED & FEELING OUT OF CONTROL, I'D CALL KAREN, AND SHE'D REASSURE ME ON THE PHONE.
I DESPERATELY TRIED TO KEEP TRACK OF WHAT WAS GOING ON WITH ME. I BOUGHT A SPIRAL-BOUND NOTEBOOK & STARTED KEEPING A JOURNAL.
HOW COULD I KEEP TRACK OF MY MIND, WITH MY OWN MIND?
I PICTURED A SPOON TRYING TO WATCH ITSELF STIR.
I DID MY BEST TO RECORD MY EMOTIONAL ROLLERCOASTER, USING WORDS & PICTURES.
100 SHEETS College Ruled
ONE SUBJECT
Micro Perforated sheets

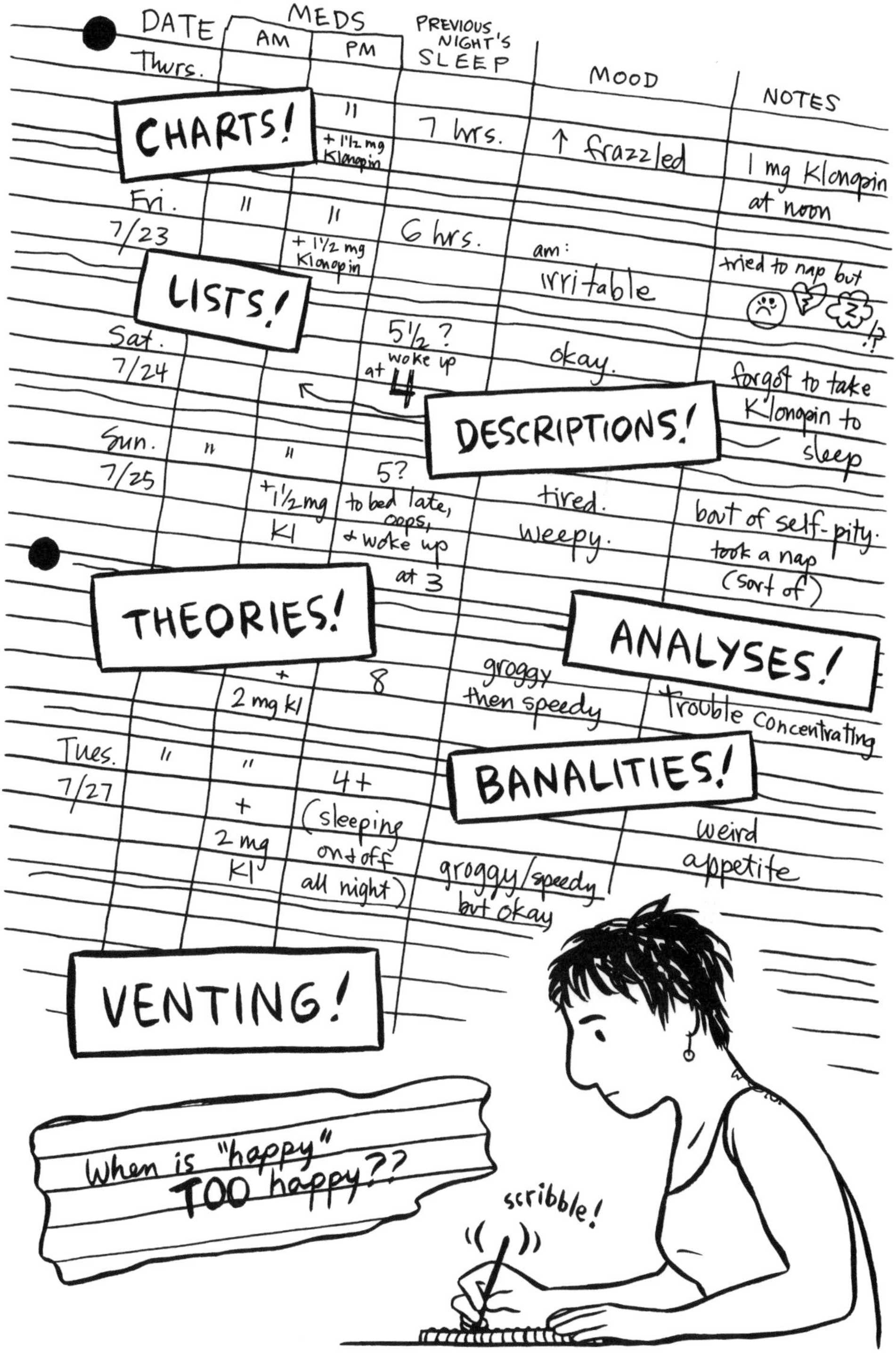

DATE
MEDS
AM
PM
PREVIOUS NIGHT'S SLEEP
MOOD
NOTES
Thurs.
CHARTS!
"
+ 1½ mg Klonopin
7 hrs.
↑ frazzled
1 mg Klonopin at noon
Fri. 7/23
"
"
+ 1½ mg Klonopin
6 hrs.
am: irritable
tried to nap but
LISTS!
Sat. 7/24
5½ ? woke up at 4
okay.
forgot to take Klonopin to sleep
DESCRIPTIONS!
Sun. 7/25
"
"
+ 1½ mg Kl
5? to bed late, oops, & woke up at 3
tired. weepy.
bout of self-pity. took a nap (sort of)
THEORIES!
ANALYSES!
+ 2 mg Kl
8
groggy then speedy
Trouble concentrating
Tues. 7/27
"
"
+ 2 mg Kl
4+ (sleeping on & off all night)
BANALITIES!
groggy/speedy but okay
weird appetite
VENTING!
When is "happy" TOO happy??
scribble!

Watch sleeping. Watch eating. Watch socializing. Watch getting work done. Watch obsessing.

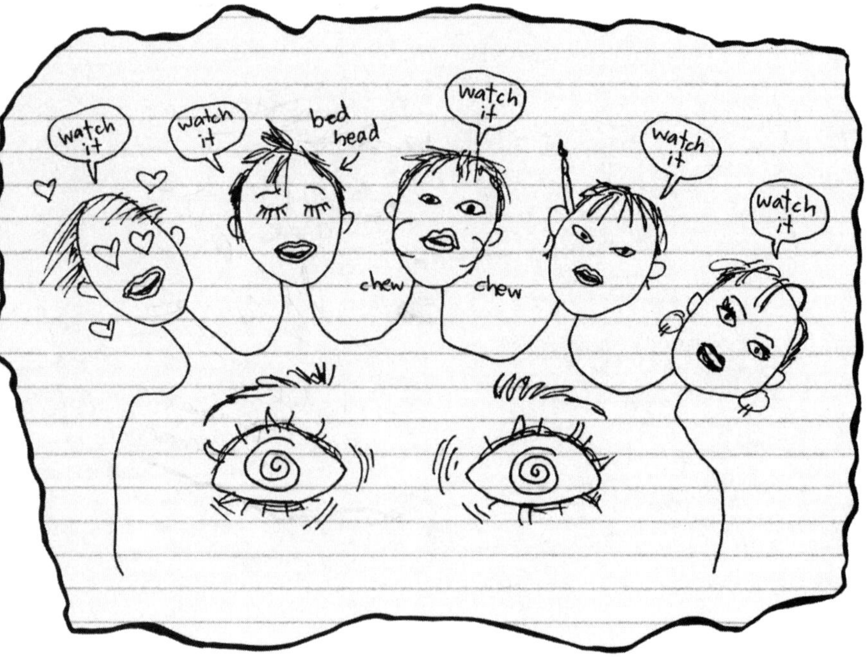
watch it
watch it
bed head
watch it
watch it
watch it
chew
chew

THERE WAS SO MUCH TO PAY ATTENTION TO.

I WAS VERY AWARE OF MY ***SYMPTOMS***, BUT I COULDN'T UNDERSTAND WHY THEY WERE SO HARD TO REALLY GET A GRIP ON.

IT WOULD BE DINNERTIME & I'D REALIZE ALL I'D EATEN ALL DAY WAS A BANANA.

OOPS. BUT HOW DID THAT HAPPEN?

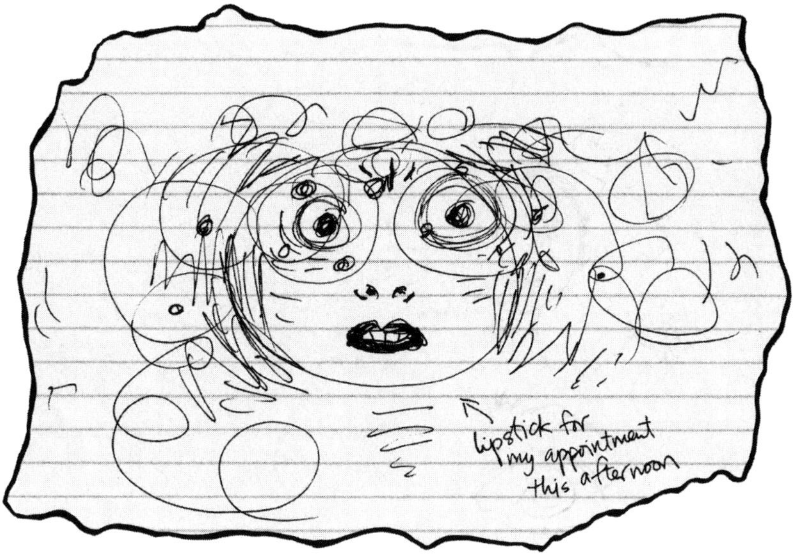
lipstick for my appointment this afternoon

MANIC OR DEPRESSED, MAC'S "PARAMOUNT" LIPSTICK WAS MY KEY TO FEELING TOGETHER.

NEATLY-APPLIED LIPSTICK = NOT CRAZY.

ONE DAY, WHILE LOOKING FOR ARTSY VAGINAL REFERENCE MATERIAL FOR A STRANGER ILLUSTRATION...

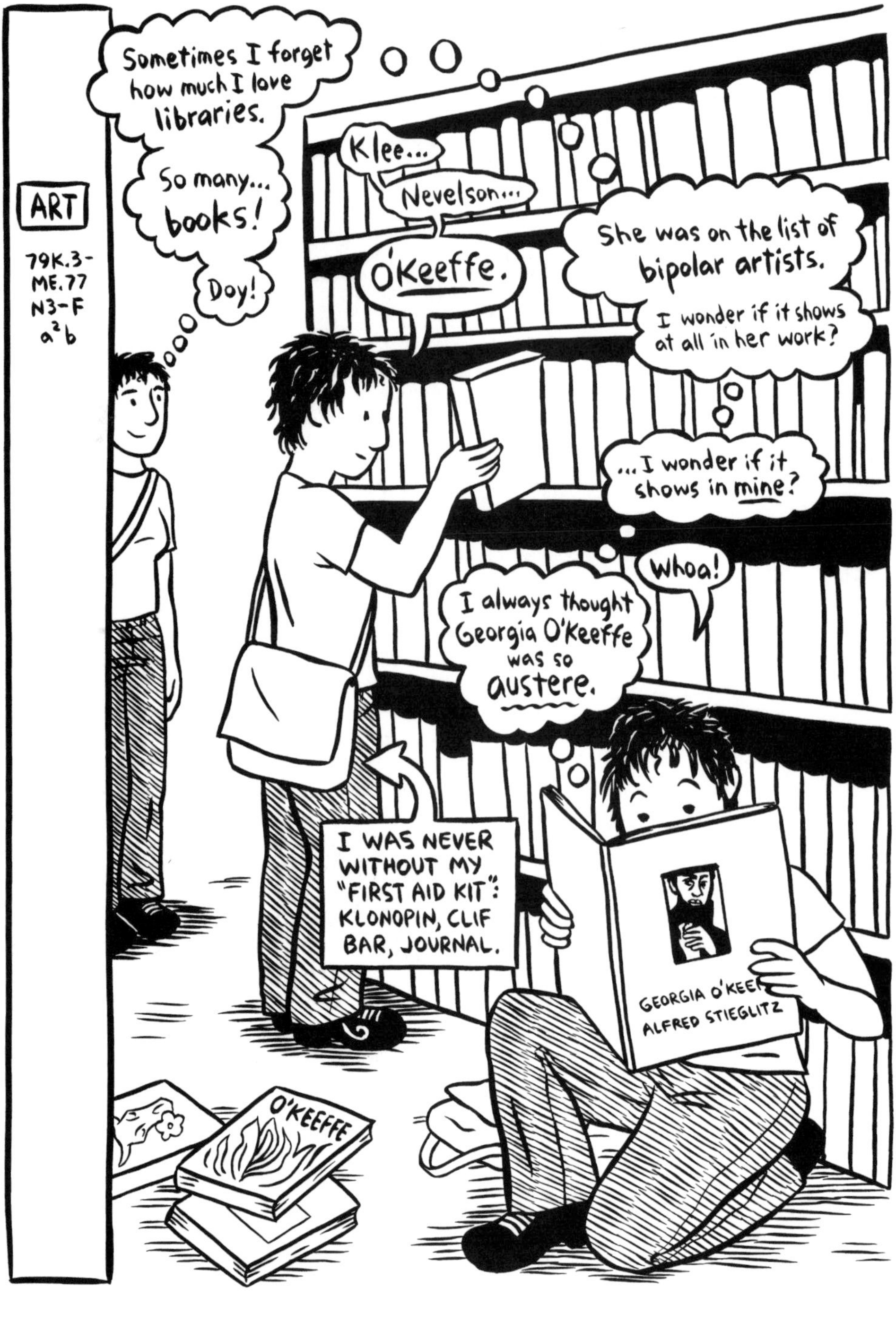

ART
79K.3-
ME.77
N3-F
a²b
Sometimes I forget how much I love libraries.
So many... books!
Doy!
Klee...
Nevelson...
O'Keeffe.
She was on the list of bipolar artists.
I wonder if it shows at all in her work?
...I wonder if it shows in mine?
Whoa!
I always thought Georgia O'Keeffe was so austere.
I WAS NEVER WITHOUT MY "FIRST AID KIT": KLONOPIN, CLIF BAR, JOURNAL.
GEORGIA O'KEEF
ALFRED STIEGLITZ
O'KEEFFE

PHOTOGRAPHER ALFRED STIEGLITZ, HER MENTOR, LOVER, HUSBAND, CHEATING HUSBAND, THEN EX-HUSBAND, TOOK PORTRAITS OF HER OVER THE COURSE OF TWENTY YEARS. SOME WERE STARTLINGLY EROTIC, WITH HER IN VARYING STATES OF UNDRESS.

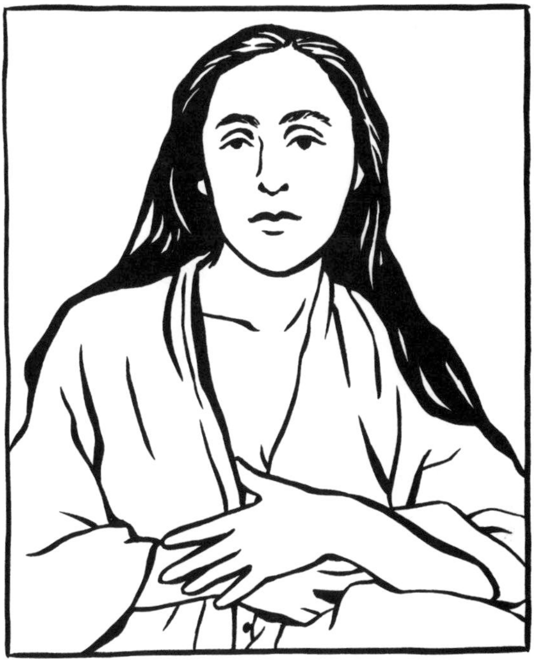

1918

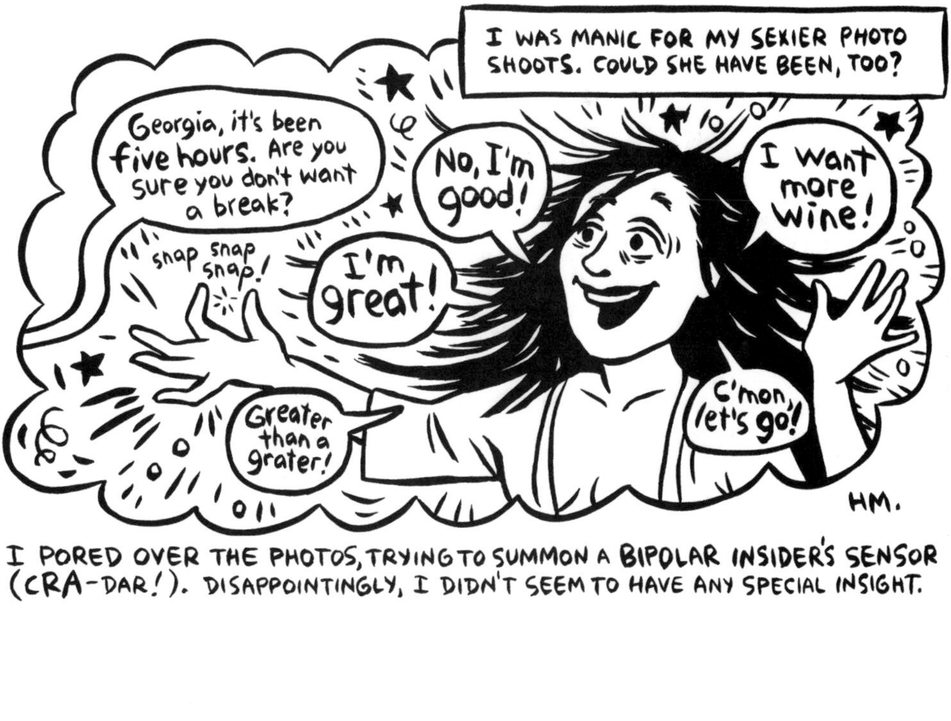
I WAS MANIC FOR MY SEXIER PHOTO SHOOTS. COULD SHE HAVE BEEN, TOO?
Georgia, it's been five hours. Are you sure you don't want a break?
No, I'm good!
I want more wine!
snap snap snap!
I'm great!
Greater than a grater!
C'mon, let's go!
HM.

I PORED OVER THE PHOTOS, TRYING TO SUMMON A **BIPOLAR** INSIDER'S SENSOR (CRA-DAR!). DISAPPOINTINGLY, I DIDN'T SEEM TO HAVE ANY SPECIAL INSIGHT.

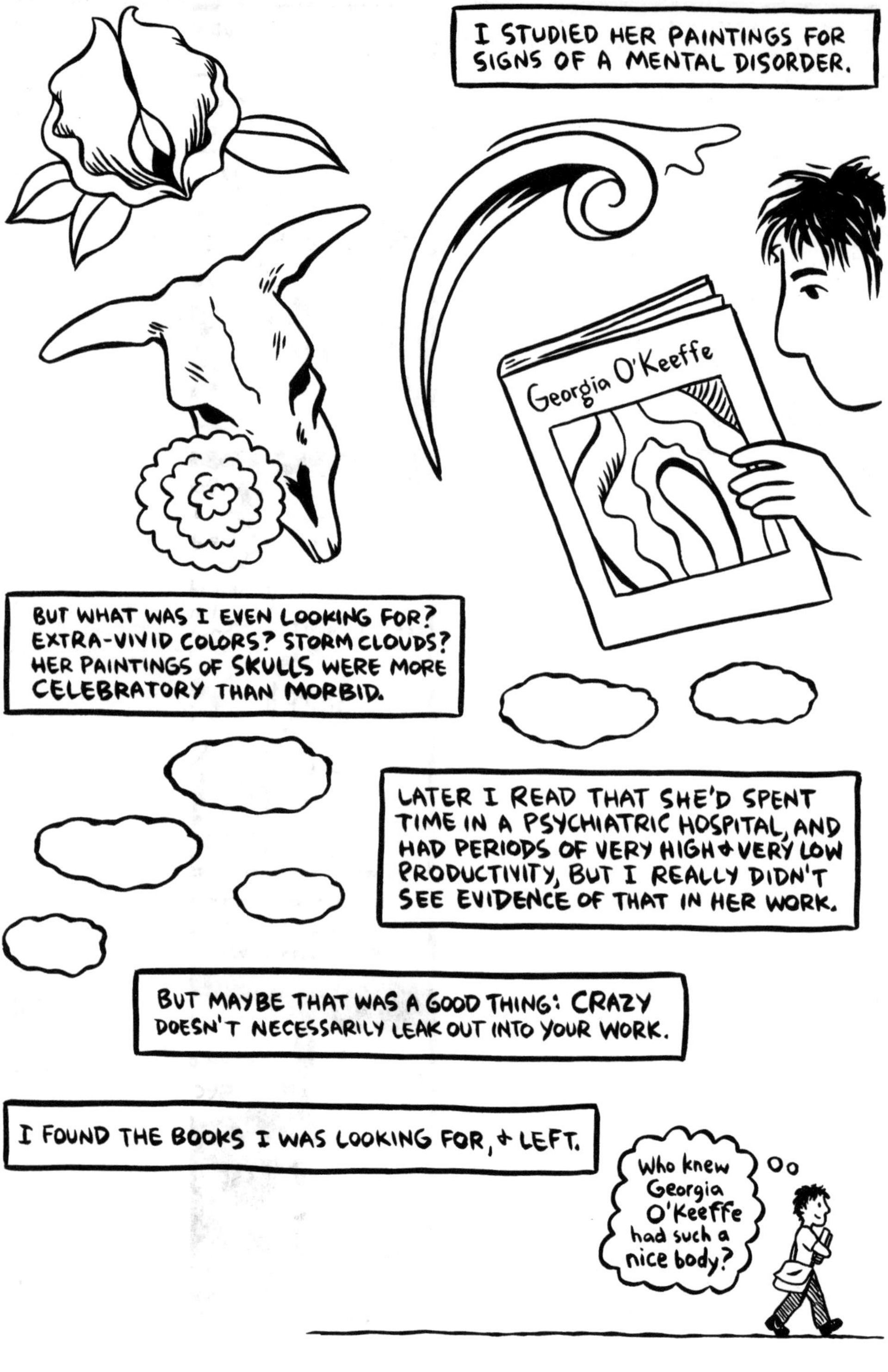
I STUDIED HER PAINTINGS FOR SIGNS OF A MENTAL DISORDER.
Georgia O'Keeffe
BUT WHAT WAS I EVEN LOOKING FOR? EXTRA-VIVID COLORS? STORM CLOUDS? HER PAINTINGS OF SKULLS WERE MORE CELEBRATORY THAN MORBID.
LATER I READ THAT SHE'D SPENT TIME IN A PSYCHIATRIC HOSPITAL, AND HAD PERIODS OF VERY HIGH & VERY LOW PRODUCTIVITY, BUT I REALLY DIDN'T SEE EVIDENCE OF THAT IN HER WORK.
BUT MAYBE THAT WAS A GOOD THING: CRAZY DOESN'T NECESSARILY LEAK OUT INTO YOUR WORK.
I FOUND THE BOOKS I WAS LOOKING FOR, & LEFT.
Who knew Georgia O'Keeffe had such a nice body?

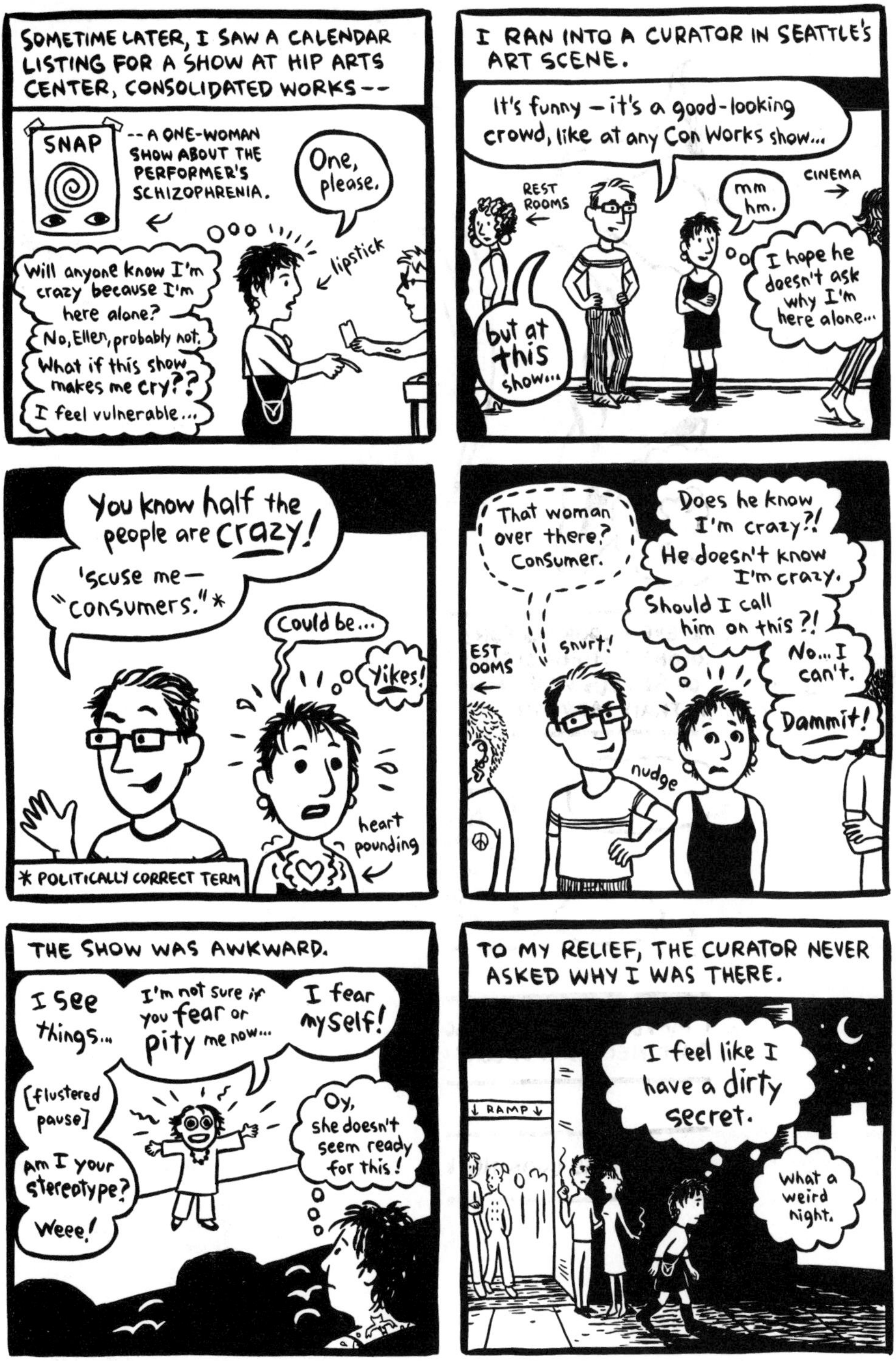
SOMETIME LATER, I SAW A CALENDAR LISTING FOR A SHOW AT HIP ARTS CENTER, CONSOLIDATED WORKS--
SNAP
--A ONE-WOMAN SHOW ABOUT THE PERFORMER'S SCHIZOPHRENIA.
One, please.
lipstick
Will anyone know I'm crazy because I'm here alone?
No, Ellen, probably not.
What if this show makes me cry??
I feel vulnerable...
I RAN INTO A CURATOR IN SEATTLE'S ART SCENE.
It's funny—it's a good-looking crowd, like at any Con Works show...
REST ROOMS
CINEMA
but at this show...
mm hm.
I hope he doesn't ask why I'm here alone...
You know half the people are crazy!
'scuse me— "consumers."*
Could be...
Yikes!
heart pounding
* POLITICALLY CORRECT TERM
That woman over there? Consumer.
snurt!
EST OOMS
Does he know I'm crazy?!
He doesn't know I'm crazy.
Should I call him on this?!
No... I can't.
Dammit!
nudge
THE SHOW WAS AWKWARD.
I see things...
I'm not sure if you fear or pity me now...
I fear myself!
[flustered pause]
Am I your stereotype?
Weee!
Oy, she doesn't seem ready for this!
TO MY RELIEF, THE CURATOR NEVER ASKED WHY I WAS THERE.
RAMP
I feel like I have a dirty secret.
What a weird night.

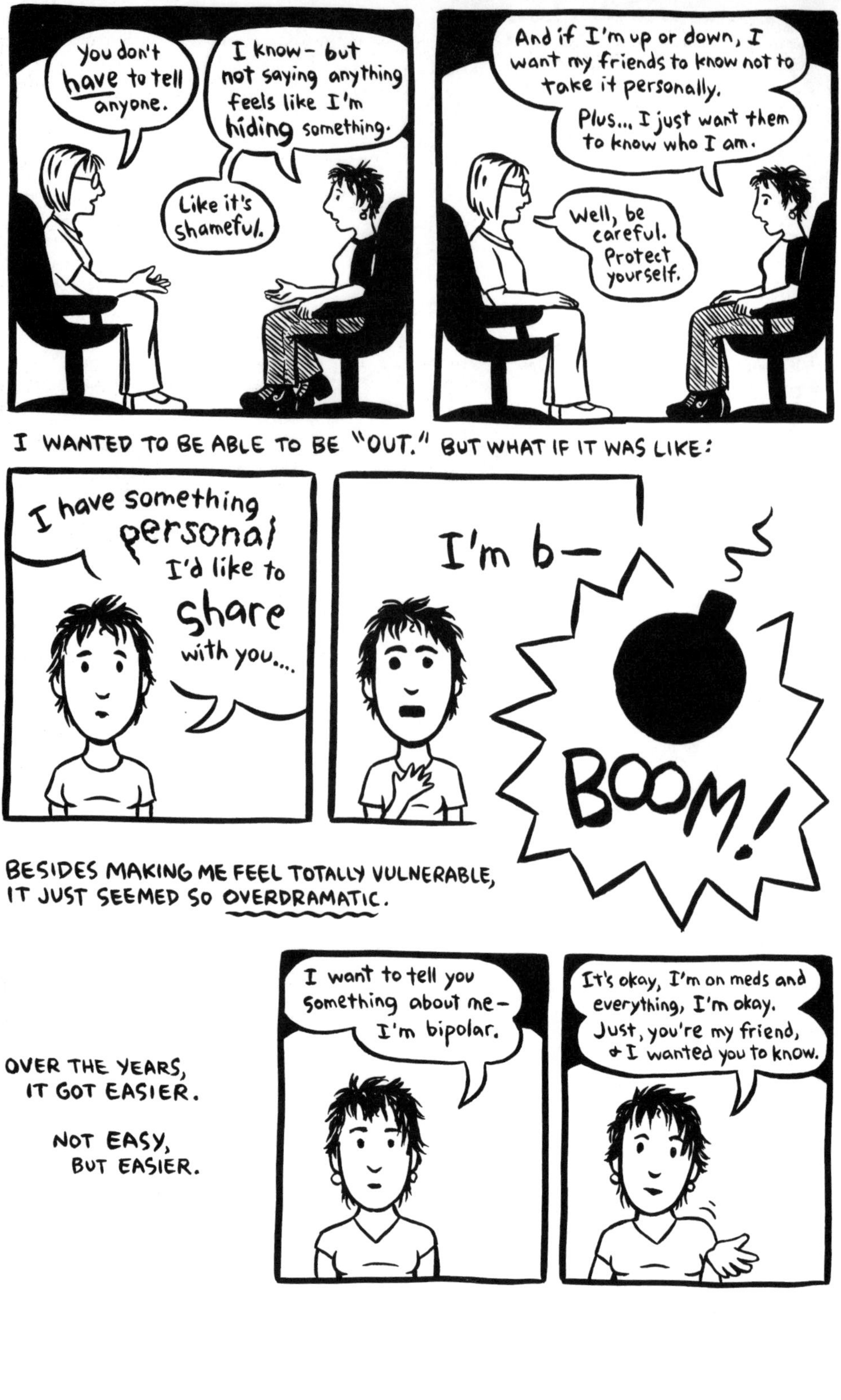

You don't have to tell anyone.
I know- but not saying anything feels like I'm hiding something.
Like it's shameful.
And if I'm up or down, I want my friends to know not to take it personally.
Plus... I just want them to know who I am.
Well, be careful. Protect yourself.
I WANTED TO BE ABLE TO BE "OUT." BUT WHAT IF IT WAS LIKE:
I have something personal I'd like to share with you....
I'm b-
BOOM!
BESIDES MAKING ME FEEL TOTALLY VULNERABLE, IT JUST SEEMED SO OVERDRAMATIC.
OVER THE YEARS, IT GOT EASIER.
NOT EASY, BUT EASIER.
I want to tell you something about me- I'm bipolar.
It's okay, I'm on meds and everything, I'm okay. Just, you're my friend, & I wanted you to know.

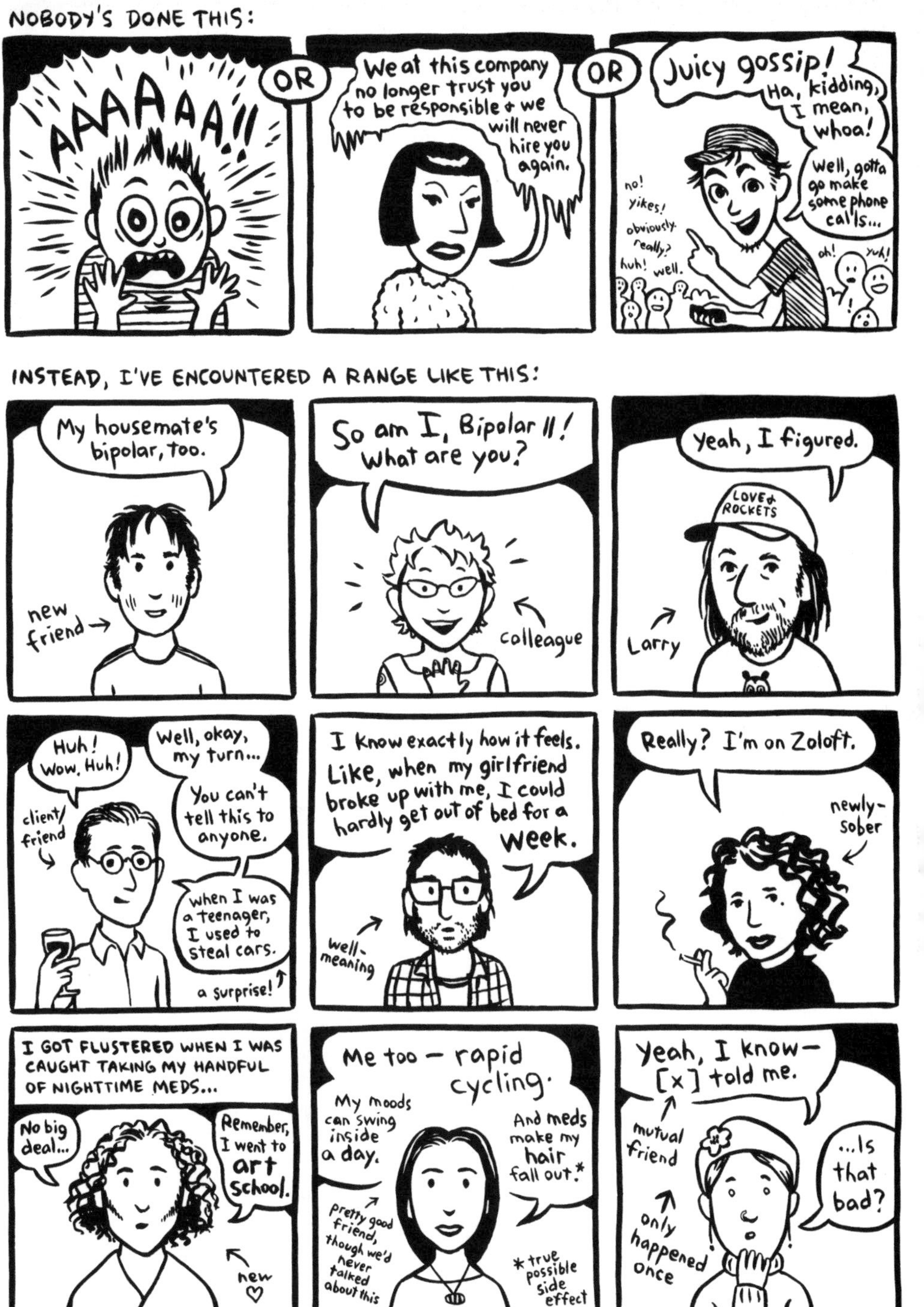
NOBODY'S DONE THIS:
AAAAAA!!
OR
We at this company no longer trust you to be responsible & we will never hire you again.
OR
Juicy gossip!
Ha, kidding, I mean, whoa!
Well, gotta go make some phone calls...
no!
yikes!
obviously.
really?
huh!
well.
oh!
yuk!
INSTEAD, I'VE ENCOUNTERED A RANGE LIKE THIS:
My housemate's bipolar, too.
new friend →
So am I, Bipolar II! What are you?
colleague
Yeah, I figured.
LOVE & ROCKETS
Larry
Huh! Wow. Huh!
Well, okay, my turn...
You can't tell this to anyone.
When I was a teenager, I used to steal cars.
client/friend
a surprise!
I know exactly how it feels. Like, when my girlfriend broke up with me, I could hardly get out of bed for a week.
well-meaning
Really? I'm on Zoloft.
newly-sober
I GOT FLUSTERED WHEN I WAS CAUGHT TAKING MY HANDFUL OF NIGHTTIME MEDS...
No big deal...
Remember, I went to art school.
new ♡
Me too — rapid cycling.
My moods can swing inside a day.
And meds make my hair fall out.*
pretty good friend, though we'd never talked about this
* true possible side effect
Yeah, I know— [x] told me.
mutual friend
only happened once
...Is that bad?
IT ALWAYS FEELS LIKE I'M DROPPING A BOMB TO SOME DEGREE, THOUGH.

MY MOODS WERE LESS EXTREME, BUT STILL UNPREDICTIBLE, PRECARIOUS. IN TURNS I'D BE OKAY, OR IN A SUSPICIOUSLY GOOD MOOD FOR DAYS, OR UNDER THE BLANKET ON MY COUCH FOR LONG STRETCHES OF TIME.

What is "normal" + "crazy"? Holidays are depressing for anyone, right?

Concentrating on drawing is so tough... the lines keep coming out wrong + it's taking so long.

I think I may be smoking too much pot — not quite every day now, mostly in the evening. But I feel groggy in the morning + decide to stop for a while, + then I change my mind.

So sensitive right now. Not depressed, exactly — ? Things keep spinning.

I must say, Led Zeppelin therapy is still working best.

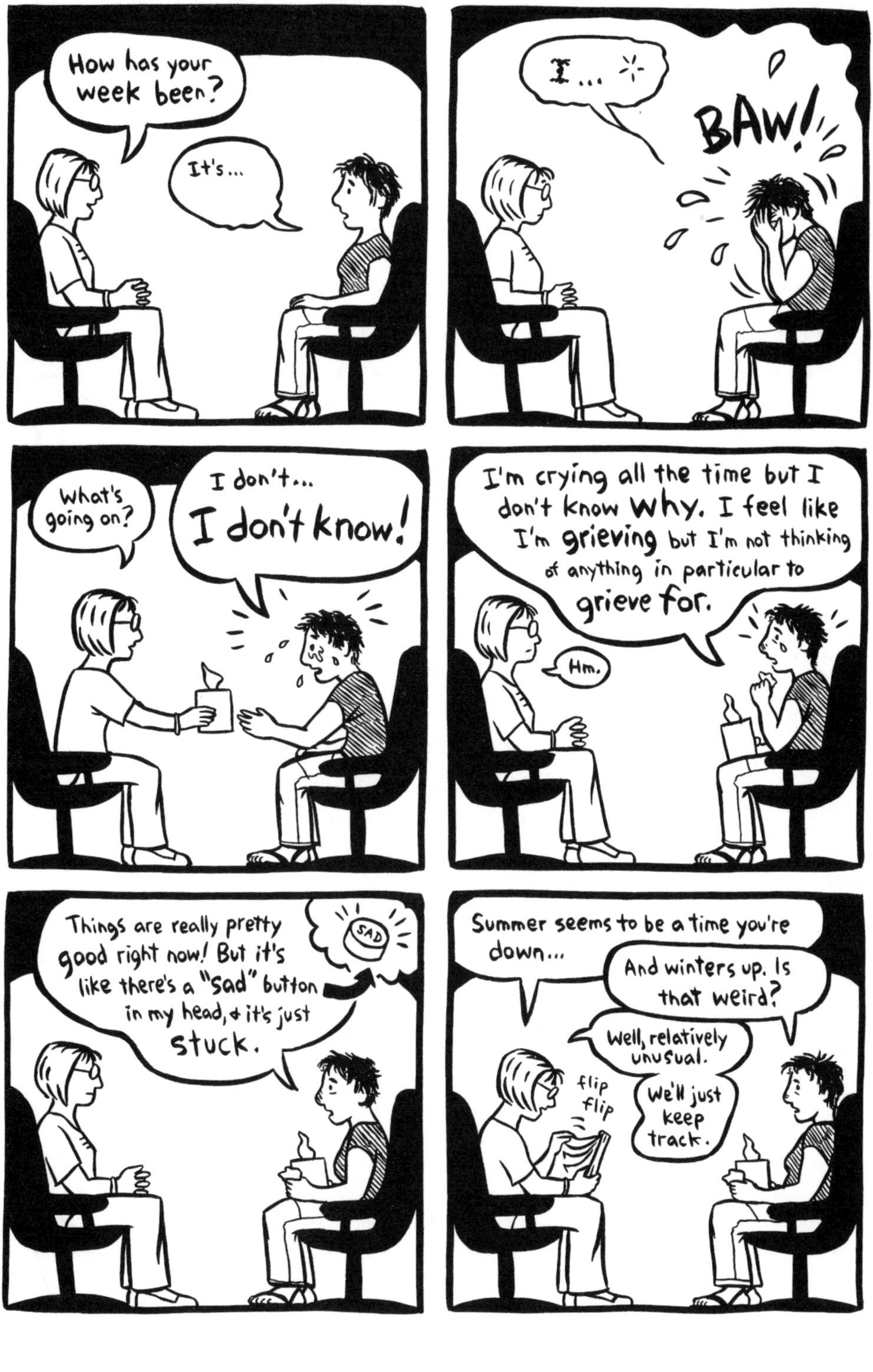
How has your week been?
It's...
I... *
BAW!
What's going on?
I don't... I don't know!
I'm crying all the time but I don't know why. I feel like I'm grieving but I'm not thinking of anything in particular to grieve for.
Hm.
Things are really pretty good right now! But it's like there's a "sad" button in my head, & it's just stuck.
SAD
Summer seems to be a time you're down...
And winters up. Is that weird?
Well, relatively unusual.
flip flip
We'll just keep track.

ON A WALK IN THE ARBORETUM, I FOUND A HALF-HIDDEN PATH, & DECIDED TO FOLLOW IT & GET AWAY FROM THE REST OF THE PEOPLE IN THE PARK.

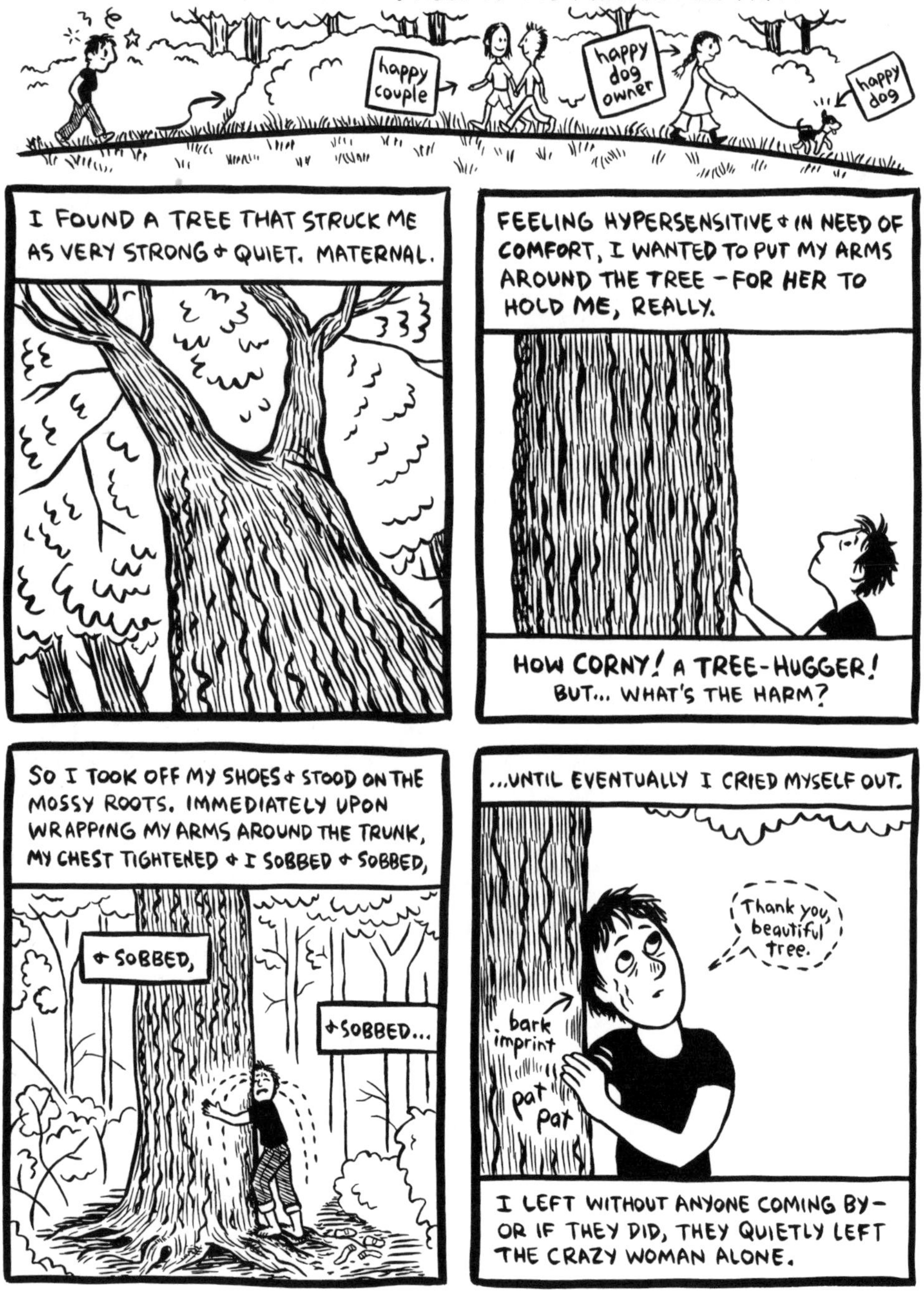
happy couple
happy dog owner
happy dog
I FOUND A TREE THAT STRUCK ME AS VERY STRONG & QUIET. MATERNAL.
FEELING HYPERSENSITIVE & IN NEED OF COMFORT, I WANTED TO PUT MY ARMS AROUND THE TREE – FOR HER TO HOLD ME, REALLY.
HOW CORNY! A TREE-HUGGER! BUT... WHAT'S THE HARM?
SO I TOOK OFF MY SHOES & STOOD ON THE MOSSY ROOTS. IMMEDIATELY UPON WRAPPING MY ARMS AROUND THE TRUNK, MY CHEST TIGHTENED & I SOBBED & SOBBED,
& SOBBED,
& SOBBED...
...UNTIL EVENTUALLY I CRIED MYSELF OUT.
Thank you, beautiful tree.
bark imprint
pat pat
I LEFT WITHOUT ANYONE COMING BY – OR IF THEY DID, THEY QUIETLY LEFT THE CRAZY WOMAN ALONE.

AND THAT WAS ME: A CRAZY WOMAN ALONE, CLINGING TO A TREE! MAYBE I WAS JUST EXHAUSTED, BUT WHEN THAT OCCURRED TO ME, I JUST FELT LIKE, "TRUE 'NUFF."

THERE WAS STILL THE PROBLEM OF INCOME. I'D REALLY LOST MOMENTUM IN MY WORK.

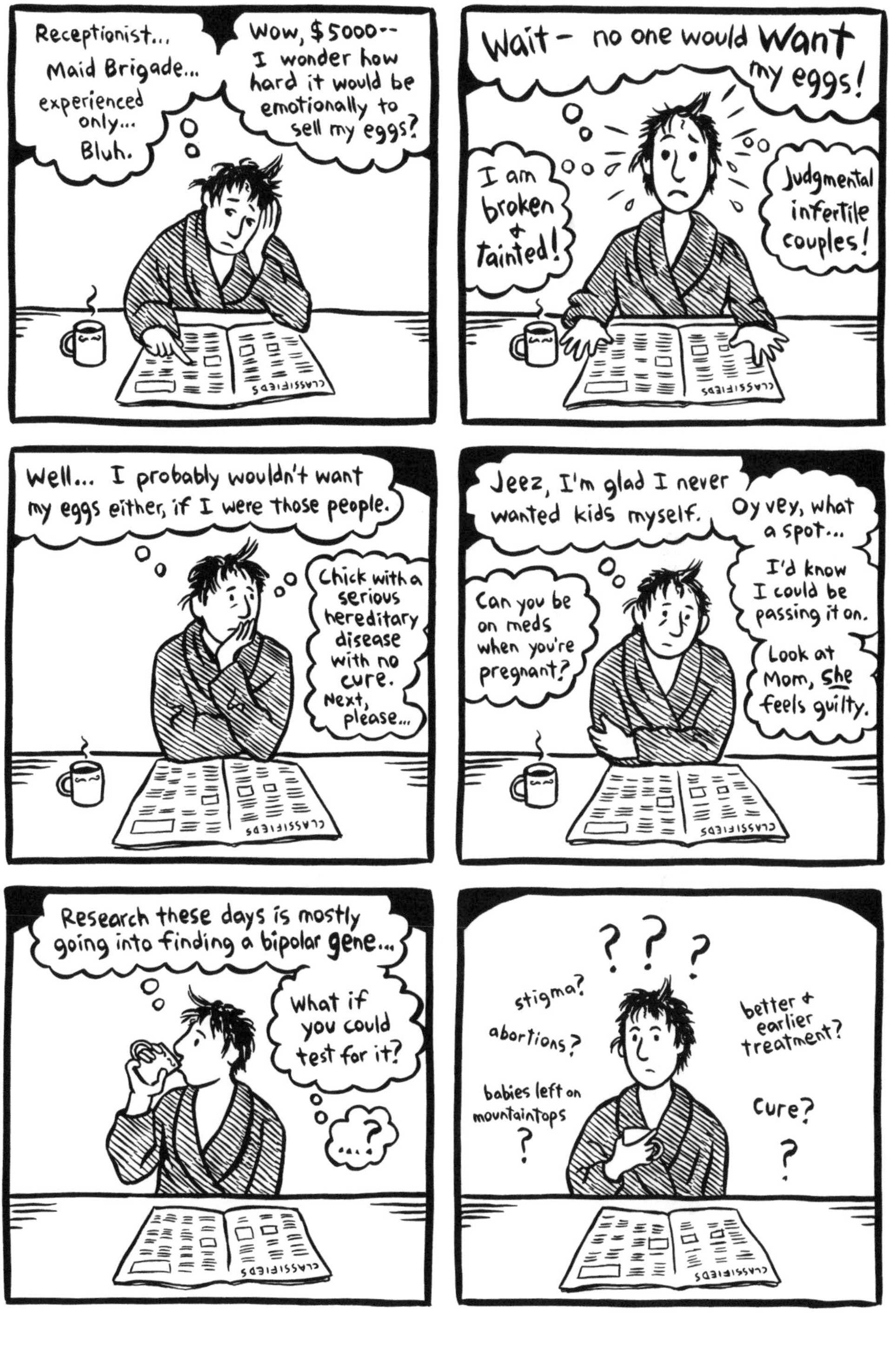

Receptionist... Maid Brigade... experienced only... Bluh.
Wow, $5000-- I wonder how hard it would be emotionally to sell my eggs?
Wait - no one would Want my eggs!
I am broken & tainted!
Judgmental infertile couples!
Well... I probably wouldn't want my eggs either, if I were those people.
Chick with a serious hereditary disease with no cure. Next, please...
Jeez, I'm glad I never wanted kids myself.
Oy vey, what a spot...
I'd know I could be passing it on.
Look at Mom, She feels guilty.
Can you be on meds when you're pregnant?
Research these days is mostly going into finding a bipolar gene...
What if you could test for it?
...?
? ? ?
stigma?
abortions?
babies left on mountaintops ?
better & earlier treatment?
Cure?
?

TOWARD THE END OF THE SUMMER, THE SAN DIEGO COMIC-CON APPROACHED, THE BIGGEST & BEST-KNOWN COMIC CONVENTION IN THE COUNTRY. I'D ONLY GONE TWICE, BUT THIS YEAR I WAS GOING FOR SURE.

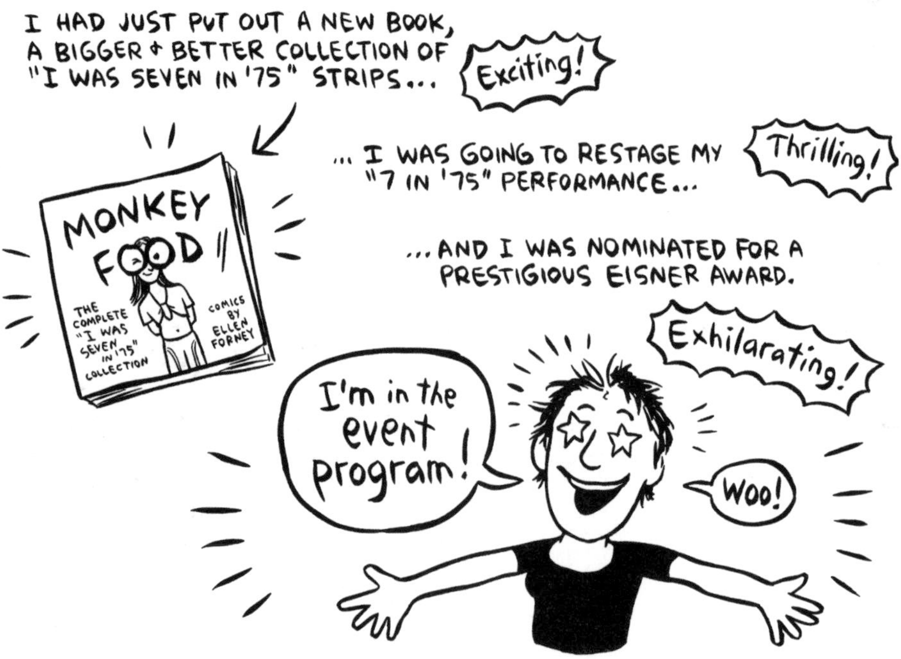
I HAD JUST PUT OUT A NEW BOOK, A BIGGER & BETTER COLLECTION OF "I WAS SEVEN IN '75" STRIPS...
Exciting!
MONKEY FOOD
THE COMPLETE "I WAS SEVEN IN '75" COLLECTION
COMICS BY ELLEN FORNEY
... I WAS GOING TO RESTAGE MY "7 IN '75" PERFORMANCE...
Thrilling!
... AND I WAS NOMINATED FOR A PRESTIGIOUS EISNER AWARD.
Exhilarating!
I'm in the event program!
Woo!

ON THE WAY TO SAN DIEGO, I STAYED WITH AN OLD FRIEND IN SAN FRANCISCO. WE SPENT FOUR DAYS LIKE THIS:

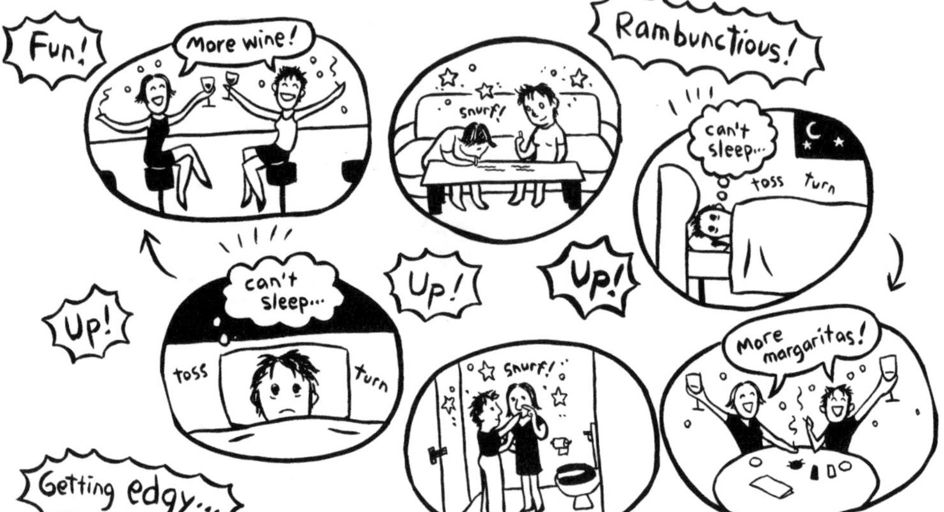
Fun!
More wine!
Rambunctious!
snurf!
can't sleep...
toss
turn
Up!
More margaritas!
snurf!
Up!
can't sleep...
toss
turn
Up!
Getting edgy...

I DIDN'T REALIZE MY EXCITEMENT HAD LIFTED INTO DANGEROUS TERRITORY.

THE FIRST DAY OF THE CON BROUGHT THOUSANDS & THOUSANDS OF PEOPLE.*

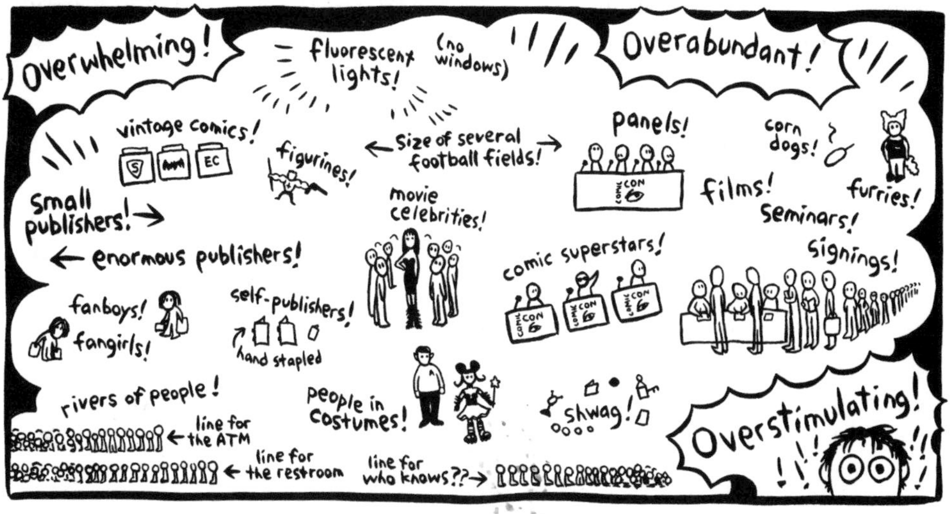

Overwhelming!
fluorescent lights!
(no windows)
Overabundant!
vintage comics!
EC
figurines!
Size of several football fields!
panels!
COMIC CON
corn dogs!
furries!
films!
seminars!
small publishers!
movie celebrities!
enormous publishers!
comic superstars!
signings!
fanboys!
fangirls!
self-publishers!
hand stapled
rivers of people!
people in costumes!
shwag!
Overstimulating!
line for the ATM
line for the restroom
line for who knows??

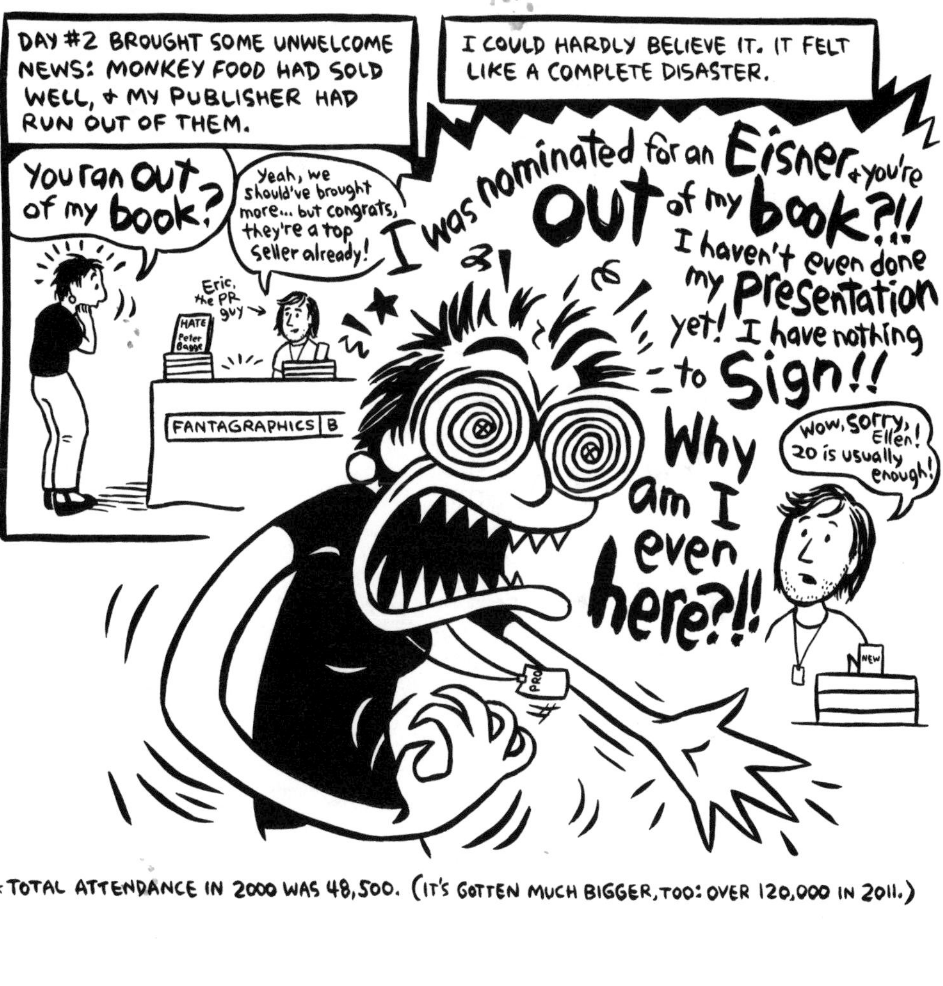

DAY #2 BROUGHT SOME UNWELCOME NEWS: MONKEY FOOD HAD SOLD WELL, & MY PUBLISHER HAD RUN OUT OF THEM.
I COULD HARDLY BELIEVE IT. IT FELT LIKE A COMPLETE DISASTER.
You ran OUT of my book?
Yeah, we should've brought more... but congrats, they're a top seller already!
Eric, the PR guy
HATE Peter Bagge
FANTAGRAPHICS B
I was nominated for an Eisner & you're OUT of my book?!! I haven't even done my Presentation yet! I have nothing to Sign!!
Why am I even here?!!
Wow, sorry, Ellen! 20 is usually enough!
PRO
NEW

*TOTAL ATTENDANCE IN 2000 WAS 48,500. (IT'S GOTTEN MUCH BIGGER, TOO: OVER 120,000 IN 2011.)

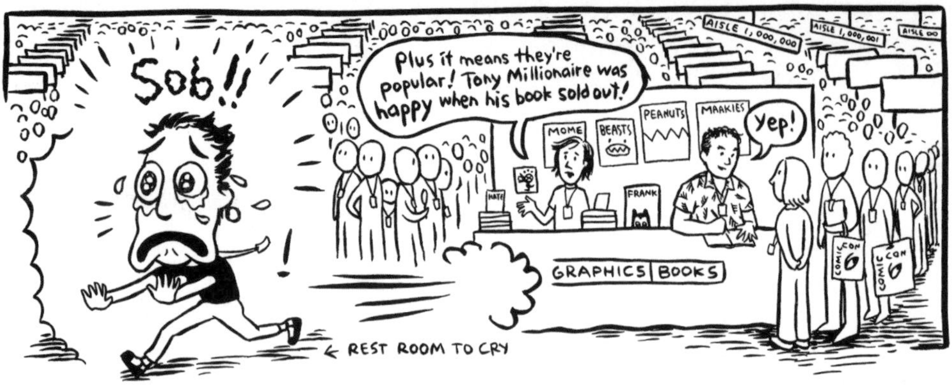
AISLE 1,000,000
AISLE 1,000,001
AISLE ∞
Sob!!
Plus it means they're popular! Tony Millionaire was happy when his book sold out!
MOME
BEASTS
PEANUTS
MAAKIES
Yep!
HATE
FRANK
GRAPHICS BOOKS
COMIC CON
COMIC CON
← REST ROOM TO CRY

I ELBOWED MY WAY THROUGH THE CROWDS TO BUY A FEW OF MY BOOKS TO SELL AT NO PROFIT. I WAS A DEVASTATED, INDIGNANT MESS FOR THE REST OF THE WEEKEND. I GOT SYMPATHY TOO, BUT I WAS INCONSOLABLE, + COULDN'T LET IT GO.

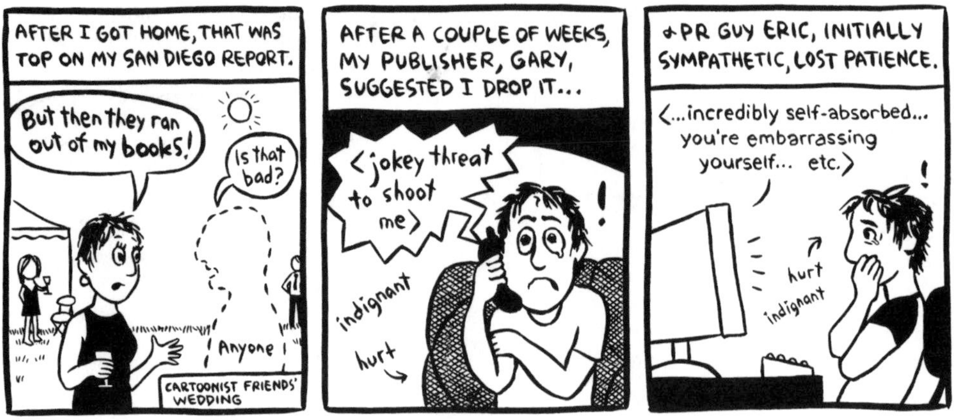
AFTER I GOT HOME, THAT WAS TOP ON MY SAN DIEGO REPORT.
But then they ran out of my books!
Is that bad?
Anyone
CARTOONIST FRIENDS' WEDDING
AFTER A COUPLE OF WEEKS, MY PUBLISHER, GARY, SUGGESTED I DROP IT...
<jokey threat to shoot me>
indignant
hurt
+ PR GUY ERIC, INITIALLY SYMPATHETIC, LOST PATIENCE.
<...incredibly self-absorbed... you're embarrassing yourself... etc.>
hurt
indignant

I KNEW THAT "PERSEVERATING," THE INABILITY TO LET SOMETHING GO, IS A SYMPTOM. BUT I HAD A GOOD, SANE REASON TO BE UPSET! IT WAS CONFUSING. EVENTUALLY, EVEN I GOT TIRED OF LISTENING TO MYSELF COMPLAIN, + I MANAGED TO REIN MYSELF IN.

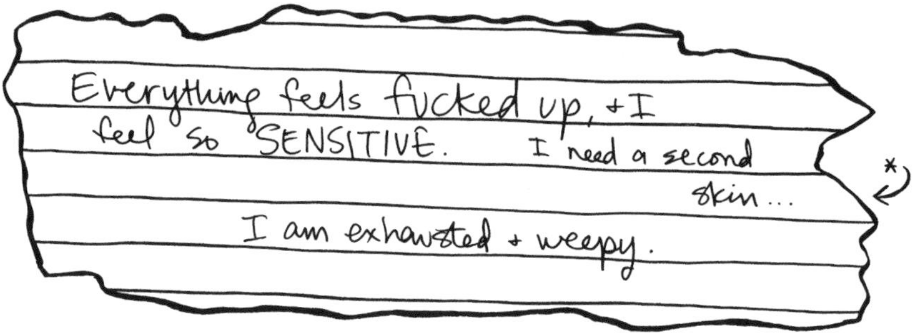
Everything feels fucked up, + I feel so SENSITIVE. I need a second skin...
I am exhausted + weepy.
*

NOTE: THE VERY DESERVING TONY MILLIONAIRE WON THE EISNER IN OUR CATEGORY.
* SONG BY THE GITS. I HIGHLY RECOMMEND IT WHEN YOU'RE FEELING TERRIBLE!

ONE FRUSTRATING THING ABOUT BIPOLAR DISORDER, & WHY IT CAN BE DIFFICULT TO TELL IF A FEELING IS "NORMAL" OR NOT, IS THAT EPISODES CAN OFTEN BE TRIGGERED BY VERY REAL STRESSES – FALLING IN LOVE, A DEATH IN THE FAMILY.

WHEN ARE EMOTIONS "OUT OF NORMAL RANGE"?

IT CAN BE HARD TO TELL FROM THE INSIDE.

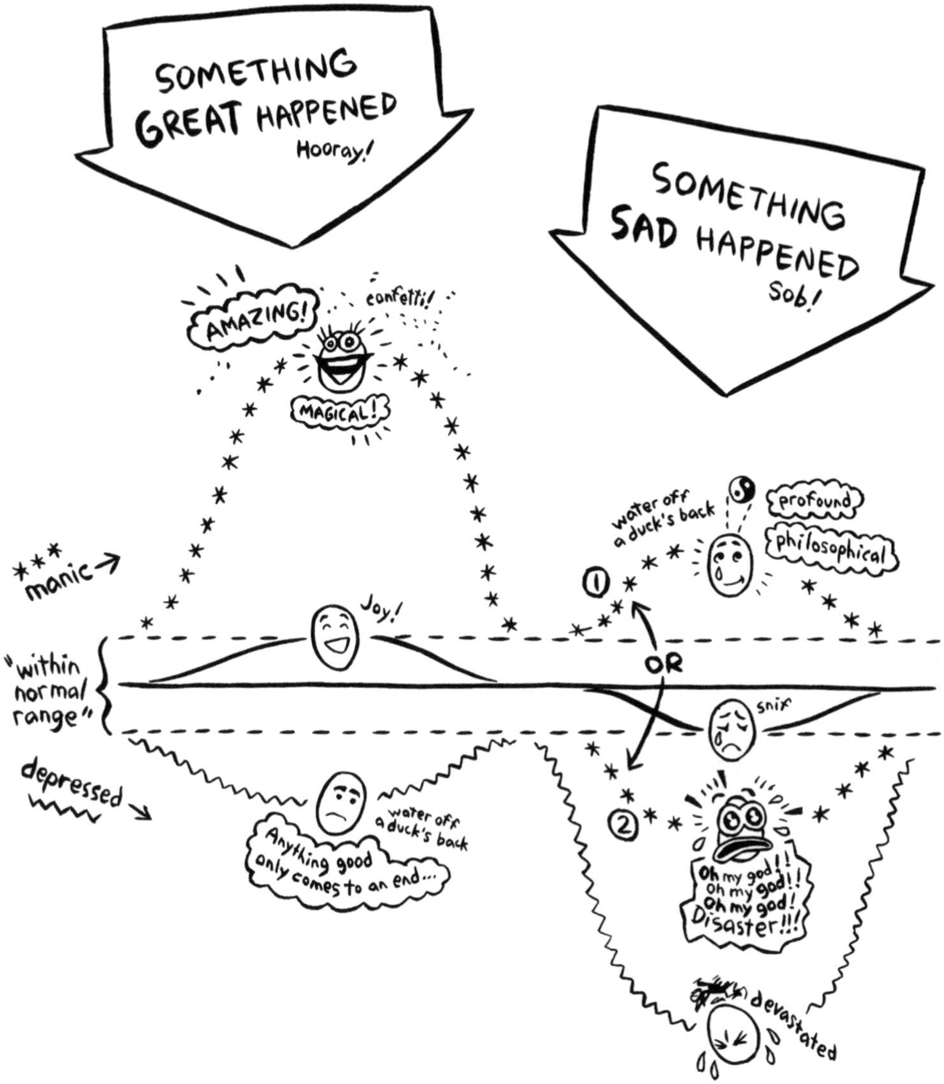
SOMETHING GREAT HAPPENED
Hooray!
SOMETHING SAD HAPPENED
Sob!
AMAZING!
confetti!
MAGICAL!
manic
Joy!
"within normal range"
depressed
water off a duck's back
Anything good only comes to an end...
water off a duck's back
profound
philosophical
①
OR
snif
②
Oh my god!! Oh my god!! Oh my god! Disaster!!!
devastated

IT WAS SUCKY THAT I DIDN'T HAVE BOOKS AT SAN DIEGO, IT WAS A BIG DEAL TO ME – BUT INSTEAD OF BEING UPSETTING, IT WAS A CATASTROPHE.

IT WAS STRANGE NOT KNOWING IF I WAS UP OR DOWN.
HOW COULD THAT NOT BE **CLEAR**?

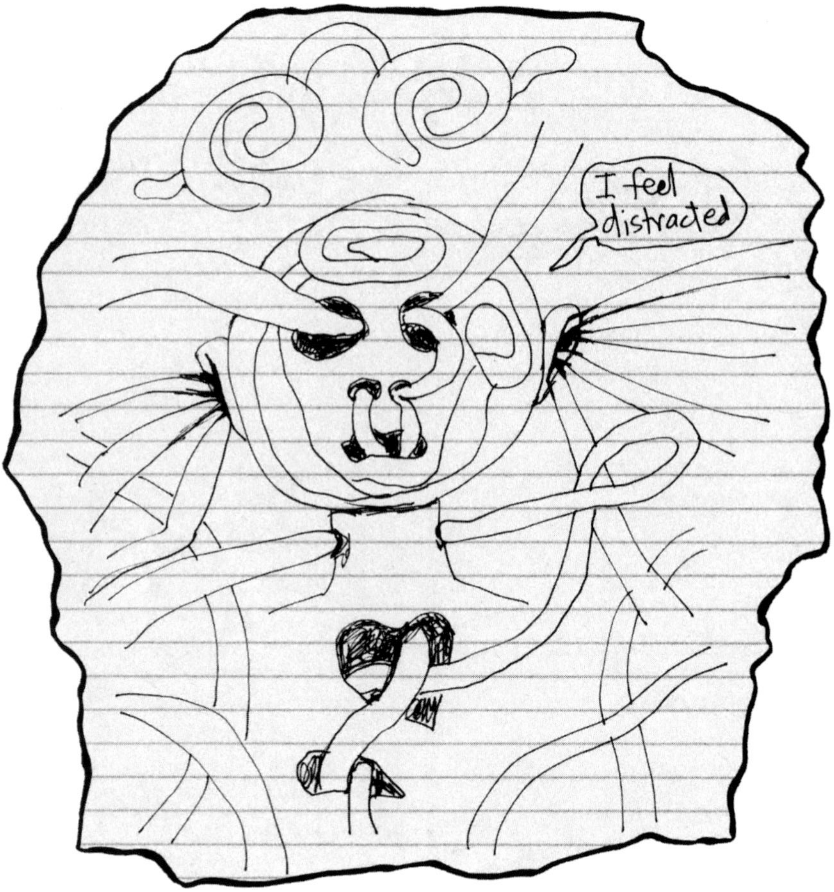
I feel distracted

I WAS SIDEWAYS, I WAS UPSIDE-DOWN.

TOO ENERGETIC TO BE DEPRESSED,
TOO ANXIOUS & SAD TO BE MANIC.

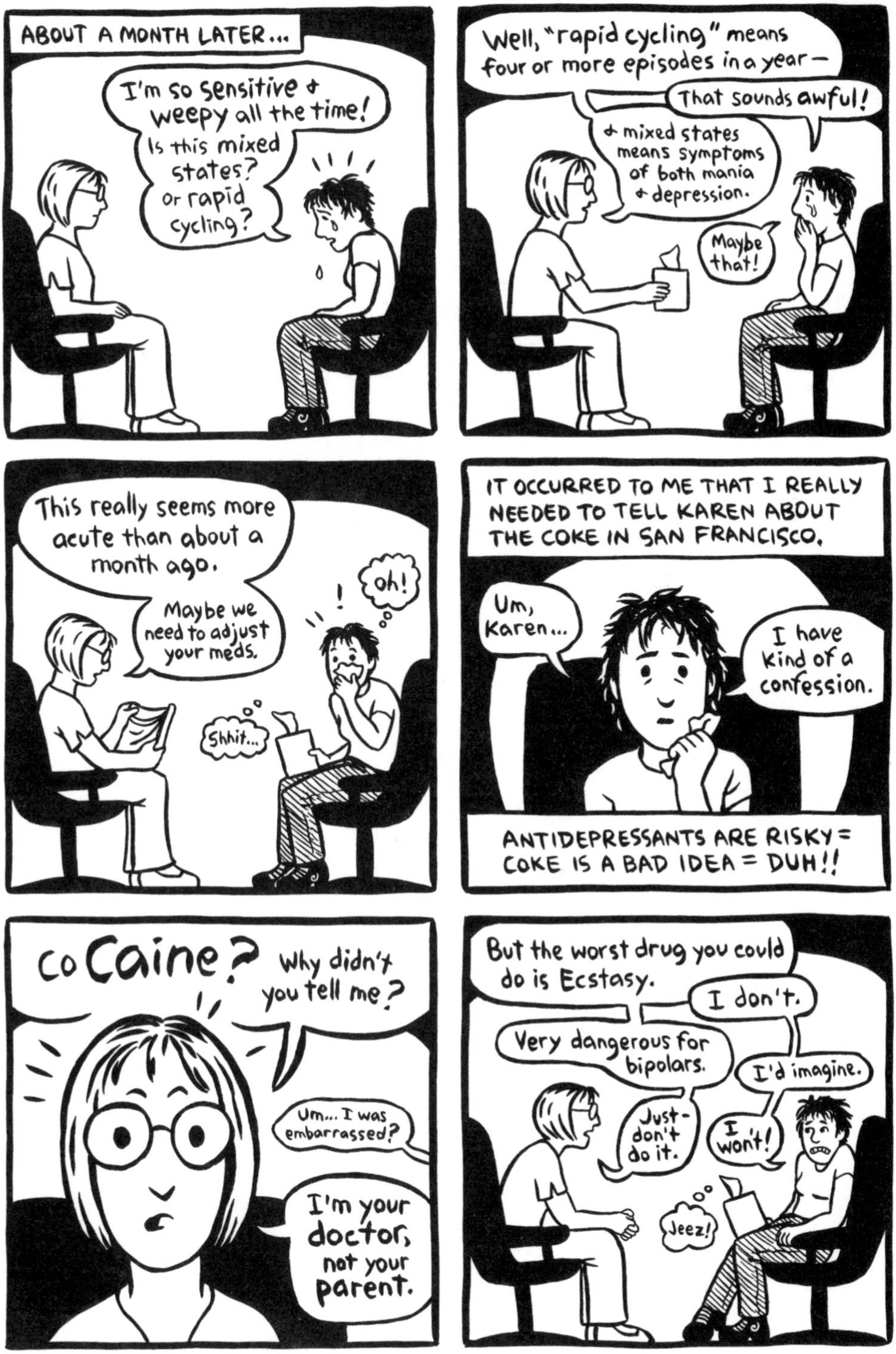
ABOUT A MONTH LATER...
I'm so sensitive & weepy all the time! Is this mixed states? or rapid cycling?
Well, "rapid cycling" means four or more episodes in a year —
That sounds awful!
& mixed states means symptoms of both mania & depression.
Maybe that!
This really seems more acute than about a month ago.
Maybe we need to adjust your meds.
oh!
Shhit...
IT OCCURRED TO ME THAT I REALLY NEEDED TO TELL KAREN ABOUT THE COKE IN SAN FRANCISCO.
Um, Karen...
I have kind of a confession.
ANTIDEPRESSANTS ARE RISKY = COKE IS A BAD IDEA = DUH!!
CoCaine?
Why didn't you tell me?
Um... I was embarrassed?
I'm your doctor, not your parent.
But the worst drug you could do is Ecstasy.
I don't.
Very dangerous for bipolars.
I'd imagine.
Just-don't do it.
I won't!
Jeez!

NO ECSTASY, NO COKE... BUT MY RISK / BENEFIT ANALYSIS STILL POINTED TO CONTINUING TO SMOKE POT.

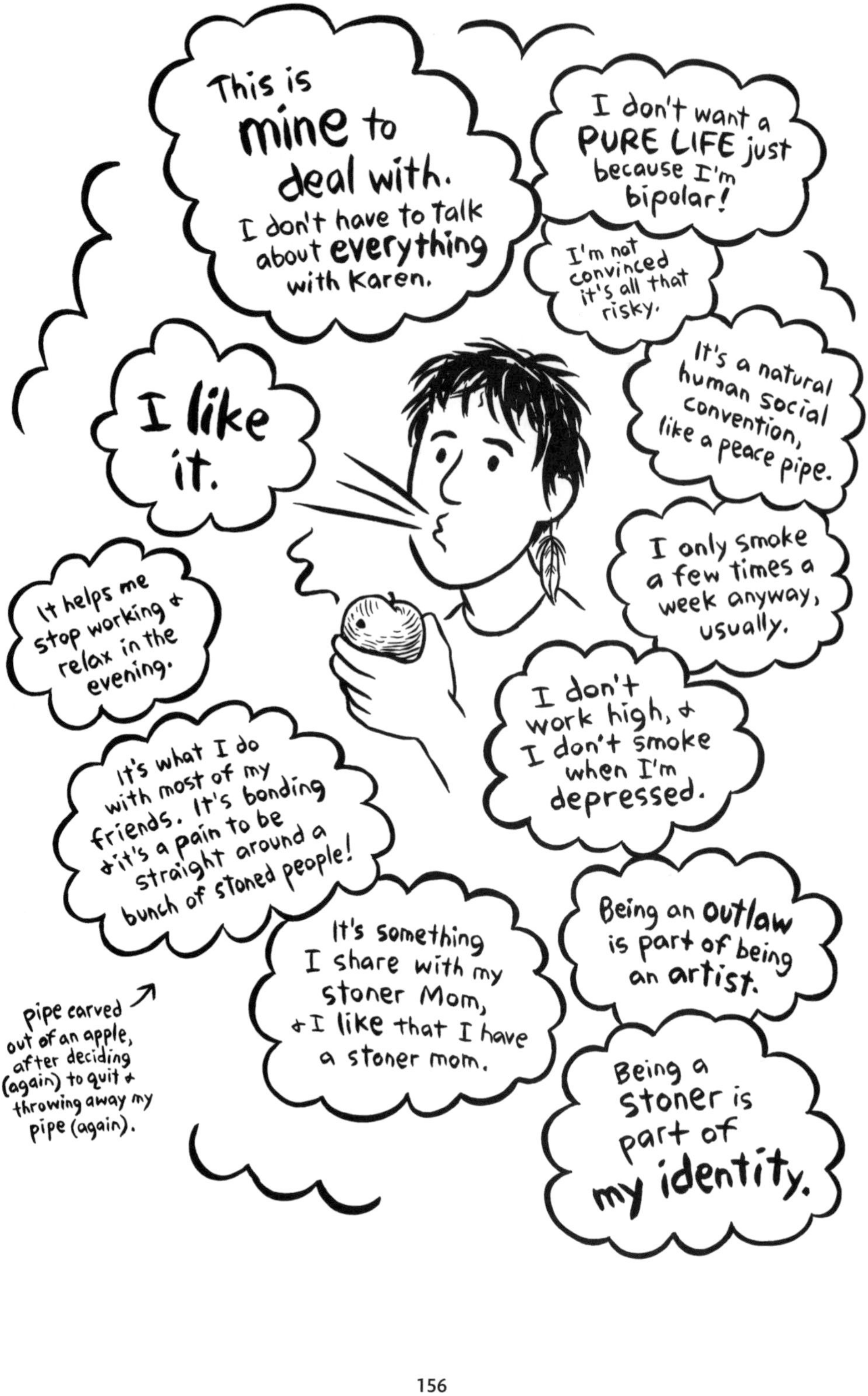
This is mine to deal with. I don't have to talk about everything with Karen.
I don't want a PURE LIFE just because I'm bipolar!
I'm not convinced it's all that risky.
I like it.
It's a natural human social convention, like a peace pipe.
I only smoke a few times a week anyway, usually.
It helps me stop working & relax in the evening.
I don't work high, & I don't smoke when I'm depressed.
It's what I do with most of my friends. It's bonding & it's a pain to be straight around a bunch of stoned people!
It's something I share with my stoner Mom, & I like that I have a stoner mom.
Being an outlaw is part of being an artist.
Being a stoner is part of my identity.
pipe carved out of an apple, after deciding (again) to quit & throwing away my pipe (again).

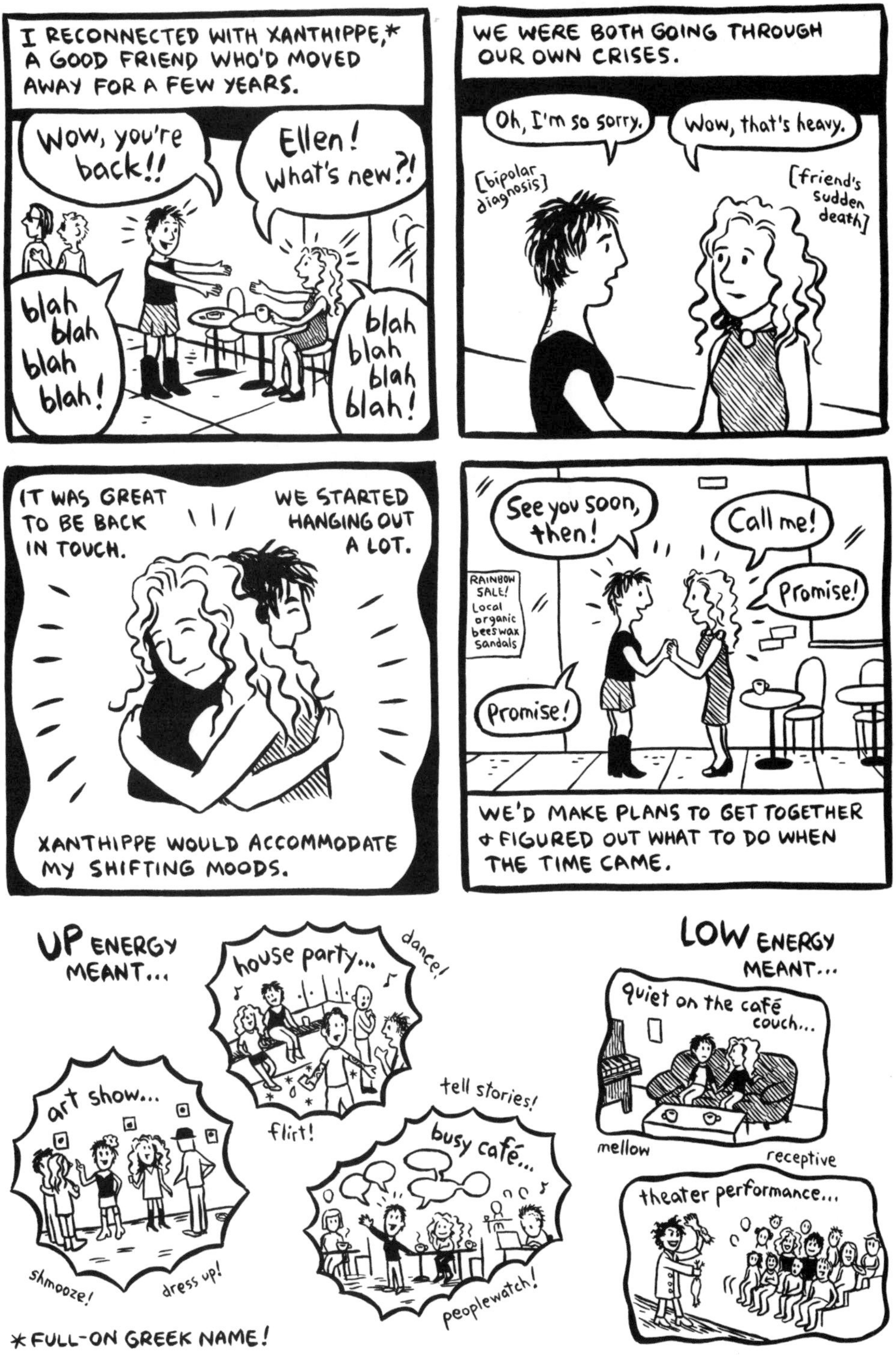
I RECONNECTED WITH XANTHIPPE,* A GOOD FRIEND WHO'D MOVED AWAY FOR A FEW YEARS.
Wow, you're back!!
Ellen! What's new?!
blah blah blah blah!
blah blah blah blah!
WE WERE BOTH GOING THROUGH OUR OWN CRISES.
Oh, I'm so sorry.
Wow, that's heavy.
[bipolar diagnosis]
[friend's sudden death]
IT WAS GREAT TO BE BACK IN TOUCH.
WE STARTED HANGING OUT A LOT.
XANTHIPPE WOULD ACCOMMODATE MY SHIFTING MOODS.
See you soon, then!
Call me!
Promise!
Promise!
RAINBOW SALE! Local organic beeswax sandals
WE'D MAKE PLANS TO GET TOGETHER & FIGURED OUT WHAT TO DO WHEN THE TIME CAME.
UP ENERGY MEANT...
house party...
dance!
flirt!
art show...
shmooze!
dress up!
busy café...
tell stories!
peoplewatch!
LOW ENERGY MEANT...
quiet on the café couch...
mellow
receptive
theater performance...
* FULL-ON GREEK NAME!

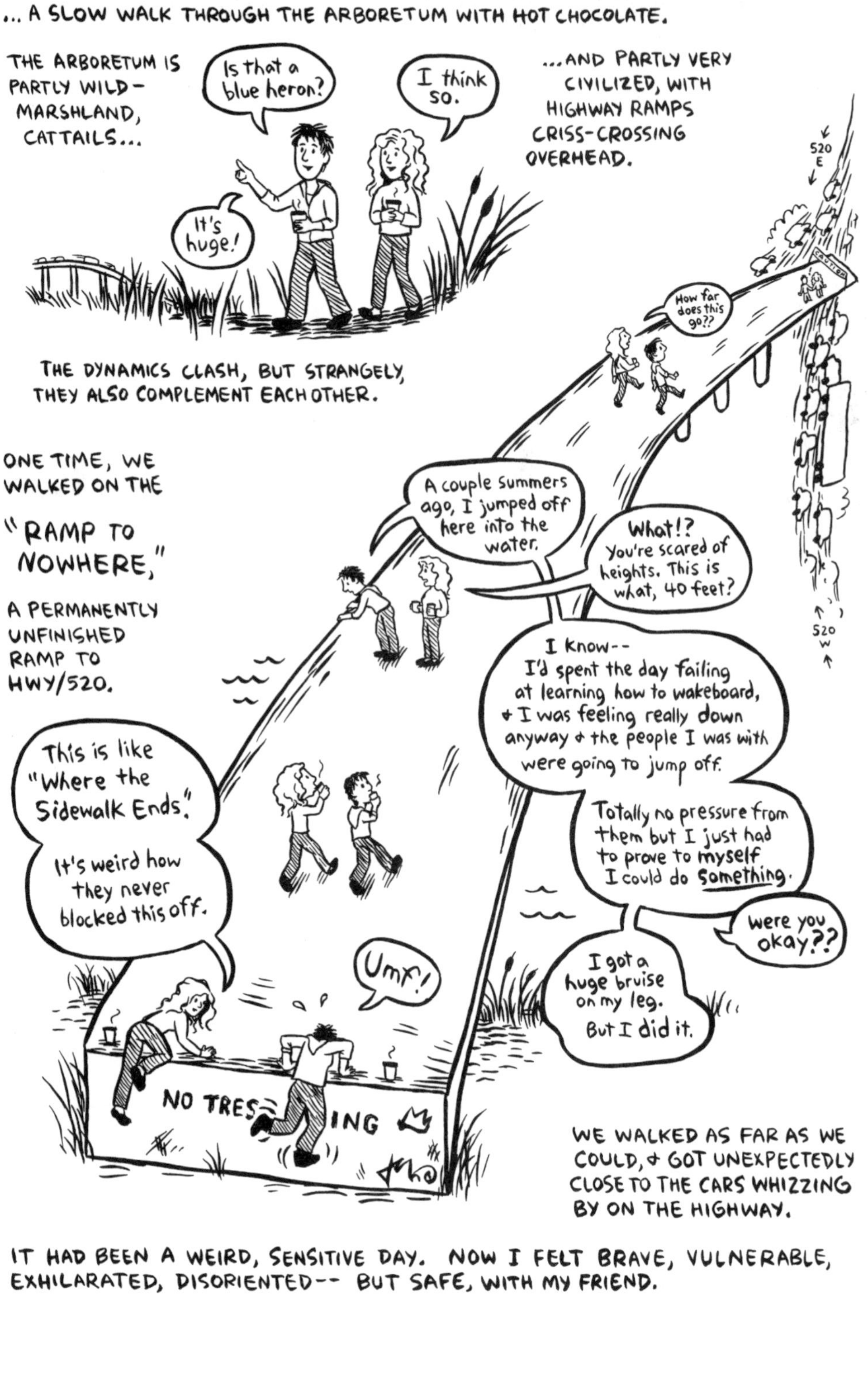
... A SLOW WALK THROUGH THE ARBORETUM WITH HOT CHOCOLATE.
THE ARBORETUM IS PARTLY WILD— MARSHLAND, CATTAILS...
Is that a blue heron?
I think so.
It's huge!
...AND PARTLY VERY CIVILIZED, WITH HIGHWAY RAMPS CRISS-CROSSING OVERHEAD.
520 E
520 W
How far does this go??
THE DYNAMICS CLASH, BUT STRANGELY, THEY ALSO COMPLEMENT EACH OTHER.
ONE TIME, WE WALKED ON THE "RAMP TO NOWHERE," A PERMANENTLY UNFINISHED RAMP TO HWY/520.
A couple summers ago, I jumped off here into the water.
What!? You're scared of heights. This is what, 40 feet?
I know-- I'd spent the day failing at learning how to wakeboard, & I was feeling really down anyway & the people I was with were going to jump off.
Totally no pressure from them but I just had to prove to myself I could do something.
Were you okay??
I got a huge bruise on my leg. But I did it.
This is like "Where the Sidewalk Ends."
It's weird how they never blocked this off.
Umf!
NO TRES ING
WE WALKED AS FAR AS WE COULD, & GOT UNEXPECTEDLY CLOSE TO THE CARS WHIZZING BY ON THE HIGHWAY.
IT HAD BEEN A WEIRD, SENSITIVE DAY. NOW I FELT BRAVE, VULNERABLE, EXHILARATED, DISORIENTED-- BUT SAFE, WITH MY FRIEND.

A YEAR AFTER SAN DIEGO, I WAS INVITED TO BE A GUEST CARTOONIST AT AN ANNUAL COMICS FESTIVAL IN PORTO, PORTUGAL, ALONG WITH A PACK OF OTHER AMERICANS (INCLUDING MEGAN, WHO WAS STILL WARY OF ME).

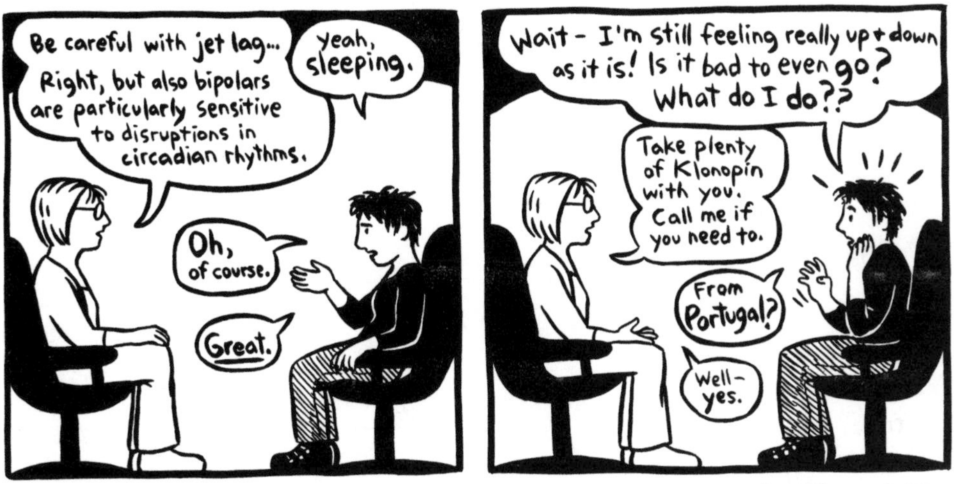
Be careful with jet lag...
Yeah, sleeping.
Right, but also bipolars are particularly sensitive to disruptions in circadian rhythms.
Oh, of course.
Great.
Wait - I'm still feeling really up + down as it is! Is it bad to even go? What do I do??
Take plenty of Klonopin with you. Call me if you need to.
From Portugal?
Well- yes.

I TOOK MY PILLBOX + MY JOURNAL TO CARRY AROUND WITH ME, + OFF I WENT. THE XI SALÃO INTERNACIONAL DE BANDA DESENHADA DO PORTO WAS IN A BEAUTIFUL OLD CAVERNOUS BUILDING IN THE CENTER OF THE CITY,

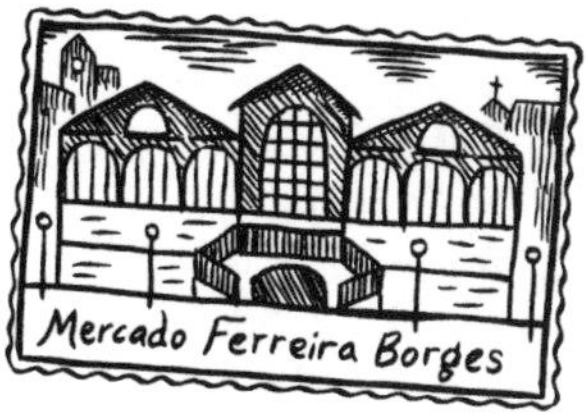
Mercado Ferreira Borges

AND THE INTERIOR WAS A LABYRINTH OF COLORFUL FREE-STANDING WALLS.

I GOT LOST REPEATEDLY, HAPPILY.

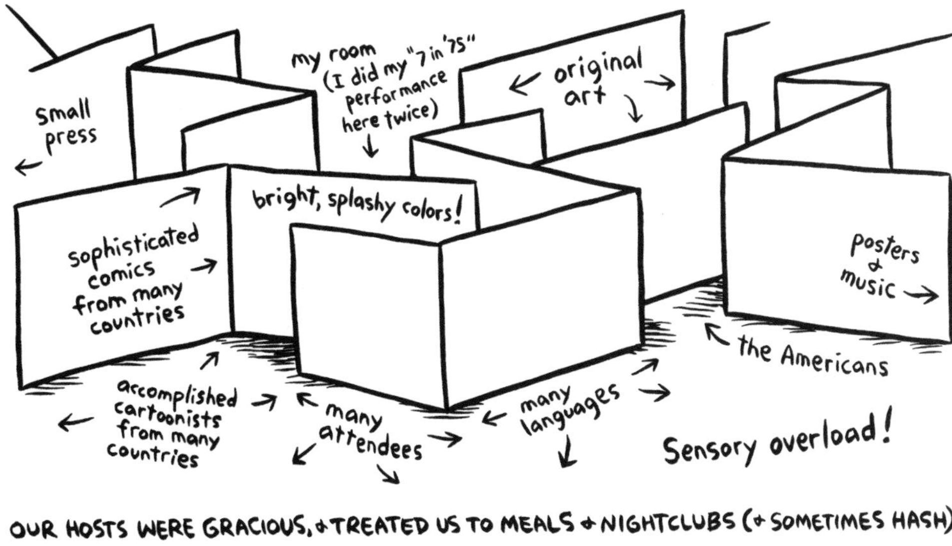
small press
my room (I did my "7 in '75" performance here twice)
original art
bright, splashy colors!
sophisticated comics from many countries
posters + music
the Americans
accomplished cartoonists from many countries
many attendees
many languages
Sensory overload!

OUR HOSTS WERE GRACIOUS, + TREATED US TO MEALS + NIGHTCLUBS (+ SOMETIMES HASH).

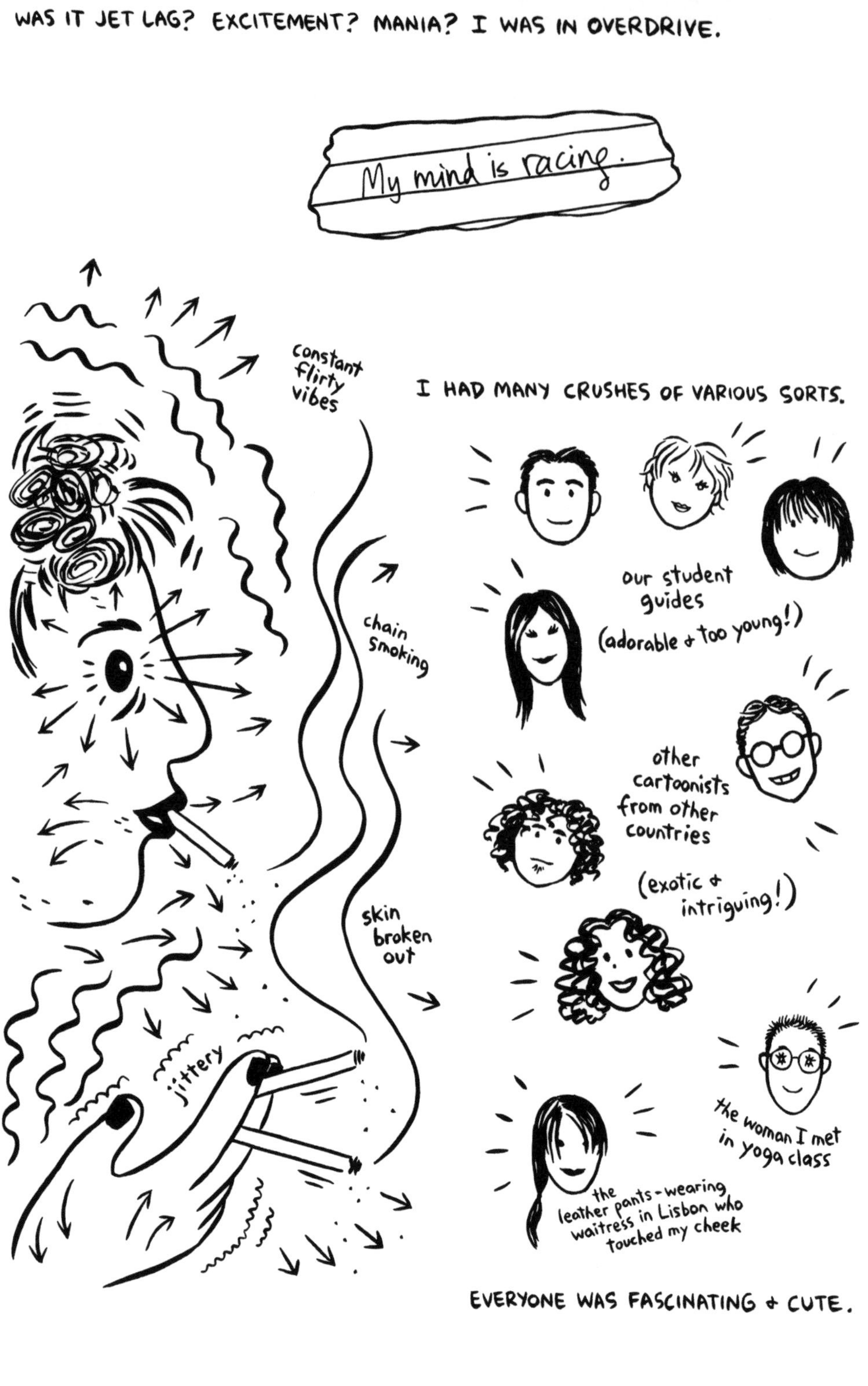
WAS IT JET LAG? EXCITEMENT? MANIA? I WAS IN OVERDRIVE.
My mind is racing.
constant flirty vibes
chain smoking
skin broken out
jittery
I HAD MANY CRUSHES OF VARIOUS SORTS.
our student guides (adorable + too young!)
other cartoonists from other countries (exotic + intriguing!)
the woman I met in yoga class
the leather pants-wearing waitress in Lisbon who touched my cheek
EVERYONE WAS FASCINATING + CUTE.

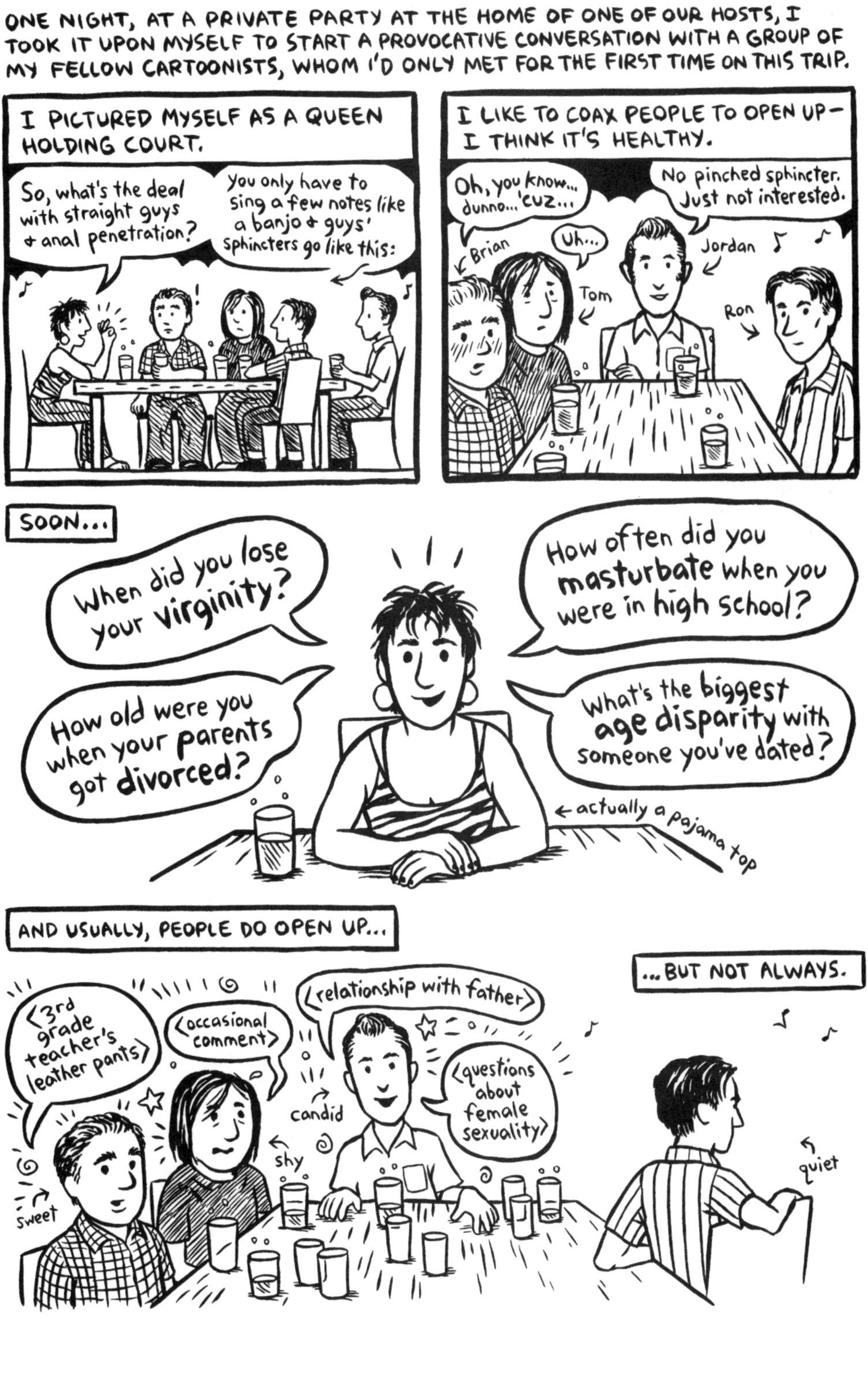
ONE NIGHT, AT A PRIVATE PARTY AT THE HOME OF ONE OF OUR HOSTS, I TOOK IT UPON MYSELF TO START A PROVOCATIVE CONVERSATION WITH A GROUP OF MY FELLOW CARTOONISTS, WHOM I'D ONLY MET FOR THE FIRST TIME ON THIS TRIP.
I PICTURED MYSELF AS A QUEEN HOLDING COURT.
So, what's the deal with straight guys & anal penetration?
You only have to sing a few notes like a banjo & guys' sphincters go like this:
I LIKE TO COAX PEOPLE TO OPEN UP— I THINK IT'S HEALTHY.
Oh, you know... dunno... 'cuz...
No pinched sphincter. Just not interested.
Brian
Uh...
Jordan
Tom
Ron
SOON...
When did you lose your virginity?
How often did you masturbate when you were in high school?
How old were you when your parents got divorced?
What's the biggest age disparity with someone you've dated?
actually a pajama top
AND USUALLY, PEOPLE DO OPEN UP...
...BUT NOT ALWAYS.
<3rd grade teacher's leather pants>
<occasional comment>
<relationship with father>
<questions about female sexuality>
candid
shy
sweet
quiet

SITTING AT MY TABLE AT THE CONVENTION, I DREW UNCHARACTERISTICALLY WEIRD CHARACTERS IN MY SKETCHBOOK.

I TOOK KLONOPIN ALL DAY LONG, EVERY DAY.

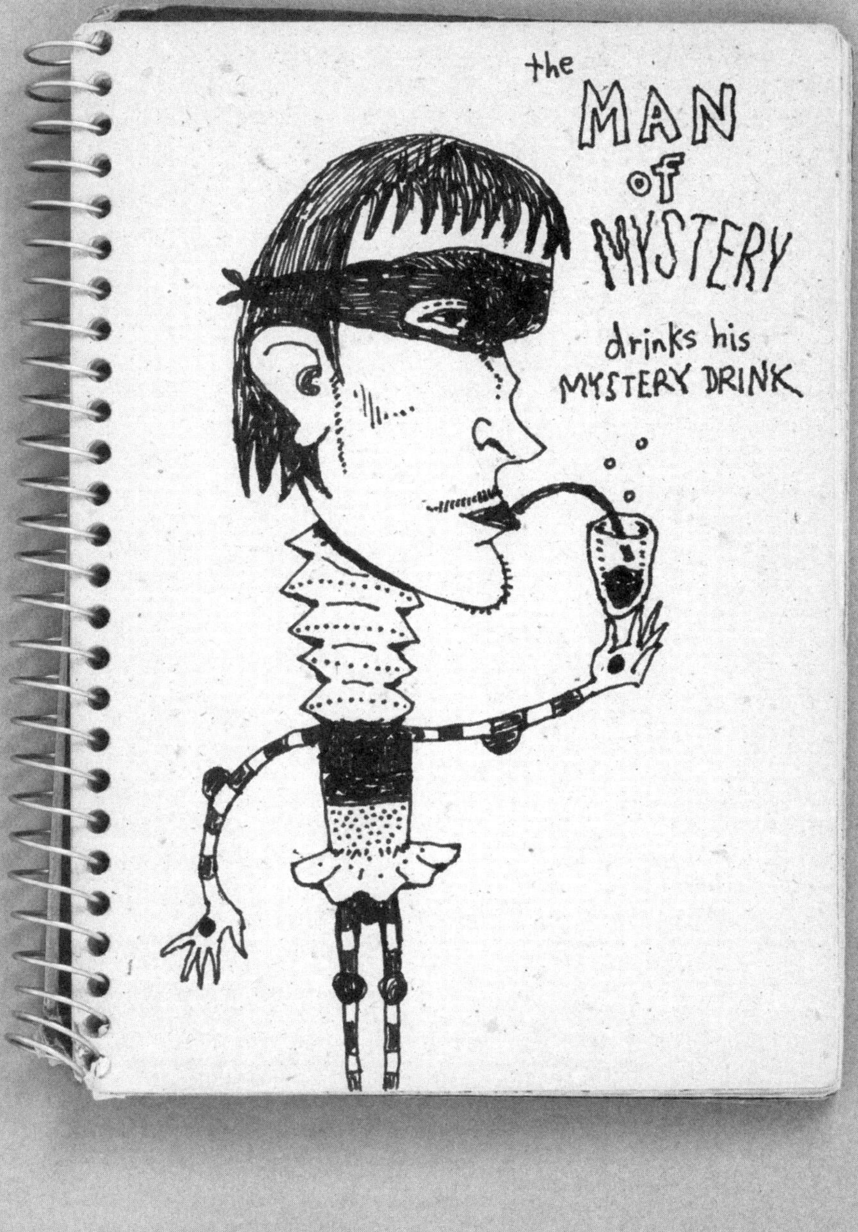
the MAN of MYSTERY
drinks his MYSTERY DRINK

I GAVE ONE OF MY DRAWINGS TO A NON-ENGLISH-SPEAKING LOCAL IN A SECOND-HAND SHOP. (WE WERE SIMULTANEOUSLY EYING THE SAME HANDMADE SKIRT & SHE LET ME HAVE IT.) IT FELT LIKE AN INTENSE CROSS-CULTURAL MOMENT, PERFECT & PROFOUND--

-- A GLIMPSE OF THE DAZZLING NETWORK OF CONNECTIONS THAT BIND THE UNIVERSE.

BREATHTAKING.

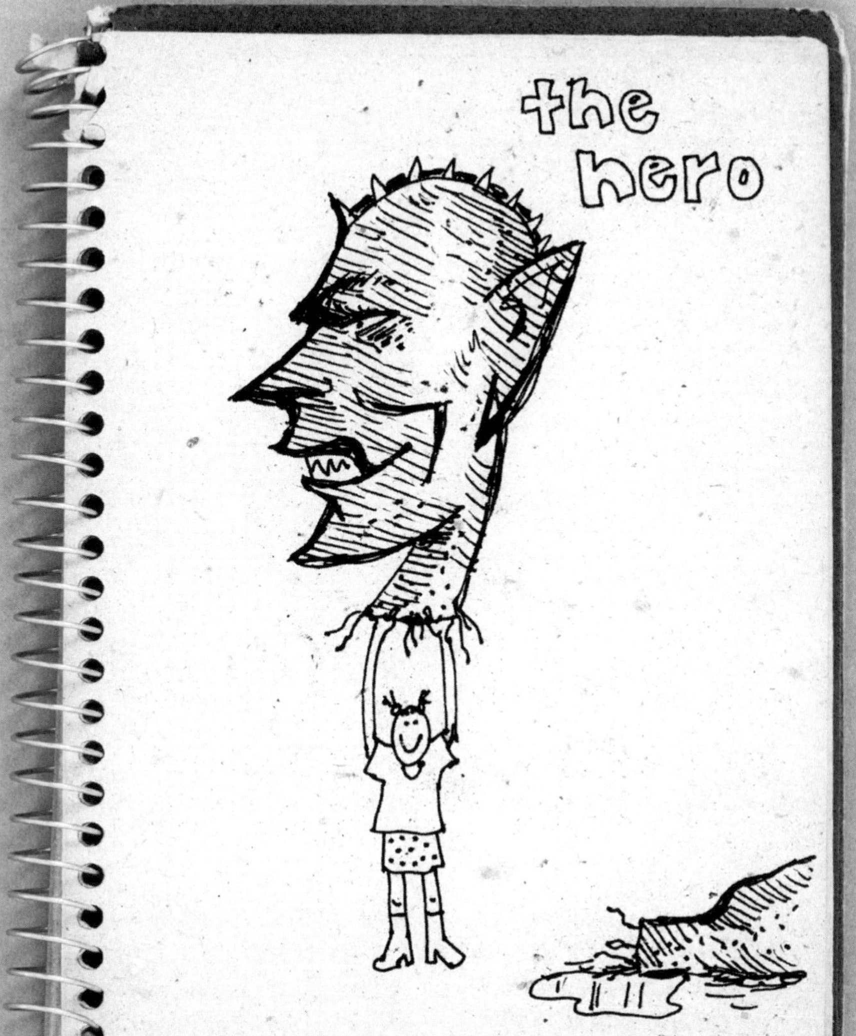
the
hero

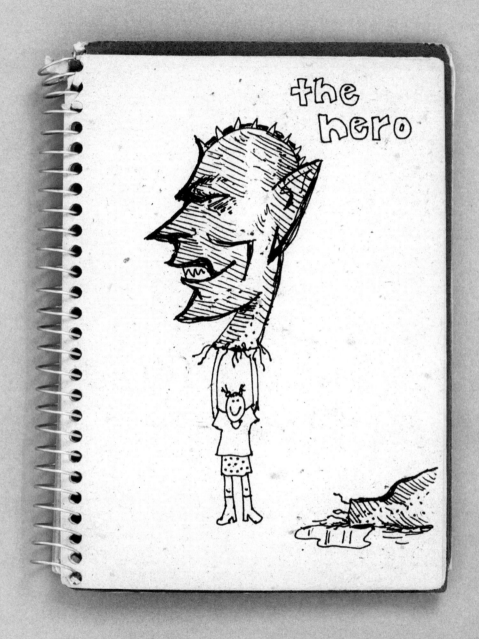

MY MIND WOULD TUMBLE OVER ITSELF
& MY BRAIN WOULD FEEL HOT,

LIKE A CAR WHEEL SPINNING ON
ASPHALT & GENERATING HEAT,

& I'D TAKE MORE KLONOPIN.

DAD MET ME IN PHILADELPHIA DURING MY LAYOVER
ON THE WAY HOME, & WE TOASTED OUR WHISKEYS IN
THE LOUNGE OF A NEARBY HOTEL.

IT WAS A RELIEF TO GET HOME TO SEATTLE. I WAS EXHAUSTED.

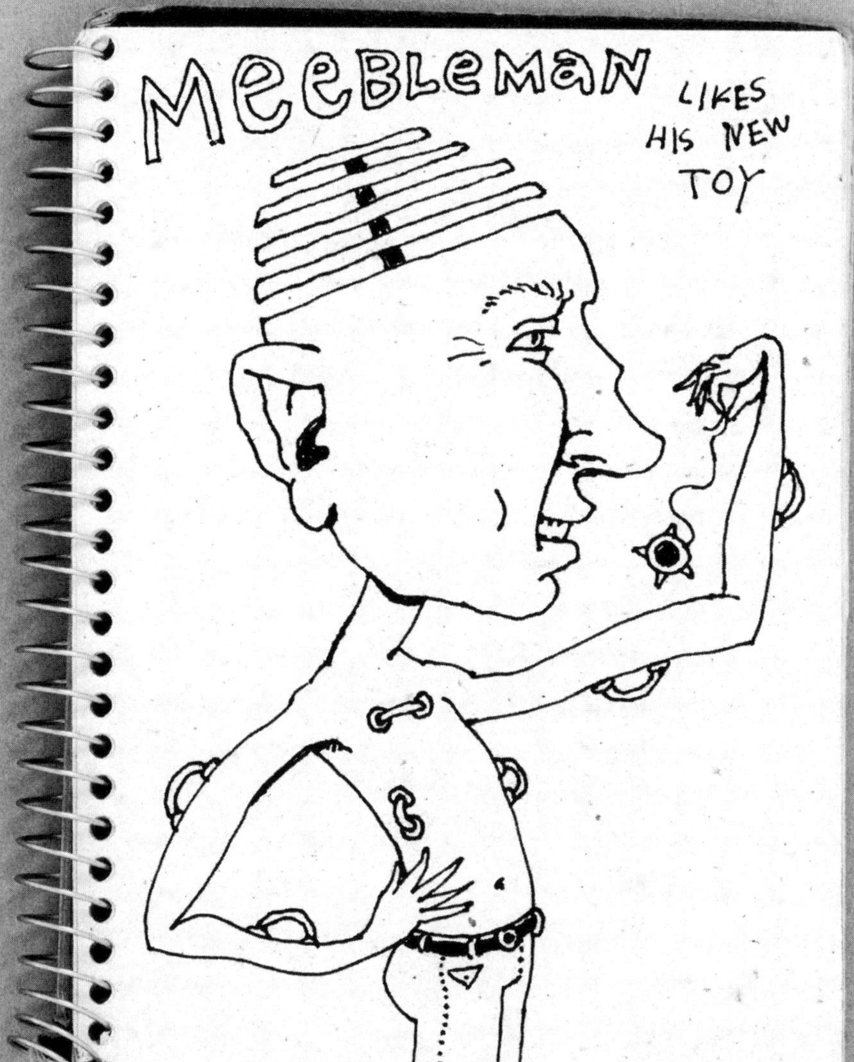
MEEBLEMAN
LIKES
HIS NEW
TOY

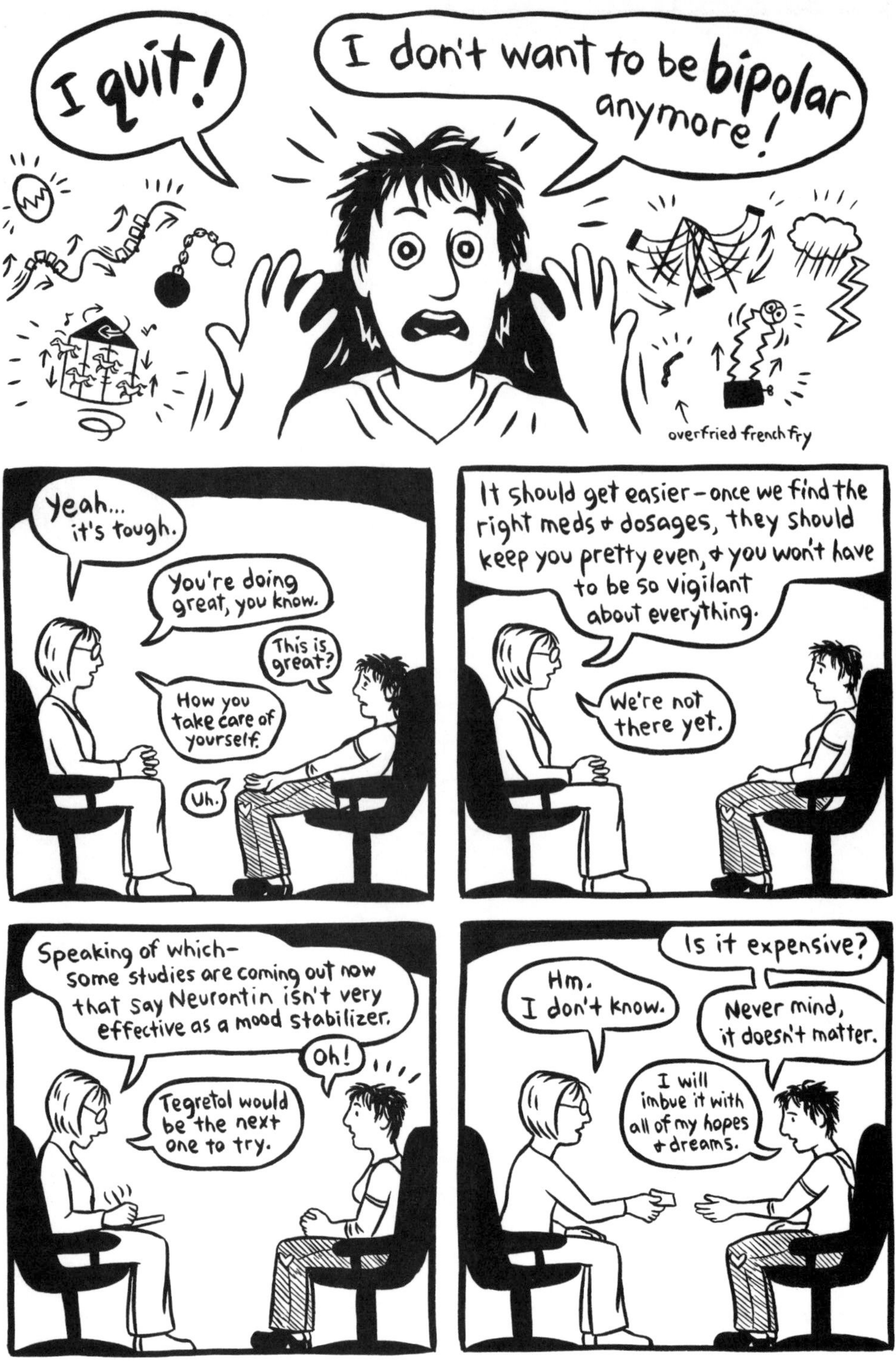

I quit!
I don't want to be bipolar anymore!
overfried french fry
Yeah... it's tough.
You're doing great, you know.
This is great?
How you take care of yourself.
Uh.
It should get easier – once we find the right meds & dosages, they should keep you pretty even, & you won't have to be so vigilant about everything.
We're not there yet.
Speaking of which– some studies are coming out now that say Neurontin isn't very effective as a mood stabilizer.
Oh!
Tegretol would be the next one to try.
Is it expensive?
Hm. I don't know.
Never mind, it doesn't matter.
I will imbue it with all of my hopes & dreams.

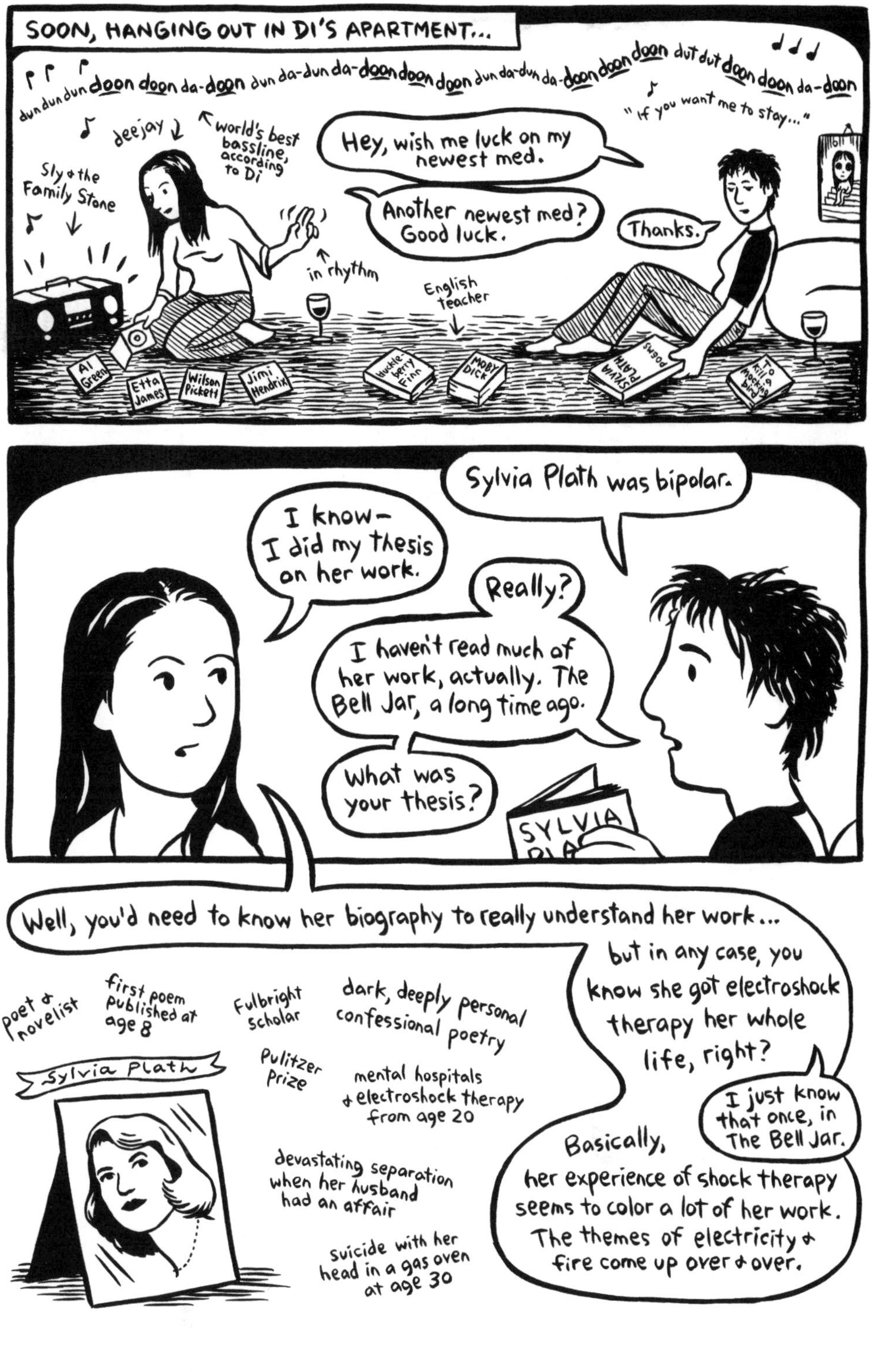
SOON, HANGING OUT IN DI'S APARTMENT...
dun dun dun doon doon da-doon dun da-dun da-doon doon doon dun da-dun da-doon doon doon dut dut doon doon da-doon
"If you want me to stay..."
deejay
world's best bassline, according to Di
Sly & the Family Stone
in rhythm
English teacher
Al Green
Etta James
Wilson Pickett
Jimi Hendrix
Huckleberry Finn
MOBY DICK
SYLVIA PLATH Poems
To Kill a mocking bird
Hey, wish me luck on my newest med.
Another newest med? Good luck.
Thanks.
Sylvia Plath was bipolar.
I know— I did my thesis on her work.
Really?
I haven't read much of her work, actually. The Bell Jar, a long time ago.
What was your thesis?
SYLVIA
Well, you'd need to know her biography to really understand her work...
but in any case, you know she got electroshock therapy her whole life, right?
I just know that once, in The Bell Jar.
Basically, her experience of shock therapy seems to color a lot of her work. The themes of electricity & fire come up over & over.
Sylvia Plath
poet & novelist
first poem published at age 8
Fulbright scholar
dark, deeply personal confessional poetry
Pulitzer Prize
mental hospitals & electroshock therapy from age 20
devastating separation when her husband had an affair
suicide with her head in a gas oven at age 30

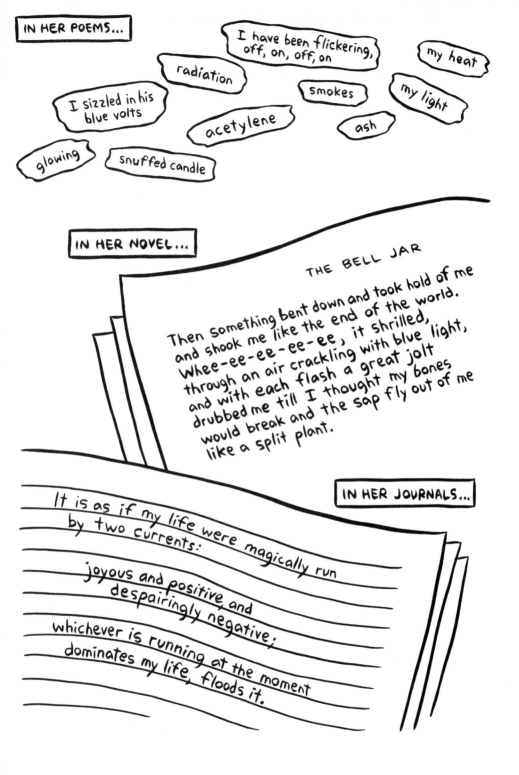

IN HER POEMS...

I have been flickering, off, on, off, on

my heat

radiation

smokes

my light

I sizzled in his blue volts

acetylene

ash

glowing

snuffed candle

IN HER NOVEL...

THE BELL JAR

Then something bent down and took hold of me and shook me like the end of the world. Whee-ee-ee-ee-ee, it shrilled, through an air crackling with blue light, and with each flash a great jolt drubbed me till I thought my bones would break and the sap fly out of me like a split plant.

IN HER JOURNALS...

It is as if my life were magically run by two currents: joyous and positive, and despairingly negative; whichever is running at the moment dominates my life, floods it.

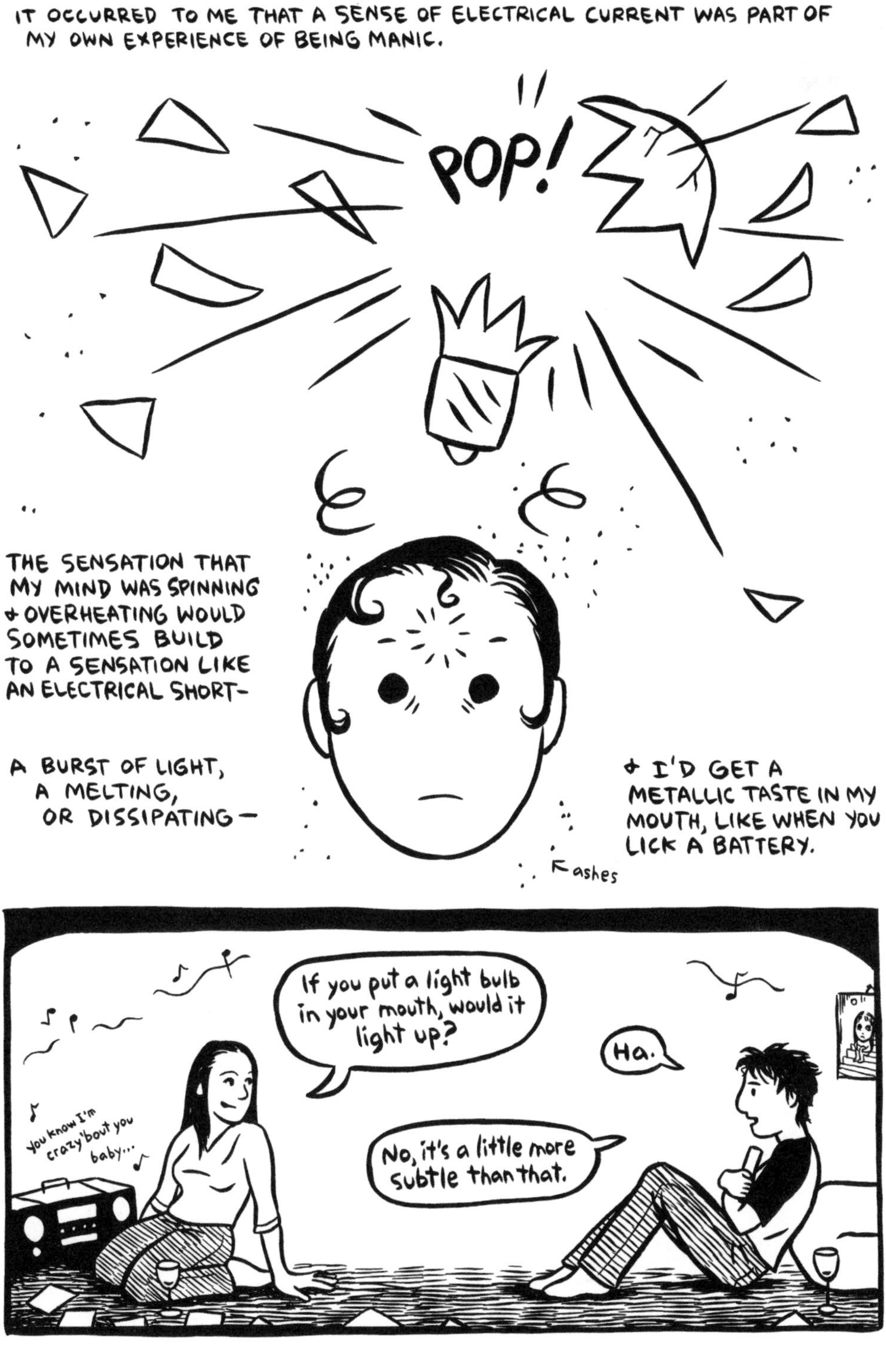
IT OCCURRED TO ME THAT A SENSE OF ELECTRICAL CURRENT WAS PART OF MY OWN EXPERIENCE OF BEING MANIC.
POP!
THE SENSATION THAT MY MIND WAS SPINNING & OVERHEATING WOULD SOMETIMES BUILD TO A SENSATION LIKE AN ELECTRICAL SHORT-
A BURST OF LIGHT, A MELTING, OR DISSIPATING —
& I'D GET A METALLIC TASTE IN MY MOUTH, LIKE WHEN YOU LICK A BATTERY.
ashes
you know I'm crazy 'bout you baby...
If you put a light bulb in your mouth, would it light up?
Ha.
No, it's a little more subtle than that.

I WAITED TO SEE IF THE TEGRETOL WOULD KICK IN. MY MIND WAS STILL SPINNING.

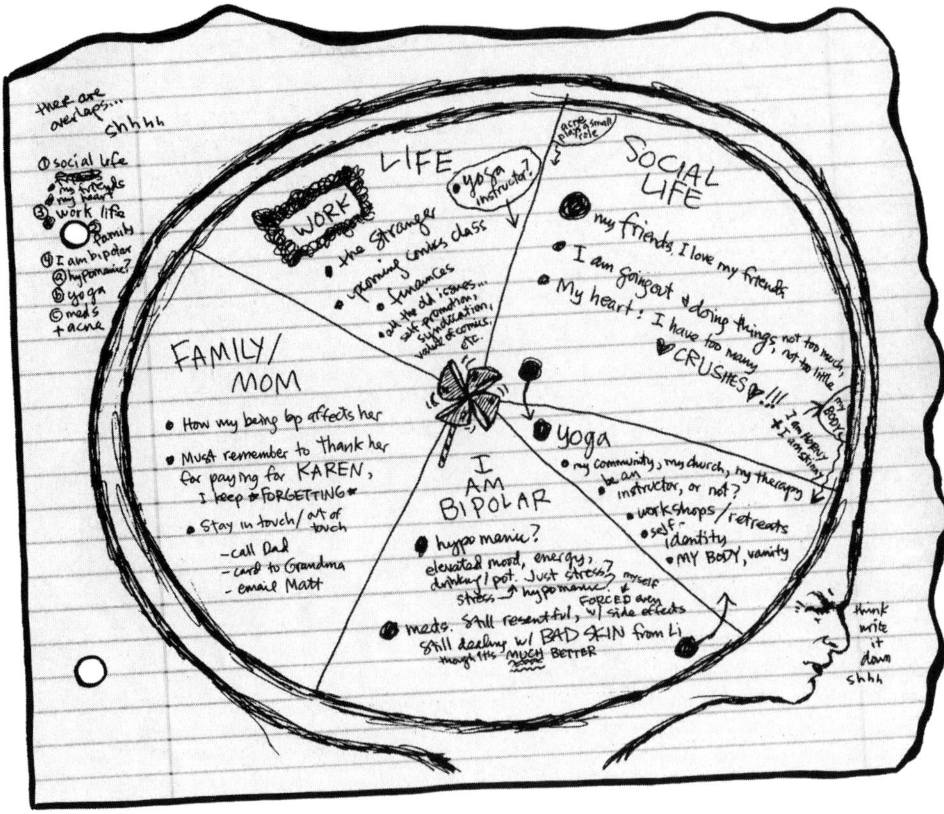
there are overlaps... shhhh
① social life
my friends
my heart
③ work life
family
④ I am bipolar
ⓐ hypomanic?
ⓑ yoga
ⓒ meds + acne
LIFE
WORK
yoga instructor?
the Stranger
upcoming comics class
finances
all the old issues... self promotion, syndication, value of comics, etc.
acne plays a small role
SOCIAL LIFE
my friends, I love my friends
I am going out & doing things, not too much, not too little
My heart! I have too many ♥CRUSHES♥!!!
my BODY
I am happy & I am skinny
FAMILY/ MOM
How my being bp affects her
Must remember to thank her for paying for KAREN, I keep FORGETTING
Stay in touch/out of touch
-call Dad
-card to Grandma
-email Matt
I AM BIPOLAR
hypomanic?
elevated mood, energy, drinking/pot. Just stress?
stress → hypomania
myself
FORCED every
meds. Still resentful, w/ side effects
Still dealing w/ BAD SKIN from Li though it's MUCH BETTER
yoga
my community, my church, my therapy
be an instructor, or not?
workshops/retreats
self-identity
MY BODY, vanity
think write it down shhh

I DIDN'T REALLY FEEL "UP" OR "DOWN"—MOSTLY EXTREMELY RESTLESS & ANXIOUS & OVERWHELMED.

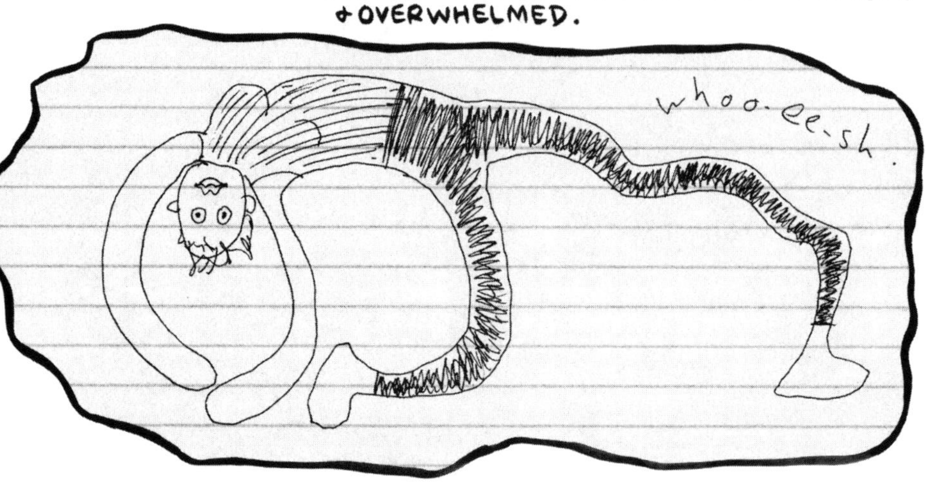
whoo-ee-sh

I STARTED HAVING TROUBLE ORGASMING,
& SOON COULDN'T AT ALL- A COMMON
SIDE EFFECT OF MANY PSYCH MEDS.

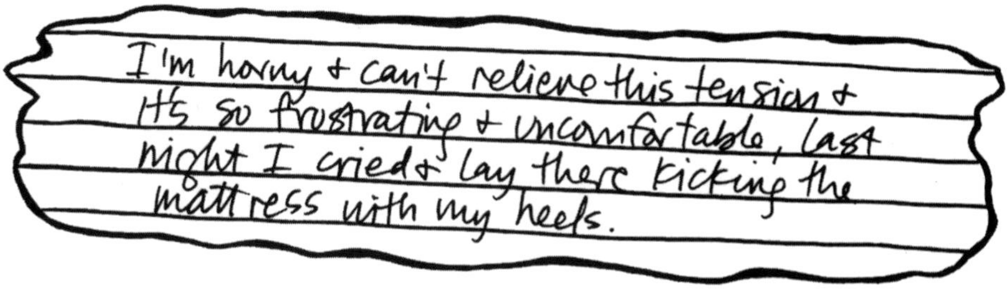
I'm horny & can't relieve this tension & it's so frustrating & uncomfortable, last night I cried & lay there kicking the mattress with my heels.

MY MOOD SWINGS WEREN'T EXTREME, BUT IT
WAS A STRUGGLE TO KEEP MYSELF GROUNDED.

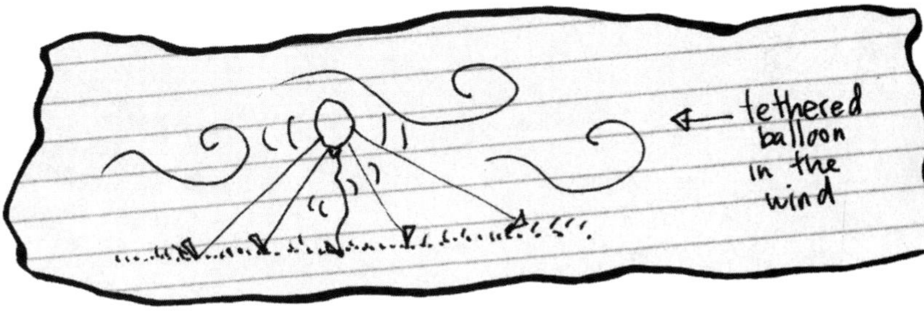
tethered balloon in the wind

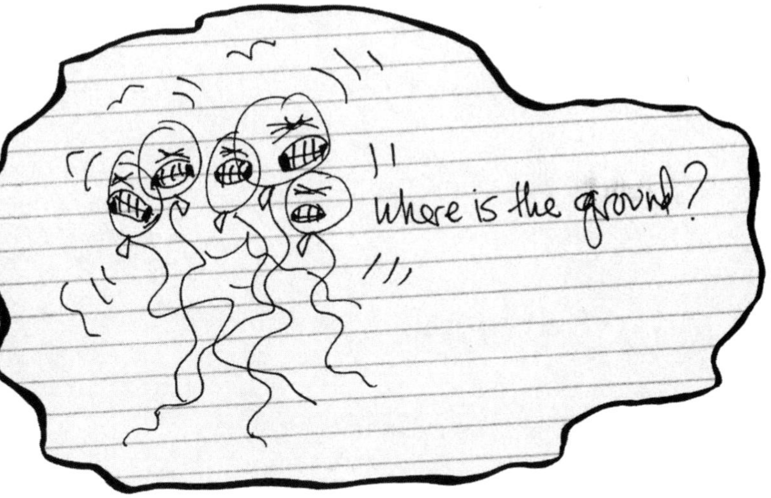
where is the ground?

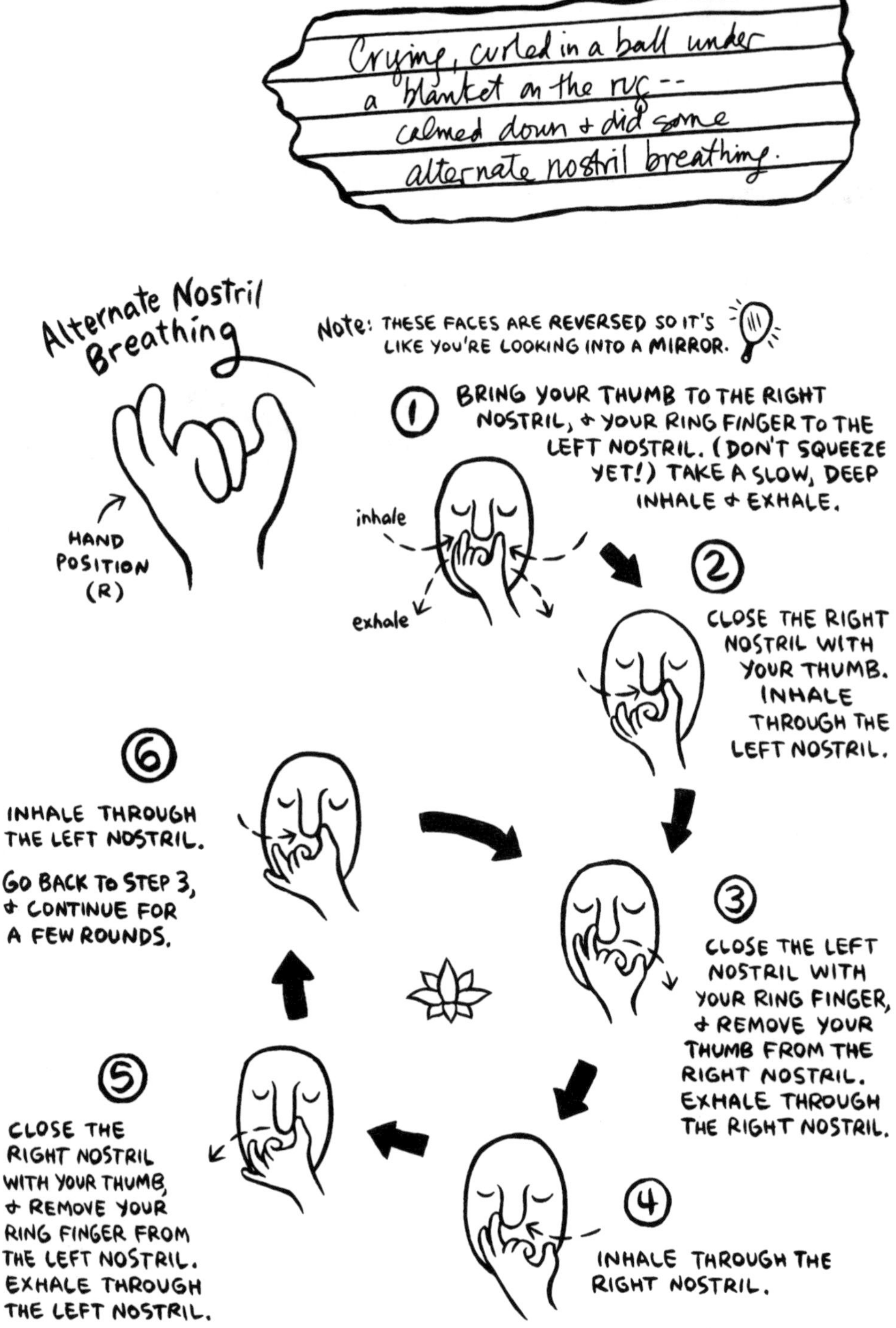
Crying, curled in a ball under a blanket on the rug -- calmed down + did some alternate nostril breathing.
Alternate Nostril Breathing
Note: THESE FACES ARE REVERSED SO IT'S LIKE YOU'RE LOOKING INTO A MIRROR.
HAND POSITION (R)
1
BRING YOUR THUMB TO THE RIGHT NOSTRIL, + YOUR RING FINGER TO THE LEFT NOSTRIL. (DON'T SQUEEZE YET!) TAKE A SLOW, DEEP INHALE + EXHALE.
inhale
exhale
2
CLOSE THE RIGHT NOSTRIL WITH YOUR THUMB. INHALE THROUGH THE LEFT NOSTRIL.
3
CLOSE THE LEFT NOSTRIL WITH YOUR RING FINGER, + REMOVE YOUR THUMB FROM THE RIGHT NOSTRIL. EXHALE THROUGH THE RIGHT NOSTRIL.
4
INHALE THROUGH THE RIGHT NOSTRIL.
5
CLOSE THE RIGHT NOSTRIL WITH YOUR THUMB, + REMOVE YOUR RING FINGER FROM THE LEFT NOSTRIL. EXHALE THROUGH THE LEFT NOSTRIL.
6
INHALE THROUGH THE LEFT NOSTRIL.
GO BACK TO STEP 3, + CONTINUE FOR A FEW ROUNDS.

MY "ANORGASMIA" FROM THE TEGRETOL WAS WEIRD – MY SEX DRIVE WAS FINE, EVEN MY PHYSICAL RESPONSE WAS FINE, UP UNTIL MY CLIMAX. I COULD FEEL MY MUSCLES CONTRACTING, BUT THERE WAS NO SENSE OF RELEASE IN MY <u>HEAD</u>, LIKE A BIG DRUMROLL WITH NOTHING AT THE END.

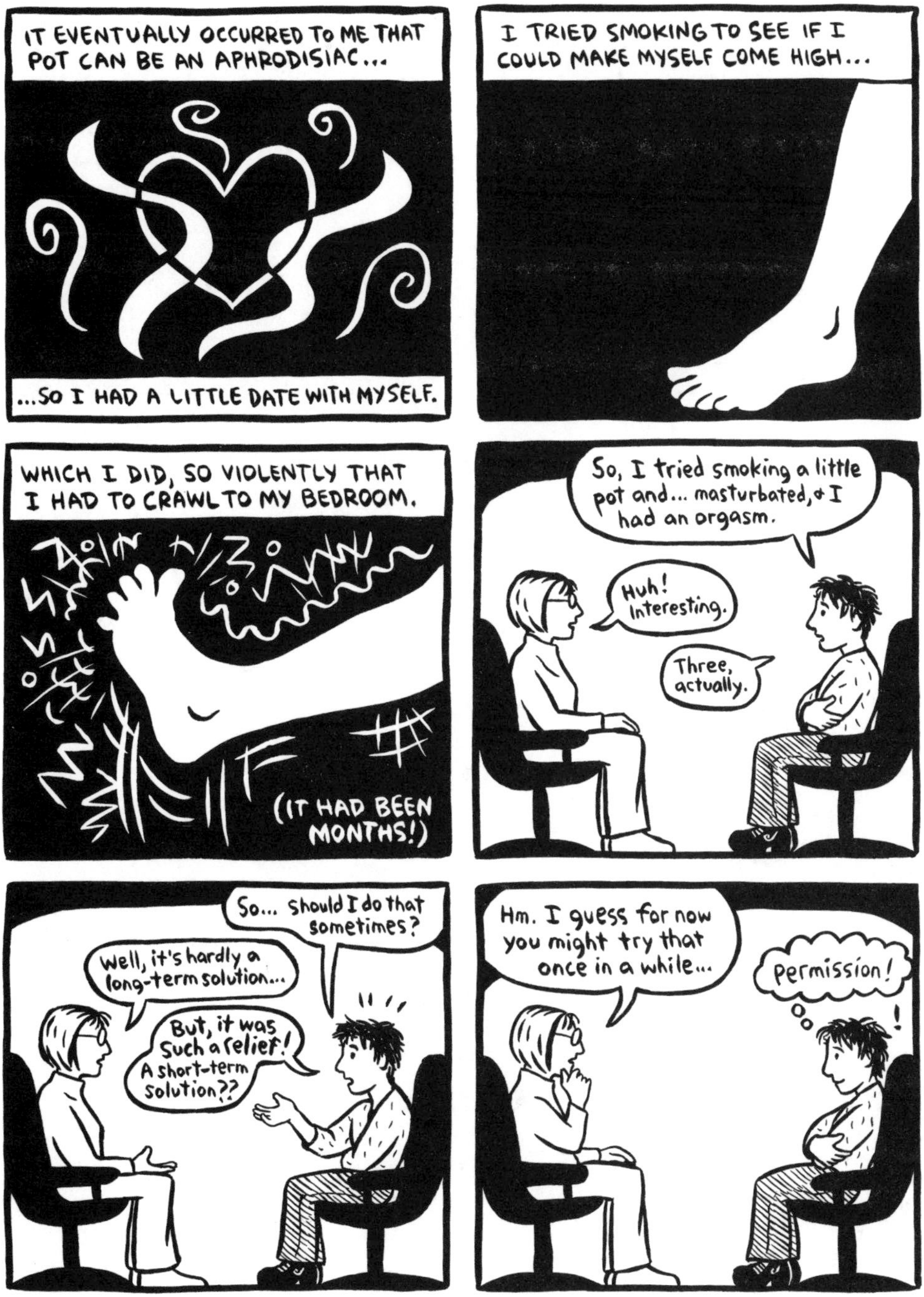
IT EVENTUALLY OCCURRED TO ME THAT POT CAN BE AN APHRODISIAC...
...SO I HAD A LITTLE DATE WITH MYSELF.
I TRIED SMOKING TO SEE IF I COULD MAKE MYSELF COME HIGH...
WHICH I DID, SO VIOLENTLY THAT I HAD TO CRAWL TO MY BEDROOM.
(IT HAD BEEN MONTHS!)
So, I tried smoking a little pot and... masturbated, & I had an orgasm.
Huh! Interesting.
Three, actually.
So... should I do that sometimes?
Well, it's hardly a long-term solution...
But, it was such a relief! A short-term solution??
Hm. I guess for now you might try that once in a while...
Permission!
!

I WAS EMOTIONALLY BOWLED OVER AT THE END OF 2001-

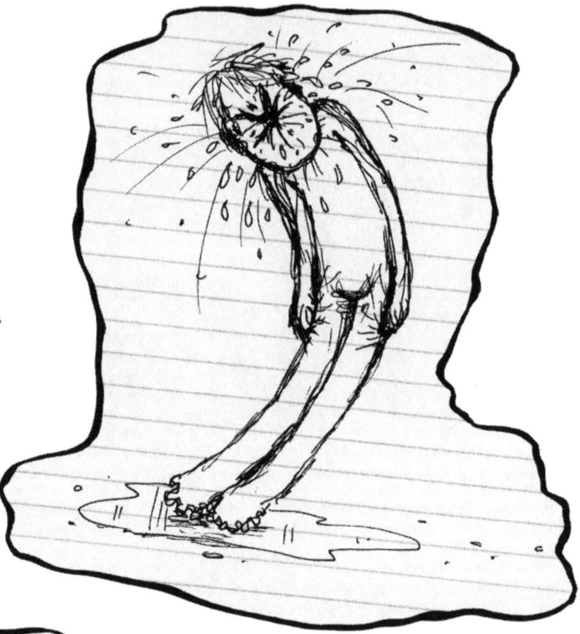

-TERRIFIED & OVERWROUGHT AFTER 9/11, & AGAIN FOR THE WEEKS THAT MY JOURNALIST BROTHER WAS REPORTING FROM AFGHANISTAN-

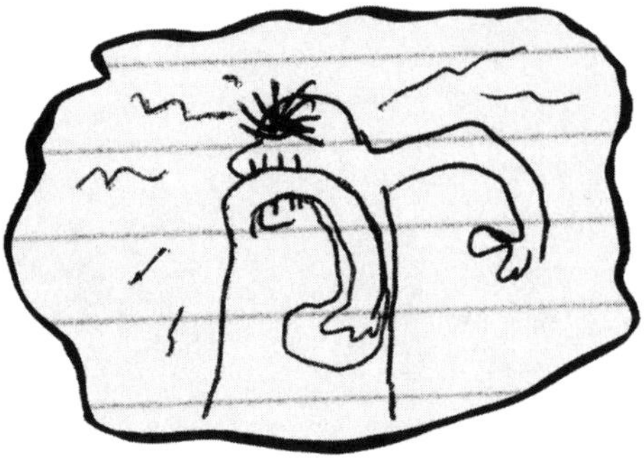

- FURIOUS & INDIGNANT WHEN I HAD A DISAGREEMENT WITH THE STRANGER'S EDITOR OVER HOW OFTEN MY COMICS WOULD RUN-

-FRUSTRATED, NERVE-WRACKED, & OVERWHELMED AT MY POWERLESSNESS OVER THE WORLD'S FUCKED-UP-NESS, MY BROTHER'S MORTALITY, MY WORK, MY HEAD.

I FELT LIKE I WOULD EXPLODE.

BY NOW IT WAS CLEAR:
THE TEGRETOL WASN'T STOPPING MY MOOD SWINGS.

HOW LONG BEFORE WE'D FIND THE RIGHT
MEDS? OR THE RIGHT COCKTAIL OF MEDS?

WE HAD BEEN TRYING
FOR YEARS.

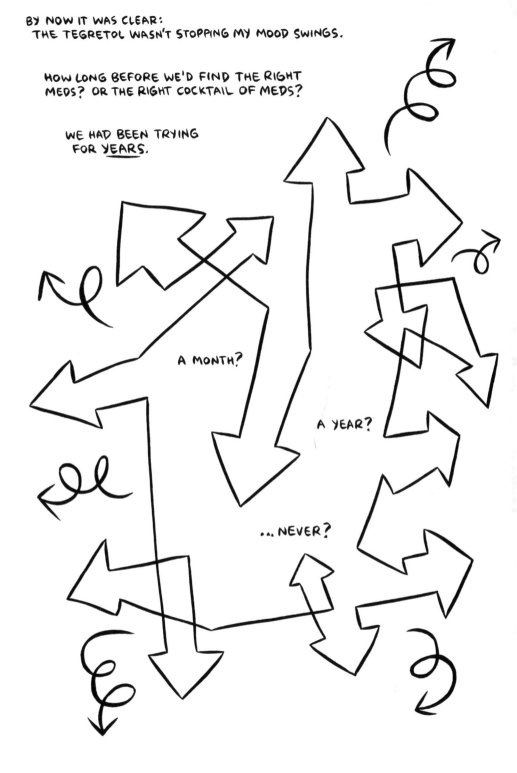

A MONTH?

A YEAR?

... NEVER?

MARCH 7, 2002: THE DAY BEFORE MY BIRTHDAY, FOUR YEARS AFTER MY DIAGNOSIS.

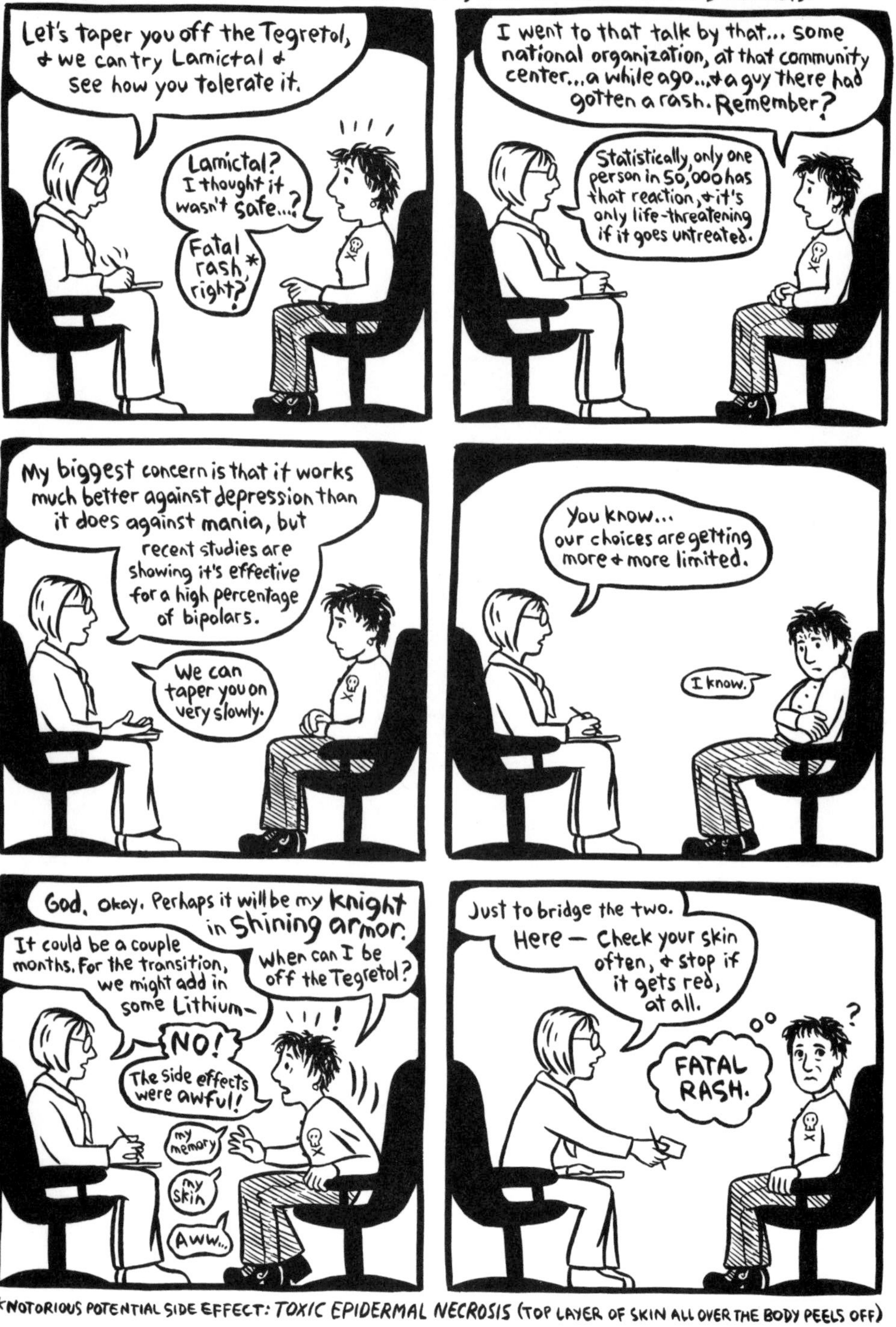
Let's taper you off the Tegretol, & we can try Lamictal & see how you tolerate it.
Lamictal? I thought it wasn't safe...?
Fatal rash,* right?
I went to that talk by that... some national organization, at that community center... a while ago... & a guy there had gotten a rash. Remember?
Statistically, only one person in 50,000 has that reaction, & it's only life-threatening if it goes untreated.
My biggest concern is that it works much better against depression than it does against mania, but recent studies are showing it's effective for a high percentage of bipolars.
We can taper you on very slowly.
You know... our choices are getting more & more limited.
I know.
God. Okay. Perhaps it will be my knight in shining armor.
When can I be off the Tegretol?
It could be a couple months. For the transition, we might add in some Lithium-
NO!
The side effects were awful!
my memory
my skin
Aww...
Just to bridge the two.
Here — Check your skin often, & stop if it gets red, at all.
FATAL RASH.

*NOTORIOUS POTENTIAL SIDE EFFECT: *TOXIC EPIDERMAL NECROSIS* (TOP LAYER OF SKIN ALL OVER THE BODY PEELS OFF)

CHAPTER 7

BIPOLAR DISORDER IS DIFFICULT TO TREAT. FINDING THE RIGHT MEDICATIONS CAN TAKE A LONG TIME, SO BIPOLARS MAY LIST OUR MED HISTORIES PROUDLY, LIKE MERIT BADGES.

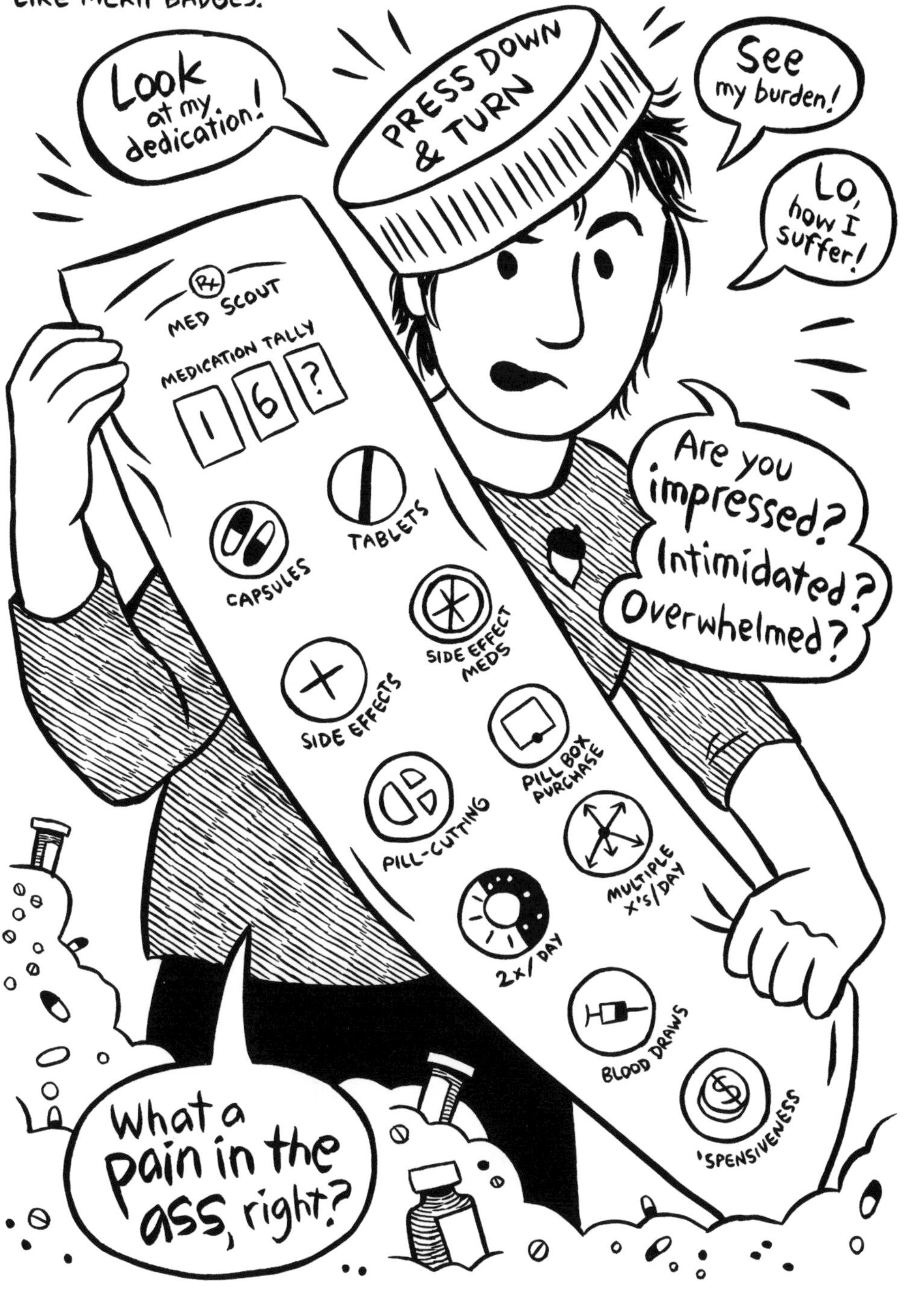

Look at my dedication!
PRESS DOWN & TURN
See my burden!
Lo, how I suffer!
Rx MED SCOUT
MEDICATION TALLY
1 6 ?
CAPSULES
TABLETS
SIDE EFFECTS
SIDE EFFECT MEDS
PILL-CUTTING
PILL BOX PURCHASE
2x/ DAY
MULTIPLE X'S/DAY
BLOOD DRAWS
'SPENSIVENESS
Are you impressed? Intimidated? Overwhelmed?
What a pain in the ass, right?

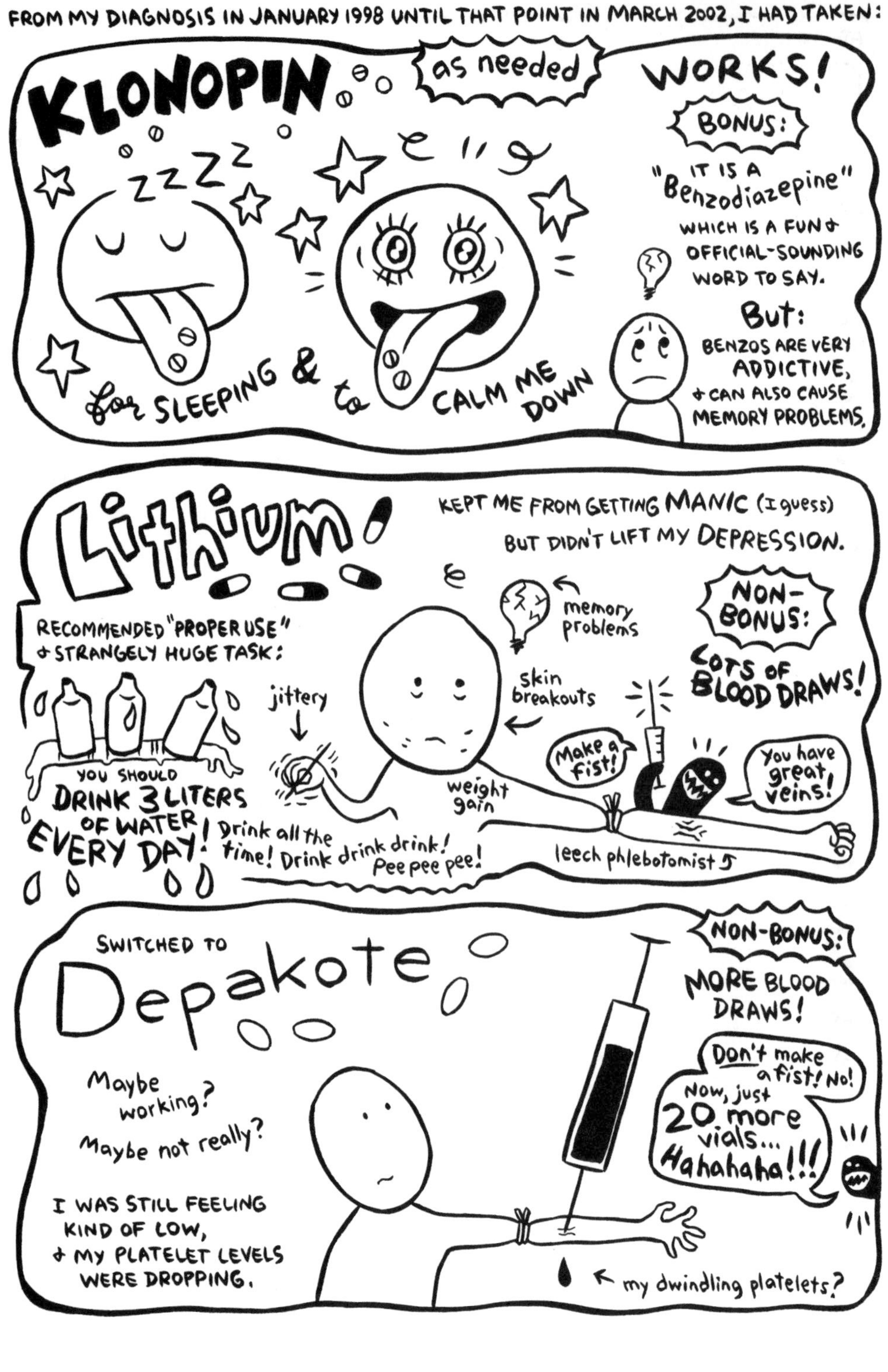
FROM MY DIAGNOSIS IN JANUARY 1998 UNTIL THAT POINT IN MARCH 2002, I HAD TAKEN:
KLONOPIN
as needed
WORKS!
BONUS:
"IT IS A "Benzodiazepine"
WHICH IS A FUN & OFFICIAL-SOUNDING WORD TO SAY.
But:
BENZOS ARE VERY ADDICTIVE, & CAN ALSO CAUSE MEMORY PROBLEMS.
zzZZ
for SLEEPING & to CALM ME DOWN
Lithium!
KEPT ME FROM GETTING MANIC (I guess)
BUT DIDN'T LIFT MY DEPRESSION.
NON-BONUS:
LOTS OF BLOOD DRAWS!
RECOMMENDED "PROPER USE" & STRANGELY HUGE TASK:
YOU SHOULD DRINK 3 LITERS OF WATER EVERY DAY!
Drink all the time! Drink drink drink! Pee pee pee!
jittery
memory problems
skin breakouts
weight gain
Make a fist!
You have great veins!
leech phlebotomist
SWITCHED TO
Depakote
NON-BONUS:
MORE BLOOD DRAWS!
Maybe working?
Maybe not really?
Don't make a fist! No!
Now, just 20 more vials... Hahahaha!!!
I WAS STILL FEELING KIND OF LOW, & MY PLATELET LEVELS WERE DROPPING.
my dwindling platelets?

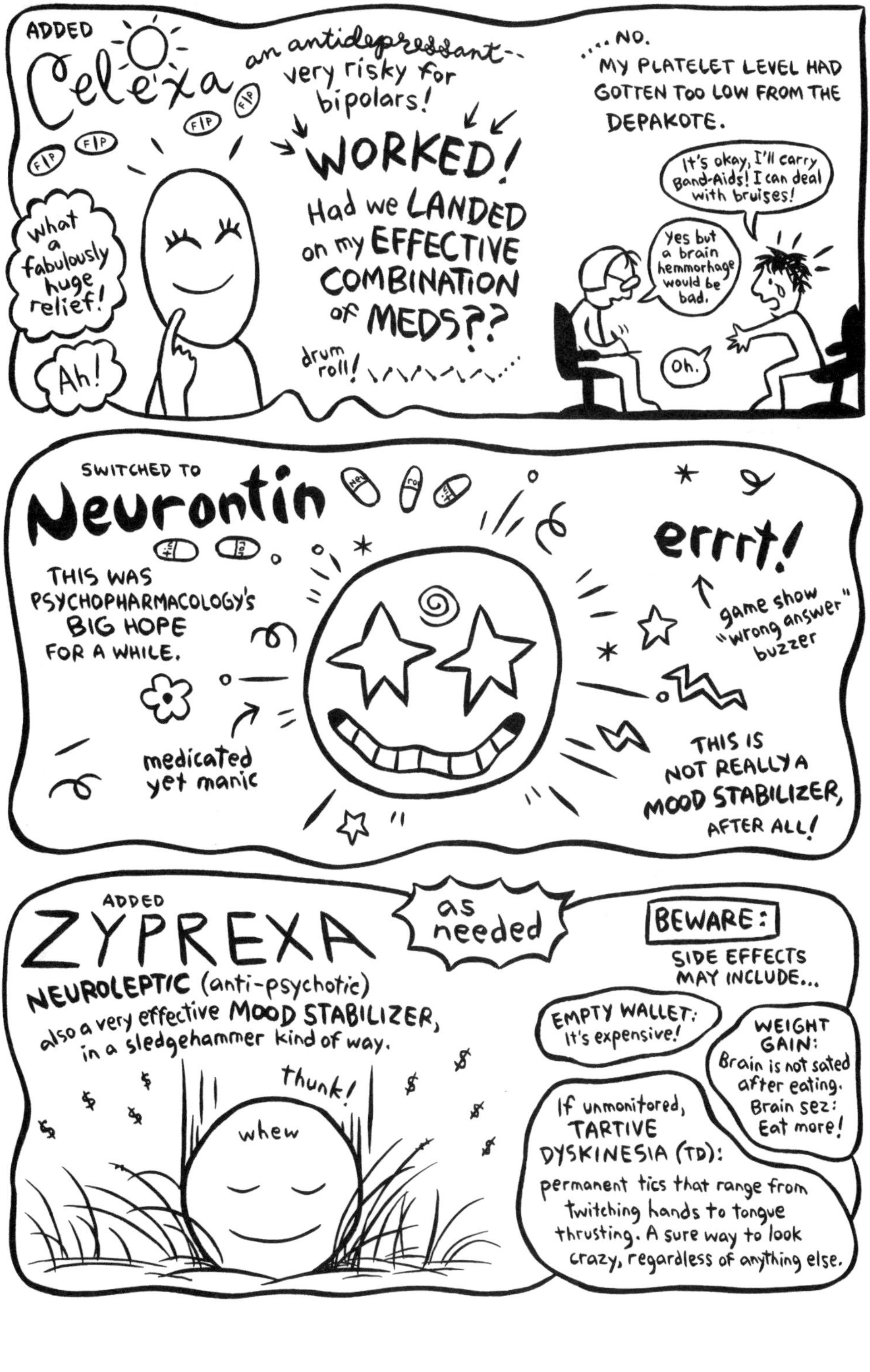
ADDED
Celexa
an antidepressant--
very risky for bipolars!
WORKED!
Had we LANDED on my EFFECTIVE COMBINATION of MEDS??
drum roll!
what a fabulously huge relief!
Ah!
F|P
....NO.
MY PLATELET LEVEL HAD GOTTEN TOO LOW FROM THE DEPAKOTE.
It's okay, I'll carry Band-Aids! I can deal with bruises!
Yes but a brain hemmorhage would be bad.
Oh.
SWITCHED TO
Neurontin
THIS WAS PSYCHOPHARMACOLOGY'S BIG HOPE FOR A WHILE.
medicated yet manic
errrt!
game show "wrong answer" buzzer
THIS IS NOT REALLY A MOOD STABILIZER, AFTER ALL!
ADDED
ZYPREXA
as needed
NEUROLEPTIC (anti-psychotic)
also a very effective MOOD STABILIZER, in a sledgehammer kind of way.
thunk!
whew
BEWARE:
SIDE EFFECTS MAY INCLUDE...
EMPTY WALLET: It's expensive!
WEIGHT GAIN: Brain is not sated after eating. Brain sez: Eat more!
If unmonitored, TARTIVE DYSKINESIA (TD): permanent tics that range from twitching hands to tongue thrusting. A sure way to look crazy, regardless of anything else.

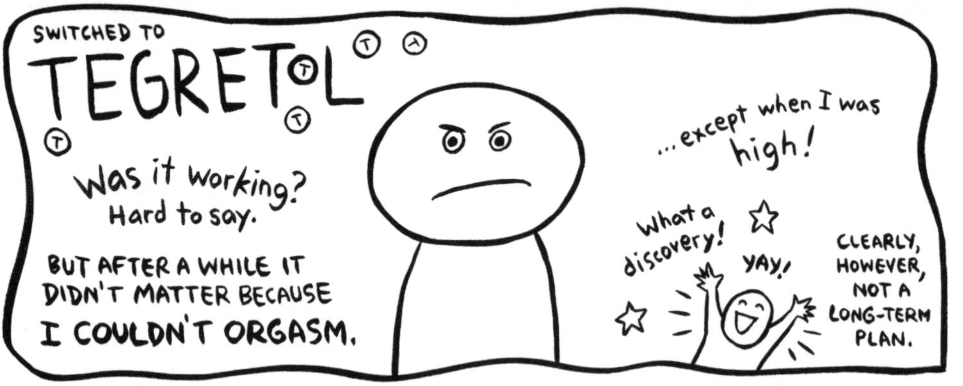
SWITCHED TO
TEGRETOL
Was it working?
Hard to say.
BUT AFTER A WHILE IT DIDN'T MATTER BECAUSE
I COULDN'T ORGASM.
...except when I was high!
What a discovery!
YAY!
CLEARLY, HOWEVER, NOT A LONG-TERM PLAN.

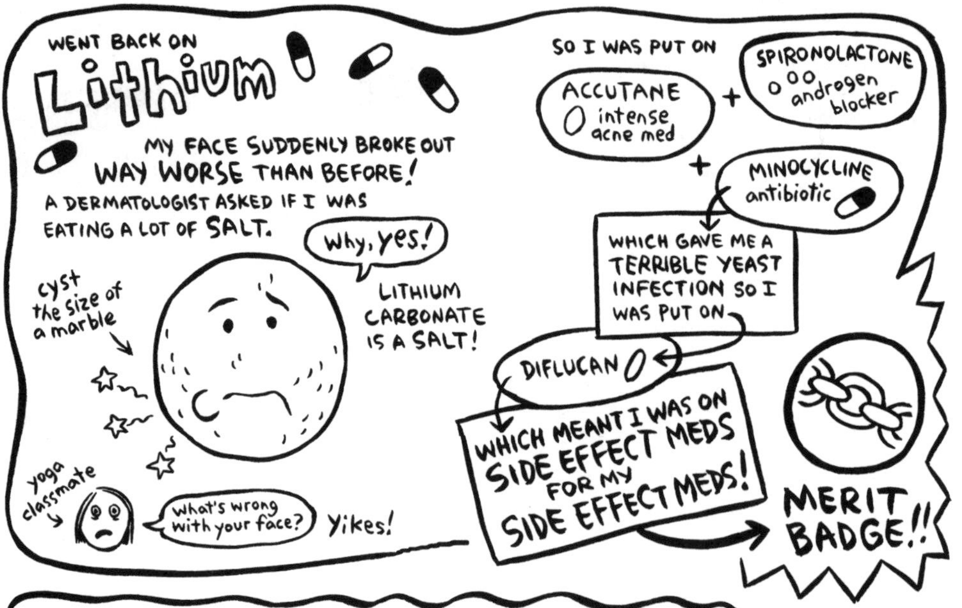
WENT BACK ON
Lithium
MY FACE SUDDENLY BROKE OUT
WAY WORSE THAN BEFORE!
A DERMATOLOGIST ASKED IF I WAS EATING A LOT OF SALT.
Why, yes!
LITHIUM CARBONATE IS A SALT!
cyst the size of a marble
yoga classmate
What's wrong with your face?
Yikes!
SO I WAS PUT ON
ACCUTANE
intense acne med
+
SPIRONOLACTONE
androgen blocker
+
MINOCYCLINE
antibiotic
WHICH GAVE ME A TERRIBLE YEAST INFECTION SO I WAS PUT ON
DIFLUCAN
WHICH MEANT I WAS ON SIDE EFFECT MEDS FOR MY SIDE EFFECT MEDS!
MERIT BADGE!!

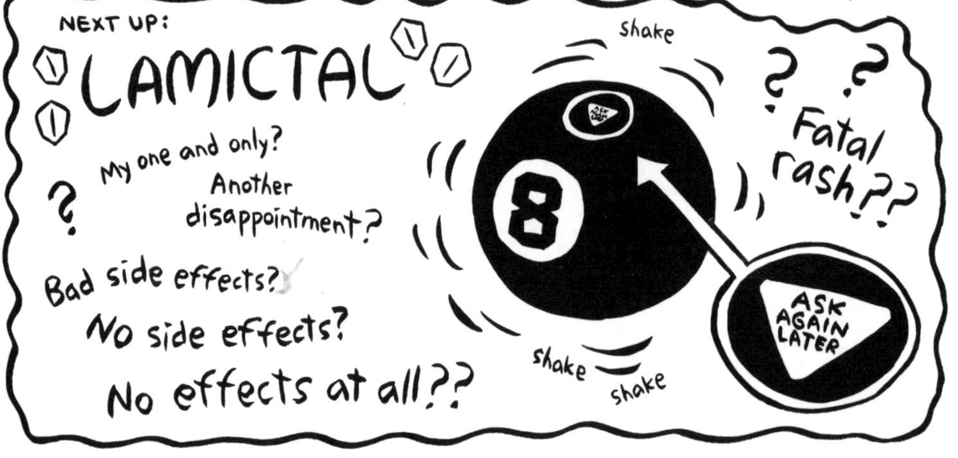
NEXT UP:
LAMICTAL
My one and only?
Another disappointment?
Bad side effects?
No side effects?
No effects at all??
shake
shake
shake
ASK AGAIN LATER
Fatal rash???

MED COMPLIANCE IS AN ESSENTIAL PART OF TREATMENT, BUT IT CAN BE **FRUSTRATING**. DO YOU TAKE YOUR MEDS DESPITE THEIR NOT **WORKING WELL**? DESPITE THEIR **SIDE EFFECTS**? DESPITE **RESENTING** THE **MULTIPLE PILL BOTTLES** THAT MAKE YOU FEEL LIKE AN **OLD PERSON** WITH **BAD BLOOD PRESSURE**??

WHAT TO DO?

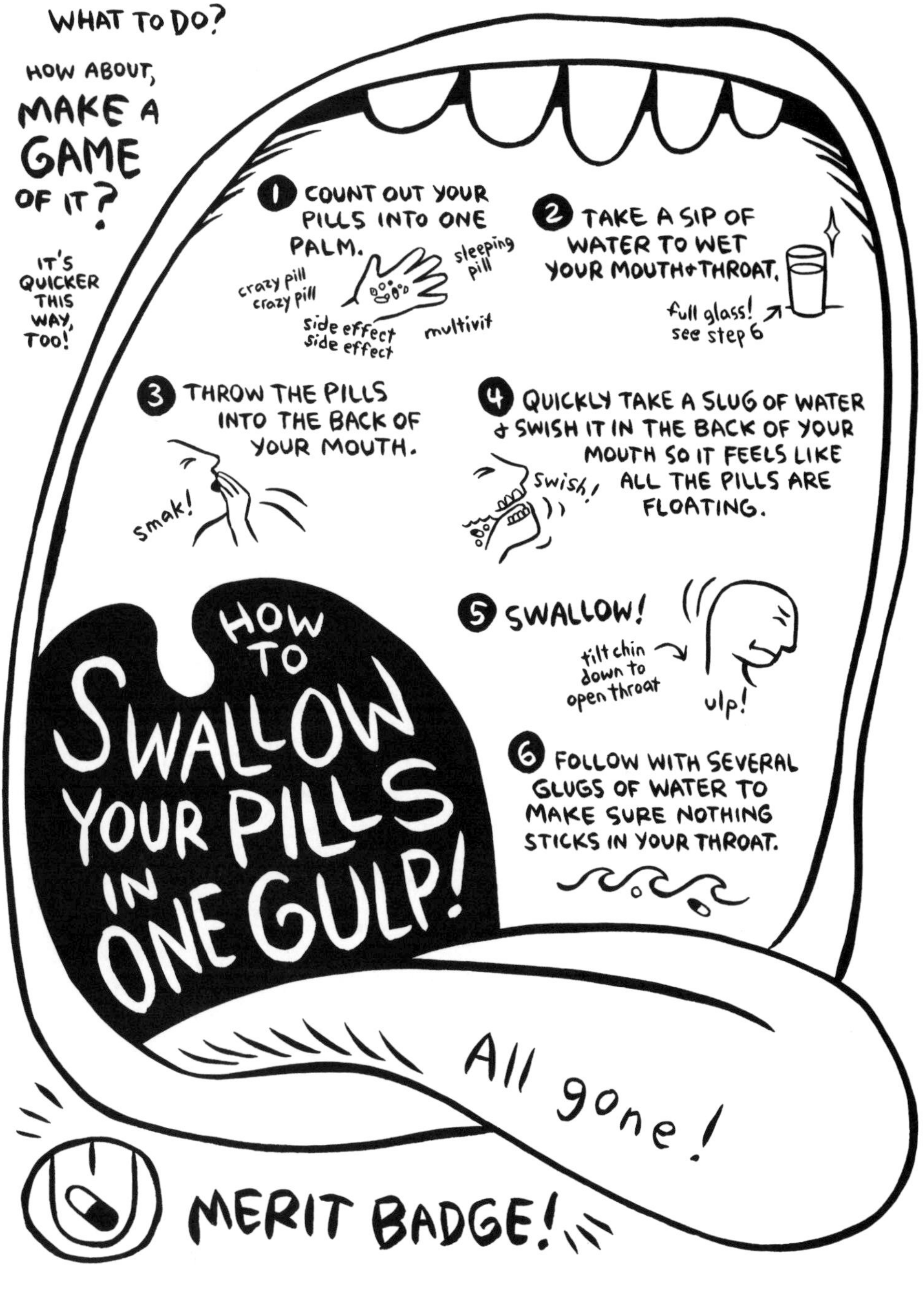
HOW ABOUT, MAKE A GAME OF IT?
IT'S QUICKER THIS WAY, TOO!
HOW TO SWALLOW YOUR PILLS IN ONE GULP!
1 COUNT OUT YOUR PILLS INTO ONE PALM.
crazy pill
crazy pill
sleeping pill
side effect
side effect
multivit
2 TAKE A SIP OF WATER TO WET YOUR MOUTH & THROAT.
full glass! see step 6
3 THROW THE PILLS INTO THE BACK OF YOUR MOUTH.
smak!
4 QUICKLY TAKE A SLUG OF WATER & SWISH IT IN THE BACK OF YOUR MOUTH SO IT FEELS LIKE ALL THE PILLS ARE FLOATING.
swish!
5 SWALLOW!
tilt chin down to open throat
ulp!
6 FOLLOW WITH SEVERAL GLUGS OF WATER TO MAKE SURE NOTHING STICKS IN YOUR THROAT.
All gone!
MERIT BADGE!

A LITTLE LESS TEGRETOL, A DETOUR ON + OFF LITHIUM, + A LITTLE MORE LAMICTAL LATER, I TOOK MYSELF TO BREAKFAST AT A LOCAL CAFE, + WROTE ON THE BACK OF A FLYER TO STAPLE INTO MY JOURNAL LATER.

Woobluum AH... sitting at the-- nonverbal!! SO blissed-out.

Yoga class this morning, then went for a long walk in this beautiful, magical neighborhood, just listening to the sounds, looking at the shapes of the branches against the blue sky, the colors of the flowers... budding trees...

Mm, this coffee is GOOD- I don't usually like drip coffee. Mmmmm

This waitress is SO CUTE! I think I'll give her my card + ask to draw her sometime.

Mm, I can feel myself hea ←ha, I wrote "healing" heading towards a nap. I didn't get enough sleep last night... how many hours? 2 to 8... 6. With 2 mg Klonopin! Jeez...

But I'm not manicky, just adjusting my prescribed + non-prescribed meds.

I am so ah at peace... what a morning!

Is this what it's like to practice yoga all the time?

"non-prescribed med" = pot

HM. NOT STABLE YET...!

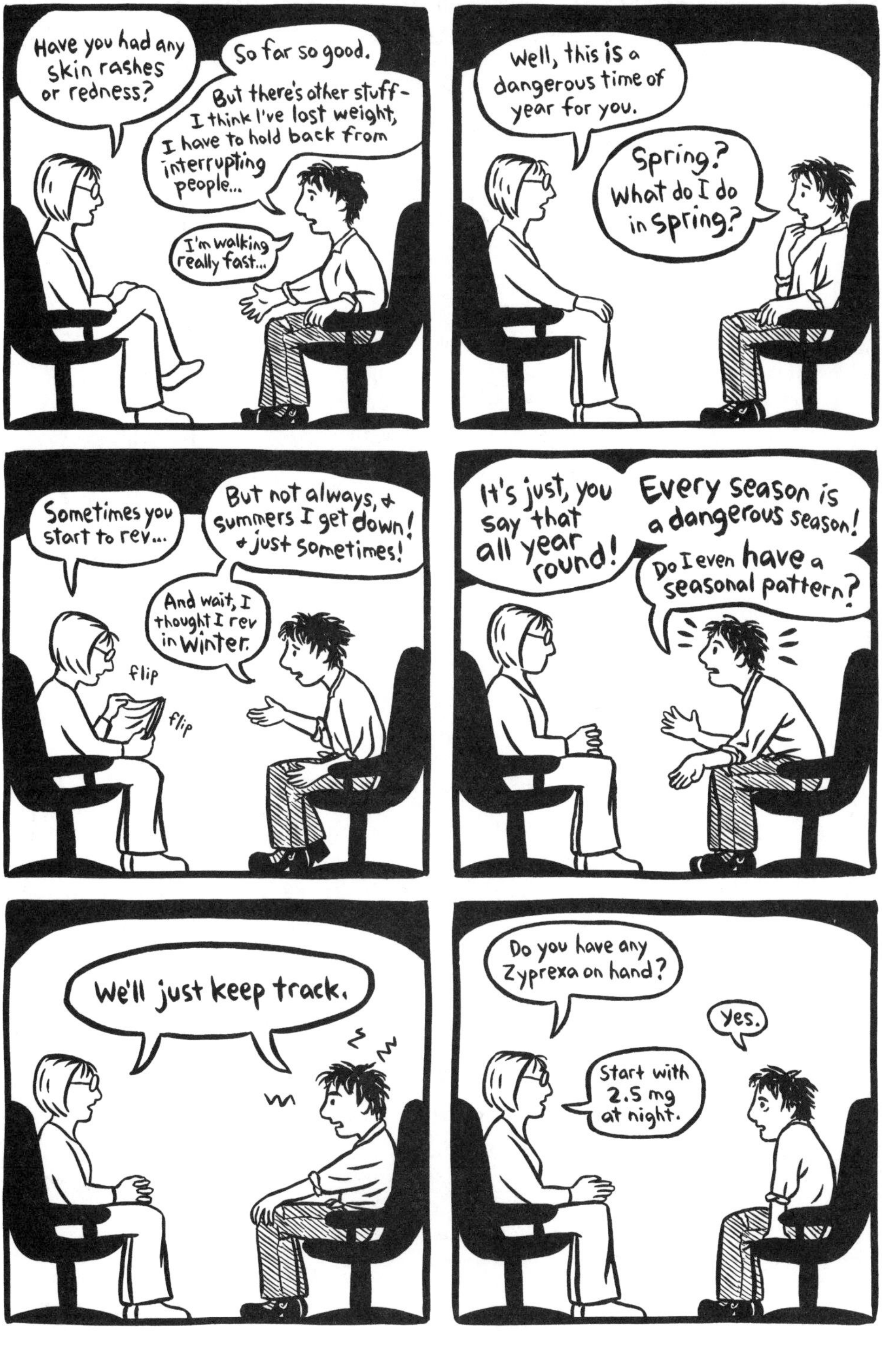
Have you had any skin rashes or redness?
So far so good.
But there's other stuff- I think I've lost weight, I have to hold back from interrupting people...
I'm walking really fast...
Well, this IS a dangerous time of year for you.
Spring? What do I do in spring?
Sometimes you start to rev...
But not always, & summers I get down! & just sometimes!
And wait, I thought I rev in winter.
flip
flip
It's just, you say that all year round!
Every season is a dangerous season!
Do I even have a seasonal pattern?
We'll just keep track.
Do you have any Zyprexa on hand?
Yes.
Start with 2.5 mg at night.

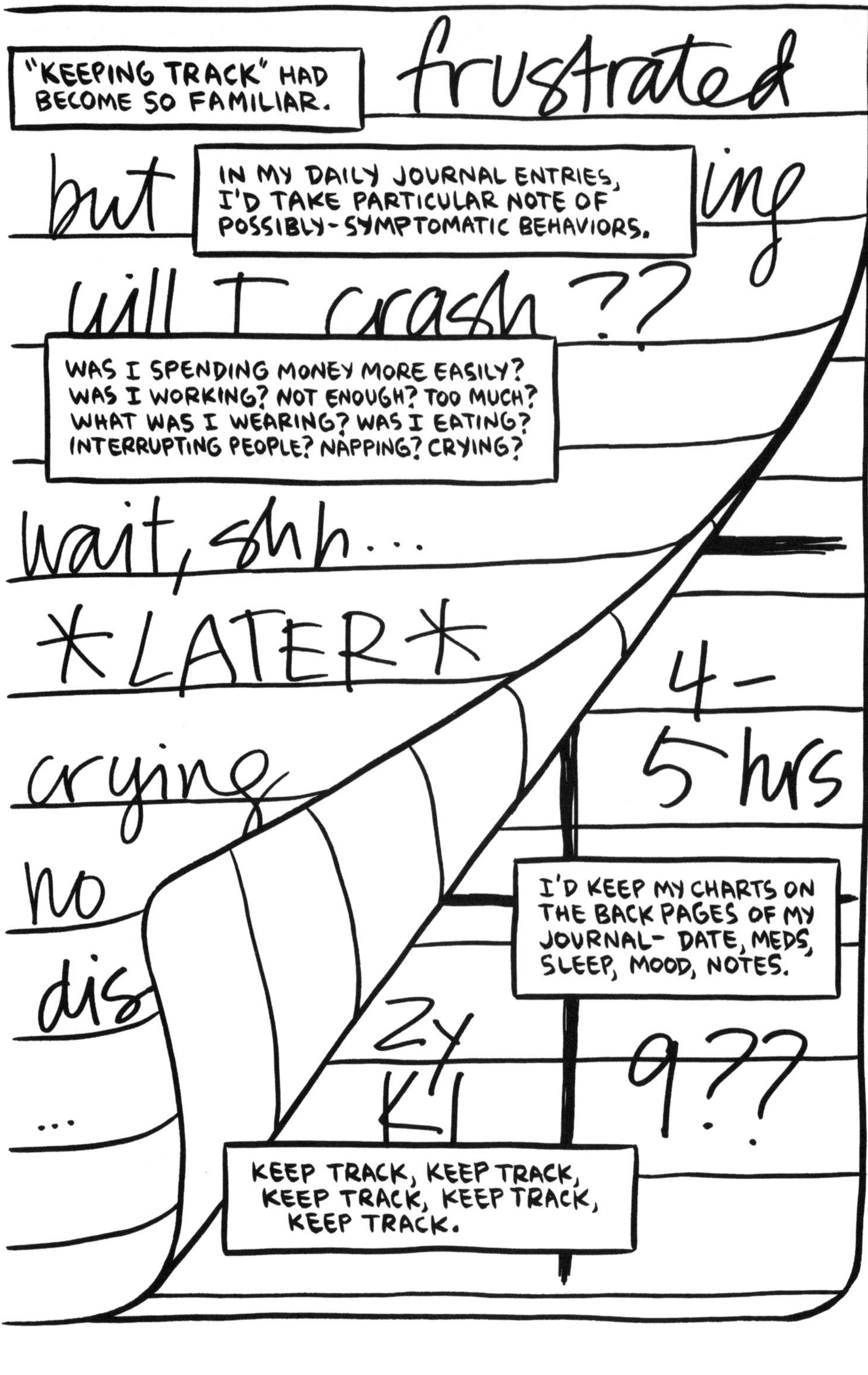
"KEEPING TRACK" HAD BECOME SO FAMILIAR.
frustrated
but
IN MY DAILY JOURNAL ENTRIES, I'D TAKE PARTICULAR NOTE OF POSSIBLY-SYMPTOMATIC BEHAVIORS.
ing
will I crash??
WAS I SPENDING MONEY MORE EASILY? WAS I WORKING? NOT ENOUGH? TOO MUCH? WHAT WAS I WEARING? WAS I EATING? INTERRUPTING PEOPLE? NAPPING? CRYING?
wait, shh...
LATER
4-5 hrs
crying
no
I'D KEEP MY CHARTS ON THE BACK PAGES OF MY JOURNAL- DATE, MEDS, SLEEP, MOOD, NOTES.
dis
9??
...
KEEP TRACK, KEEP TRACK, KEEP TRACK, KEEP TRACK, KEEP TRACK.

PRE-DIAGNOSIS MANIA WAS A LOT MORE FUN THAN POST-DIAGNOSIS MANIA. NOW, WITH INSIGHT ABOUT MY EFFECT ON THE PEOPLE CLOSE TO ME, & AN ACUTE AWARENESS OF MY INEVITABLE POST-MANIA DEPRESSION, FEELING "UP" WAS SCARY.

RRRRR
Klonopin

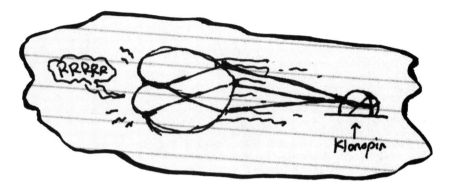

I HAD COME TO REALLY APPRECIATE MY PILLBOX OF KLONOPIN, RATTLING AROUND IN MY BAG.

straining at my own bit

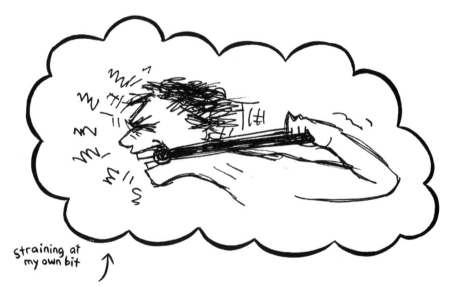

I GOT THIS MENTAL IMAGE A LOT, THOUGH I NEVER DREW IT IN ANY OF MY JOURNALS OR SKETCHBOOKS. THE IMAGE WAS SATISFYING ENOUGH JUST IN MY HEAD, I'M NOT SURE WHY.

AT LEAST I FELT LIKE I WAS FINALLY LEARNING HOW TO HOLD MY OWN REINS.

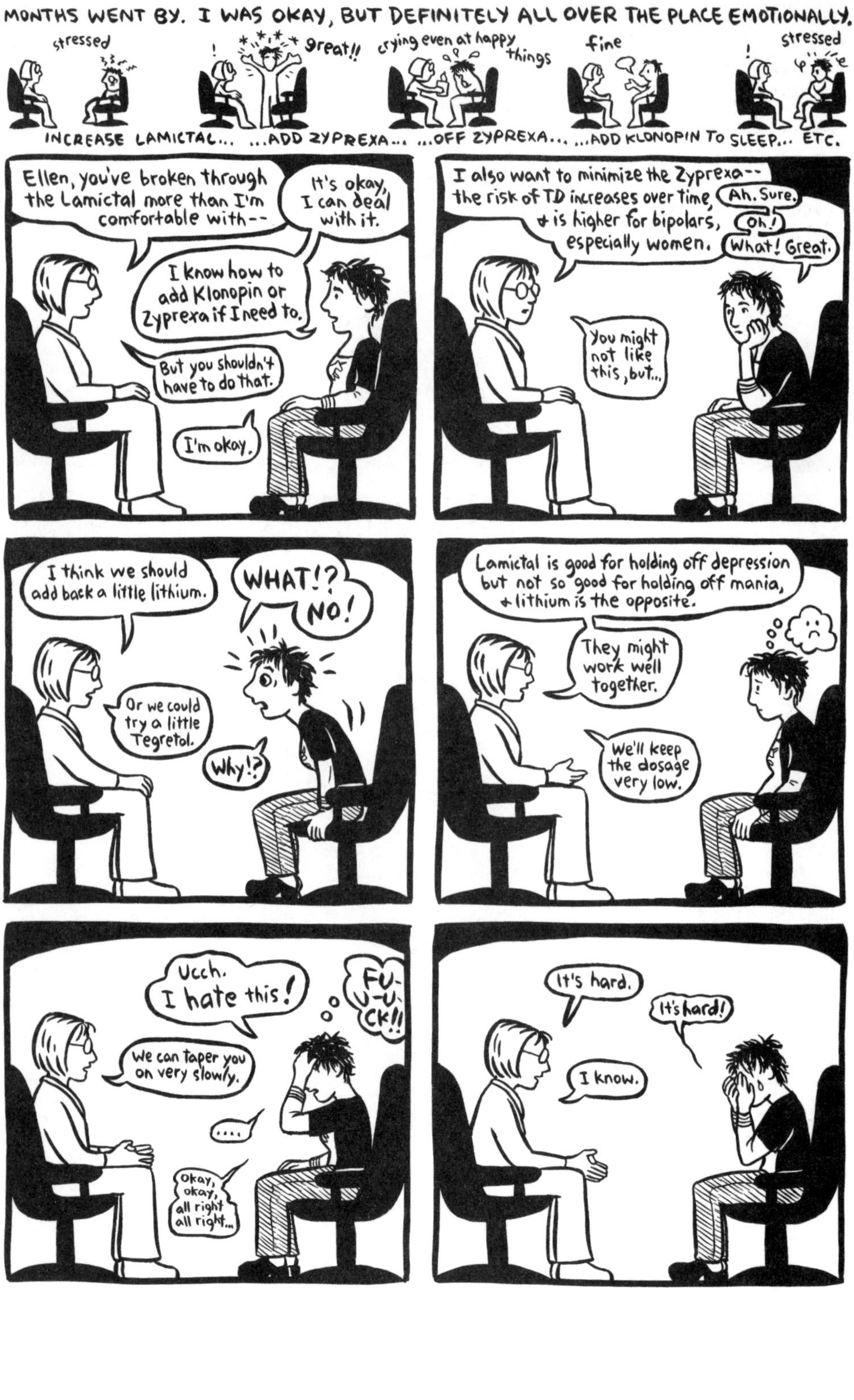

MONTHS WENT BY. I WAS OKAY, BUT DEFINITELY ALL OVER THE PLACE EMOTIONALLY.
stressed
great!!
crying even at happy things
fine
stressed
INCREASE LAMICTAL... ...ADD ZYPREXA... ...OFF ZYPREXA... ...ADD KLONOPIN TO SLEEP... ETC.
Ellen, you've broken through the Lamictal more than I'm comfortable with--
It's okay, I can deal with it.
I know how to add Klonopin or Zyprexa if I need to.
But you shouldn't have to do that.
I'm okay.
I also want to minimize the Zyprexa-- the risk of TD increases over time, & is higher for bipolars, especially women.
Ah. Sure.
Oh!
What! Great.
You might not like this, but...
I think we should add back a little lithium.
WHAT!? NO!
Or we could try a little Tegretol.
Why!?
Lamictal is good for holding off depression but not so good for holding off mania, & lithium is the opposite.
They might work well together.
We'll keep the dosage very low.
Ucch. I hate this!
FU-U-U-CK!!
We can taper you on very slowly.
....
Okay, okay, all right all right...
It's hard.
It's hard!
I know.

OF COURSE KAREN WANTED ME ON LITHIUM. IT WAS THE GOLD STANDARD, THE OLDEST BIPOLAR MED, WITH THE BEST TRACK RECORD. BUT WOULD A LOWER DOSE EASE THE SIDE EFFECTS ON MY SKIN? MY MEMORY? THE MEMORY PROBLEMS REALLY MADE ME FEEL CRAZY.

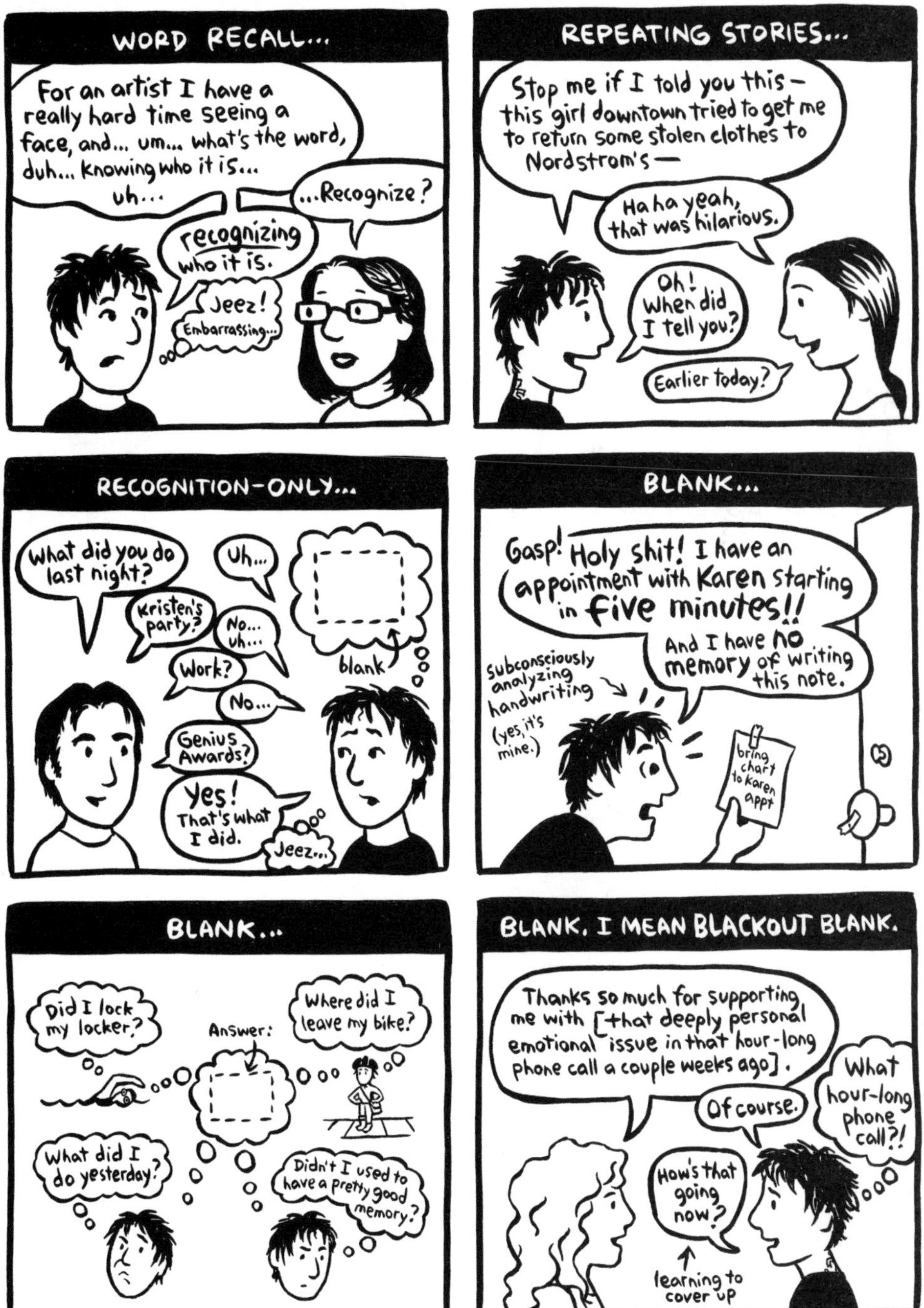
WORD RECALL...
For an artist I have a really hard time seeing a face, and... um... what's the word, duh... knowing who it is... uh...
...Recognize?
recognizing who it is.
Jeez! Embarrassing...
REPEATING STORIES...
Stop me if I told you this— this girl downtown tried to get me to return some stolen clothes to Nordstrom's—
Ha ha yeah, that was hilarious.
Oh! When did I tell you?
Earlier today?
RECOGNITION-ONLY...
What did you do last night?
Uh...
Kristen's party?
No... uh...
Work?
No...
blank
Genius Awards?
Yes! That's what I did.
Jeez...
BLANK...
Gasp! Holy shit! I have an appointment with Karen starting in five minutes!!
And I have no memory of writing this note.
Subconsciously analyzing handwriting
(yes, it's mine.)
bring chart to Karen appt
BLANK...
Did I lock my locker?
Answer:
Where did I leave my bike?
What did I do yesterday?
Didn't I used to have a pretty good memory?
BLANK. I MEAN BLACKOUT BLANK.
Thanks so much for supporting me with [that deeply personal emotional issue in that hour-long phone call a couple weeks ago].
Of course.
What hour-long phone call?!
How's that going now?
learning to cover up

AT LEAST LITHIUM WAS CHEAP.

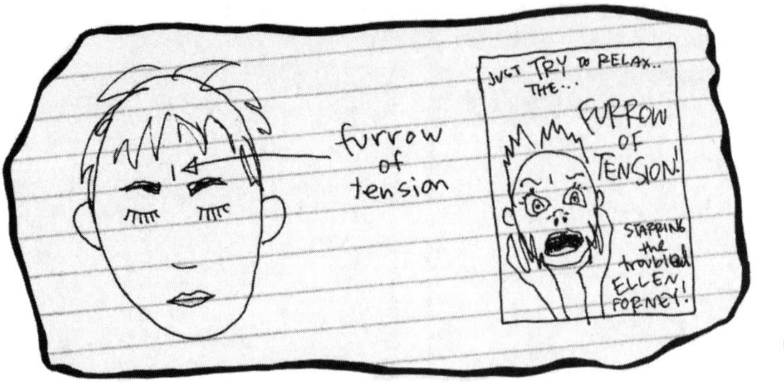
furrow of tension
JUST TRY TO RELAX.. THE...
FURROW OF TENSION!
STARRING the troubled ELLEN FORNEY!

HOLD TIGHT, RELAX, WAIT.

KEEP WATCH FOR SIDE EFFECTS.

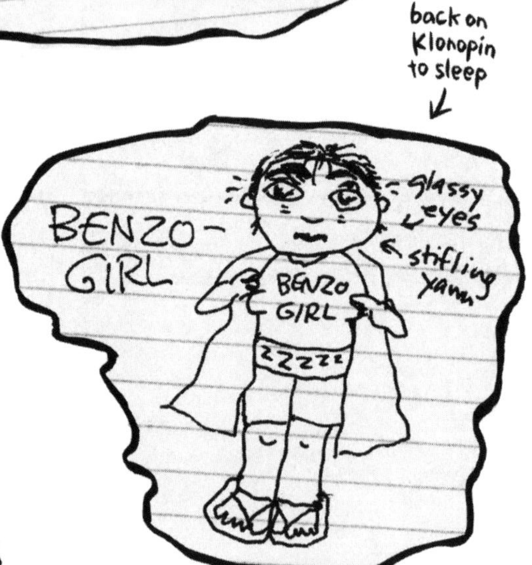
back on Klonopin to sleep
BENZO-GIRL
glassy eyes
stifling yawn
BENZO GIRL
ZZZZZ

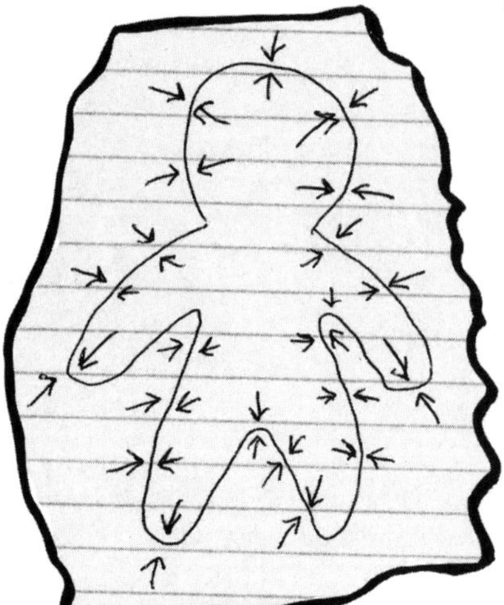

KEEP TRACK.

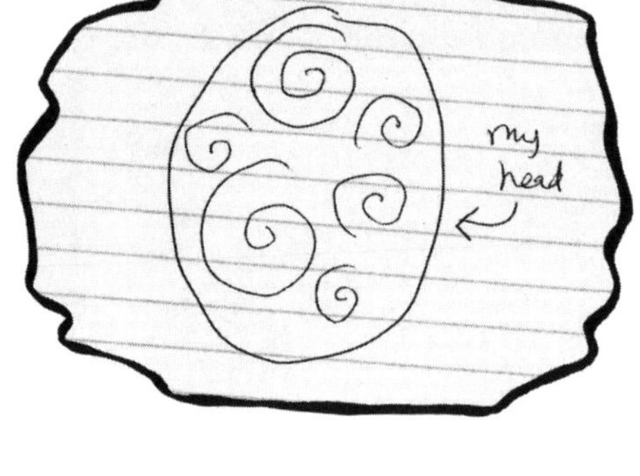
my head

BREATHE.

SEVERAL MONTHS LATER, I HADN'T HAD ANY NOTABLE MOOD SWINGS, & MY SKIN WAS OKAY.

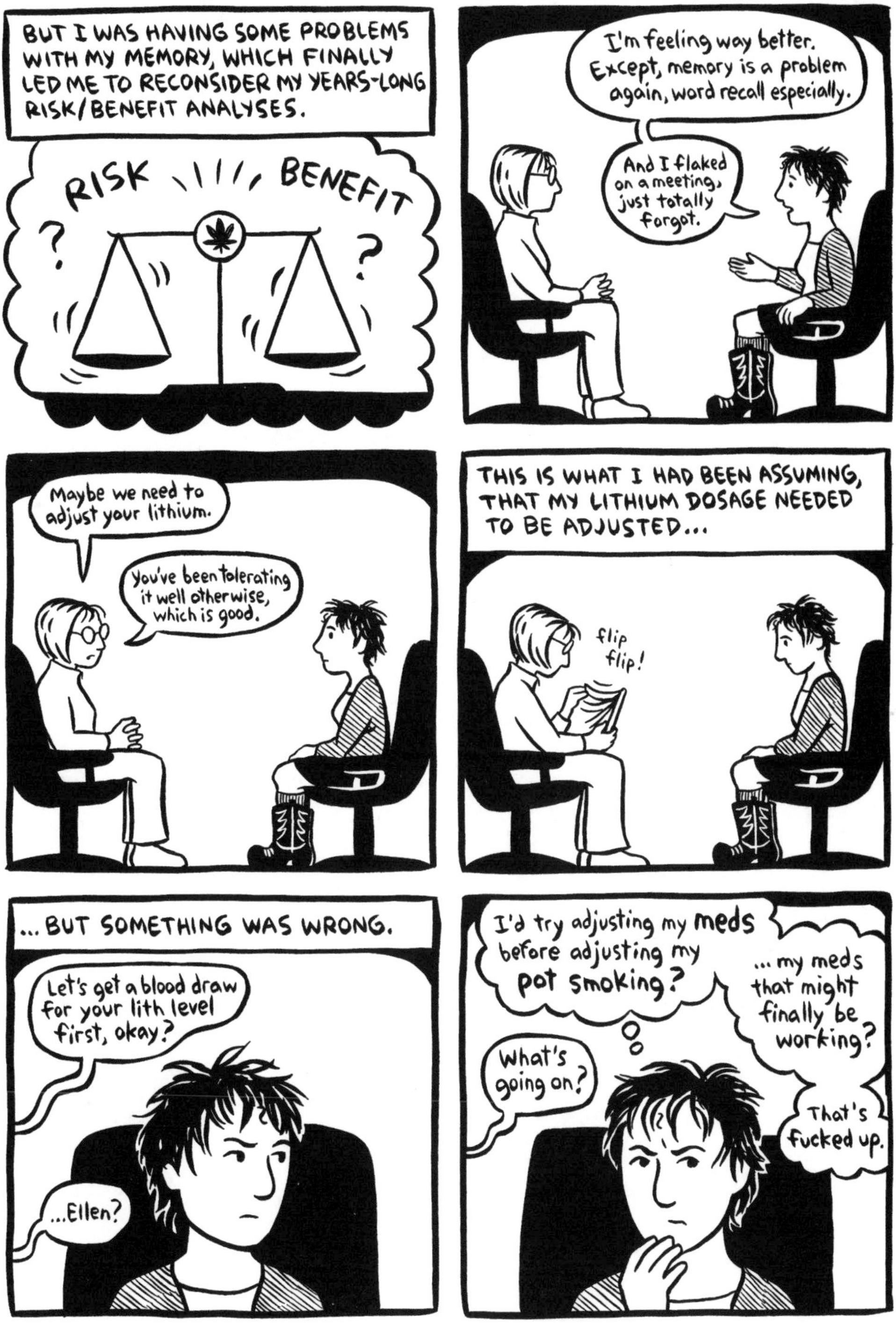
BUT I WAS HAVING SOME PROBLEMS WITH MY MEMORY, WHICH FINALLY LED ME TO RECONSIDER MY YEARS-LONG RISK/BENEFIT ANALYSES.
RISK
BENEFIT
?
?
I'm feeling way better. Except, memory is a problem again, word recall especially.
And I flaked on a meeting, just totally forgot.
Maybe we need to adjust your lithium.
You've been tolerating it well otherwise, which is good.
THIS IS WHAT I HAD BEEN ASSUMING, THAT MY LITHIUM DOSAGE NEEDED TO BE ADJUSTED...
flip flip!
... BUT SOMETHING WAS WRONG.
Let's get a blood draw for your lith level first, okay?
...Ellen?
I'd try adjusting my meds before adjusting my pot smoking?
... my meds that might finally be working?
What's going on?
That's fucked up.

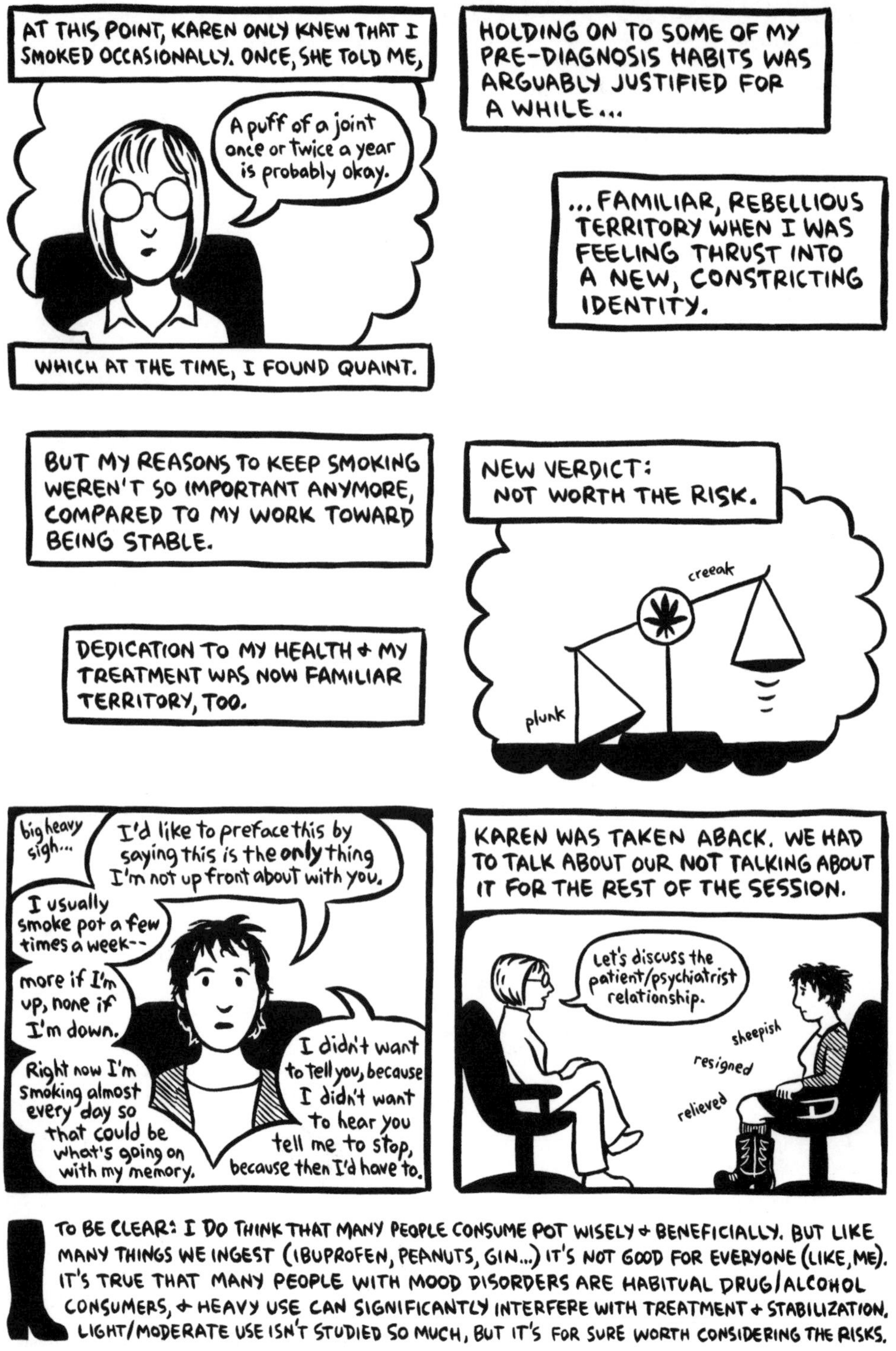
AT THIS POINT, KAREN ONLY KNEW THAT I SMOKED OCCASIONALLY. ONCE, SHE TOLD ME,
A puff of a joint once or twice a year is probably okay.
WHICH AT THE TIME, I FOUND QUAINT.
HOLDING ON TO SOME OF MY PRE-DIAGNOSIS HABITS WAS ARGUABLY JUSTIFIED FOR A WHILE...
...FAMILIAR, REBELLIOUS TERRITORY WHEN I WAS FEELING THRUST INTO A NEW, CONSTRICTING IDENTITY.
BUT MY REASONS TO KEEP SMOKING WEREN'T SO IMPORTANT ANYMORE, COMPARED TO MY WORK TOWARD BEING STABLE.
DEDICATION TO MY HEALTH + MY TREATMENT WAS NOW FAMILIAR TERRITORY, TOO.
NEW VERDICT: NOT WORTH THE RISK.
creeak
plunk
big heavy sigh...
I'd like to preface this by saying this is the only thing I'm not up front about with you.
I usually smoke pot a few times a week--
more if I'm up, none if I'm down.
Right now I'm smoking almost every day so that could be what's going on with my memory.
I didn't want to tell you, because I didn't want to hear you tell me to stop, because then I'd have to.
KAREN WAS TAKEN ABACK. WE HAD TO TALK ABOUT OUR NOT TALKING ABOUT IT FOR THE REST OF THE SESSION.
Let's discuss the patient/psychiatrist relationship.
sheepish
resigned
relieved
TO BE CLEAR: I DO THINK THAT MANY PEOPLE CONSUME POT WISELY + BENEFICIALLY. BUT LIKE MANY THINGS WE INGEST (IBUPROFEN, PEANUTS, GIN...) IT'S NOT GOOD FOR EVERYONE (LIKE, ME). IT'S TRUE THAT MANY PEOPLE WITH MOOD DISORDERS ARE HABITUAL DRUG/ALCOHOL CONSUMERS, + HEAVY USE CAN SIGNIFICANTLY INTERFERE WITH TREATMENT + STABILIZATION. LIGHT/MODERATE USE ISN'T STUDIED SO MUCH, BUT IT'S FOR SURE WORTH CONSIDERING THE RISKS.

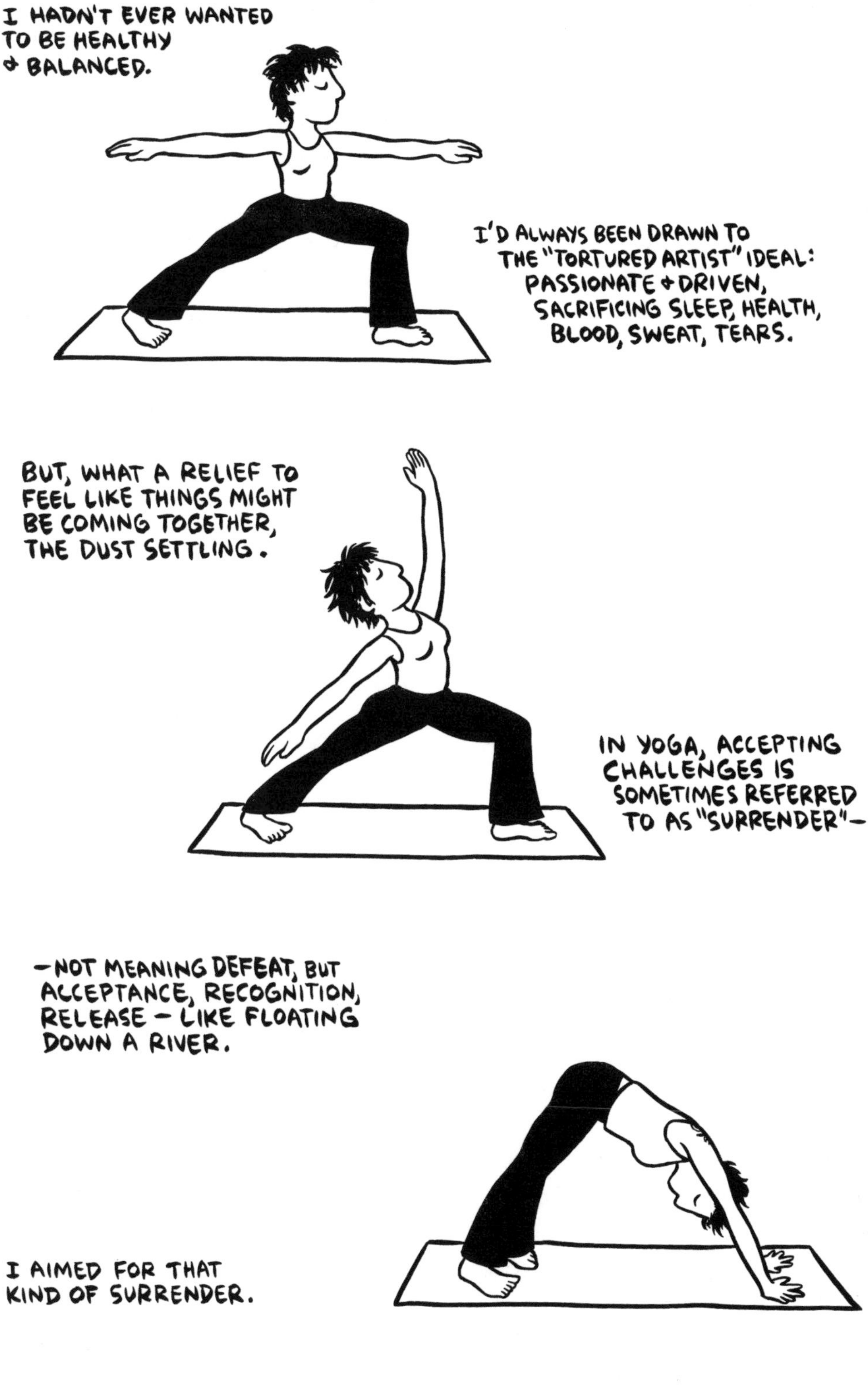
I HADN'T EVER WANTED TO BE HEALTHY & BALANCED.
I'D ALWAYS BEEN DRAWN TO THE "TORTURED ARTIST" IDEAL: PASSIONATE & DRIVEN, SACRIFICING SLEEP, HEALTH, BLOOD, SWEAT, TEARS.
BUT, WHAT A RELIEF TO FEEL LIKE THINGS MIGHT BE COMING TOGETHER, THE DUST SETTLING.
IN YOGA, ACCEPTING CHALLENGES IS SOMETIMES REFERRED TO AS "SURRENDER"—
—NOT MEANING DEFEAT, BUT ACCEPTANCE, RECOGNITION, RELEASE — LIKE FLOATING DOWN A RIVER.
I AIMED FOR THAT KIND OF SURRENDER.

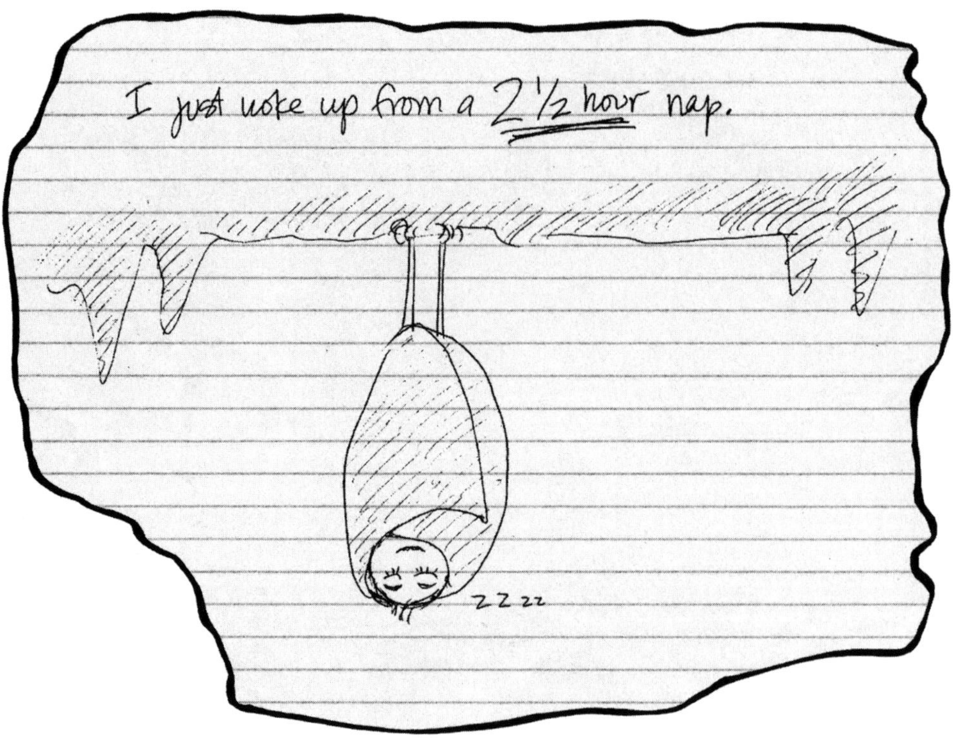
I just woke up from a 2½ hour nap.
ZZzz

I WAS LANDING.

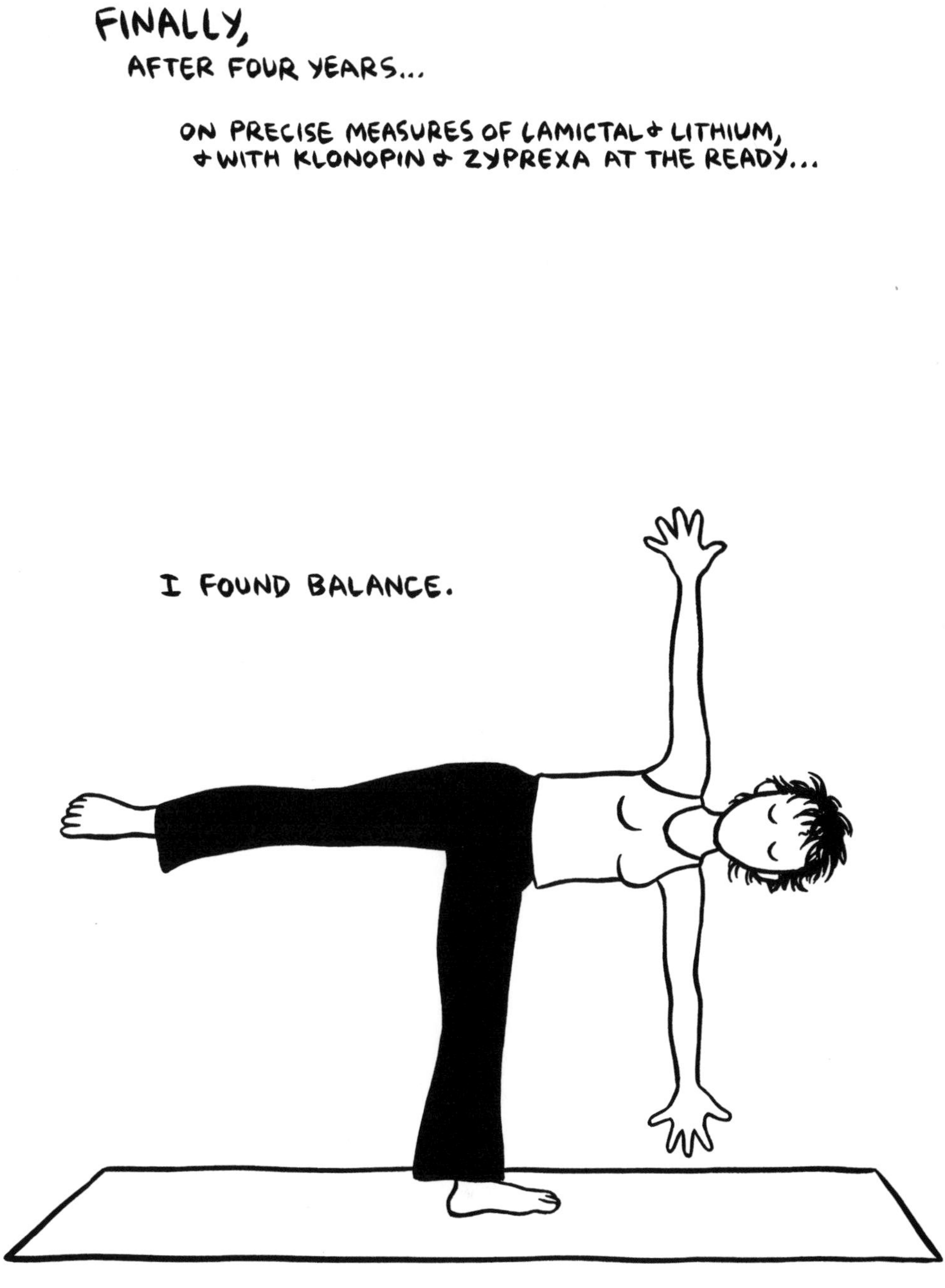
FINALLY,
AFTER FOUR YEARS...
ON PRECISE MEASURES OF LAMICTAL & LITHIUM,
& WITH KLONOPIN & ZYPREXA AT THE READY...
I FOUND BALANCE.

CHAPTER 8

AT LONG LAST, AFTER FINDING MY OWN PATH, IT WAS TIME TO TACKLE SOME OLD QUESTIONS & ASSUMPTIONS ABOUT CLUB VAN GOGH. PART OF ME STILL WONDERED IF "CRAZY ARTIST" MIGHT BE JUST A STEREOTYPE.

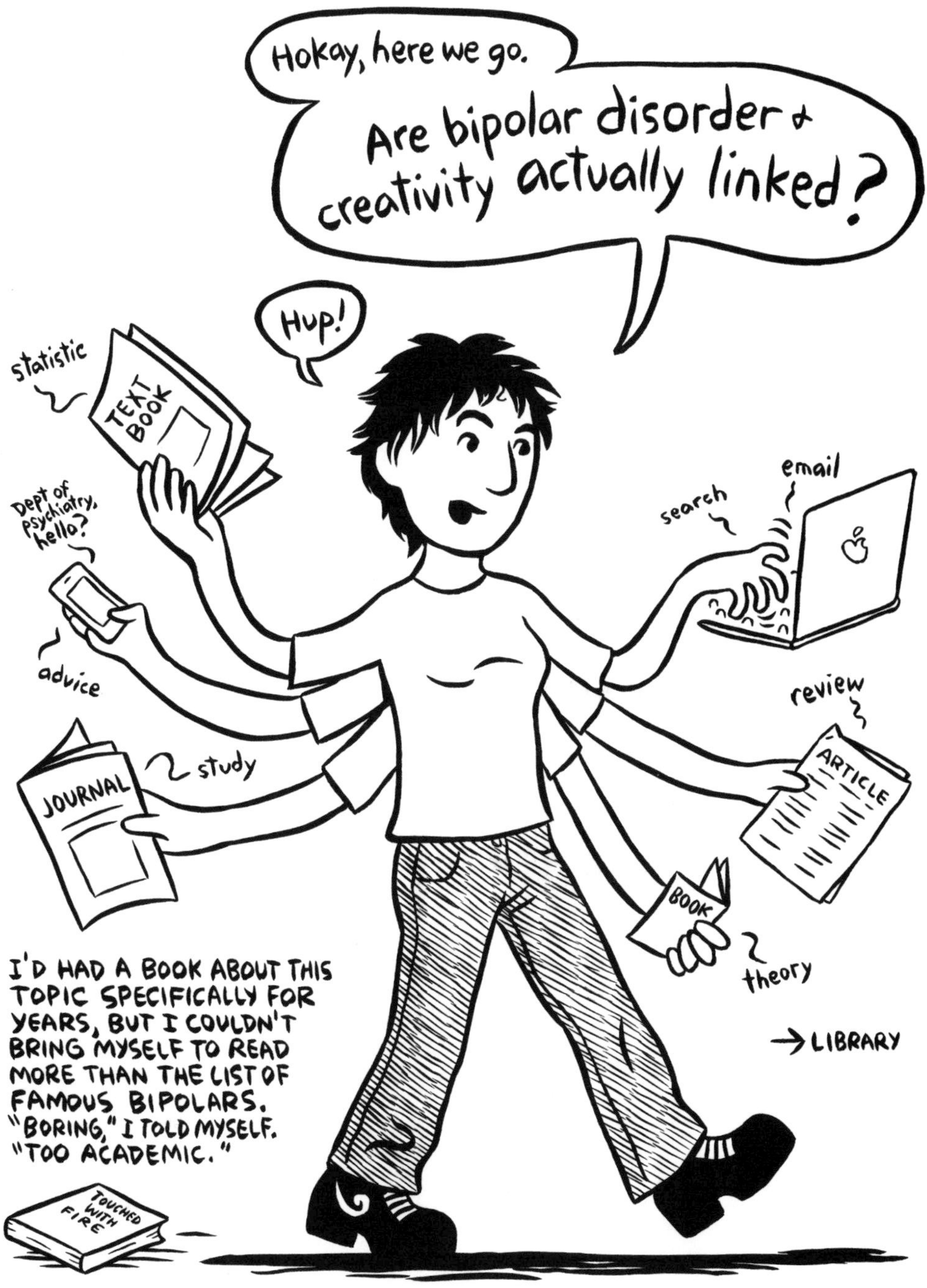
Hokay, here we go.
Are bipolar disorder & creativity actually linked?
Hup!
statistic
TEXT BOOK
Dept of psychiatry, hello?
advice
JOURNAL
study
email
search
review
ARTICLE
BOOK
theory
→ LIBRARY
TOUCHED WITH FIRE

I'D HAD A BOOK ABOUT THIS TOPIC SPECIFICALLY FOR YEARS, BUT I COULDN'T BRING MYSELF TO READ MORE THAN THE LIST OF FAMOUS BIPOLARS. "BORING," I TOLD MYSELF. "TOO ACADEMIC."

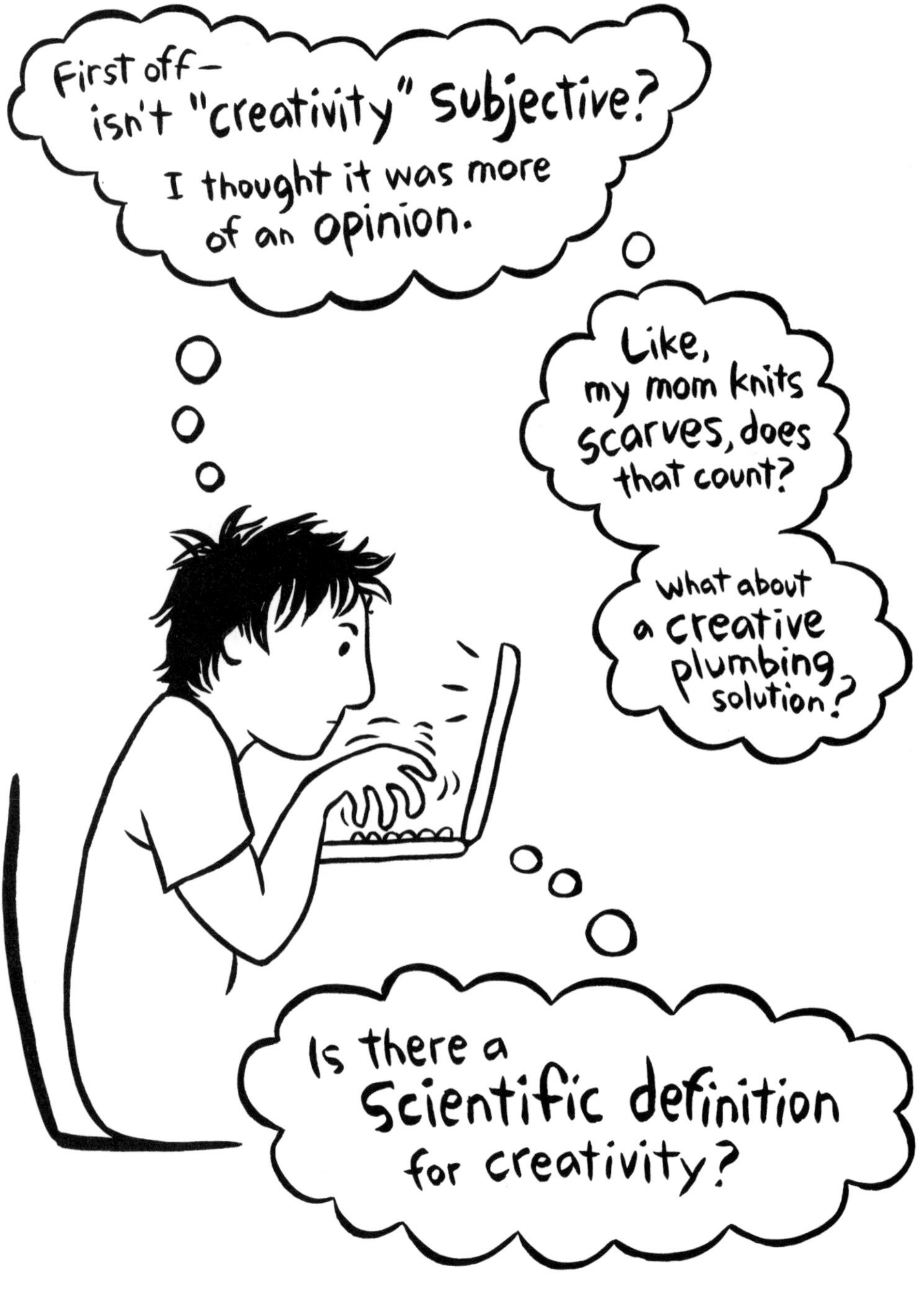
First off— isn't "creativity" subjective?
I thought it was more of an opinion.
Like, my mom knits scarves, does that count?
What about a creative plumbing solution?
Is there a scientific definition for creativity?

CREATIVITY ISN'T EASY TO PINPOINT, BUT MOST RESEARCHERS AGREE ON THIS PARTICULAR

DEFINITION OF CREATIVITY:

n. THOUGHTS & BEHAVIORS THAT ARE ORIGINAL & USEFUL.

(ANDREASEN, 2005)

ITS THREE COMPONENTS ARE:

① PERSON

THEIR CHARACTERISTICS

I free-associate and wear unusual clothes!

OR CHOSEN OCCUPATION

I am a *poet.*

ESPECIALLY IN THE "CREATIVE ARTS," INCLUDING:
- ART
- ARCHITECTURE
- DESIGN
- MUSIC
- THEATER
- WRITING
- POETRY

(LUDWIG, 1992)

② PROCESS OF THINKING

I problem-solve in an interesting way!

toink!

③ PRODUCT

OR IDENTIFIABLE OUTCOME

Eh voilà!

applause! applause!

ting ting!

ORIGINAL & USEFUL!

bouncing baby

SPY camera!

NOTE | FREE TICKET TO BEING DEEMED CREATIVE: BE AN ACCLAIMED ARTIST. e.g. PULITZER PRIZE-WINNING PIANIST = CREATIVE!

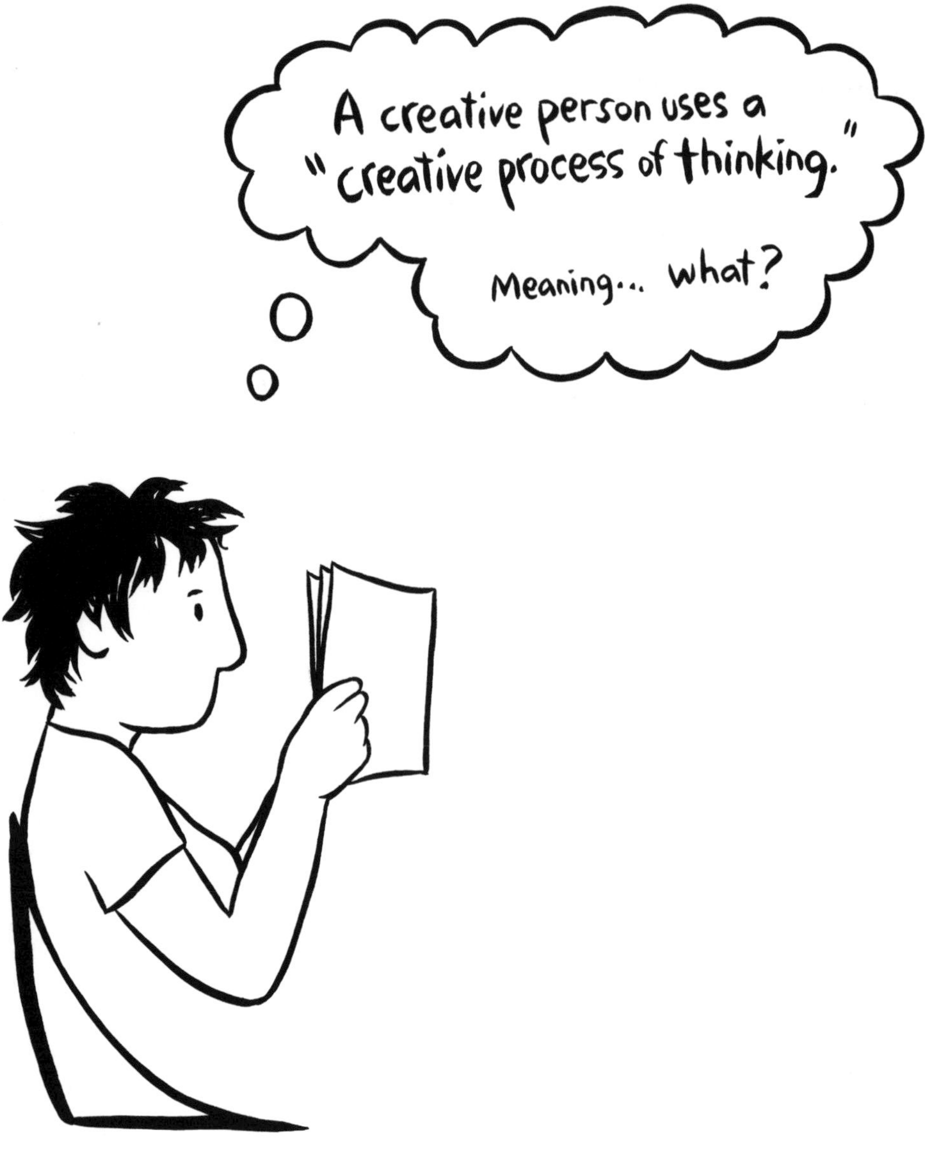
A creative person uses a "creative process of thinking."
Meaning... what?

SOUNDS VAGUE, BUT SCIENCE HAS AN ANSWER FOR THIS, TOO!

CREATIVE THOUGHT

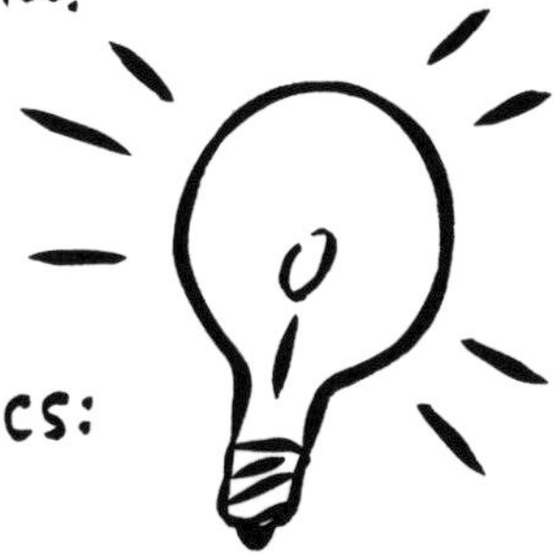

INVOLVES A FEW DIFFERENT CHARACTERISTICS:

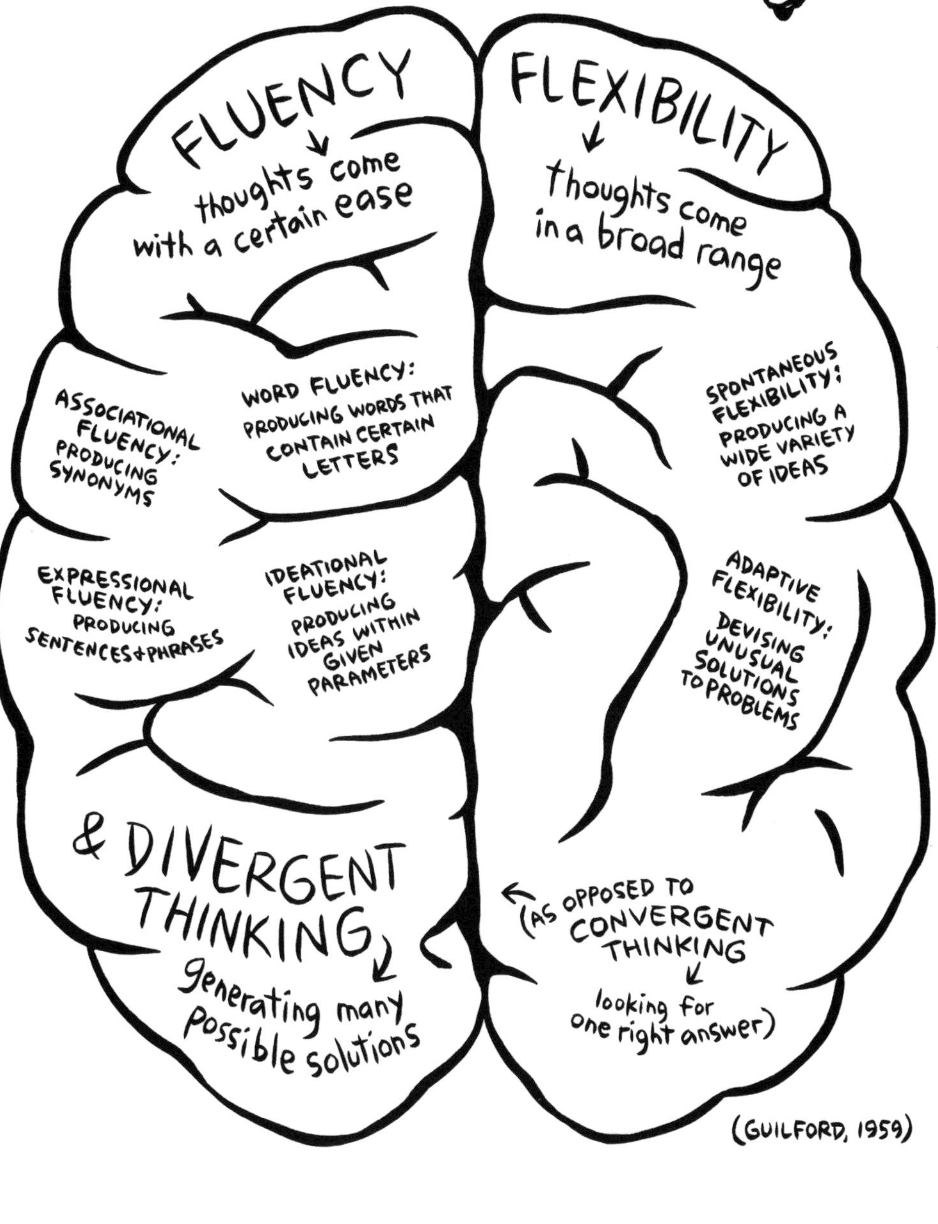
FLUENCY
thoughts come with a certain ease
FLEXIBILITY
thoughts come in a broad range
ASSOCIATIONAL FLUENCY: PRODUCING SYNONYMS
WORD FLUENCY: PRODUCING WORDS THAT CONTAIN CERTAIN LETTERS
SPONTANEOUS FLEXIBILITY: PRODUCING A WIDE VARIETY OF IDEAS
EXPRESSIONAL FLUENCY: PRODUCING SENTENCES & PHRASES
IDEATIONAL FLUENCY: PRODUCING IDEAS WITHIN GIVEN PARAMETERS
ADAPTIVE FLEXIBILITY: DEVISING UNUSUAL SOLUTIONS TO PROBLEMS
& DIVERGENT THINKING
generating many possible solutions
(AS OPPOSED TO CONVERGENT THINKING
looking for one right answer)

(GUILFORD, 1959)

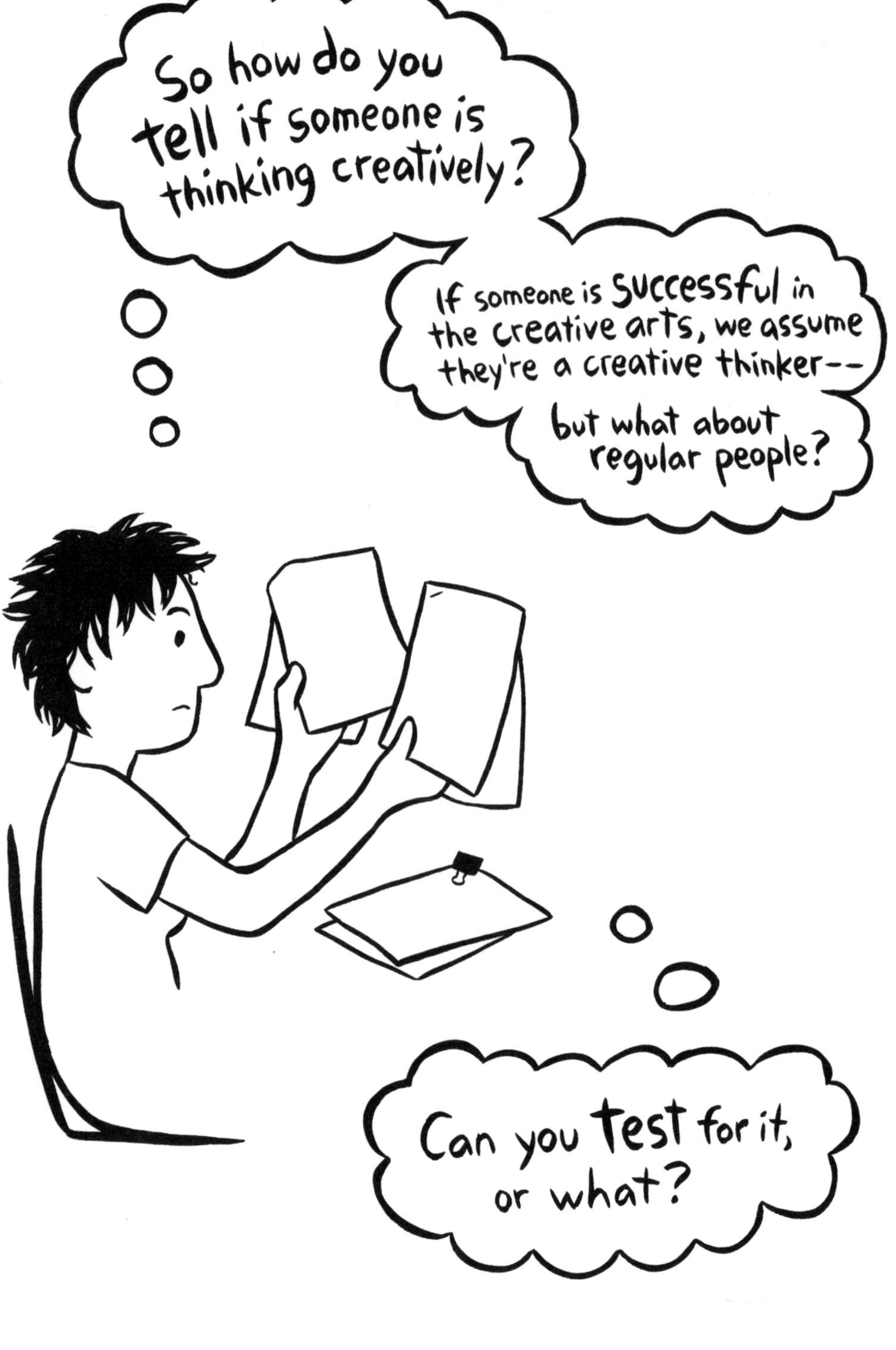
So how do you tell if someone is thinking creatively?
If someone is successful in the creative arts, we assume they're a creative thinker--
but what about regular people?
Can you test for it, or what?

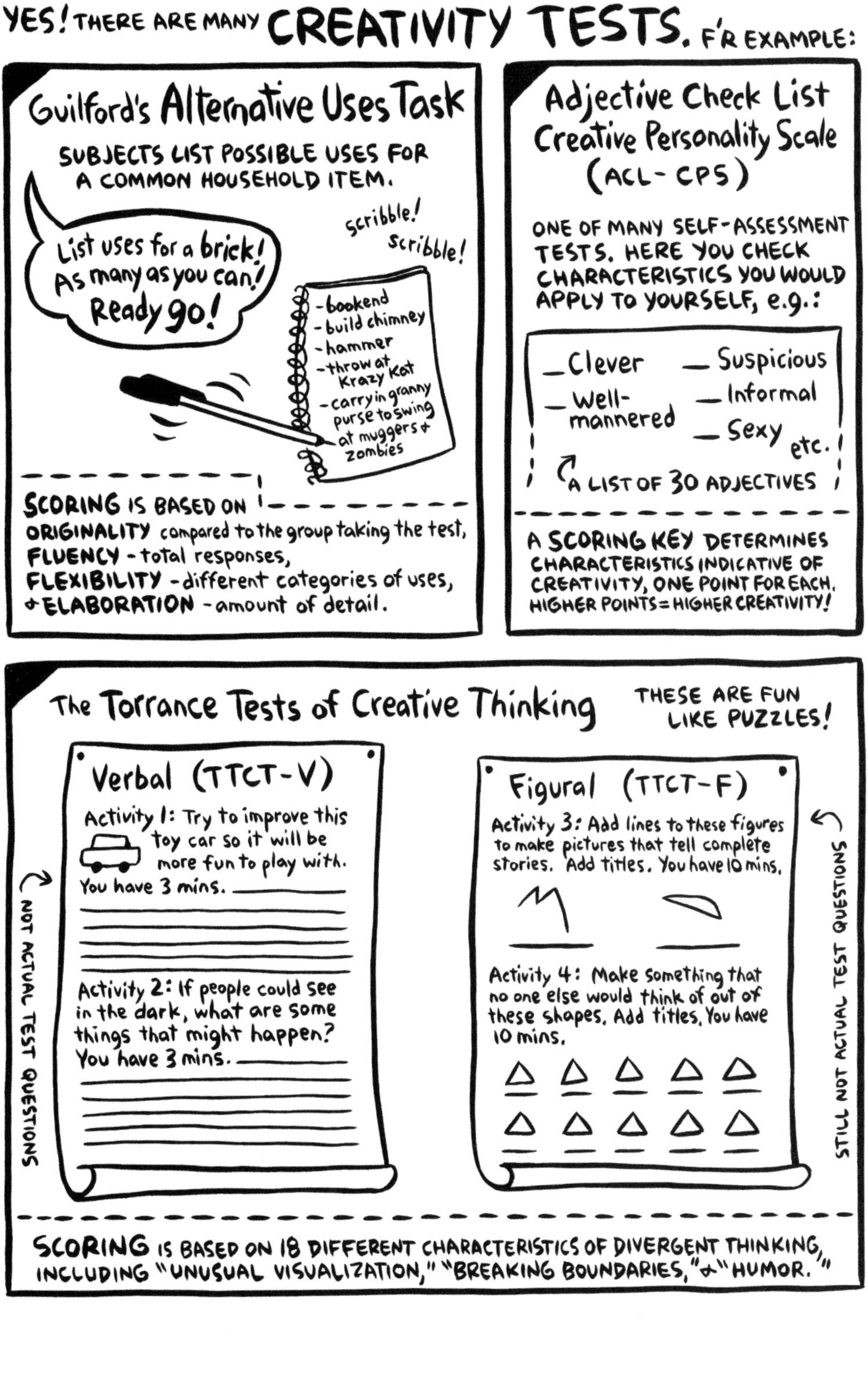
YES! THERE ARE MANY CREATIVITY TESTS. F'R EXAMPLE:
Guilford's Alternative Uses Task
SUBJECTS LIST POSSIBLE USES FOR A COMMON HOUSEHOLD ITEM.
List uses for a brick! As many as you can! Ready go!
scribble! scribble!
-bookend
-build chimney
-hammer
-throw at Krazy Kat
-carry in granny purse to swing at muggers & zombies
SCORING IS BASED ON
ORIGINALITY compared to the group taking the test,
FLUENCY - total responses,
FLEXIBILITY - different categories of uses,
& ELABORATION - amount of detail.
Adjective Check List Creative Personality Scale (ACL-CPS)
ONE OF MANY SELF-ASSESSMENT TESTS. HERE YOU CHECK CHARACTERISTICS YOU WOULD APPLY TO YOURSELF, e.g.:
_Clever
_Suspicious
_Well-mannered
_Informal
_Sexy
etc.
A LIST OF 30 ADJECTIVES
A SCORING KEY DETERMINES CHARACTERISTICS INDICATIVE OF CREATIVITY, ONE POINT FOR EACH. HIGHER POINTS = HIGHER CREATIVITY!
The Torrance Tests of Creative Thinking
THESE ARE FUN LIKE PUZZLES!
Verbal (TTCT-V)
Activity 1: Try to improve this toy car so it will be more fun to play with. You have 3 mins.
Activity 2: If people could see in the dark, what are some things that might happen? You have 3 mins.
NOT ACTUAL TEST QUESTIONS
Figural (TTCT-F)
Activity 3: Add lines to these figures to make pictures that tell complete stories. Add titles. You have 10 mins.
Activity 4: Make something that no one else would think of out of these shapes. Add titles. You have 10 mins.
STILL NOT ACTUAL TEST QUESTIONS
SCORING IS BASED ON 18 DIFFERENT CHARACTERISTICS OF DIVERGENT THINKING, INCLUDING "UNUSUAL VISUALIZATION," "BREAKING BOUNDARIES," & "HUMOR."

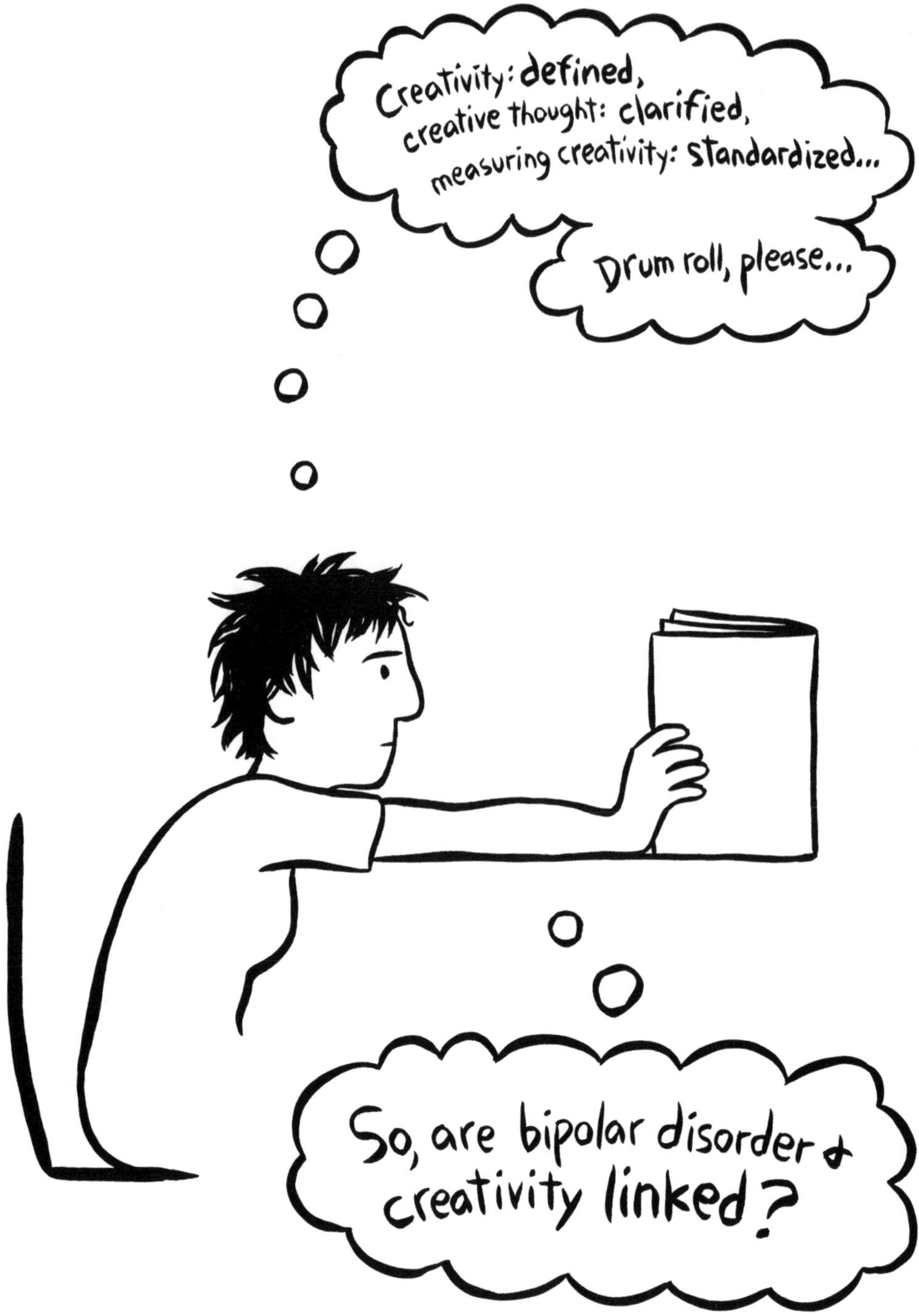
Creativity: defined,
creative thought: clarified,
measuring creativity: standardized...
Drum roll, please...
So, are bipolar disorder & creativity linked?

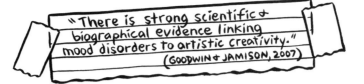

"There is strong scientific & biographical evidence linking mood disorders to artistic creativity."
(GOODWIN & JAMISON, 2007)

MANY RESEARCHERS OVER MANY YEARS HAVE EXAMINED THIS CORRELATION, USING CASE STUDIES, FAMILY STUDIES, CREATIVITY TESTS, & MORE.

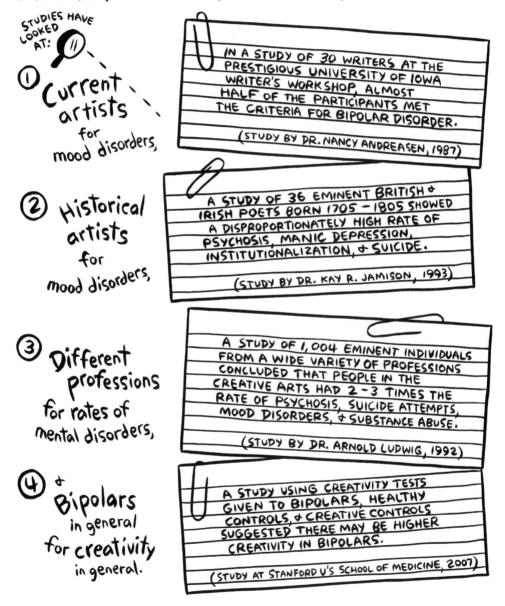

STUDIES HAVE LOOKED AT:

① Current artists for mood disorders,

IN A STUDY OF 30 WRITERS AT THE PRESTIGIOUS UNIVERSITY OF IOWA WRITER'S WORKSHOP, ALMOST HALF OF THE PARTICIPANTS MET THE CRITERIA FOR BIPOLAR DISORDER.

(STUDY BY DR. NANCY ANDREASEN, 1987)

② Historical artists for mood disorders,

A STUDY OF 36 EMINENT BRITISH & IRISH POETS BORN 1705 – 1805 SHOWED A DISPROPORTIONATELY HIGH RATE OF PSYCHOSIS, MANIC DEPRESSION, INSTITUTIONALIZATION, & SUICIDE.

(STUDY BY DR. KAY R. JAMISON, 1993)

③ Different professions for rates of mental disorders,

A STUDY OF 1,004 EMINENT INDIVIDUALS FROM A WIDE VARIETY OF PROFESSIONS CONCLUDED THAT PEOPLE IN THE CREATIVE ARTS HAD 2–3 TIMES THE RATE OF PSYCHOSIS, SUICIDE ATTEMPTS, MOOD DISORDERS, & SUBSTANCE ABUSE.

(STUDY BY DR. ARNOLD LUDWIG, 1992)

④ & Bipolars in general for creativity in general.

A STUDY USING CREATIVITY TESTS GIVEN TO BIPOLARS, HEALTHY CONTROLS, & CREATIVE CONTROLS SUGGESTED THERE MAY BE HIGHER CREATIVITY IN BIPOLARS.

(STUDY AT STANFORD U'S SCHOOL OF MEDICINE, 2007)

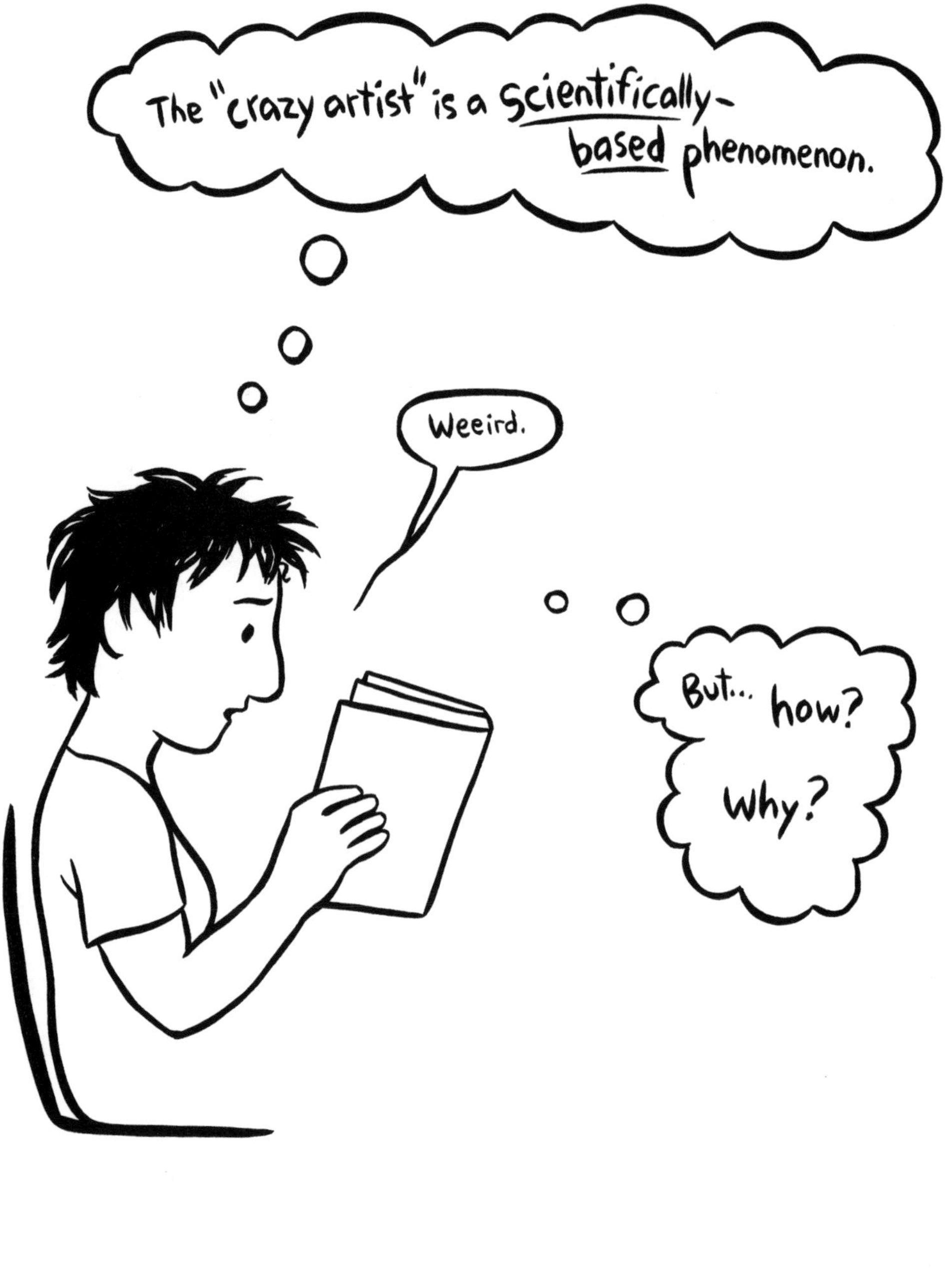
The "crazy artist" is a scientifically-based phenomenon.
Weeird.
But... how?
Why?

HOW? WHY?

WELL, THE BRAIN, IT IS A MYSTERIOUS THING. IT'S GENERALLY ACCEPTED THAT THERE **IS** A CONNECTION, BUT NOBODY SEEMS TO KNOW **WHY**.

OF THE MANY THEORIES, HERE ARE A COUPLE THAT MAKE SENSE TO ME:

① CHARACTERISTICS OF **CREATIVES** **AND** CHARACTERISTICS OF **BIPOLARS**

HAVE A LOT OF **OVERLAP,**

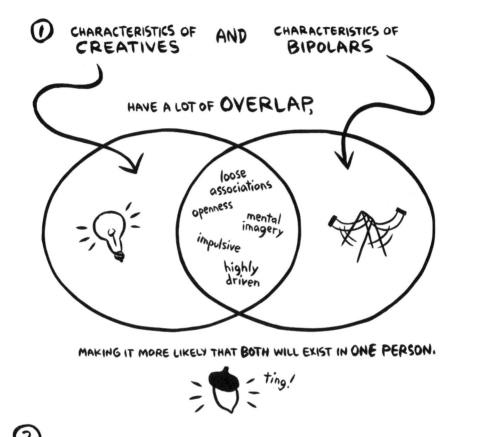

loose associations
openness
mental imagery
impulsive
highly driven

MAKING IT MORE LIKELY THAT **BOTH** WILL EXIST IN **ONE PERSON.**

ting!

② SOME OTHER ASPECTS OF THE CREATIVE ARTS PROFESSIONS, WHILE NOT <u>CAUSING</u> A MENTAL DISORDER, MIGHT PROLONG OR DEEPEN ONE THAT EXISTS.

INTENSE EMOTIONS TEND TO BE HIGHLY VALUED

DRUG & ALCOHOL USE IS COMMON (CULTURALLY & AS A PERFORMANCE ENHANCER)

IRREGULAR SCHEDULE = IRREGULAR SLEEP = OFF-KILTER CIRCADIAN RHYTHMS

HIGH GOALS BUT WITH EXTREME UPS & DOWNS IN RECOGNITION FOR WORK

COMMON LACK OF: JOB SECURITY... FINANCIAL STABILITY... HEALTH INSURANCE... =STRESS

Wow, this is kind of disconcerting.
Some of these studies correlate creativity just with mania.
Mad genius/crazy artist was much easier to think about as a stereotype.
I guess my real question now is...

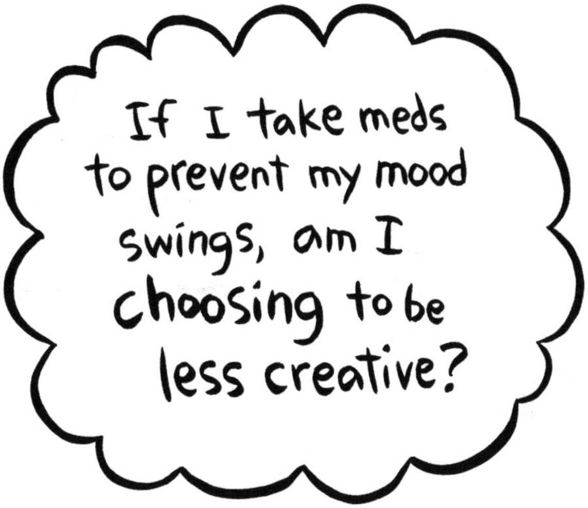
If I take meds to prevent my mood swings, am I choosing to be less creative?

That was my question
Specifically, when Karen first recommended I take lithium.
It terrified me.
For all these years, ever since I first started taking meds, I haven't wanted to confront that question again.

LOOKING THROUGH THE RESEARCH WAS UNSETTLING. THE INFORMATION WAS AMBIGUOUS, VARYING FROM PERSON TO PERSON & STUDY TO STUDY.

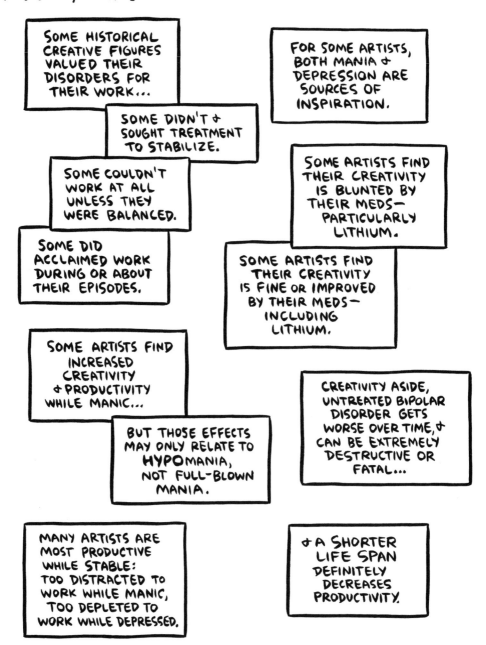

SOME HISTORICAL CREATIVE FIGURES VALUED THEIR DISORDERS FOR THEIR WORK...

SOME DIDN'T & SOUGHT TREATMENT TO STABILIZE.

SOME COULDN'T WORK AT ALL UNLESS THEY WERE BALANCED.

SOME DID ACCLAIMED WORK DURING OR ABOUT THEIR EPISODES.

FOR SOME ARTISTS, BOTH MANIA & DEPRESSION ARE SOURCES OF INSPIRATION.

SOME ARTISTS FIND THEIR CREATIVITY IS BLUNTED BY THEIR MEDS— PARTICULARLY LITHIUM.

SOME ARTISTS FIND THEIR CREATIVITY IS FINE OR IMPROVED BY THEIR MEDS— INCLUDING LITHIUM.

SOME ARTISTS FIND INCREASED CREATIVITY & PRODUCTIVITY WHILE MANIC...

BUT THOSE EFFECTS MAY ONLY RELATE TO HYPOMANIA, NOT FULL-BLOWN MANIA.

CREATIVITY ASIDE, UNTREATED BIPOLAR DISORDER GETS WORSE OVER TIME, & CAN BE EXTREMELY DESTRUCTIVE OR FATAL...

MANY ARTISTS ARE MOST PRODUCTIVE WHILE STABLE: TOO DISTRACTED TO WORK WHILE MANIC, TOO DEPLETED TO WORK WHILE DEPRESSED.

& A SHORTER LIFE SPAN DEFINITELY DECREASES PRODUCTIVITY.

THE ISSUES WERE PART MEDICAL, PART PHILOSOPHICAL.

I'm glad I didn't read all this back when I was first diagnosed. It was so confusing, trying to make the right choices--
--though really, I didn't choose to take meds, it was a basic survival instinct.
I never want to experience pain like that again.
Thank god my meds don't flatten me.
Actually, I guess they help my creativity, because it's when I'm balanced that I can really focus & get my work done.

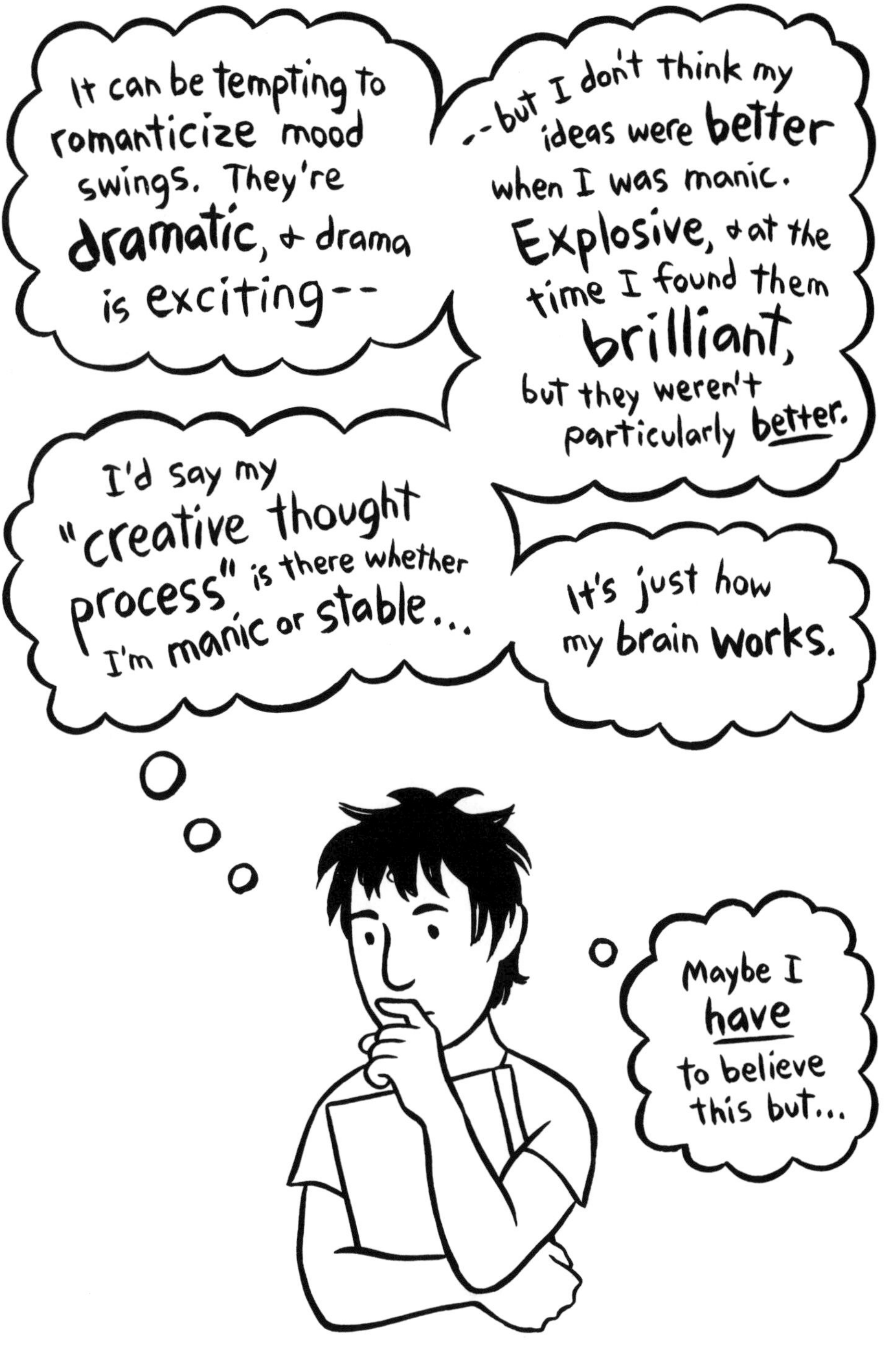
It can be tempting to romanticize mood swings. They're dramatic, & drama is exciting--
--but I don't think my ideas were better when I was manic. Explosive, & at the time I found them brilliant, but they weren't particularly better.
I'd say my "creative thought process" is there whether I'm manic or stable...
It's just how my brain works.
Maybe I have to believe this but...

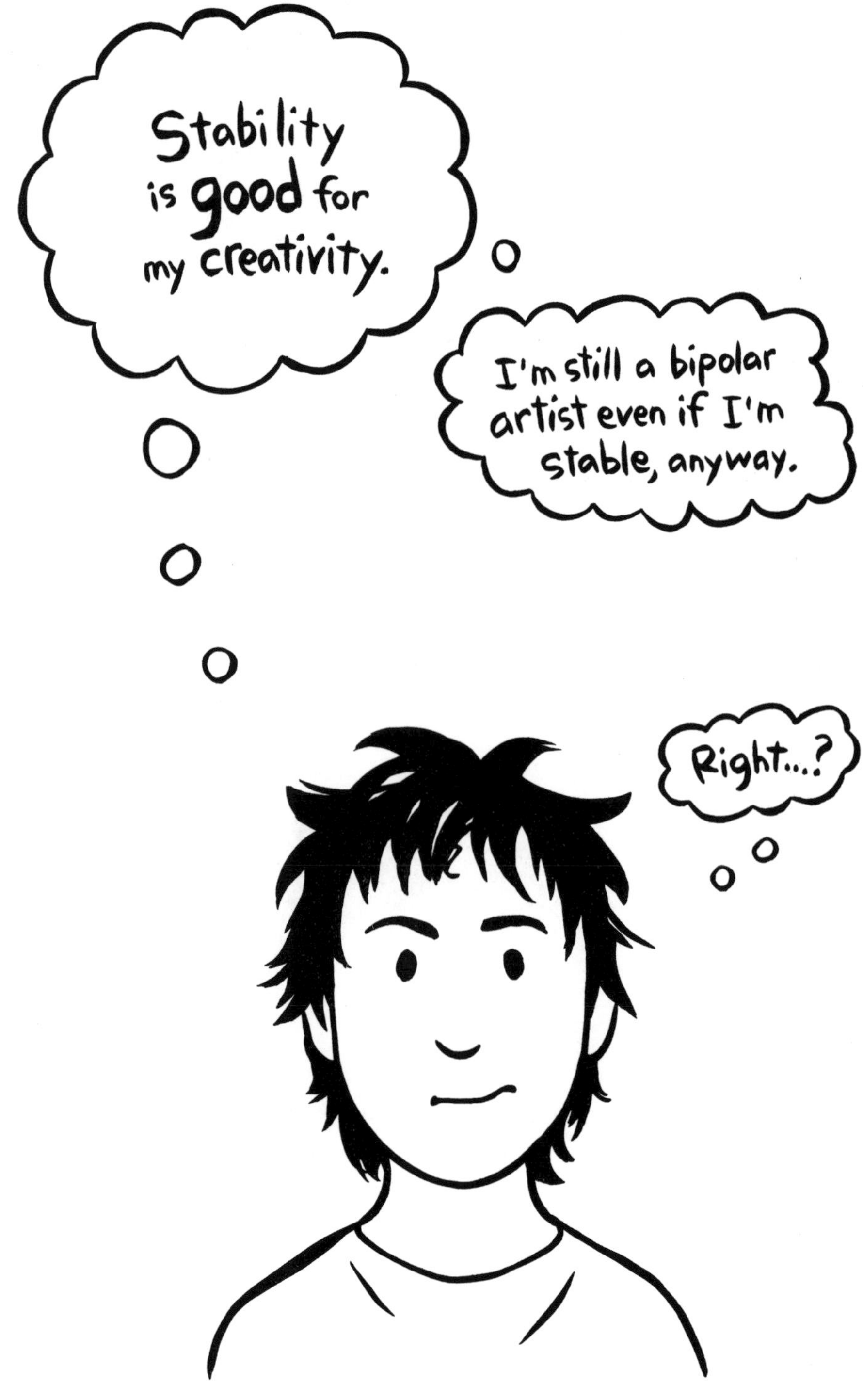
Stability is good for my creativity.
I'm still a bipolar artist even if I'm stable, anyway.
Right...?

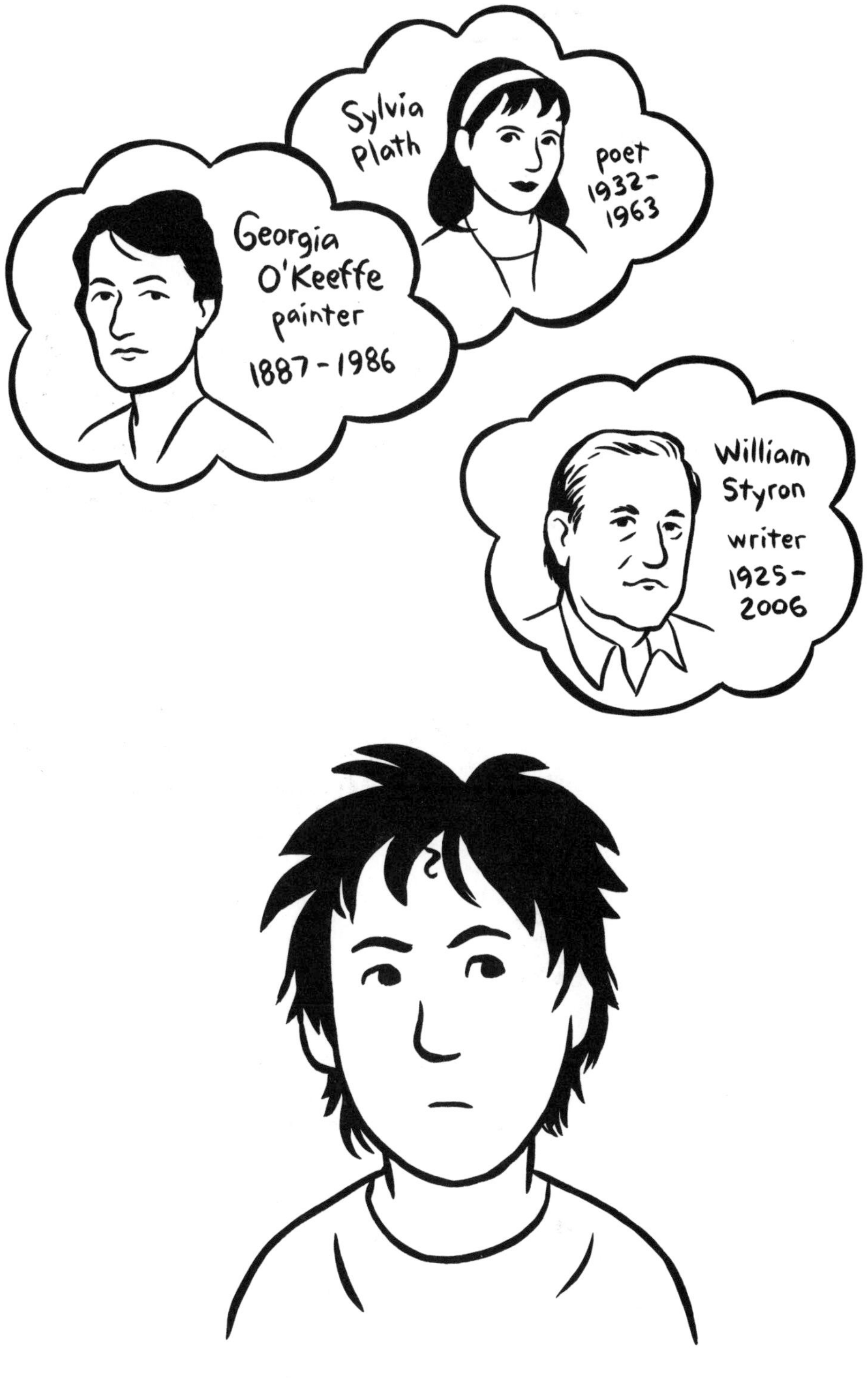
Sylvia Plath
poet 1932-1963
Georgia O'Keeffe
painter
1887-1986
William Styron
writer
1925-2006

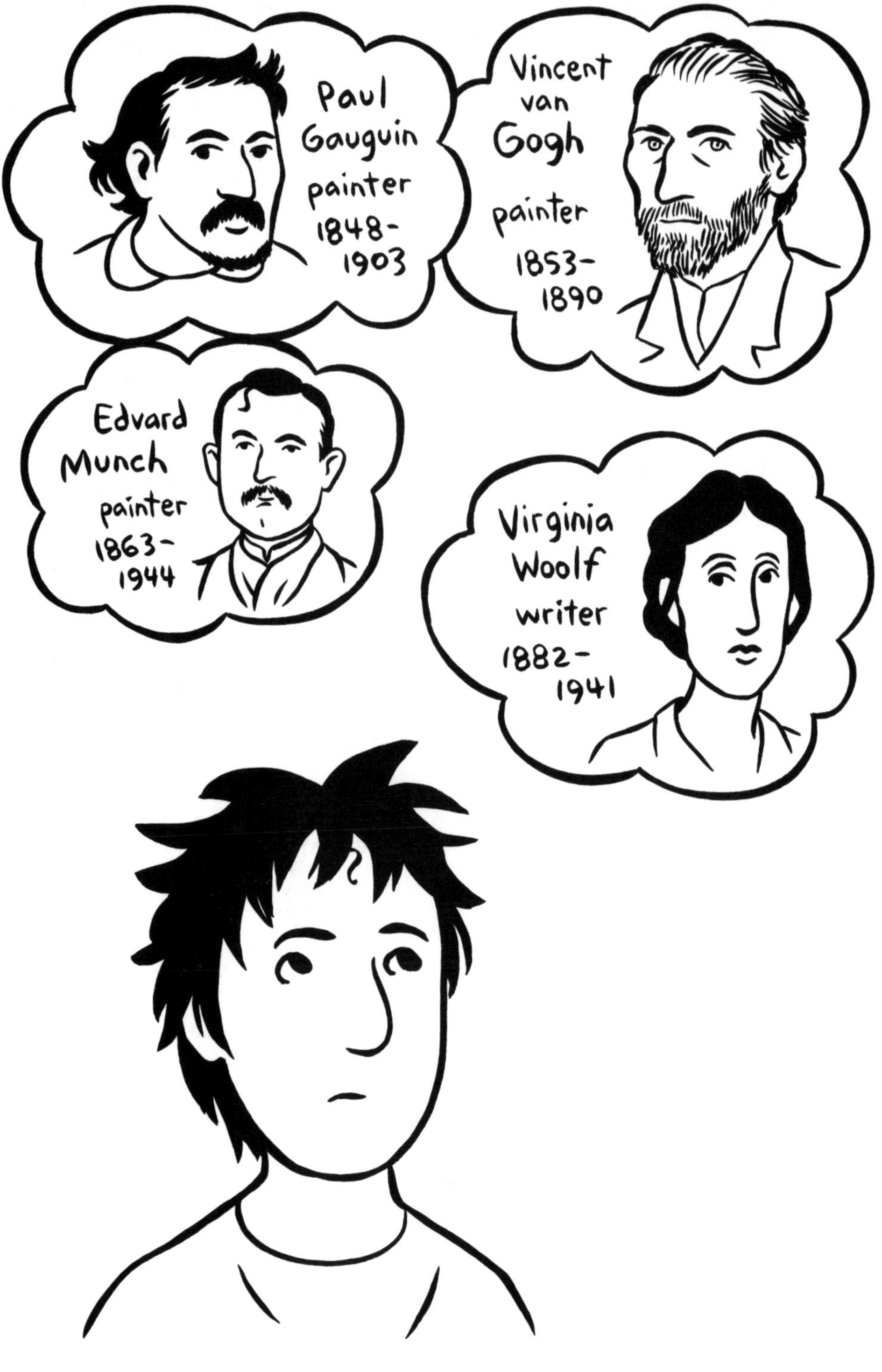
Paul Gauguin painter 1848-1903
Vincent van Gogh painter 1853-1890
Edvard Munch painter 1863-1944
Virginia Woolf writer 1882-1941

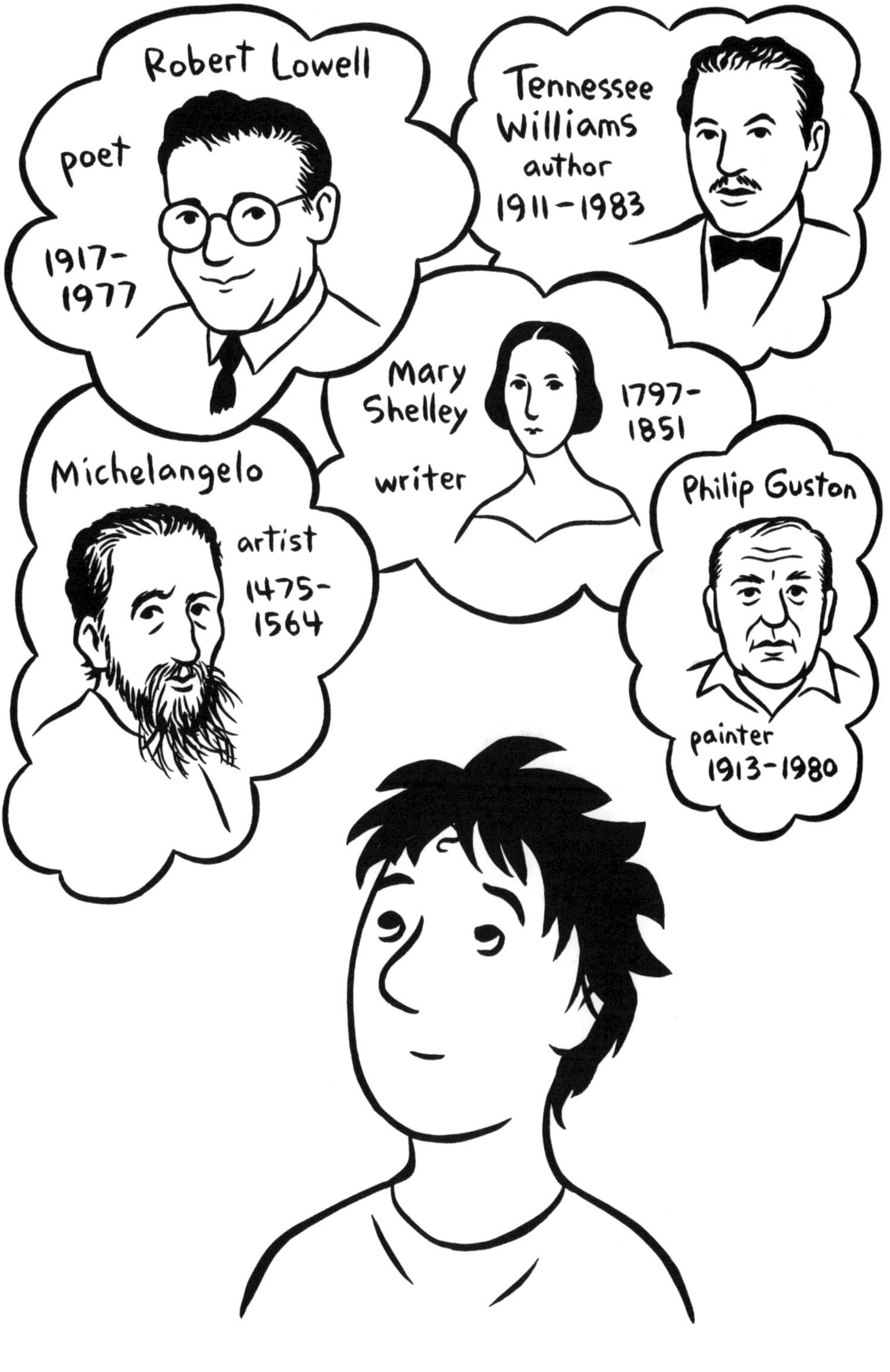
Robert Lowell
poet
1917-
1977
Tennessee
Williams
author
1911-1983
Mary
Shelley
1797-
1851
writer
Michelangelo
artist
1475-
1564
Philip Guston
painter
1913-1980

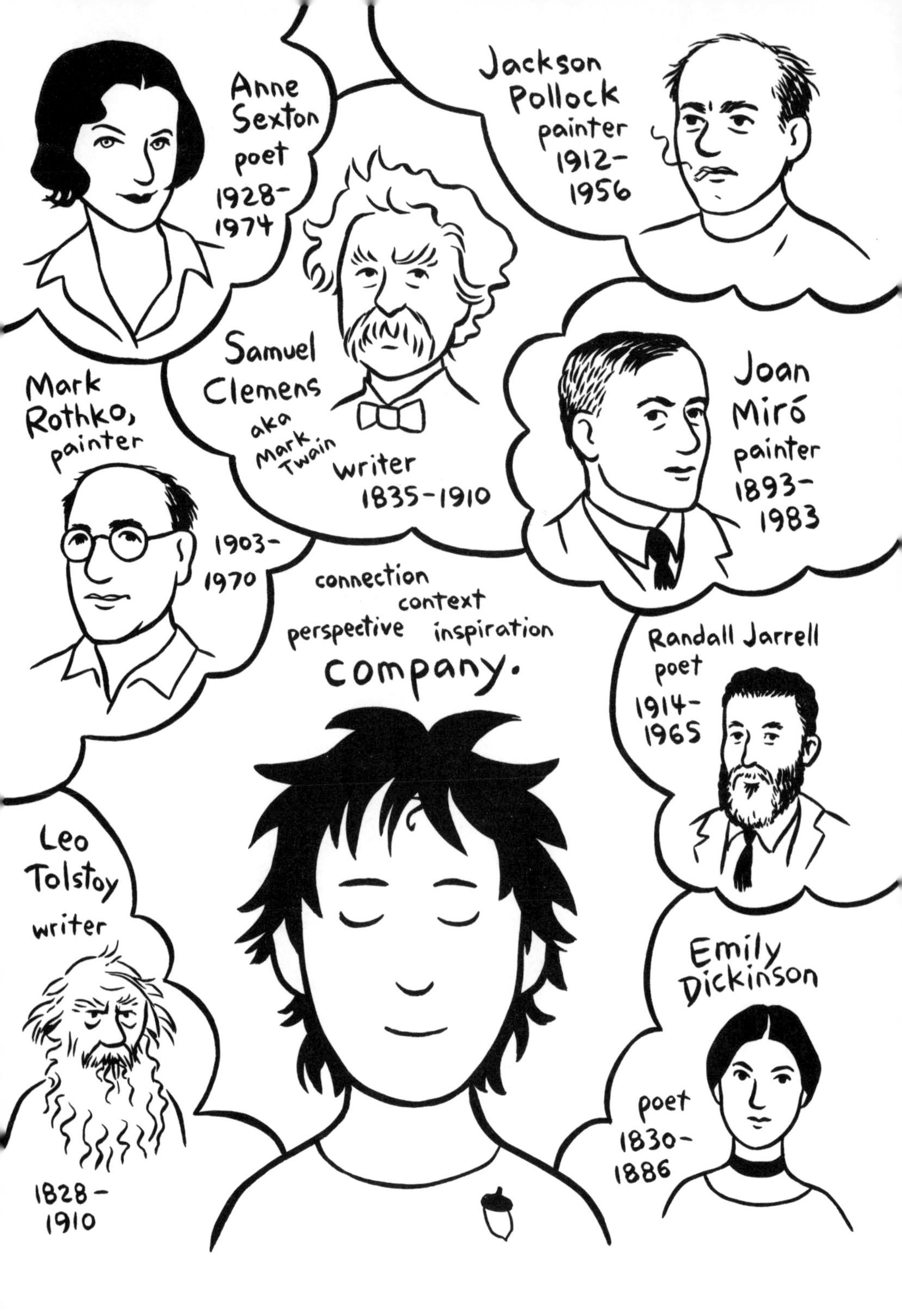

Anne Sexton poet 1928-1974
Jackson Pollock painter 1912-1956
Samuel Clemens aka Mark Twain writer 1835-1910
Mark Rothko, painter 1903-1970
Joan Miró painter 1893-1983
connection
context
perspective
inspiration
company.
Randall Jarrell poet 1914-1965
Leo Tolstoy writer 1828-1910
Emily Dickinson poet 1830-1886

CHAPTER 9

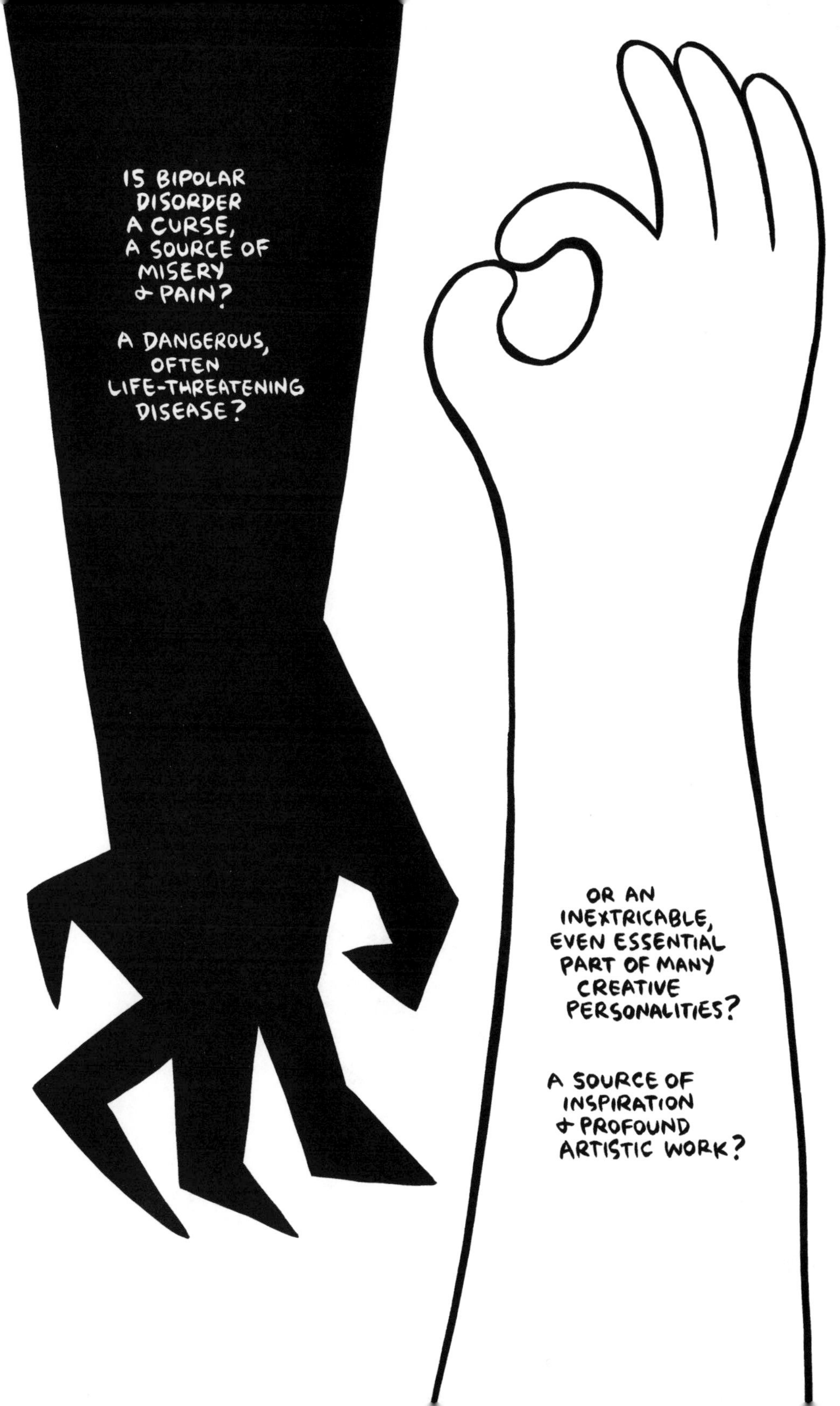
IS BIPOLAR DISORDER A CURSE, A SOURCE OF MISERY & PAIN?
A DANGEROUS, OFTEN LIFE-THREATENING DISEASE?
OR AN INEXTRICABLE, EVEN ESSENTIAL PART OF MANY CREATIVE PERSONALITIES?
A SOURCE OF INSPIRATION & PROFOUND ARTISTIC WORK?

I SUPPOSE IT'S BOTH.

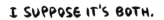

FOR BETTER & WORSE, BIPOLAR DISORDER IS
AN IMPORTANT PART OF WHO I AM & HOW I THINK.

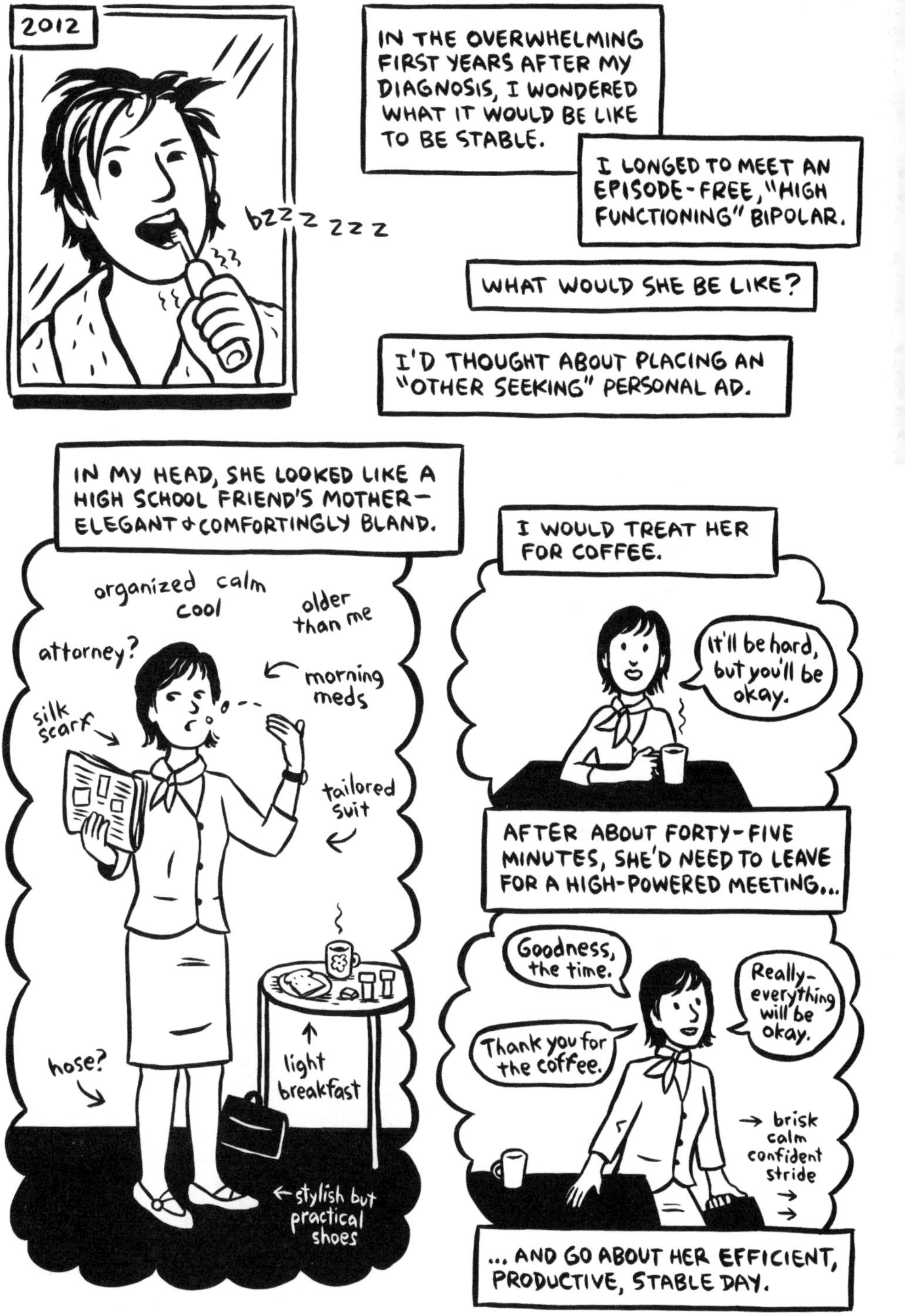
2012
IN THE OVERWHELMING FIRST YEARS AFTER MY DIAGNOSIS, I WONDERED WHAT IT WOULD BE LIKE TO BE STABLE.
bzzz zzz
I LONGED TO MEET AN EPISODE-FREE, "HIGH FUNCTIONING" BIPOLAR.
WHAT WOULD SHE BE LIKE?
I'D THOUGHT ABOUT PLACING AN "OTHER SEEKING" PERSONAL AD.
IN MY HEAD, SHE LOOKED LIKE A HIGH SCHOOL FRIEND'S MOTHER— ELEGANT & COMFORTINGLY BLAND.
organized calm
cool
older than me
attorney?
morning meds
silk scarf
tailored suit
light breakfast
hose?
stylish but practical shoes
I WOULD TREAT HER FOR COFFEE.
It'll be hard, but you'll be okay.
AFTER ABOUT FORTY-FIVE MINUTES, SHE'D NEED TO LEAVE FOR A HIGH-POWERED MEETING...
Goodness, the time.
Really— everything will be okay.
Thank you for the coffee.
brisk calm confident stride
... AND GO ABOUT HER EFFICIENT, PRODUCTIVE, STABLE DAY.

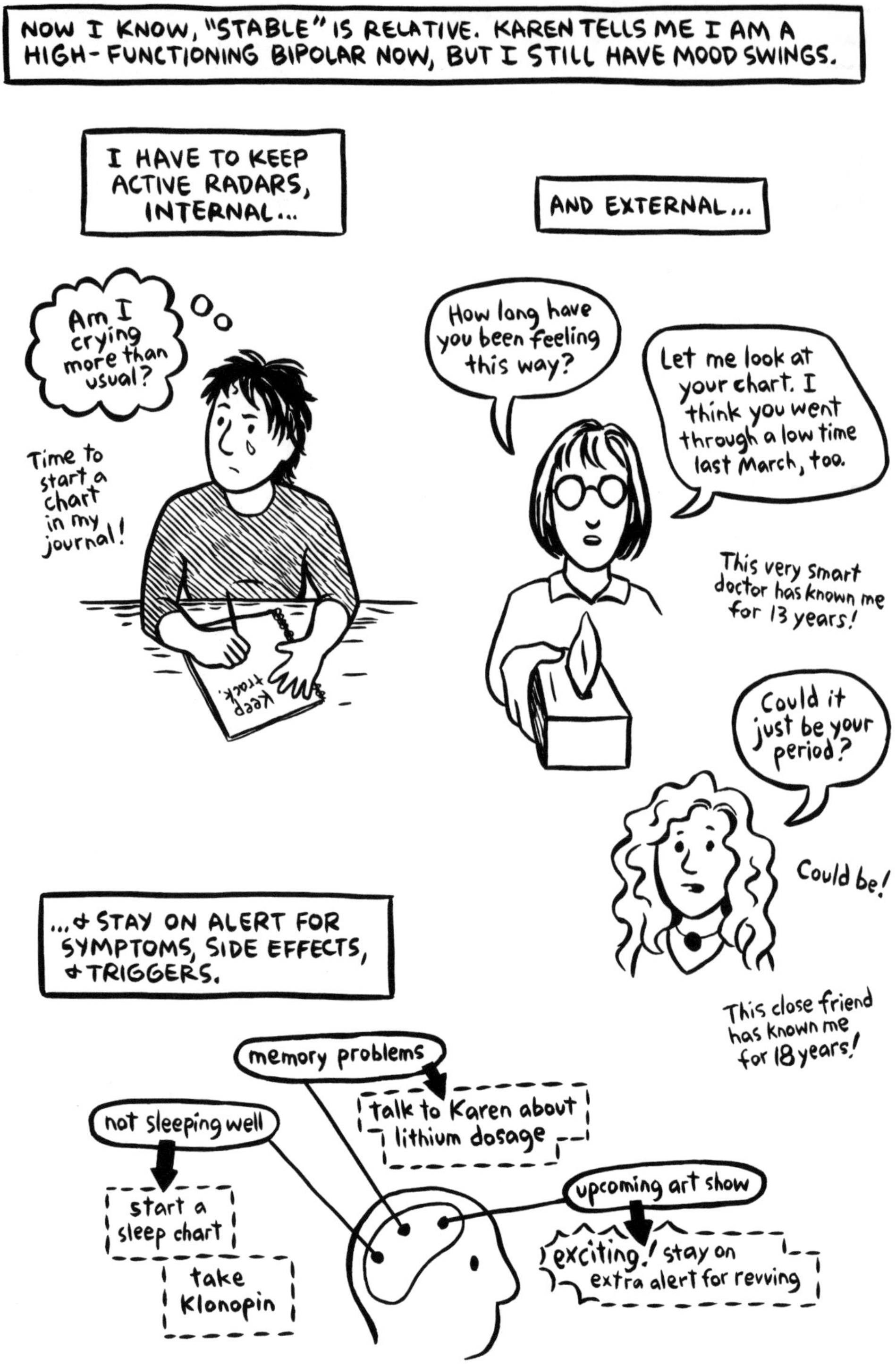
NOW I KNOW, "STABLE" IS RELATIVE. KAREN TELLS ME I AM A HIGH-FUNCTIONING BIPOLAR NOW, BUT I STILL HAVE MOOD SWINGS.
I HAVE TO KEEP ACTIVE RADARS, INTERNAL...
Am I crying more than usual?
Time to start a chart in my journal!
keep track.
AND EXTERNAL...
How long have you been feeling this way?
Let me look at your chart. I think you went through a low time last March, too.
This very smart doctor has known me for 13 years!
Could it just be your period?
Could be!
This close friend has known me for 18 years!
...& STAY ON ALERT FOR SYMPTOMS, SIDE EFFECTS, & TRIGGERS.
memory problems
talk to Karen about lithium dosage
not sleeping well
start a sleep chart
take Klonopin
upcoming art show
exciting! stay on extra alert for revving

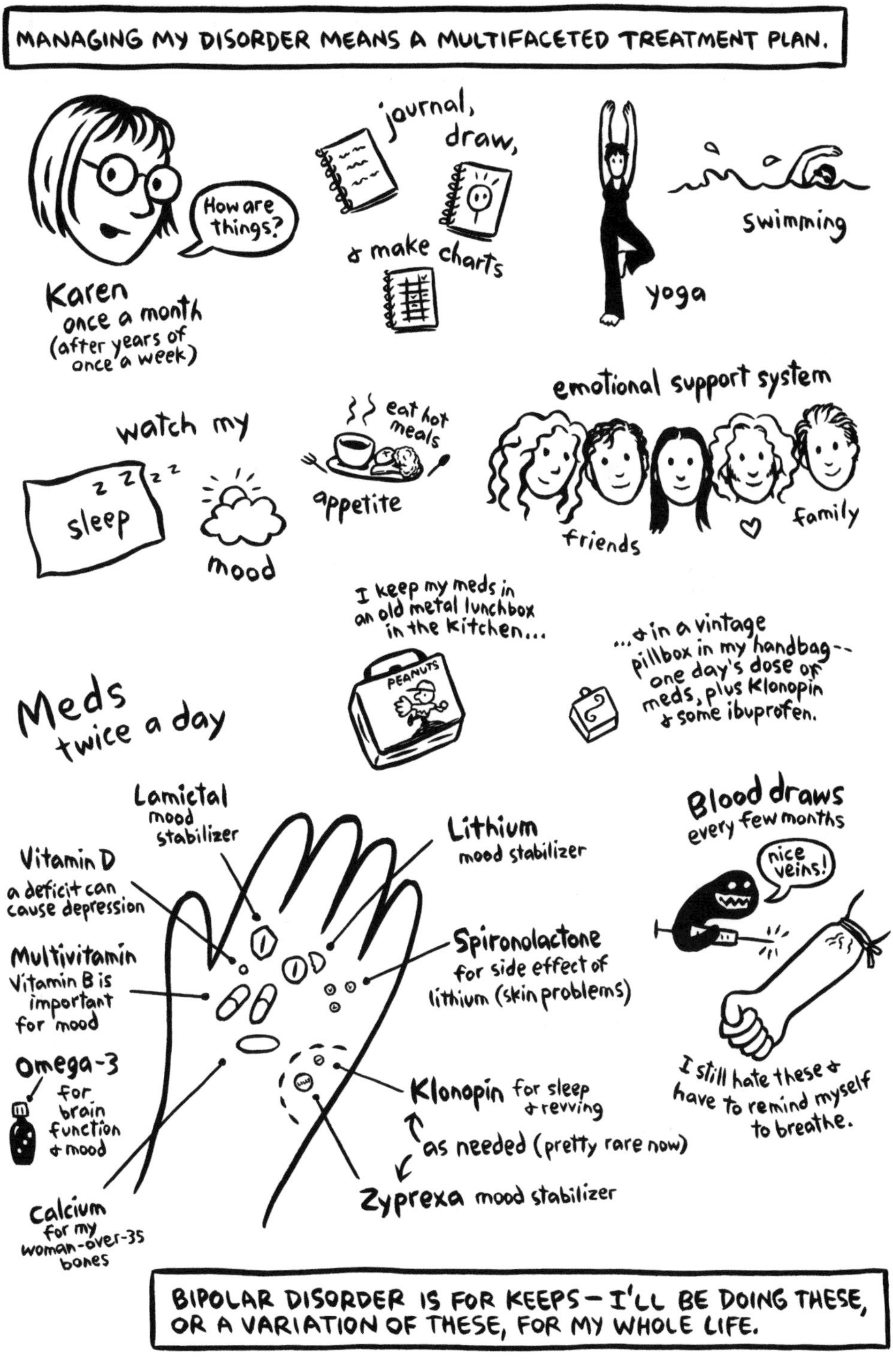
MANAGING MY DISORDER MEANS A MULTIFACETED TREATMENT PLAN.
How are things?
Karen once a month (after years of once a week)
journal, draw, & make charts
yoga
swimming
watch my
z z z z
sleep
mood
eat hot meals
appetite
emotional support system
friends
family
I keep my meds in an old metal lunchbox in the kitchen...
PEANUTS
...& in a vintage pillbox in my handbag-- one day's dose of meds, plus Klonopin & some ibuprofen.
Meds twice a day
Lamictal mood stabilizer
Lithium mood stabilizer
Vitamin D a deficit can cause depression
Multivitamin Vitamin B is important for mood
Spironolactone for side effect of lithium (skin problems)
Omega-3 for brain function & mood
Klonopin for sleep & revving
as needed (pretty rare now)
Zyprexa mood stabilizer
Calcium for my woman-over-35 bones
Blood draws every few months
nice veins!
I still hate these & have to remind myself to breathe.
BIPOLAR DISORDER IS FOR KEEPS — I'LL BE DOING THESE, OR A VARIATION OF THESE, FOR MY WHOLE LIFE.

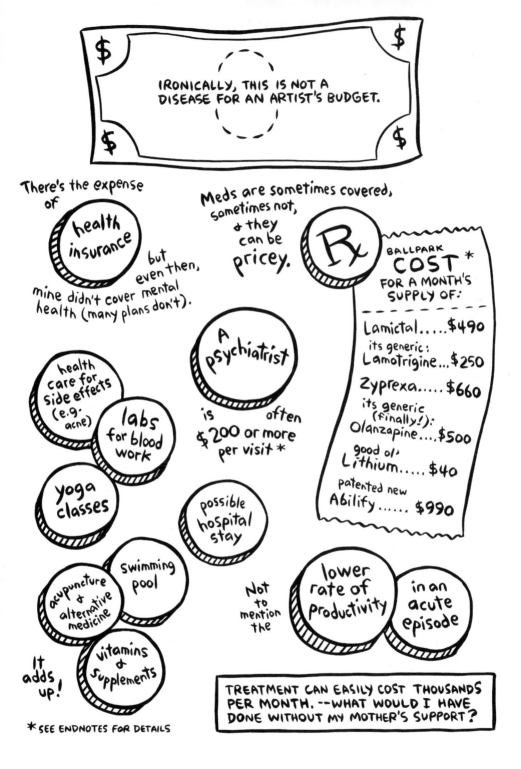

IRONICALLY, THIS IS NOT A DISEASE FOR AN ARTIST'S BUDGET.

There's the expense of health insurance but then, even then, mine didn't cover mental health (many plans don't).

Meds are sometimes covered, sometimes not, & they can be pricey.

health care for side effects (e.g. acne)

labs for blood work

yoga classes

A psychiatrist is often $200 or more per visit *

acupuncture & alternative medicine

swimming pool

possible hospital stay

vitamins & supplements

It adds up!

* SEE ENDNOTES FOR DETAILS

R
BALLPARK COST *
FOR A MONTH'S SUPPLY OF:

Lamictal.....$490
its generic:
Lamotrigine...$250

Zyprexa.....$660
its generic (finally!):
Olanzapine....$500

good ol'
Lithium.....$40

patented new
Ability......$990

Not to mention the lower rate of productivity in an acute episode

TREATMENT CAN EASILY COST THOUSANDS PER MONTH. --WHAT WOULD I HAVE DONE WITHOUT MY MOTHER'S SUPPORT?

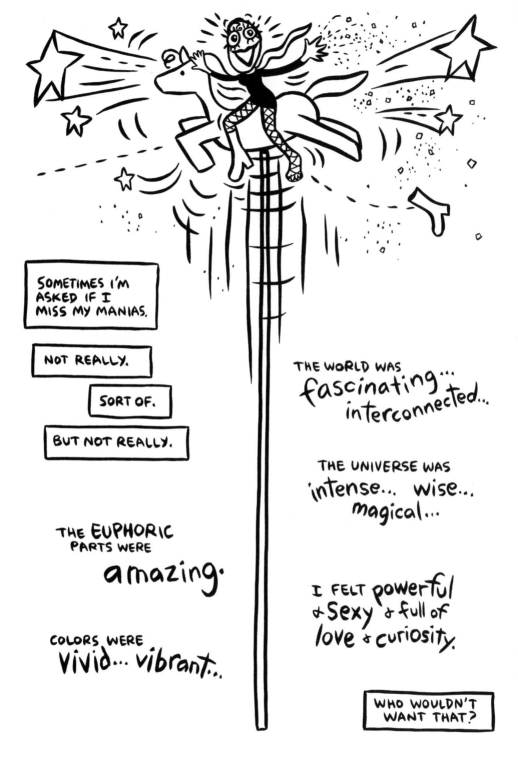

SOMETIMES I'M ASKED IF I MISS MY MANIAS.

NOT REALLY.

SORT OF.

BUT NOT REALLY.

THE WORLD WAS fascinating... interconnected...

THE UNIVERSE WAS intense... wise... magical...

THE EUPHORIC PARTS WERE amazing.

COLORS WERE vivid... vibrant...

I FELT powerful & sexy & full of love & curiosity.

WHO WOULDN'T WANT THAT?

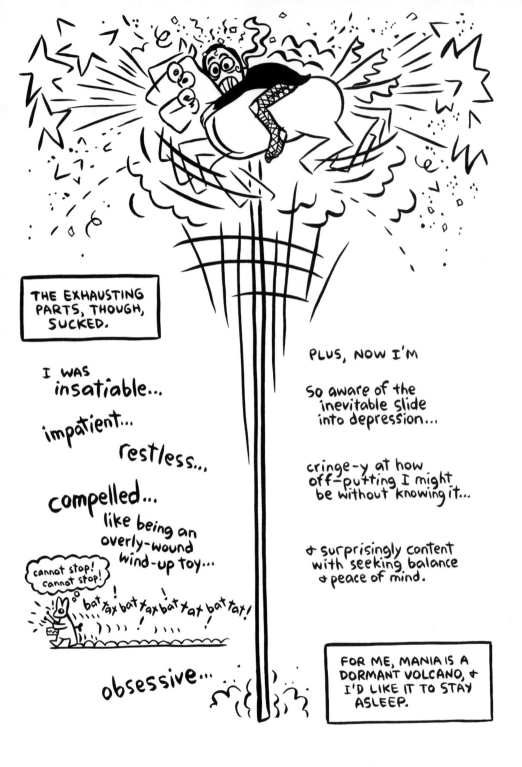

THE EXHAUSTING PARTS, THOUGH, SUCKED.

I WAS insatiable...

impatient...

restless...

compelled...

like being an overly-wound wind-up toy...

cannot stop! cannot stop!

bat tat bat tat bat tat bat tat!

obsessive...

PLUS, NOW I'M

so aware of the inevitable slide into depression...

cringe-y at how off-putting I might be without knowing it...

& surprisingly content with seeking balance & peace of mind.

FOR ME, MANIA IS A DORMANT VOLCANO, & I'D LIKE IT TO STAY ASLEEP.

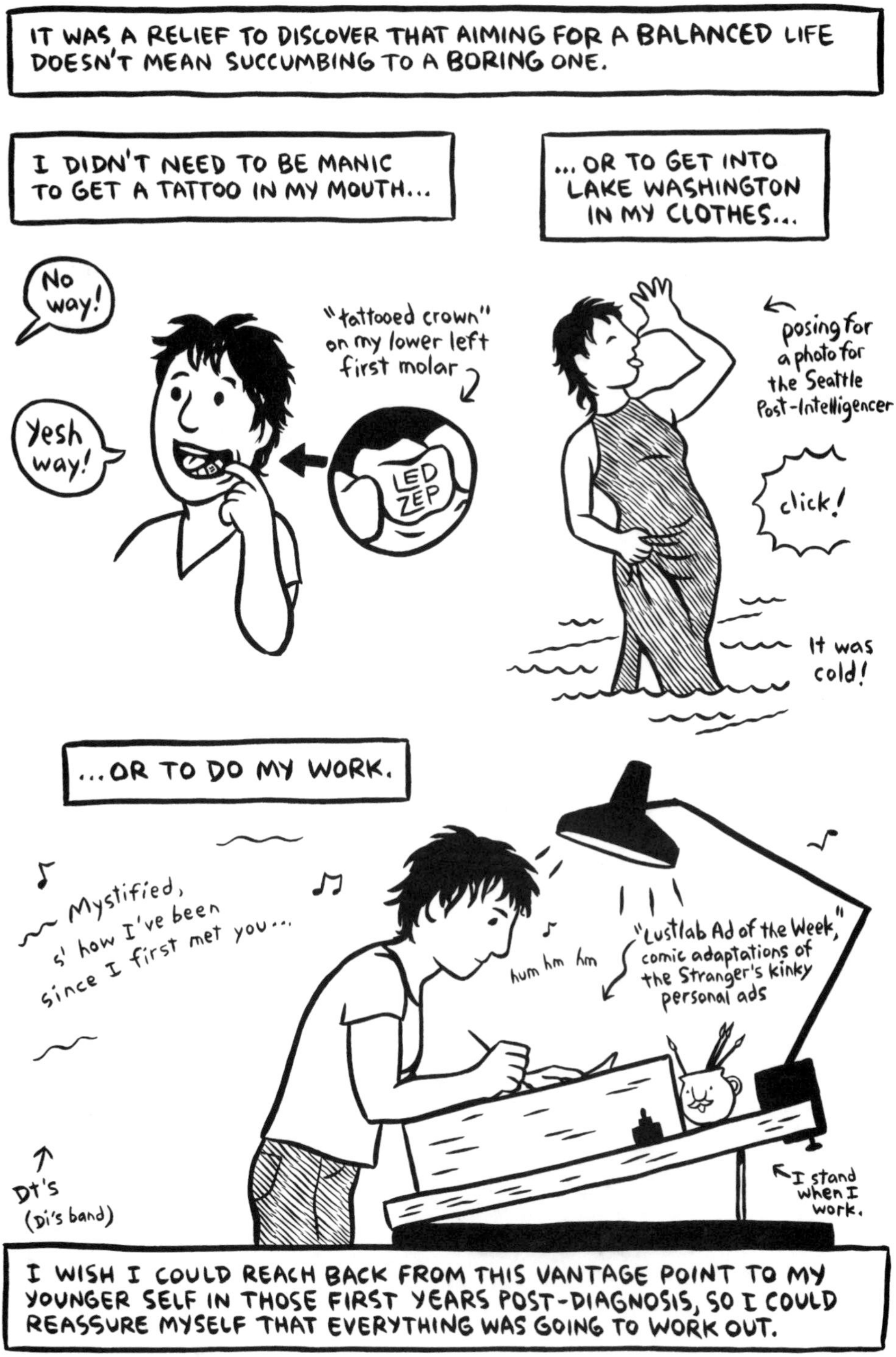
IT WAS A RELIEF TO DISCOVER THAT AIMING FOR A BALANCED LIFE DOESN'T MEAN SUCCUMBING TO A BORING ONE.
I DIDN'T NEED TO BE MANIC TO GET A TATTOO IN MY MOUTH...
No way!
Yesh way!
"tattooed crown" on my lower left first molar
LED ZEP
...OR TO GET INTO LAKE WASHINGTON IN MY CLOTHES...
posing for a photo for the Seattle Post-Intelligencer
click!
It was cold!
...OR TO DO MY WORK.
Mystified, s' how I've been since I first met you...
hum hm hm
"Lustlab Ad of the Week," comic adaptations of the Stranger's kinky personal ads
DT's (Di's band)
I stand when I work.
I WISH I COULD REACH BACK FROM THIS VANTAGE POINT TO MY YOUNGER SELF IN THOSE FIRST YEARS POST-DIAGNOSIS, SO I COULD REASSURE MYSELF THAT EVERYTHING WAS GOING TO WORK OUT.

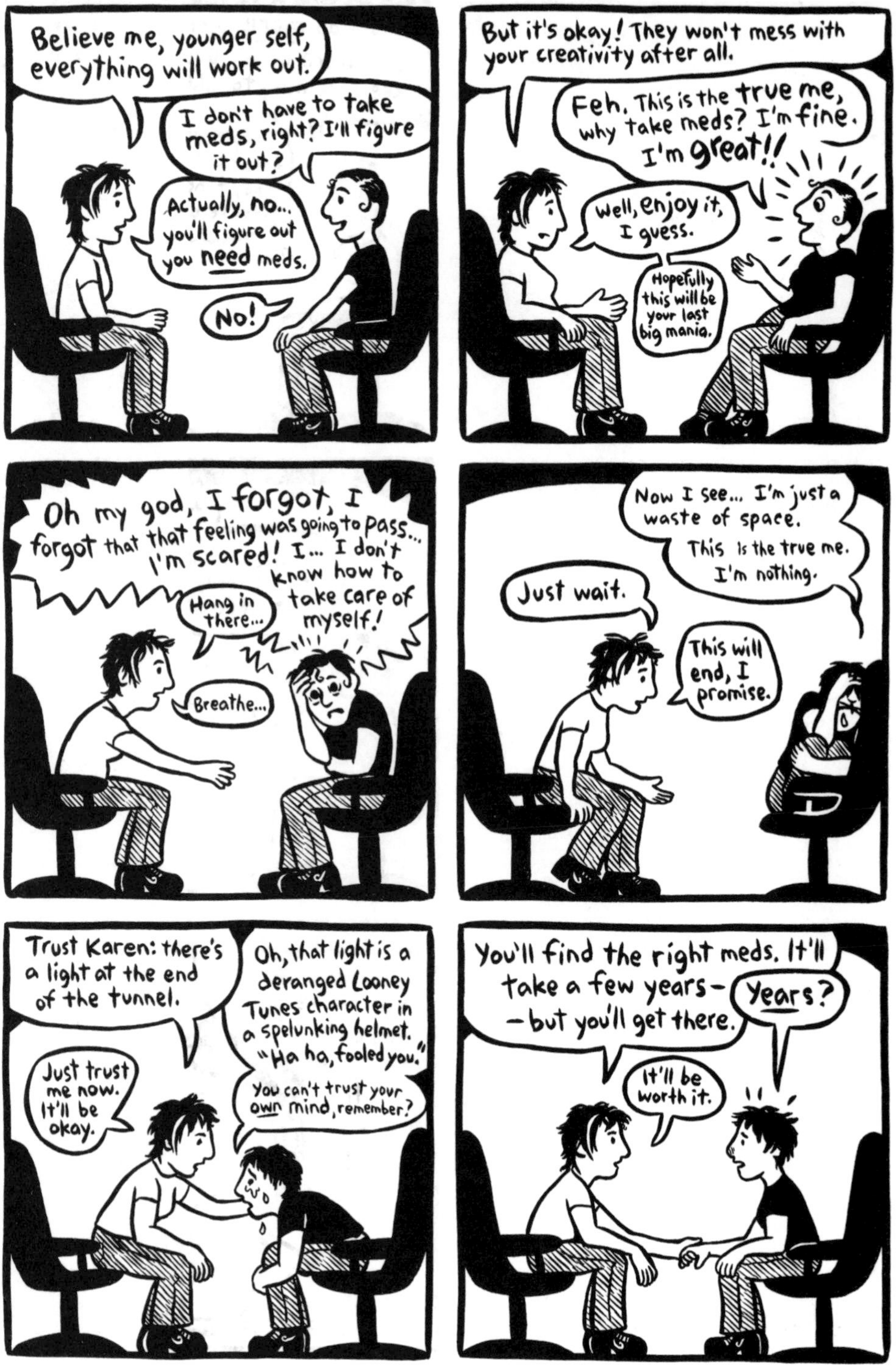
Believe me, younger self, everything will work out.
I don't have to take meds, right? I'll figure it out?
Actually, no... you'll figure out you need meds.
No!
But it's okay! They won't mess with your creativity after all.
Feh. This is the true me, why take meds? I'm fine. I'm great!!
Well, enjoy it, I guess.
Hopefully this will be your last big mania.
Oh my god, I forgot, I forgot that that feeling was going to pass... I'm scared! I... I don't know how to take care of myself!
Hang in there...
Breathe...
Now I see... I'm just a waste of space.
This is the true me. I'm nothing.
Just wait.
This will end, I promise.
Trust Karen: there's a light at the end of the tunnel.
Oh, that light is a deranged Looney Tunes character in a spelunking helmet. "Ha ha, fooled you."
You can't trust your own mind, remember?
Just trust me now. It'll be okay.
You'll find the right meds. It'll take a few years—
—but you'll get there.
Years?
It'll be worth it.

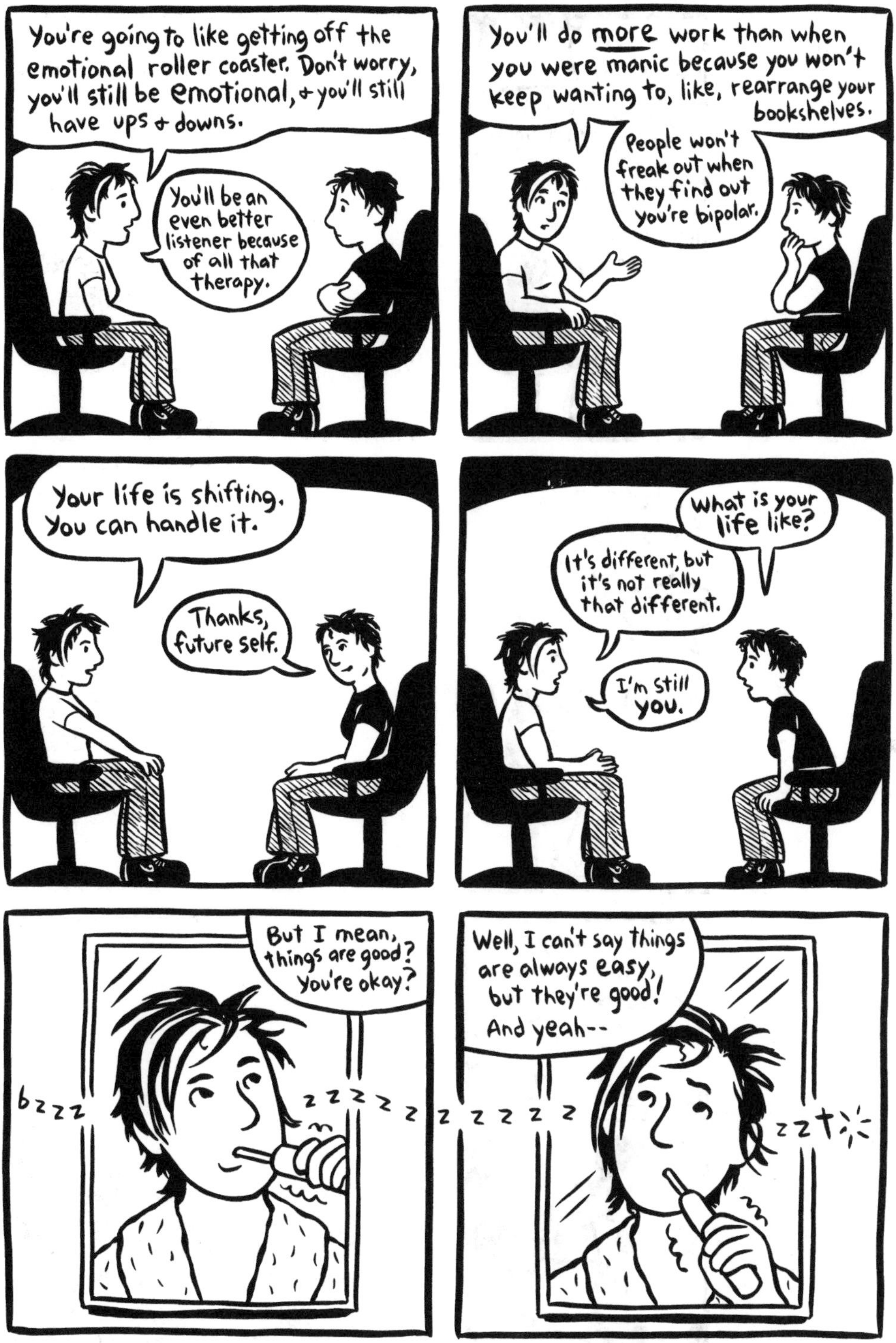
You're going to like getting off the emotional roller coaster. Don't worry, you'll still be emotional, + you'll still have ups + downs.
You'll be an even better listener because of all that therapy.
You'll do more work than when you were manic because you won't keep wanting to, like, rearrange your bookshelves.
People won't freak out when they find out you're bipolar.
Your life is shifting. You can handle it.
Thanks, future self.
What is your life like?
It's different, but it's not really that different.
I'm still you.
But I mean, things are good? You're okay?
bzzz
zzzzz z z zzzzz
Well, I can't say things are always easy, but they're good! And yeah--
zzt

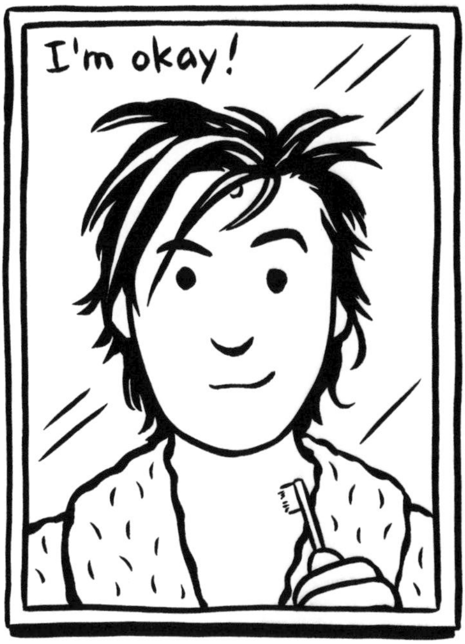
I'm okay!

ACKNOWLEDGMENTS

Worlds of thanks to my mother, Diane Gabe; my father, LeRoy Forney; and my brother, Matthew Forney; for the long phone calls, for rooting for me as I was writing this book, and for a lifetime of unconditional love.

To cartoonists Alison Bechdel, Megan Kelso, Jim Woodring, Craig Thompson, Kaz, and comics editor Chris Duffy, for professional and editorial support, and much-appreciated spirit boosting.

To Lucia Watson, my editor at Gotham; and my agent, Holly Bemiss; for having confidence in me and offering enormously helpful and insightful guidance.

To Dr. John Neumaier, MD; Mark Wittow of Washington Lawyers for the Arts; Dr. Paula J. Clayton, MD, JoEllen McNeal, and Wylie Tene of American Foundation for Suicide Prevention; Susan Pittman of Insure Northwest; and Jamie Vann; for invaluable research assistance and advice.

To Maré Odomo, my indispensable production assistant, and interns Rosie Heffernan and Elaine Lin, for additional help with production.

To Richard Hugo House, Therese Charvet and Tere Carranza of Sacred Groves, and Alix Wilbur, for much-needed space to develop my work.

Namaste to my yoga teachers, especially Denise Benitez, the Seattle Yoga Arts community, Lisa Holtby, and Douglas Ridings, for inspiring me to set out on the path of yoga and to maintain my practice with joy.

A zillion thanks to those I am so fortunate to call my friends, for supporting me with understanding and grace, and for trusting me to support you, too, in particular Risa Blythe, Anthippy Petras, and Diana Young-Blanchard; also to treasured friends, family, and community, including Laurel Ehrenfreund, Tamara Burke, Kristen Fisher Ratan, Ariel Meadow Stallings, Nathaniel Wice, Grace Gabe, Ariel Bordeaux, Larry Reid, Gary Groth, Kim Thompson, Eric Reynolds, Fantagraphics Books, Owen Connell and Parlor F Tattoo, Ron Regé Jr., Brian Ralph, and Jordan Crane.

And to everyone else who appeared in this book, named and unnamed, for being a part of my story, and in doing so, sharing a small piece of your own story with me.

I'd especially like to thank Jacob Peter Fennell, who helped me every step of the way with technical, editorial, and production tasks and snafus, and fed me hot meals, and most important, was always ready with frequently needed emotional support, patience, love, enthusiasm, and generosity. You rock.

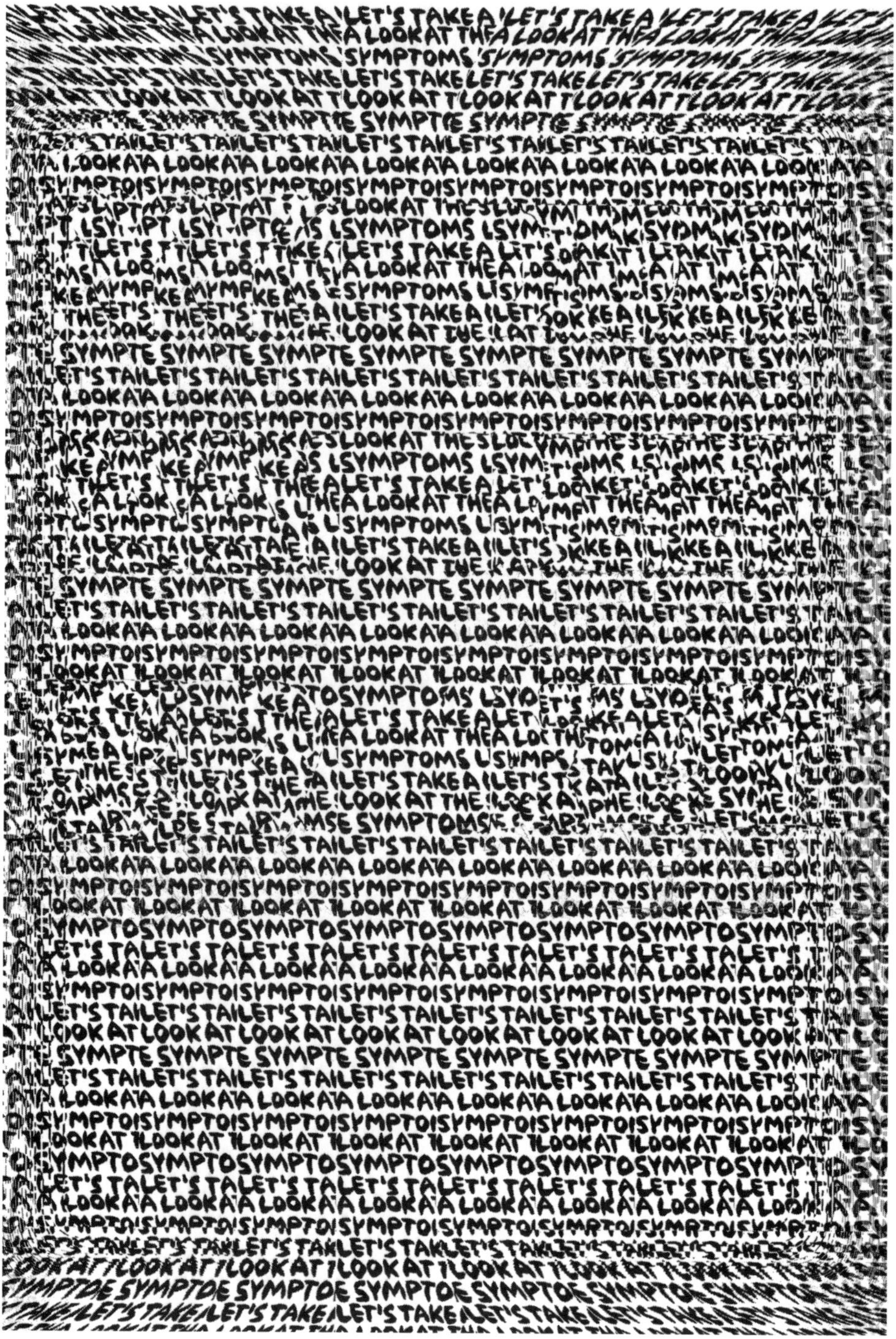
LET'S TAKE A
LOOK AT THE
SYMPTOMS

APPENDIX

The drawing on page 20 is a simulation of a "single-image stereogram," a computer-generated pattern that creates an illusion of three-dimensionality from a two-dimensional object (like in the *Magic Eye* books). I had originally intended to use a real stereogram right on that page in Chapter 2, but decided it would stall the story too much. But here it is! By crossing and uncrossing your eyes slowly as you look at the pattern, you will see YOU ARE CRAZY floating a few inches above the paper.

ENDNOTES

CHAPTER 1

page 8
Comic panel © Kaz, from *Bare Bulbs: Underworld Two* (Seattle: Fantagraphics Books, 1996), p. 55.

page 10
Tattoo artwork by Kaz (1997).

CHAPTER 2

pages 15–18
American Psychiatric Association: *Diagnostic and Statistical Manual of Mental Disorders*, Fourth Edition, Text Revision. Washington, DC, American Psychiatric Association, 2000, p. 362.

page 28
Kay Redfield Jamison, *An Unquiet Mind: A Memoir of Moods and Madness* (New York: Random House, 1995), p. 80.

page 33
Drawings based on photographs by Jimmy Malecki (1998).

pages 34–38
Drawings based on photographs by Victoria Renard (1998).

pages 40–41
Kay Redfield Jamison, *Touched with Fire: Manic-Depressive Illness and the Artistic Temperament* (New York: Simon & Schuster, 1993), pp. 267–270.

page 44
Suicide and suicide attempt rates for the general population: Center for Disease Control and Prevention (2007) and the American Foundation for Suicide Prevention.

Note: The rates vary widely depending on demographic. For example, rates are higher for men than for women, and the age group with the highest rate is 45–54.

Suicide and suicide attempt rates for bipolars: F. K. Goodwin & K. R. Jamison, *Manic-Depressive Illness: Bipolar Disorders and Recurrent Depression* (New York: Oxford University Press, 2007), pp. 249–251.

Note: The book's review of 30 studies of completed suicides (1937–1988) showed widely varying results, but all were higher than the average rates for the general populationw. The researchers note that rates for the earlier studies may not reflect current rates, since modern treatment has become more effective, the use of lithium in particular.

CHAPTER 3

page 50
Ellen Forney, *I Was Seven in '75* (Seattle: Self-published with a Xeric Foundation grant, 1997).

page 54
Poster design by Shawn Wolfe (1998).

page 59
American Psychiatric Association: *Diagnostic and Statistical Manual of Mental Disorders,* pp. 346–347.

page 72
US Food and Drug Administration, www.fda.gov.

CHAPTER 4

page 78
Judy Blume, *Forever.* New York: Simon & Schuster, 1975.

Judy Blume, *Summer Sisters.* New York: Delacorte Press, 1998.

page 79
"My Interview with Judy Blume," *Seattle Weekly,* June 11, 1998, p. 45.

page 86
American Psychiatric Association: Diagnostic and Statistical Manual of Mental Disorders, p. 356.

page 87
David D. Burns, MD, *Feeling Good: The New Mood Therapy* (New York: HarperCollins, 1980), pp. 42–43.

page 88
David D. Burns, MD, *Feeling Good: The New Mood Therapy* (New York: HarperCollins, 1980), pp. 62–65.

page 89
Madeleine L'Engle, *A Wrinkle in Time* (New York: Dell Publishing, 1962).

P. L. Travers, *Mary Poppins*, illustrated by Mary Shepard (London: HarperCollins; New York: Harcourt, Brace, 1934).

Norton Juster, *The Phantom Tollbooth*, illustrated by Jules Feiffer (New York, Random House, 1961).

C. S. Lewis, *The Lion, the Witch and the Wardrobe*, illustrated by Pauline Baynes (London: Geoffrey Bles, 1950; New York: Collier Books, 1970).

pages 90–91
William Styron, *Darkness Visible: A Memoir of Madness* (New York: Random House, 1990).

page 104
Note: I did use those notes one year later, to write a one-page comic, "So' Cal' Travel Journal," for *The Stranger* (April 1999), reprinted in *I Love Led Zeppelin* by Ellen Forney (Seattle: Fantagraphics Books, 2006), p. 38.

CHAPTER 5

page 118
Drawing based on *Starry Night* (1889), which Van Gogh painted while voluntarily hospitalized in the asylum at Saint-Rémy, France.

Van Gogh Museum, Amsterdam, www.vangoghmuseum.nl.

Dietrich Blumer, "The Illness of Vincent van Gogh," *American Journal of Psychiatry*, Vol. 159, No. 4 (2002), pp. 519–526.

Bernard Denvir, *Vincent: A Complete Portrait: All of Vincent van Gogh's Self-Portraits, with Excerpts from His Writings* (Philadelphia: Courage Books, 1997).

page 121
Edvard Munch collected writings, Munch Museum, Oslo, Norway.

Sue Prideaux, *Edvard Munch: Behind the Scream* (Yale University Press, 2005).

pages 125–126
"Wednesday Morning Yoga" was originally published in *Scheherazade: Comics About Love, Treachery, Mothers, and Monsters*, Megan Kelso, ed. (New York: Soft Skull Press, 2004), and reprinted in *I Love Led Zeppelin*, pp. 42–43.

Note: Admittedly, "I didn't find inspiration from my depression" is a questionable statement in the middle of a graphic novel about my mood disorder!

page 127
Pierluigi de Vecchi & Gianluigi Colalucci, *Michelangelo: The Vatican Frescoes* (New York: Abbeville Press, 1997).

page 128
Jamison, *Touched with Fire*, pp. 58–59.

Goodwin & Jamison, *Manic-Depressive Illness*, p. 383.

CHAPTER 6

page 141
Alfred Stieglitz, *Georgia O'Keeffe, A Portrait* (New York: Metropolitan Museum of Art, 1978). Drawing based on Plate 24 (1918).

page 150
Ellen Forney, *Monkey Food: The Complete "I Was Seven in '75" Collection* (Seattle: Fantagraphics Books, 1999).

page 153
Based on discussions with two clinical psychiatrists.

page 169
Sly and the Family Stone. "If You Want Me to Stay." *Fresh*. Epic, 1973.

page 170
Sylvia Plath, "Fever 103," "Lady Lazarus," and "The Hanging Man," *Collected Poems* (Faber and Faber, 1981). **Note:** "The Hanging Man" is specifically about Plath's experience of electroshock therapy.

Sylvia Plath, *The Bell Jar* (New York: Harper & Row, 1971), p. 171.

Sylvia Plath, *The Unabridged Journals of Sylvia Plath* (entry for Friday, June 20, 1958), ed. Karen V. Kukil (Anchor Books, 2000), p. 395.

Note: Plath was also a visual artist. She drew several illustrations in *The Bell Jar*, and in 2011, the Mayor Gallery in London exhibited "Sylvia Plath: Her Drawings," featuring over forty of her ink drawings.

"Crazy 'Bout You Baby," written by Sonny Boy Williamson II (1951), performed by Ike and Tina Turner (1968), covered by Dt's, *Nice 'N' Ruff: Hard Soul Hits, Vol. 1.* Get Hip Recordings, 2006.

CHAPTER 8

page 203

Nancy Andreasen, *The Creating Brain: The Neuroscience of Genius* (Dana Press, 2005), p. 17.

Arnold M. Ludwig, "Creative achievement and psychopathology: Comparison among professions," *American Journal of Psychotherapy*, Vol. 46, No. 3 (1992): pp. 344–345.

page 205

J. P. Guilford, "Traits of creativity," in H. H. Anderson, ed., *Creativity and Its Cultivation* (New York: Harper, 1959), pp. 142–161, quoted in Jamison's *Touched with Fire*, pp. 105–106.

page 207

"Guilford's Alternative Uses Task" (1967) was developed by psychologist J. P. Guilford, who also defined the traits of creative thinking.

H. G. Gough, "A creative personality scale for the Adjective Check List," *Journal of Personality and Social Psychology*, 37 (1979): 1,398–1,405. The words in this sample considered to reflect a creative personality are "clever," "informal," and "sexy."

E. Paul Torrance developed the Torrance Tests of Creative Thinking (TTCT) in 1966; it is currently the most widely used creativity test. Copyright held by Scholastic Testing Service, Inc.

page 209

Goodwin & Jamison, *Manic-Depressive Illness*, p. 406.

Andreasen, *The Creating Brain*, pp. 93–96.

Jamison, *Touched with Fire*, pp. 61–72.

Ludwig, "Creative achievement and psychopathology," pp. 330–356.

C. M. Santosa, C. M. Strong, C. Nowakowska, P. W. Wang, C. M. Rennicke, T. A. Ketter, "Enhanced creativity in bipolar disorder patients: A controlled study," *Journal of Affective Disorders*, 100 (2007): 31–39.

Note: Even researchers that endorse a correlation between mood disorders and creativity recognize that the studies have potential problems. For example, in studies of historical figures, biographers may be biased, sources may be unreliable, or information may be affected by cultural norms and expectations. In studies of living figures, reliability may be compromised by small sample sizes, inconsistent definitions of creativity and psychiatric illness, or nonrandom selection of subjects (Goodwin & Jamison, *Manic-Depressive Illness*, pp. 381–383). That said, many studies over many years point to this correlation, using many different methods and different populations, so it seems like a good bet.

page 211
G. Murray & S. Johnson, "The clinical significance of creativity in bipolar disorder," *Clinical Psychology Review*, 30 (2010), 721–732.

page 215
Examination of lithium's effect on creativity:

Goodwin & Jamison, *Manic-Depressive Illness*, pp. 403–405.

CHAPTER 9

page 230
The cost of treatment is very individual, of course. It's like asking what a house costs. What kind of house? Where? There are too many factors to really give an answer that's both short and accurate, but I hope this gives a general idea, or at least some issues to consider.

Cost for a psychiatrist varies hugely. Factors include length of appointment (e.g., a fifty-minute session is more than a fifteen-minute "med check"), region (e.g., Los Angeles is typically more expensive than Seattle), practice (a community clinic might have a sliding scale, a psychiatrist in private practice can cost up to $500 an hour), and insurance coverage (appointments may be entirely covered, or entirely *not* covered). Patients' frequency of appointments also varies (e.g., several times a week, or just once every few months as maintenance).

Cost for medications is unregulated in this country, so there's an enormous range, from pharmacies to clinics, online wholesalers to online hucksters. The difference in price between patented drugs and generics is extreme, and drug companies tend to keep the prices as high as possible before their patents run out.

I list Walgreens cash prices rounded to the nearest $10, January 2012, as follows: Lamictal (lamotrigine), 200 mg x 60#; Zyprexa (olanzapene), 10 mg x 30#; lithium (capsules), 600 mg x 60#; Abilify (aripiprazole), 20 mg x 30#.

page 233
The Dt's. "Mystified." *Filthy Habits*. Get Hip Recordings, 2007.